The Early Christian Church

A History of Its First Five Centuries

The Early Christian Church

A History of Its First Five Centuries

J. G. Davies

Edward Cadbury Professor of Theology
University of Birmingham

Baker Book House
Grand Rapids, Michigan

Reprinted 1980 by Baker Book House Company
with permission of copyright holder

ISBN: 0-8010-2906-6

PHOTOLITHOPRINTED BY CUSHING - MALLOY, INC.
ANN ARBOR, MICHIGAN, UNITED STATES OF AMERICA

CONTENTS

ILLUSTRATIONS

Between pages 146 *and* 147

Acknowledgments

The author wishes to thank the following for providing illustrations for this volume: Alinari, Pls 5, 7, 9, 12a, 13, 30; Anderson, Pls 23, 24, 25, 28, 29; Messrs Barrie and Rockliff, Pls 26, 27; The Trustees of the British Museum, Pls 8, 11, 12b; Bayerisches Nationalmuseum, Munich, Pl 10; The Syndics of the Fitzwilliam Museum, Cambridge, Pls 2, 16; Courtauld Institute of Art, Pl 19; Denise Fourmont (From 'Ampoules de Terre Sainte' by Professor Grabar (Editions C. Klincksieck)), Pl 15; André Held, Pls 3, 14, 31; Pont. Comm. Arch. Sacra., Pls 17, 18, 20, 21; The John Rylands Library, Manchester, Pl 1; Victoria and Albert Museum, Pls 4 and 6

PREFACE

ANYONE who would undertake the writing of an account of the Early Church for inclusion within a series devoted to the History of Religion, and therefore within certain necessarily confined limits, is faced with two acute problems concerning the selection and the arrangement of the material. The volume of facts known about the first centuries of the Church's existence is immense and to record all would require the production not of a single book but of an entire library. How then is the historian to decide which events he will include and which he will omit? Clearly his choice will be determined by his understanding of the relative importance of the several items and he will judge that importance in the light of his over-all interpretation of the development of Christian life and thought. Those incidents and ideas will be chronicled that, in his view, make the development clear, and those that do not will be passed over. There is, however, room for considerable divergence of opinion concerning this development and what has produced it. It has been held that the early history of the Church represents a perversion of the simple primitive gospel preached by Jesus; the story of the Church then becomes an account of the obscuring of Christian truth. Or again it has been argued that the history of Christian belief is to be understood solely as the attempt by Christian thinkers to grapple with the situation created by the failure of Christ to come again. No one can produce a coherent account without adopting a position *vis-à-vis* these and other evaluations. This is not the place to discuss at length my own critical standpoint, but the reader should be given some insight into what an author's presuppositions are.

I see the history of the Church as the record of a steady progress, to be understood in terms of a primary creative impulse given by Jesus of Nazareth. I see the development as in the main an advance and an enrichment of an inner life which was naturally influenced by political, social, economic and philosophical pressures – from one aspect the history of the Church is the record of how it adapted itself to and assimilated these. I would repudiate any simplification that would reduce these factors to one of supreme importance, such as the influence of mystery religions or the impact of Hellenistic thought. History and human life are too complex to explain or describe by means of a single supposedly key-category. In what follows therefore the material has been selected both to illustrate this complexity and at the same time to present a continuous and coherent account of a progression.

The arrangement of the material gives rise to other problems. There are so many facets of the life of the Church: the growth of its structure, the illumination of its beliefs, the elaboration of its worship, etc. These are aspects of one indivisible entity and could ideally be represented only in musical terms in the form of a fugue, each theme related to the others and inseparable from them. But words and not musical notation must be used and so, inevitably, each aspect must be treated separately, while it is constantly remembered that they should be fused in the mind of the reader into a single whole. The six inter-related aspects I have chosen are as follows: the environment, the sources, the expansion and development, the beliefs, the worship and the social life. Each chapter, with the exception of the first, has therefore six main sections. The reader can, if he wishes, follow each section throughout: he would then have a miniature history of the Roman empire and of the general background of the Church's growth; he would have an abbreviated patrology, a consecutive account of the missionary endeavour and of internal progress and struggles; a history of Christian doctrine and of worship, and finally a short social history.

The first chapter, which is included at the request of the General Editor of the series, is somewhat different because it is devoted to the origins of Christianity. It has therefore only three main sections: the background, the sources and the message and ministry of Jesus. This subject in itself bristles with critical difficulties, but since the good historian is not he who carries scepticism to extremes, but he who, on the basis of a careful analysis of the material, seeks to make sense of the past, I have endeavoured to give a coherent account which, by the very nature of historical study, can only be regarded as tentative. It is never possible to catalogue the *assured* results of New Testament criticism, for the conclusions of one generation of scholars raise new problems and provide the basis for the researches of their successors. For this very reason, accounts of the origins of the Church and indeed of the history of the Church as a whole need to be rewritten in each generation – finality in this kind of study is impossible.

This work is intended both for the general reader and for the student; for the latter I have included full references so that he may check the statements made against the original sources, if he so chooses, and may have the basis for further reading of the original texts. In order that these notes may not distract the general reader, they have been printed at the end of this volume, where they may remain neglected by those who wish to go no further. A select bibliography has also been provided, which lists many books that contain information about additional reading.

I wish to record my gratitude to my wife for drawing the plans and to the publishers for the care and attention they have given to this work.

BIRMINGHAM J. G. DAVIES

CHAPTER ONE

THE ORIGINS OF CHRISTIANITY

The Background – The Sources – The Message and Ministry of Jesus

THE BACKGROUND

THE ORIGINS of Christianity go back to the activities of a Palestinian Jew, by the name of Jesus, who was born in the reign of Herod the Great and conducted his mission under Pontius Pilate, the Roman procurator from AD 26–36. Since Jesus was a Jew and his relations were mainly, though not exclusively, with those of his own race, if he is to be set firmly within his historical context something must be said of the Judaism in which he was nurtured and grew up. Like any other Jew of the period, Jesus cannot but have been conscious of his nation's past and have shared with his contemporaries their hopes and aspirations which were based upon that past. Its record was contained in their sacred writings, which were divided into three sections: the Law, being the Pentateuch or first five books of the Old Testament; the prophets, consisting of the Former, i.e. Joshua, Judges, I and II Samuel, and I and II Kings, and the Latter, i.e. the major and minor prophets; and the writings, i.e. Psalms, Proverbs, Song of Songs, Ruth, Lamentations, Ecclesiastes, Esther, Daniel, Ezra, Nehemiah and I and II Chronicles.

From these holy books the Jew learned of God's dealings with Israel from the time when the twelve tribes were united under Moses to form a nation. This story was set within a universal context by the opening chapters of Genesis which tell how God created heaven and earth and man in his own image. Then followed man's rebellion against God and his consequent corruption. The divine method of coping with this situation was to select one individual, Abraham, out of the fallen mass of mankind that his descendants might be taught the will of God and be the medium whereby all nations could be brought back to serve their Creator.

Israel's past

It was these descendants who were delivered by God from bondage in Egypt and were united to him by a covenant ratified on Mount Sinai. The Terms of this agreement were specified in the law promulgated through Moses, and henceforth the Jews were the chosen people of God, elected not to privilege but to service as the agents of his purpose. So they were brought into the Promised Land and given a king as the divine representative, and with him too God entered into a covenant, which however contained no stipulation but rested on the firm promise: 'thy throne shall be established for ever'.[1] Now began that period which to the Jew of Jesus' day was the Golden Age of Israelite history – the age of the shepherd king, David, the Lord's Messiah or Anointed One, the age of his son Solomon, when the kingdom stretched from Kadesh in the north to Eziongeber in the south and when the Temple, the shrine of the Ark and the focus of the divine presence, was built in Jerusalem; the age of freedom, independence and peace. But, so the story continues, the glory soon passed; the one people split into two, organized into the northern and southern kingdoms; the Israelites went a-whoring after other gods; they failed to persevere in the way of righteousness. Despite the warnings of the prophets that this disobedience to the divine will could not but issue in disaster, despite the bitter denunciations of an Amos (*c.* 750 BC), the laments of his near contemporary Hosea, and the alarm sounded by Isaiah, first the northern kingdom was swept away by the Assyrians under Sennacherib, its capital Samaria falling in 722. Then the southern half, equally unheeding the admonitions of a Jeremiah, came under the rule of the Babylonians led by Nebuchadnezzar, its capital Jerusalem being devastated in 587 and its leading citizens deported.

The experience of the Exile bit deep into the Jewish soul. It gave him an acute sense of sin, since he accepted the prophetic interpretation of these events as punishment for failure to obey the divine commands, and hence the Day of Atonement became the major religious festival of the year; it gave him abhorrence of all that might contaminate him in his daily life, and hence he sought to separate himself from the non-Jew or Gentile; it gave him an earnest desire to know the divine will and to do it, so as to avoid the repetition of such a calamity, and hence the codification of the law. This belief in divine retribution – a retribution of the strictest juristic kind – affected the Israelite understanding of the covenant, which was also interpreted legalistically; the people *had* to observe the law given by God. This law or Torah, contained in the Pentateuch, was to be applied to every circumstance, and this became the primary function of the scribe, for prophecy had ceased and would only make its reappearance with the dawn of the Age to Come. So, for example, the brief prohibition of work on the Sabbath day does not enter into details; hence the scribes sought to define accurately what work was forbidden and eventually concluded that there were thirty-nine different categories of labour to be condemned. In this way the oral law of the Jews developed, being concerned with Halakah, i.e. legal precepts of the kind just mentioned, and Haggadah, i.e. moral exhortations and narratives which closed the gaps in the history of the race. Nevertheless, despite this Haggadic material, the sacred scriptures were no longer regarded as the historical record of God's dealings with his people; they were a book of divine law. In binding herself to her past, thus understood, Israel loosed her ties with the present; God was not so much the God of history but the God about to come and the chosen people were conceived to be not those with a mission to fulfil but the holy nation, separated from all worldly interests and ideals.

This belief in the God about to come was also the product of historical circumstances, not of the Exile but of the succeeding centuries. In 538 BC, after his conquest of Babylonia, Cyrus, king of the Persians, adopted a policy of calculated leniency towards local autonomy, and the first Jews returned from exile. It was not however until eighteen years later, due to the efforts of the prophets Haggai and Zechariah, that work on rebuilding the Temple began. Hopes ran high for a national restoration, but with the removal of Zerubbabel, a legitimate descendant of the Davidic house, the monarchy ceased to exist and the yoke of foreign oppression was fastened firmly upon the Israelites. Persian domination, brought to an end by the conquests of Alexander the Great (*c.* 333), was followed by that of his successors, first the Ptolemies in Egypt and then, from 198, by that of Seleucids in Syria. Some thirty years later a short-lived independence under the Maccabean house was achieved, but came to an end, with none of its promise realized, when the Roman legions entered under Pompey in 63 BC. The dream of a neo-Davidic empire and of the establishment of the era of righteousness and peace had come to nothing, and it was as a puppet king of the Romans that Herod the Great reigned in Judaea from 37 to 4 BC. After his death his kingdom was subdivided between his sons and grandsons, Judaea proper being ruled by Archelaus (4 BC–AD 6), until it finally came under the control of the Roman procurators, of whom Pontius Pilate began his ten-year term of office in AD 26 during the reign of the emperor Tiberius (AD 14–37).

Israel's hope

The contrast between this oppression and suffering and the divine promises contained in the books of the law induced in the Jew a profound pessimism about the present age and a fervent hope in the intervention of God to bring it to an end, to overthrow the forces of evil and to honour his covenant with the Davidic house. This hope was fostered by the writings of the apocalyptic school, such as the book of Daniel, a genre of literature, owing not a little to Iranian influence, which described visions of the future, often regarded as imminent, and expressed the certainty of the ultimate triumph of God and the glorification of his people Israel. So a new Golden Age was envisaged, when God's Kingdom or rule would be set up, exercised either directly or through his promised Messiah.

Judaism thus had two poles: the hope of the future and the fulfilment of the law; but it would be a mistake to assume that there was a rigidly uniform attitude to these. Just as the apocalyptists did not agree amongst themselves in presenting an identical blue-print of the expected end, so the Jews as a whole differed in their understanding of the law, and these differences were reflected in the several parties that emerged in the post-exilic period and were distinct and active at the time of Jesus. Indeed it has been said, with some justice, that 'Christianity simply intensified a fissiparous process within Judaism that had already been going on for centuries, ever since the split between the northern and southern kingdoms.'[2]

Parties in Judaism

One source of divergent views was disagreement as to the extent of the law. The Sadducees, who were in the main the aristocratic priestly party, accepted the authority of the written Torah and refused to countenance any additions to it. The Pharisees, who developed out of the lay scribes, upheld the equal importance of the oral tradition. The beliefs of the two groups were consequently dissimilar; the Sadducees rejected the idea of a resurrection and were opposed to any developed angelology, since they could find little or no support for these in the written records, while the Pharisees proclaimed a future life and a complex angelology and demonology, since these had become essential features of the apocalyptic teaching. The Sadducees endorsed the strictest fulfilment of the written law, but challenged the Pharisees' readiness to modify it. The Pharisees asserted the unlimited obligation of the living tradition and opposed the Sadducean political prudence[3] and willingness to co-operate with the authorities of the occupying power, which allowed freedom to Temple worship and the Jewish courts, in particular the Sanhedrin. Both however had a certain common ground in the worship of the Temple and the synagogue, for while the former was the primary sphere of influence of the Sadducean priesthood, it was supported by the punctilious payment of tithes by the Pharisees, and while the latter gave an opportunity for the exposition of the law in terms of the oral tradition, its services included a priestly blessing, if a priest were present, and were linked with the rites of the Temple. Both too had common ground in their opposition to the Essenes who combined different elements from Sadduceeism and Pharisaism. Thus, like the former, they were adherents of the traditions of priesthood with their own rites of purification and a sacred meal corresponding to the sacerdotal ritual bath and the partaking of the Shew-bread.[4] Like the latter they practised a rigorous observance of the law, cherished apocalyptic hopes and claimed to be the true people of God. Unlike either, however, the Essenes formed an ascetic monastic society withdrawn from common life; they supplemented the Torah with sacred books of their own and they looked for a Messiah of the Aaronic line. That despite their isolation they were not quietists is evidenced by *The War of the Sons of Light against the Sons of Darkness*, a Qumran text which is 'a kind of G.H.Q. Manual for the guidance of the Brotherhood'[5] in the campaign or battle that will usher in the New Age.

Nevertheless, the Essenes shunned the direct political action which was the policy of the Zealots. These were groups of partisans who stimulated and supported rebellious movements against the occupying power and were characterized by the profession of a theocratic ideal and fervent Messianic hopes. The chain of plots and insurrections, for which they were in part or wholly responsible, stretches from the time of Herod to the Jewish War, when in AD 70 Jerusalem was destroyed, and even into the reign of Hadrian, when Bar Cochba headed yet another unsuccessful revolt. Part of their success with the people lay in the claim of their several leaders to be prophets or even the Messiah. According to Josephus 'these were such men as deceived and deluded the people under the pretence of divine inspiration, but were for procuring innovations and changes of the government; and these prevailed with the multitude to act like madmen, and went before them into the wilderness, as pretending that God would there show them the signal of liberty.'[6]

John the Baptist

Not all these prophetic figures earned the condemnation of Josephus; there was one, who had no association with the Zealots, whom he was prepared to praise. Commenting on the defeat of Herod the Tetrarch by the forces of Aretas, king of the Nabataeans, Josephus says:

> Now some of the Jews thought that the destruction of Herod's army came from God, and that very justly, as a punishment for what he did against John,

who was surnamed the Baptist. For Herod had him killed, although he was a good man, and commanded the Jews to exercise virtue, to be just towards one another, and pious towards God. He invited them to unite themselves by a baptism. For it is on this condition that God regarded baptism with favour, if it served not only for remission of certain faults, but also to purify the body after the soul had already been purified by justice. Now when some came to crowd about him, for they were greatly moved by hearing his words, Herod, who feared lest the great influence John had over the people might put it into his power and inclination to raise a rebellion (for they seemed ready to do anything he should advise), thought it best, by putting him to death, to prevent any mischief he might cause, and not bring himself into difficulties by sparing a man who might make him repent of it when it should be too late.[7]

In this brief account of John the Baptist's activity there is no hint of Messianism or of an eschatological outlook, which would explain Herod's concern to be rid of John for fear of a possible rebellion. But Josephus would be careful to pass over such matters since they were anti-Roman, and his omission can be supplied from the Synoptic Gospels.

In the Marcan and Matthean reports John appears abruptly on the scene – Luke alone provides some information about his childhood. John is dressed in the traditional garb of a prophet, with a leather girdle around his loins, like Elijah of old.[8] Here is a new note in post-exilic Judaism; the divine moratorium on prophecy has come to an end, since a genuine prophet, accepted as such by the crowds that flock to him, has now appeared. This could have only one meaning: the decisive action of God was imminent. This indeed was the burden of the Baptist's message: 'Who warned you to flee from the wrath to come? . . . And even now is the axe also laid unto the root of the trees: every tree therefore that bringeth not forth good fruit is hewn down, and cast into the fire'.[9] John thus stood in the line of the Old Testament prophets and his message was a solemn warning of judgement to come, coupled with a call to repentance. Its difference lay in the stress on the urgent nearness of the time of God's Kingdom. John himself prepared his hearers for this coming by administering a baptism in water; in so doing he was performing an act which had parallels in the widespread baptizing movement of the first century BC, but it was to be distinguished from proselyte baptism, in that it was offered to Jews, and from Essene purification, in that it was performed on Gentiles. By so doing John was not abandoning the idea of a chosen people but the assumption that the chosen people and the visible Israel were to be identified. Moreover, this baptism was a prophetic sign, like the mark on the forehead of Ezekiel ix, a guarantee, more than a mere promise, that those who were sealed in this way would pass safely through the impending tribulation and secure a place in the Kingdom.

John also specified the agent of this impending judgement: 'there cometh he that is mightier than I, the latchet of whose shoes I am not worthy to unloose . . . whose fan is in his hand, throughly to cleanse his threshing-floor, and to gather the wheat into his garner; but the chaff he will burn up with unquenchable fire.'[10] Here is no fulfiller of political aspirations, but the judge of the world who brings a baptism of fire. According to the Christian tradition this person is none other than Jesus of Nazareth; hence at this point we must pass from a consideration of the background to Jesus himself, after first surveying the sources at our disposal for reconstructing his life and teaching.

THE SOURCES

Jewish and Pagan

The principal sources for the life and teaching of Jesus of Nazareth are to be found in the pages of the New Testament. Outside these books the evidence is very scanty indeed. This extra-Biblical material emanates on the one hand from Jewish writers and on the other from pagan authors. The sole certainly authentic reference to Jesus in the works of the Jewish historian Flavius Josephus is to be found in his *Antiquities of the Jews* which he published in AD 93 or 94. This is no more than the statement that James was 'the brother of Jesus who was called the Christ'.[1] The Talmud[2] contains a number of passages relating to Jesus, but it is doubtful if they have any independent historical value and they are largely an interpretation of the Christian tradition in order to discredit it; so Jesus is declared to have practised magic, to have led the people astray and to have been hanged on the eve of the Passover.

Amongst pagan writers the first in point of time is Thallus the Samaritan, whose *Chronicle* (*c.* AD 50) indicates that he was familiar with the Passion Narrative at Rome and sought to give a naturalistic explanation of the incidents, e.g. that the darkness at noon was the result of an eclipse. Pliny the Younger, who was governor of Bithynia in 110, wrote to his imperial master Trajan for instructions as to what action he should take with regard to the Christians; his remark, that they sing 'a hymn to Christ as to a god', is however no independent evidence but is derived from his examination of the believers who had been brought before him.[3] The friend and correspondent of Pliny was the historian Tacitus and from his *Annals* we have a more explicit statement which seems to have been derived from neither Jewish nor Christian sources; in his account of Nero's reign he mentions Christ 'whom the Procurator Pontius Pilate, under the rule of Tiberius, had handed over to the torture'.[4] Also writing about Nero, some decades later, Suetonius records the persecution of the Christians, but says nothing of Christ. However, in his *Life of Claudius*,[5] he mentions the expulsion of the Jews from Rome on account of the disturbances instigated by a certain Chrestos – by this he most probably meant Christ and was reporting troubles between the Jewish and Christian communities.

This testimony, briefly summarized, is unquestionably meagre, but this is only to be expected, since the majority of the citizens of the Roman Empire would have had neither opportunity to acquire, nor interest in obtaining, information about an obscure man executed as a criminal in a distant province. We may note, *en passant*, that Herodotus could similarly speak of Persian religion without a mention of Zoroaster and that Dion Cassius could describe the Jewish revolt of AD 130 without once naming Bar Cochba, its leader.

Christian Sources – Paul

Within the New Testament the earliest documents are the letters of Paul, the first of which was written *c.* AD 48, thus post-dating the death of Jesus by some two decades, and the last just over twenty years later. Paul's letters were the product of particular circumstances and related to specific problems that had arisen in the communities for which he was responsible; the life of Christ was therefore not his primary concern in writing and he mentions details only incidentally. If we assemble these passing allusions from the genuine epistles we find that, according to Paul, Jesus was a Jew,[6] a descendant of the royal Davidic house,[7] who, being under the Law, had been circumcised.[8] He had a brother named James[9] and a number of followers, including Peter, James and John.[10] Paul gives no account of a ministry but indicates that he knew Jesus to have been a teacher, since he records one of his sayings.[11] This Jesus was eventually betrayed, but immediately before this, at the Passover season,[12] he had an evening meal with his disciples during which he said some mysterious words in relation to bread, which he blessed, broke and distributed, and to wine, which he similarly blessed and passed round, calling the former his body and the latter his blood.[13] The responsibility for his ensuing death was largely that of his fellow-countrymen[14] and the manner of his dying was by crucifixion[15] or nailing to a cross.[16] He was buried and on the third day rose from the dead and appeared to Peter, to the twelve Apostles, to a gathering of five hundred of his followers, to James and then to the Apostles once more.[17] Paul does not list the sources of his information but he was trained in Jerusalem under the rabbi Gamaliel at approximately the time when Jesus was active; according to the Acts of the Apostles he was also in the capital shortly after Jesus' execution.[18] He himself records his interview with Peter and James, the brother of Jesus,[19] and some of the passages, referred to above, are clearly reproductions of an already existing tradition. Thus Paul may have been, though there is no certainty of this, an eyewitness of some of the events in Jesus' life; he certainly did have conversations with those who were eyewitnesses and he had access to some stereotyped traditions about Jesus.

The Gospels

The outline of Jesus' life to be derived from Paul in no way contradicts the fuller accounts contained in the basic documents, the gospels according to Matthew, Mark, Luke and John. But if these sources are to be appreciated, something must be said of their inter-relationship, of their antecedents and of their nature.

If the texts of Matthew, Mark and Luke are arranged in a table or synopsis consisting of parallel columns, it immediately becomes apparent that these are not distinct documents, since not only do we find a great number of the same sayings and incidents repeated in each, but identical words and phrases are used to describe them,[20] e.g.

Mark i	Matt. viii	Luke iv
32 And at even, when the sun did set, they brought unto him all that were sick, and them that were possessed with devils.	16 And when even was come, they brought unto him many possessed with devils:	40 And when the sun was setting, all they that had any sick with divers diseases brought them unto him; and he laid his hands on every one of them,
33 And all the city was gathered together at the door.		
34 And he healed many that were sick with divers diseases, and cast out many devils;	and he cast out the spirits with a word, and healed all that were sick:	and healed them. ([34] . . . with divers diseases . . .)
		41 And devils also came out from many, crying out, and saying, Thou art the Son of God. And rebuking them,
and he suffered not the devils to speak, because they knew him.		he suffered them not to speak, because they knew that he was the Christ.
	17 that it might be fulfilled which was spoken by Isaiah the prophet, saying, Himself took our infirmities, and bare our diseases.	

This similarity may be explained on the grounds either that each evangelist or gospel-writer drew on the same original document or that one or other of them copied the third. The general consensus of scholarly opinion is to the effect that Matthew and Luke used Mark which was, therefore, the first gospel to be published, being written, probably at Rome, *c.* AD 66, shortly after the Neronian persecution. The principal grounds for assigning priority to Mark are as follows. First, of Mark's 661 verses Matthew reproduces the substance of over 600 in language largely identical with Mark, while Luke does the same for more than fifty per cent of Mark. Second, in any one passage which stands in all three gospels, the majority of Mark's words are found in Matthew and Luke, either alternately or both together. Third, the order of Mark's narrative is mainly reproduced by Matthew and Luke, and where either of these two desert the Marcan order the other is usually found to support him. This identity of content, wording and order is scarcely explicable except on the basis that Matthew and Luke had each a copy of Mark when they came to produce their gospels.

To recognize that Matthew and Luke used Mark and that Mark therefore has chronological priority is not to exhaust the subject of their inter-relationship, since further study of a synopsis reveals that Matthew and Luke have much material in common, some 200 verses in effect, which they have not derived from Mark, e.g.

LUKE XI	MATT. XII
24 The unclean spirit	43 But the unclean spirit,
when he is gone out of the man,	when he is gone out of the man,
passeth through waterless places,	passeth through waterless places,
seeking rest;	seeking rest,
and finding none, he saith,	44 and findeth it not. Then he saith,
I will turn back unto my house	I will return into my house whence I
whence I came out.	came out;
25 And when he is come,	and when he is come,
he findeth it swept and garnished.	he findeth it empty, swept, and
	garnished.
26 Then goeth he, and taketh to him	45 Then goeth he, and taketh with
	himself
seven other spirits more evil than	seven other spirits more evil than
himself;	himself,
and they enter in and dwell there;	and they enter in and dwell there;
and the last state of that man	and the last state of that man
becometh worse than the first.	becometh worse than the first.
	Even so shall it be also unto this evil
	generation.

Again there is a twofold possibility; either the one copied the other or both drew on the same source. Against the first explanation are the facts that the common material appears in totally different contexts and in a different order in each gospel and that the wording is by no means always identical. Hence scholars have concluded that Matthew and Luke made use of a common source, which is usually referred to as Q, from the German *Quelle* meaning a source. But both the extent and nature of Q are difficult to determine with precision. Just as Matthew has copied certain verses of Mark which Luke omits, and vice versa, so each may have included passages from Q which the other has left out. Moreover, Q may not have been a single written document; it could have consisted of both written and oral material. Whatever its exact form, Q was in the main a collection of the sayings of Jesus, together with a few incidents such as the Temptation narrative.

If we remove from Matthew and Luke the material they have each copied from Mark and that which each has taken from Q, then there are left some 400 verses peculiar to Matthew and some 500 peculiar to Luke, the former material being usually referred to as M and the latter as L. But there is no adequate reason for supposing that either M or L were single written documents; each may have consisted of one or more manuscripts together with one or more groups of oral tradition.

It will have become apparent that in discussing the inter-relationship of the first three gospels, we have also begun to consider their antecedents. So it has been seen that Luke, writing between AD 80 and 90, possibly in Greece, drew upon Mark, Q and L, and that Matthew, writing between AD 70 and 100, possibly at Antioch, likewise employed Mark and Q and incorporated M. Can we postulate any other sources? We have already referred to Q as consisting mainly, though not exclusively, of sayings of Jesus, and this is evidence that such collections were in circulation, in written or oral form or both. There are also in existence a number of sayings, not found in the gospels, which are attributed to Jesus, and some of them most probably derived from collections of this type, e.g. 'It is more blessed to give than to receive'.[21] As an illustration of what such a collection was like we may turn to the papyrus discovered in 1897 at Oxyrhynchus in Egypt.[22] This is a fragment of the third century containing sayings of Jesus, written down one after the other with no connecting narrative or indication of circumstances. So we read: 'and then you will see to cast out the mote which is in the eye of your brother', and this is all but identical with Lk. vi. 42b. Or again: 'Says Jesus; a city built on the summit of a high mountain and fortified cannot fall nor be concealed' – this is a variant of Matt. v. 14.

Testimonies

In addition to sayings collections we must also reckon with the existence of catenae of Old Testament texts. The evangelists, as we shall see, interpreted the life and teaching of Jesus as the fulfilment of the Old Testament hope; they therefore quoted frequently from the Jewish Scriptures; but since these books were bulky, costly and had no divisions into chapters and verses, to look up a quotation was anything but easy. To assemble apposite extracts was a simple means of dealing with this problem and an example of such a ready reference booklet is the *Testimonies* of Cyprian of Carthage (*c.* AD 250) described by its author as 'an abridged compendium'. In this work he groups, under appropriate headings, passages from the Bible, which by his day included the New Testament, and so under 'That he would rise again from the dead on the third day', Cyprian writes out Hos. vi. 2; Exod. xix. 10, 11 and Matt. xii. 39, 40. That such collections existed in the first century is rendered probable by the fact that otherwise unrelated texts are associated in the same order and quoted by different writers, so Is. xxviii. 16 and viii. 14 are used both in Rom. ix. 32, 33 and I Peter ii. 6–8. Moreover, the citations frequently agree neither with the Hebrew text of the Old Testament nor with any extant Greek version: this is particularly noticeable in Matthew who in all probability took them from a pre-existing Christian testimony book.

Gospel antecedents

In considering the antecedents of the gospels attention has so far been concentrated upon Matthew and Luke, with Mark as one of their antecedents. But what of Mark itself? It is possible, although not certain, that the author had a set of Old Testament proof texts; he may have had further a collection of the sayings of Jesus, but if so his material was less in quantity than that available to Matthew and Luke. It is likely that he had before him a continuous narrative of the Passion. The reasons for this supposition are: first, the concluding chapters have the nature of a consecutive historical account, although it must be admitted that the order of events was in a sense inevitable, since the arrest must have preceded the trial and the execution must have followed the sentence; second, the narration of single incidents, detached from the close sequence of events, would have satisfied no conceivable need within the life of the early Church. It is indeed in the life of the early Church that we seek further the traces of the tradition about Jesus between his death and our first written accounts. But before so doing the nature of the material must be characterized.

The records about Jesus can, for this purpose, be divided into sayings and doings. We have already noted that the former category was preserved with little or no connecting narrative or indication of the circumstances in which the words or parables were uttered. The same would appear to have been the situation in general with regard to Jesus' actions; quite a number of incidents recorded in the gospels are lacking in information as to where or when they happened. Thus the story of the healing of the leper in Mk. i. 40–45 is detached from any topographical or temporal setting. After an editorial comment – 'And he went into their synagogues throughout all Galilee, preaching and casting out devils' – the bald statement follows: 'And there cometh to him a leper'. Similarly the healing of the deaf mute (Mk. vii. 32–37) is presented without any attempt at a precise location beyond the preceding editorial statement which suggests that it was somewhere in the region of the sea of Galilee. Moreover, in several cases where a particular day is specified, it is clear that this is no more than a deduction from the story itself. So when the disciples pluck ears of corn, the Pharisees ask: 'Why do they on the sabbath day that which is not lawful?' Hence the evangelist can introduce the event with the words: 'And it came to pass, that as he was going on the sabbath day through the cornfields . . .'[23] It is evidence of this kind that leads us to conclude that in the preliterary period of the gospel tradition stories about Jesus, with the probable exception of the Passion narrative, circulated as isolated units in the same way that his sayings were remembered divorced from time and place. Consequently, further study of the antecedents of the written gospels has been conducted in accordance with the methods of Form Criticism, which directs attention to the separate units, seeks to classify them according to their form, then tries to recover the original form which may have been modified during the oral period, and finally attempts to define the *Sitz im Leben* or life-situation out of which the material sprang.

Form Criticism

The several forms of the tradition are commonly reduced to four principal ones. First there are the *Pronouncement-Stories*, which are characterized by their brevity and simplicity and by their lack of interest in portraiture; they culminate in, and are rounded off by, a saying of Jesus that expresses an ethical or religious precept. Thus the story of the Tribute Money[24] reaches its climax in the pronouncement: 'Render unto Caesar the things that are Caesar's, and unto God the things that are God's.' Next there are the *Miracle-Stories*; unlike the former these have a certain wealth of detail and, where a healing is involved, they provide a miniature history of the illness, describe its severity, the technique used to cure it and its outcome. So in the story of the epileptic boy[25] the sufferer is stated to have been subject to fits from infancy; the effects – foaming at the mouth and grinding of teeth – are graphically set forth; Jesus speaks to him, takes him by the hand, 'and he arose'. The *Sayings*, our third category, are by no means uniform. They include aphorisms and proverbs as well as parables. They may be short and evidence Hebrew parallelism, according to which what is stated in the first line of a couplet is reproduced in a different way in the second line, e.g.

> Be not anxious for your life, what ye shall eat;
> nor yet for your body, what ye shall put on.
> For the life is more than the food,
> And the body than the raiment.[26]

They may be extended stories, such as the parable of the Prodigal Son.[27] Equally the *Stories about Jesus* cannot be reduced to a single sharply defined form, and include such incidents as the calling of the disciples[28] and the visit to Nazareth.[29]

To attempt to detect the modifications which these forms have undergone during the oral period is a delicate task and agreement is by no means always possible, since arguments brought forward by one critic in favour of a supposed 'original' may not convince another, and in any case the balance of probabilities does not bring certainty. Nevertheless such detection is on occasion quite possible, so the example of Hebrew parallelism quoted above from Luke appears in Matthew with an addition to the first line of the words 'or what ye shall drink'.[30] Since this extra clause destroys the balance of the couplet, we may reasonably assume that it represents a modification of the original saying, and that the Lucan version is to be preferred to the Matthean.

In considering the life-situation of this material, it has to be recognized that this is twofold; there is first the *Sitz im Leben* in the early Church, and there is second the *Sitz im Leben* in the ministry of Jesus. Each unit of the tradition has had its connexion with certain interests in the life of the Church and with the expression of that life. In other words the gospel tradition was closely related to the Church's life, in part grew out of it and was designed for it. Amongst these interests may be specified preaching, teaching, polemics, apologetics, confession and worship. The task of preaching was to bring the hearers to repentance and belief; it was to force upon them the crisis of decision. Hence we can understand the importance of the Miracle-Story for this purpose; the story of the Stilling of the Storm reaches its climax with the disciples' question, which is also the question of the preacher to his possible converts, 'Who then is this, that even the wind and the sea obey him?'[31]

The sayings collections preserve material needed for the teaching of candidates for baptism; they are a kind of primitive Christian catechism. Again the accounts of the Last Supper provide the charter deeds and the pattern of eucharistic worship. But to suppose that the material was nothing more than the creation of the early Christian community to answer its contemporary needs would be to make an unwarrantable assumption, and hence the need to seek a further *Sitz im Leben* in the ministry of Jesus. This task too bristles with difficulties and the critic is in danger of finding himself within a vicious circle. His knowledge of Jesus' ministry rests upon the gospels; if, on this basis, he reaches some conception of the nature of that ministry and then attempts to fit the separate units into that conception, he is liable to replace the gospel record with a hypothetical construction of his own, the validity of which can also be questioned. This does not mean that the attempt should not be made, but he would be a rash man who would claim for his conclusion more than a tentative character.

Whatever the forms of the material, whatever the needs to which it answered, it was passed on at first by word of mouth. Within the Judaism of Jesus' day oral transmission of the law was a widespread practice. There were those who learned it off, parrot-like, and repeated it when required, and there were those who added an interpretation. Since the first Christians were Jews, familiar therefore with these techniques, we may reasonably conclude that a similar practice of transmission and interpretation of the sayings and acts of Jesus was pursued. Moreover since the oral law was by its very nature *oral*, it was not written down, although some brief notes were permitted. A similar attitude on the part of the first Christians serves to explain the delay in writing down the tradition about Jesus. This reserve as regards the written word would have broken down as Christianity moved out into the Gentile world, and so eventually transcription began, issuing in the gospels we now possess, whose nature and purpose must be finally surveyed.

Nature and Purpose of the Gospels

Whatever the gospels were, they were certainly not biographies. They were not attempts either to trace the course of Jesus' life or to depict the development of his personality. Mark begins abruptly with the baptism of John, when Jesus was some thirty years old, and finishes his record with Jesus' death twelve months later. Similarly, the fourth gospel confines itself to the public ministry, although it stretches it out to some three years' duration. Matthew and Luke supply birth stories, and the latter records one incident when Jesus was twelve years old, but they tell us virtually nothing of his childhood, youth and early manhood. Indeed it is impossible to fit the gospels into any known genre of literature contemporary with their production. Because of this unique character, because there is no other literary form with which they can be compared, any judgement upon their nature must be based in the first instance upon them alone.

When the structure of the gospels is examined, we recognize the correctness of the assertion that they are 'passion narratives with extended introduction'.[32] This is particularly true of Mark, six of whose sixteen chapters are devoted to the final week in Jerusalem, but it is also applicable to the writings of the other evangelists. How is this disproportionate space allotted to the few days of the Passion to be explained? Recognizing that each complete gospel, as distinct from the separate units from which it has been composed, had a life-setting in the early Church, we have to acknowledge the centrality of the cross of Jesus in the primitive preaching. 'We preach Christ crucified . . . I determined not to know anything among you, save Jesus Christ, and him crucified.'[33]

Thus the attention devoted to the Passion in the gospels corresponds to its importance in the primitive preaching, and this indicates a connexion between the two, i.e. between written gospel and oral preaching. As a specimen of this preaching we may take the sermon ascribed to Peter at Joppa; he refers to the good news 'which was published throughout all Judaea, beginning from Galilee, after the baptism which John preached; even Jesus of Nazareth, how that God anointed him with the Holy Ghost and with power: who went about doing good, and healing all that were oppressed of the devil; for God was with him. And we are witnesses of all things which he did both in the country of the Jews, and in Jerusalem; whom also they slew, hanging him on a tree. Him God raised up the third day, and gave him to be made manifest.'[34] These words are as good a brief summary of the contents and order of the Marcan gospel as could be found, and they point the way to a definition of the nature of the gospels. They are the preaching, the kerygma, written down; they are not objective history, as this is commonly understood today, they are kerygmatic history. The title given to these documents, i.e. gospels, leads to the same conclusion, for gospel means good news. Thus these works are the proclamation that something has happened, that this constitutes good news, and the news is that God's promises, the fulfilment of which was eagerly awaited at the time of Jesus, as we have seen from our sketch of the background, were in the process of realization through Jesus of Nazareth.

To say that the gospels are kerygmatic history is to re-emphasize their peculiar character. The evangelists and their fellow believers did not view Jesus as a figure of the past but rather as the risen Lord, present with his power and word, so that in relating his ministry they proclaimed who he is and not who he was. Similarly they reproduced his sayings not as recollections out of the past but as directions for the present and the future. Thus the gospels are at one and the same time both the testimony of the Church's faith in Jesus and the narration, however summary, of his history.

So closely are these two interwoven, viz. the Jesus of history and the Jesus of faith, that it is all but impossible to separate them. Indeed many would contend that such an attempt is vain, that the Christian faith in Jesus is true and that any other interpretation would not do justice to the facts. Moreover, it may be argued that the historical method alone cannot resolve the question since the Jesus of faith is clearly unique, while the historical approach rests on the belief that 'the universe and society possess sufficient uniformity to exclude the possibility of overly pronounced deviations'.[35] Indeed, 'historical investigation proceeds on the assumption that a study of the past is only possible if the supernatural is shouldered out of the way, for historical study knows no techniques or methods for evaluating the supernatural. Faith stakes its all on the interpenetration of the natural and the supernatural most clearly revealed in gospel history',[36] and so the inquiry into the Jesus of history cannot be divorced from the pronouncements of faith. This does not mean that the techniques of the historian's craft are not to be applied to the gospels; it does mean that the application of these techniques cannot be expected to validate the Christian claim. The historian may legitimately determine that the crucifixion of Jesus was an historical fact; he cannot say that God was in Christ reconciling the world unto himself. Yet the historical question is of supreme importance, since the centre and authority of the Christian religion is to be sought in the action or revelation of God in the person of the man Jesus whose historical life is a necessary dynamic part of that religion. Were this not so, were this authority to be found in spiritual experience alone, then the reality of the historical life would not matter and the story of Jesus could be no more than a myth or fable providing a terminology for the rationalization of that spiritual experience. To this view the evangelists were themselves opposed; despite the kerygmatic nature of their writing, they were concerned with the historical reality of the events, and one of them, Luke, goes out of his way to assert: 'Many writers have undertaken to draw up an account of the events that have happened among us, following the traditions handed down to us by the original eyewitnesses and servants of the Gospel. And so I in my turn, your Excellency, as one who has gone over the whole course of these events in detail, have decided to write a connected narrative for you, so as to give you authentic knowledge about the matters of which you have been informed.'[37] But while relating the events, they were concerned above all with their meaning, and they affirmed that certain of the things that Jesus had said and done were not understood even by the chosen circle of his disciples.[38] It was only in the light of subsequent experience, so they believed, that the correct importance and interpretation of them could be given, and this they proceeded to do.

If the nature of the gospel material is kerygmatic, then the over-all purpose of the evangelists may be defined as the setting down of the preaching in written form. But this conclusion does not exclude the possibility that each evangelist had a subsidiary purpose or purposes in mind, and some of these may be briefly indicated. According to Papias, bishop of Hierapolis about 140, Mark based his gospel upon the reminiscences of Peter and wrote it down after the latter's death. There is much to be said for accepting the accuracy of this statement, since the gospel contains a number of unnecessary details which are best explained as the preservation of individual recollections (e.g. the 'green grass' in vi. 39) in which case Mark's motive was to give the gospel a permanent written form in view of the passing of the first generation of believers. It is to be noted that he gives explanations of Jewish customs and thus intended to make the Jewish milieu intelligible to Gentile readers. Luke's gospel which, as we have seen, is an enlarged edition of Mark was also directed towards Gentile readers and this is made clear by the preface quoted above. Luke was also influenced by an apologetic aim, viz. to show how from the beginning the Christian faith was not condemned willingly by the Roman authorities, and so he frequently intimates that the government representatives refused to take up a hostile attitude to Jesus. Matthew is decidedly Jewish in flavour and to that extent commends the faith not to the Gentiles but to the Jews. From the structure of the work and from the alterations made to the principal source, Mark, it has been concluded that the book was intended for reading at the gatherings for worship. John's gospel, probably the latest to be written *c.* 100, is more theological in its outlook than the three Synoptics. The author, possibly a disciple of the apostle John with the same name and the title 'Elder', states his purpose in these words: 'these are written, that ye may believe that Jesus is the Christ, the Son of God; and that believing ye may have life in his name.'[39] Hence he seeks to draw out the meaning of Jesus' actions in the form of an inspired meditation. With the needs of the contemporary Church before him, he was also interested in showing the relevance of the historical life of Jesus to the present life of the Christians, and so intimates how the sacramental acts, Baptism and the Eucharist, make that past history a present experience.

These then are the principal sources for our knowledge of the life and teaching of Jesus, the account of which can now be taken up from the preaching of John the Baptist, who announced the imminence of God's intervention and the advent of one greater than he.

THE MESSAGE AND MINISTRY OF JESUS

The message of John the Baptist, as we have seen, was a call to repentance and to baptism in view of the imminence of the Kingdom. According to our sources – and their historicity at this point cannot be doubted since the baptism of the *sinless* Jesus presented a problem to later Christians – Jesus answered this summons, thus identifying himself with his people.[1] But although to Herod Jesus was John the Baptist all over again,[2] the gospels draw a sharp contrast between the two. John was the harbinger of the Kingdom, while Jesus was not a herald but the very one through whom the Kingdom was to be established. The difference is like that between the eleventh and twelfth hours. According to Jesus' message the Kingdom of God was already dawning: 'Blessed are the eyes which see the things that ye see: for I say unto you, that many prophets and kings desired to see the things which ye see, and saw them not; and to hear the things which ye hear, and heard them not.'[3]

Here then is a new feature: the apocalyptists and even John were concerned with the future; Jesus was concerned with the present eschatologically conceived, i.e. understood in terms of the eschaton or end actually taking place. So 'the kingdom of God is come upon you.'[4] It is true that Jesus could nevertheless teach his disciples to pray: 'Thy kingdom come', but this future consummation is already a present reality in the message and mission of Jesus. Thus, according to him, the decisive moment of God's action had arrived, the exercise of the divine sovereign power was inaugurated. God was no longer the one about to come, rather the essential mystery of Jesus was to make the reality of God and of his rule present.

The Parables of Jesus

In his parables, which were not allegories but short stories each with its central point, Jesus sought both to convey some understanding of the nature of the Kingdom and also to involve his hearers so that they ceased to be mere onlookers and were presented with a crisis of decision. The majority of the Jews conceived the Kingdom in political terms: the day would come when they would rise in revolt and, with God's help, would overthrow the occupying power and restore the glory of David's reign under one of his descendants. Jesus repudiated this political ideal; to him the Kingdom was the outcome of a hidden process which depended entirely, not upon human effort, but upon the divine action. So he likened the Kingdom to yeast, fermenting within the dough until it swells and bubbles, even as his ministry was now permeating the dead lump of official Judaism;[5] he compared it with a seed growing secretly which, without human assistance, develops and ripens.[6] While insisting in this way on the divine initiative, Jesus also sought to elicit a response from the crowds that flocked to hear him. Like the man who found a treasure hid in a field, they were to give their all that they might have this heavenly treasure.[7] Like the Unjust Steward, whose malpractices had been detected, they were to take urgent and decisive action in view of the crisis before them.[8] Other parables, like that of the Marriage Feast[9] relate to Israel's rejection of Jesus' proclamation of the Kingdom, and the consequent summons to publicans and sinners.

The Miracles of Jesus

Inseparably connected with this are the miracles ascribed to Jesus. 'No one,' argues Dibelius, 'would have told such stories about Jesus if he had not actually held the role of miracle-worker. Generally speaking these narratives also testify . . . to the fact that Jesus actually did such astonishing things. Nothing of the sort was related of John the Baptist, although he had a prophet's call.'[10] But what was the meaning of these actions? Since the good news is basically occurrence, something which happens, the miracles proclaimed in deed what the parables conveyed in words: they were signs of the coming of the Kingdom. Just as, when God had intervened to save his chosen people from Egypt, Pharaoh's servants had admitted: 'This is the finger of God',[11] so Jesus, questioned about his miracles, declared: 'If I by the finger of God cast out devils, then is the kingdom of God come upon you.'[12] The exorcisms were signs that the power of evil was being broken, that God's dominion over a fallen world was being restored and that consequently the eschatological reign of God was being inaugurated. The battle in which Jesus was engaged was not one involving chariots and legions, but a spiritual campaign to overthrow Satan, and the liberation of the demon-possessed was indicative of his success, for no one can spoil the goods of a strong man without first rendering him powerless.[13] So Isaiah's prophecy of the release of the captives and of the restoration of the sight of the blind was being fulfilled.[14]

Inevitably this raised the question: who is this man who does these things? Hence John the Baptist, imprisoned by Herod, sent two of his followers to ask: 'Art thou he that cometh, or look we for another?'

Jesus' reply, which in all essentials probably represents a reliable tradition, was: 'Go your way, and tell John what things ye have seen and heard; the blind receive their sight, the lame walk, the lepers are cleansed, and the deaf hear, the dead are raised up, the poor have good tidings preached to them.'[15] Thus the miracles are not only signs of the Kingdom, they are proof that its inauguration takes place in Jesus and his activity. They contain therefore a clue to the nature of his ministry. He is the divine agent, and the age of the promised Messiah is dawning. Moses fed the chosen people with manna in the wilderness: Jesus feeds the five thousand with bread in the wilderness and gives them a foretaste of the Messianic banquet, of the great feast of the blessed which will take place, according to eschatological expectation, when the Kingdom is consummated.[16]

Jesus' ethical teaching

It follows from this that Jesus was not primarily a teacher, one with some information or instruction to impart; he had come to *do* something, viz. to proclaim and establish the Kingdom of God. Nevertheless, this message and activity carried certain implications. Entrance into the Kingdom involves a radical transformation; as John had asserted, it required repentance, which is to be understood not as a mere *feeling* of sorrow for past misdeeds but as a complete change of heart, an entirely fresh orientation. The kind of life that is to issue from such a *volte-face* was illustrated by Jesus in what is usually called his ethical teaching. The picture of human life that he drew is a picture of human life in the Kingdom of God on earth, and his moral demands consequently presuppose a changed nature. In this respect there was a fundamental difference between Jesus and the scribes for whom the law was the embodiment of all moral requirements. As such it formalized the authority of the divine will, which was understood to be expressed in a series of legal enactments; any changes, if at all possible, were changes in the law not in the human heart. So the law, rather than God, had become man's real authority, and instead of encouraging a divine human-encounter, it frustrated it. The opposition between Jesus and the scribes was thus on a difference of principle; to him right living was the spontaneous activity of a transformed character; to them it was obedience to a discipline imposed from without. While the scribes were concerned to interpret the law and apply it to every situation, Jesus refused to legislate[17] and did not promulgate a series of rules.

This basic variance of outlook is to be seen in the question put by the scribe to Jesus: what commandment is the first of all?[18] The Rabbis were prepared to admit that one commandment might have priority in that all the others could be deduced from it; this priority however was not absolute but logical, since each commandment was as important as another. Jesus' reply, to the effect that we must love God and our neighbours as ourselves, reveals his antinomianism. These precepts are not 'legal'; they neither prescribe nor forbid any specific action; they cannot be enforced and they apply entirely to man's inner disposition. Outward behaviour should not be the result of conformity to a rule, but the fruit of an inward revolution. Jesus demanded not a reformation of behaviour but a transformation of character, for to him sin was not primarily a matter of omissions and commissions but a condition of the soul which, through the divine forgiveness, could be radically altered. The ethics of the law issue in self-righteousness, for it is man alone who thereby achieves his own perfection;[19] the ethics of Jesus centre in man's believing response to his proclamation of the Kingdom, in the repentance and re-creation thereby involved.

The scribes and Pharisees correctly perceived that their ideal and that of Jesus were incompatible, because Jesus was not a reformer of the law but one who superseded its authority: 'Ye have heard that it was said . . . But I say unto you . . .'[20] The gospels represent a mounting hostility on the part of the official guardians of Judaism to the Nazarene prophet as he pursued his itinerant ministry, now preaching in the open air, now taking the opportunity to proclaim his message in the setting of the synagogue services, and although we may be uncertain of the exact chronological sequence of the events, there is no reason to doubt the general picture.

Jesus' ministry

According to Mark, the scribes first of all indulged in silent criticism:[21] their next step was to question the disciples,[22] then to challenge Jesus directly,[23] and finally to lay plans to have him silenced.[24] The same source describes a sustained campaign to discredit him. His opponents spread the rumour that his activities were the consequence of demon possession:[25] they asked him to produce a sign from heaven:[26] they demanded that he should declare by what authority he did these things,[27] and they wanted to know whether it was right to pay taxes to the Roman government,[28] confident that if his reply was affirmative they could compromise him in the eyes of the people, and if negative that they could embroil him with the civil authorities. With considerable dialectical skill Jesus refused to be trapped, and this failure on the part of his opponents left them with only one possible course: he had to be silenced once and for all. According to the records, Jesus foresaw this outcome and foretold his eventual suffering and death. While the details of these prophecies[29] have in all probability been written up after the events, it would be the height of scepticism to doubt that Jesus did expect a violent death, for commonsense would tell him that there could be no other end to the path he was treading and, moreover, he had the example of John before him. These same prophecies all affirm that the expected death would not be final, but that he would rise from the dead. Jesus' consciousness of his divine mission, coupled with his realization that death awaited him, combined naturally to convince him that whatever the immediate result, his vindication by God would follow – again scepticism about this element in the prophecies is scarcely necessary.

On Friday, April 3, AD 33, according to one feasible computation of the date, Jesus was executed. The final sequence of events that led to this is given in great detail by the four evangelists, and if allowance is made for their apologetic purpose, which was to play down the responsibility of the Roman authorities, a coherent account emerges.

On the Sunday before the feast of the Passover, Jesus came to Jerusalem and was acclaimed by his followers.[30] According to John,[31] the messianic significance of this entry, in fulfilment of Zechariah ix. 9, was not immediately appreciated, and this is confirmed by the apparent unconcern of both the Jewish authorities and the Roman administration. After registering a protest against trading in the Temple area, which was reported to the hierarchs and further incensed them against him,[32] Jesus withdrew to the nearby village of Bethany, where he made his temporary headquarters, coming into the Holy City each morning.

On the Thursday night Jesus gathered his disciples around him for a meal in Jerusalem[33] and then withdrew to an olive grove for prayer. Meanwhile the Jewish leaders had intimated to the Roman governor that Jesus was politically suspect and was likely to cause trouble, especially as feelings often ran high during a major festival. Pilate, who, according to Philo[34] and Josephus,[35] supported by a passage in Luke,[36] was both cruel and ruthless, acted swiftly. A detachment of Roman troops, assisted by a posse of Temple police, and guided by one of Jesus' own disciples, Judas, went to the garden of Gethsemane, arrested Jesus and took him in custody to the High Priest's residence. Early in the morning, after a brief deliberation by the Sanhedrin, the supreme Jewish court, Jesus was despatched to Pilate, who examined him as an agitator or a person who might become the occasion of a political disturbance. The death sentence was passed and, following a scourging and a mockery by Pilate's soldiers, Jesus was removed from the procurator's court to the place of execution, where he was crucified, a summary statement of the cause for which he had been condemned being affixed above him: The King of the Jews.[37] Since the Jews regarded it as a duty to ensure that the bodies of executed persons were given decent burial before nightfall, one, Joseph of Arimathea, obtained the necessary permission from the procurator and the body of the dead Jesus was laid in a nearby tomb.

The sources do not represent this as the end of the story of Jesus of Nazareth, but before considering the sequel, it is necessary to integrate the events outlined with the previous account of Jesus' message and ministry. In effect, this involves the attempt to answer two inter-related questions: how did Jesus understand his death and, in particular, its relation to the Kingdom? how did Jesus conceive of himself and, in particular, his relation to the Kingdom?

The Messiahship of Jesus

There seems little reason to doubt that Jesus' choice of twelve Apostles involved the claim, by symbolic action akin to prophetic symbolism, that he was to be the founder of a Messianic community that should replace the Old Israel as the elect of God. There is further the fact that he was executed as a political agitator and this must have involved on his part the acknowledgement of some sort of Messianic pretension. Yet the first three gospels never attribute to Jesus any explicit affirmation of Messiahship, and even when Peter confesses him to be such,[38] he neither accepts nor rejects the title. Since the beginning of this century it has been customary to interpret this silence in terms of the 'Messianic secret'. As first propounded this thesis was to the effect that this was no more than a literary device of the evangelists to explain how Jesus, later believed to be the Messiah, was not recognized during his lifetime. The true history of Jesus was thus a non-Messianic history which has been reinterpreted in the light of the Church's faith. This scarcely seems to accord with the facts: there is no reason to suppose that Jesus did not awaken Messianic expectations by his coming or that his followers, during his lifetime, did not believe him to be the Messiah. 'We hoped that it was he which should redeem Israel',[39] say the two disciples on the Emmaus road, voicing quite accurately the conviction of Jesus' followers before his death. Inevitably the death would disappoint this hope and, if it were the end, finally destroy it, but that the hope existed prior to the crucifixion it is unnecessary to deny. What then of Jesus' silence?

Jesus' restraint in the use, and not rejection, of the title is readily understandable when it is remembered that, although there was no single fixed concept of the Messiah, to many of his contemporaries it was charged with a political significance which Jesus was not prepared to endorse. To claim openly to be the Messiah would have been to place himself at the head of an insurrection, and this, it cannot be questioned, was contrary to his intention. Moreover it was believed that the Messiah would only be known and accepted when he had revealed his identity through his work of salvation. 'According to Jewish thought,' states S. Mowinckel, 'it is only then that he will be Messiah in the full sense of the term. Before that time we may say that he is *Messias designatus*, a claimant to Messianic status'[40] – so it is the Messianic work that makes him the Messiah and manifests him as such. Thus Jesus during his ministry was Messiah designate and only when he had accomplished his mission was he enthroned as Messiah; prior to this any claim would be premature.

Because of Jesus' reticence in the use of this title, since it would give rise to misconception, it is legitimate to speak of his self-consciousness, although, in the absence of a certain chronology, it is not possible to trace any development. Thus, *pace* certain critics,[41] it may be accepted that Jesus reflected upon his mission, and his understanding of it crystallized in a further title, that of the Son of man. It is difficult to believe that this title, which is hardly used at all in the New Testament outside the gospels and which is unintelligible in Greek, could have been other than what it is repeatedly represented to be, i.e. a self-designation of Jesus. The Son of man sayings attributed to him are of three kinds: those in which he identified himself during his ministry with the Son of man;[42] those in which he refers to the coming suffering and resurrection of the Son of man,[43] and those in which he speaks of the future glory of the exalted Son of man and appears to distinguish himself from him.[44] The origin of the concept is most probably to be sought in Daniel vii. 13ff. where 'one like unto a son of man' comes to God and 'there was given him dominion, and glory, and a kingdom'. The Son of man is thus primarily a triumphant figure, and the groups of sayings just listed may be integrated if it is recognized that just as Jesus, while being Messiah designate, had yet to enter on his Messiahship, so he had yet to become the exalted Son of man, while exercising, by anticipation, the functions appertaining to that glorified state.

Jesus and his death

The inter-relation of our two questions – Jesus' understanding of himself and of his death – has now become apparent, in that according to one group of these sayings the Son of man is to receive dominion *after* suffering. This association of suffering and glory is already apparent in the Daniel passage, for there the Son of man, who is identified with the saints of the Most High, is, prior to his exaltation, subjected to a succession of oppressors. Daniel voices the majority view of the Old Testament writers, so forcibly expressed by Job's three friends, that suffering is the consequence of one's sin.[45] There is however an alternative interpretation of suffering and death to be found in the Old Testament, both in the so-called Servant Songs of Deutero-Isaiah[46] and in the regulations for sacrifice. The Servant, whose exact identity is uncertain but may be the ideal Israel, bears the consequences not of his own sin but of the sin of others: his suffering is representative. 'He was wounded for our transgressions, he was bruised for our iniquities . . . the Lord hath laid on him the iniquity of us all . . . when thou shalt make his soul an offering for sin. . . . Behold, my servant shall deal wisely, he shall be exalted and lifted up.' It is a matter of much debate how far Jesus interpreted his mission in these terms.[47] If he did not, then it remains an insoluble problem why Jesus, who foresaw his death and was thoroughly familiar with the Old Testament, should have neglected the most apposite series of passages that could have given meaning to it – passages which were certainly appreciated and applied by his followers.[48] To suppose that Jesus knew he was to suffer but could see no reason for so doing is to place him in the category of Job – Christians have always rated him much higher.

Within the Servant Songs themselves and amongst the catenae just quoted, there is clear evidence of an association between his suffering and death and sacrificial ideas: 'thou shalt make his soul an offering for sin'. To the Jew the sacrificial system was the God-given means for removing sin; by sacrifice he believed that his sin was covered so that it no longer stood as an obstacle between himself and God. It was the way of restoring fellowship with God to whom life was offered. At the Last Supper, according to Mark,[49] Jesus took a cup of wine and said: 'This is my blood of the covenant which is shed for many.' These words have as their background the ceremony in Exodus xxiv when God brought his chosen people into covenant with him, and they have a parallel in Isaiah xlii. 6 where it is stated that God will give the Servant 'for a covenant of the people'. The primary meaning is that Jesus' death is an atoning or reconciling death whereby a new covenant is sealed and ratified through his self-offering. In the Matthean account the blood is said to be poured out 'unto remission of sins'[50] and this is a correct exegesis of the words 'shed for many' by which Jesus' death is interpreted as an expiatory sacrifice for sin. In Mark the verse immediately following connects this with the Kingdom: 'Verily I say unto you, I will no more drink of the fruit of the vine, until that day when I drink it new in the kingdom of God.' So the cup not only foreshadows the approaching death but heralds the joy of the Kingdom. Even under the threat of the cross Jesus is confident that the Kingdom will be set up. This hope can only mean that he believed his death to be a necessary step to the establishment of the Kingdom.[51] Beyond the suffering and death, he saw his exaltation which would be his vindication.

This concept of a suffering Messiah was unknown to the Judaism of Jesus' day, and indeed, while it would be wrong to attempt to detach Jesus from his environment, he himself stands out from it and defies all attempts to fit him into contemporary categories. Although he was addressed as 'Rabbi', he was quite unrabbinic in his teaching and behaviour; he did not wait for the people to come to him, he went out to them; he did not just attract disciples, he sought and called them; he did not confine his teaching to the synagogue, he made use of every opportunity, frequently teaching in the open air to all sorts and conditions of men; he spoke with an immediacy and an authority which astonished his hearers. Unlike John the Baptist, he was no prophet of the ancient school; he said nothing, as far as one can tell, of a calling and never employed the prophetic formula: 'Thus saith the Lord.' Again he cannot be classified as an apocalyptic visionary, since he made no claim to have seen visions nor did he rest his authority on ecstatic states. On the contrary the authority with which he spoke was the same authority that gave the Jewish law its form and substance. He was conscious that he was bringing in a new order and that his life and death were not just a human act but an act of God in flesh and blood. It is true that Jesus did not 'indulge publicly in theological reflection with regard to his own Person',[52] but it is clear that he regarded himself as standing in a unique relationship to God, so that God was not only acting through him but in him.

To Jesus God was Father – but it has to be noted that he is not represented as speaking of the Fatherhood of God save within the confined circle of his closest followers. The reason for this reticence may be sought in the fact that the Father was the supreme reality in Jesus' life. 'His experience of the Father is something so profound and so moving that it will not bear to be spoken about except to those who have shown themselves to be fitted to hear.'[53] Jesus' absolute obedience to his Father is revealed in his prayer in the garden of Gethsemane, which there is no reason to doubt was audible to his disciples, and he addresses him not in the normal fashion of the Aramaic-speaking Jew as *ahbi*, but as *abba*, which is the more familiar term used of one's earthly progenitor. Thus one may speak of a conscious identification with God on the part of Jesus, or, in Cullmann's phrase, one may say 'he is related to God as no other man is'.[54]

His Jewish opponents, so we are informed, appreciated this claim implicit in Jesus' mission. When he said to the paralytic: 'Son, thy sins are forgiven', they reasoned: 'Who can forgive sins but one, even God?'[55] Since to them the expected Messiah would come to bring triumph to the righteous, while this man concerned himself with sinners and outcasts, they were not prepared to admit that his action was the action of God, and so they brought him to his death. This, humanly speaking, should have been the end of the story of Jesus of Nazareth. That it was not was the conviction of the early Christians, who believed him to have been raised from the dead and to have ascended into heaven.

Jesus' resurrection

Although to speak of Jesus' resurrection at this point in the account of his ministry and message is chronologically accurate, to do so is to treat the basic documents with some violence, since they were written in the light of that event. The resurrection is not just the climax of the gospels; without it, there would be no gospels or gospel at all. It was the resurrection that created belief in Jesus as Lord and illuminated both his death and the ministry that preceded it. Nor is this event capable of direct historical investigation: no account of it is given, since the early Christians were concerned only with the fact and not with the method, and if the claim be justified that here was no mere survival but an actual raising from the dead then this was something unique and miraculous which involves the acceptance of the reality of the divine action in history. The accounts of the resurrection appearances, impossible though it may be to reconcile them, are evidence that Jesus' followers were convinced that they had seen him risen and had had a personal encounter not with a ghost but with one who had died but was now alive, having broken the power of death. But the 'resurrection itself belongs to Christian faith since it is described . . . as the ratification by God of the obedience of Jesus and of his righteousness. The resurrection is therefore meaningless and ultimately trivial apart from the belief in the active power of the living God and in the ultimate truth of what Jesus said and did. It is also meaningless apart from the recognition that a particular historical life and death can have universal and ultimate significance.'[56]

It was because of this event, accepted on the evidence of the Apostles and tested in their own experience, that the first Christians came to look upon the man Jesus of Nazareth as the direct revelation of God, not only for the past but for the present. To them the story of Jesus was the story of the eschatological action of God, culminating in Calvary and the victory of the resurrection so that the power of God's reign was established in history. It was this Jesus, the risen and ascended Christ, who was the Founder of Christianity, according to the view of its earliest adherents, as a new religion, the principal features of which were to be worked out in what is usually known as the Apostolic Age.

CHAPTER TWO

THE APOSTOLIC AGE

The Background – Sources – Expansion and Development – Beliefs – Worship – Social Life

THE BACKGROUND

Hellenistic Judaism

SINCE the birthplace of Christianity was Palestine, its founder a Jew by race and its first adherents were of the same nationality, the environment of the Church in its earliest days was that of first-century Judaism, the main characteristics of which have been already surveyed in the preceding chapter. Indeed, initially, Christianity seemed indistinguishable from its parent and was regarded by many as no more than another sect within Judaism, and so Gallio, proconsul of Achaia, refused to intervene in a controversy between the Jewish community at Corinth and some Christian missionaries on the grounds that the trouble related to 'questions about words and names and your own law'.[1] It was not long, however, before the Good News of Jesus the Christ was carried beyond the confines of Galilee and Judaea and was proclaimed to the Hellenistic world, thus bringing a necessary change of background. A bridge between the two, between Judaism and Hellenism, already existed in the form of Hellenistic Judaism, but the difference between Judaism within and outside Palestine should not be exaggerated; such differences as existed were largely matters of emphasis.

The religious life of these Jewish communities, scattered the length and breadth of the Roman Empire, centred in the synagogues, where the version of the Old Testament in use was the Septuagint, a Greek translation made at Alexandria some two hundred years before the birth of Christ. To these synagogues were also attached a not inconsiderable number of 'God-fearers', pagans who were attracted by the monotheism and way of life, but who refused to take the final step of being circumcised and acquiring Jewish citizenship. Here was fertile ground for the Christian message, since these people were familiar with the Old Testament whose fulfilment was being proclaimed.

Pagan religion

The non-Jews or pagans, who formed the bulk of the population of the Roman world were also susceptible, but for different reasons. The breakdown of the city state, for which the conquests of Alexander were not a little responsible, had led to the decay of local patriotism. The establishment of the Empire, after Octavius' victory at Actium in 4 BC and his acceptance of the title Augustus four years later, produced a political system that seemed world-wide in its scope and beyond the comprehension of the individual citizen; he could neither control it nor contribute directly to it. In this condition of apparent helplessness small solace was to be found in the worship of the ancient gods. The scepticism of the closing decades of the Republic persisted among the educated classes, as typified by Pliny the Elder, AD 23–79, despite the restoration of the cultus under Augustus, who assumed the office of Pontifex Maximus. His successors, with the exception of Nero, continued his policy, but for most it was no more than a formality, being, together with Emperor-worship which began with Julius Caesar and derived ultimately from Alexander, a reasonable expedient to provide a unifying focus for the many peoples now united within the one domain.

The Philosophical Schools

To this disregard for the gods of the past the various schools of philosophy contributed in no small measure. Neither the Academic or Platonic nor the Peripatetic or Aristotelian were much in vogue in the first century AD, but the Stoic, founded by Zeno of Citium *c.* 300 BC, and the Epicurean, which derived from Epicurus, 341–270 BC, had their adherents and these two systems each undermined the current mythology. The Epicureans denied that the gods had any concern for human life, while the Stoics were contemptuous of the Olympian hierarchy, regarded the stories of the gods as allegories and affirmed that the supreme reality was immanent in the universe as a refined form of matter. Stoicism as expounded by Seneca, who was executed on the orders of Nero in 65, was a not ignoble creed, with its emphasis on the brotherhood of men and the need for moral endeavour, but it was in the main esoteric and aristocratic. Such popularization as it achieved was the work of the Cynics, itinerant philosophic missionaries who were the mendicant monks of paganism, but while some of them earned a deserved reputation, most were ignorant and corrupt pretenders who brought discredit on the name.

The character of philosophy during this period was no longer the same as in previous centuries. The intellectual curiosity that had provided the initial impulse had waned, and instead of speculation, the study of moral problems had come to the fore. Stoics and Epicureans were concerned with the culture of the individual moral life; they sought for an inner peace. They propounded a standard of values different from that of the world outside and sought to convert men to their ideals of conduct. So Epictetus, who was amongst the philosophers banished by Domitian in AD 93, describing the perfect philosophic preacher, asserts that 'he must know that he has been sent by Zeus to men as a messenger, in order to show them that in questions of good and evil they have gone astray and are seeking the true nature of good and evil where it is not, while never noticing where it is.'[2] This movement indubitably produced a number of pagan saints, and it advanced the moral education of the masses, stimulating their religious hunger, but its negative success, in bringing the gods into disrepute, was greater than its positive, in winning men to a new way of life. The majority of the populace continued to regard itself as the plaything of fate.

Fate, Astrology and the Mysteries

'Throughout the whole world,' said the elder Pliny, 'at every place and hour, by every voice, Fortune alone is invoked and her name spoken: she is the one defendant, the one culprit, the one thought in men's minds, the one object of praise, the one cause. She is worshipped with insults, counted as fickle and often as blind, wandering, inconsistent, elusive, changeful, and friend of the unworthy. We are so much at the mercy of chance that Chance is our god.'[3] The arbiters of this Fate, so it was believed under the influence of Babylonian observations of the heavenly bodies purveyed by Syrian merchants, slaves and mercenaries, were the planets and the stars. Consequently, astrology assumed a position of great importance: Augustus had his horoscope published and minted coins bearing Capricorn, the sign of his birth, while Tiberius neglected worship as useless because of the certainty of astrological predestination.[4] If these ideas emanating from the East served only to render man's plight the more hopeless, from the same area came cults which provided some relief – these were the mystery religions.

The appeal of Mithra, whose worship derived ultimately from Persia, lay not a little in the fact that he was represented as a saviour who could release men from the hostile control of the Zodiac and the planets, the agents of unseeing Fate. The devotees of Isis and Osiris, a cult of

Egyptian origin, could pray with conviction: 'Your hand alone can disentangle the hopelessly knotted skeins of Fate, terminate every bad spell of weather, and restrain the stars from harmful conjunction.'[5]

Initially suspect in the eyes of the old senatorial nobility, these cults came increasingly to the fore as the equestrian class, recruited from self-made men uninfluenced by traditional Roman aristocratic feelings of superiority towards the worship of subject races, rose in importance from the Flavian period onwards. Many of the deities of these cults, such as Attis and Adonis, were originally vegetation gods and although, with their exportation, they lost some of their former associations, the rites with which they were honoured retained primitive features. With the exception of Mithraism, the central figure was a divine being who died and rose again, union with whom was obtained through an initiation ceremony which also gave assurance of immortality. Under the tutelage of the god it seemed possible to escape from the wheel of fate and to be preserved from the machinations of the predatory demons to which the world was believed to be subject. Nevertheless the Mysteries were without wide popular appeal; their adherents were the well born, the well educated and the well-to-do. The greater part of the inhabitants of the Roman Empire had neither the intelligence nor the discretion to qualify for membership, and only a limited number could afford the high fees demanded. From some women were excluded and all laid such stress on a dualism of body and soul, the latter being the unfortunate prisoner of the former, that they made no impression upon the whole man.

Gnosticism

This dualism was given its most extreme formulation in Gnosticism. This diffuse atmosphere of thought, which eventually found expression in innumerable sects, seems to have arisen late in the first century[6] and, like the Mysteries, to have spread from Syria and Egypt into the Graeco-Roman world. Syncretistic in character, it claimed to mediate a gnosis or knowledge that would bring salvation. Although the details of this redemptive myth differed from group to group, its underlying structure remained the same. It affirmed a complete antithesis of spirit and matter; it postulated a primordial catastrophe in heaven when the original man fell and his being was shattered into a myriad fragments. These elements were seized upon by demons as nuclei to create a world out of the chaos of darkness and they still survive as the souls of men. Although stupefied and held in bondage by the evil powers, they yearn to ascend to their former home in eternity. The supreme deity, who is at an infinite distance from evil matter, takes pity on these imprisoned sparks of light and sends a saviour, who descends to overcome the demons and ascends in triumph; it is through him that the captive spirits may obtain release. Knowledge of this conveys enlightenment and redemption. The full elaboration of this esoteric teaching must be dated in the post-apostolic era, but already within the first century such ideas were current, inculcating, with the Mysteries, the need for a saviour and so, in a measure, preparing the way for Christianity with its message of redemption.

Pax Romana

The climate of thought and religious practice within the Roman Empire in the first century was particularly favourable to the nascent Christian Church. The bankruptcy of the ancient cults left a void which neither the philosophical schools nor the Mysteries could adequately fill; if anything, they intensified it, by the insistence of the one on moral ideals and of the other on the need for a saviour: Christianity could and did provide both. It supplied the religious hunger; it lifted men from the depths of the moral degradation into which contemporary pagan society had plunged them; it brought assurance of a personal Redeemer which could liberate them from evil and from death itself; it satisfied the desire for escape from Fate; it answered a social need and secured men against loneliness. Through its exorcists it set men free from demon possession; through its rites of unction and the laying on of hands it cared for the sick. To the Christians God had indeed sent his Christ 'in the fullness of the times', i.e. when the time was ripe. But there were factors other than the spiritual and intellectual that favoured the spread of this new religion.

First and foremost there was the existence of Rome itself. The victory of Augustus brought an end to the civil war and inaugurated an unprecedented period of comparative peace (27 BC–AD 14), which was maintained under his successors: Tiberius (AD 14–37), Gaius (37–41), Claudius (41–54) and Nero (54–68). It is true that there were occasional revolts in the provinces, as in Africa and Gaul under Tiberius or in Judaea beginning during the principate of Galba and the year of the Four Emperors (68–69), but under the Flavians, Vespasian (69–79), Titus (79–81) and Domitian (81–96), no serious disturbances took place. This absence of strife and the prevalence of the *pax Romana* assisted considerably the spread of Christianity and this indeed was fully appreciated, as witness the statement of Origen:

There is abundance of peace which began at the birth of Christ, God preparing the nations for his teaching, that they might be under one prince, the king of the Romans, and that it might not be more difficult, owing to the lack of unity between the nations due to the existence of many kingdoms, for Jesus' apostles to accomplish the task laid upon them by their Master, when he said: 'Go and teach all nations'. Now the existence of many kingdoms would have been a hindrance to the preaching of the doctrine of Jesus throughout the entire world because of men everywhere engaging in war, and fighting for their native country, which was the case before Augustus, and in periods still more remote.[7]

Peace was accompanied by the growth of commerce and the development of communications. The Roman system of roads remains justly famous; even in such remote areas as Britain some 5,000 miles were laid down, and throughout the Empire a veritable network of highways provided the means for easy travel. The virtual, but not total, suppression of brigandage and piracy facilitated the movement of men and ideas. The Christian gospel was borne along the trade routes and its earliest strongholds were those cities which were centres of commerce. Moreover the conquests of Alexander had carried the Greek culture, and with it its language, far beyond the confines of his native land. Apart from some few pockets of resistance, such as North Africa where the Punic tongue survived or Egypt where Coptic was spoken, the Κοινή or common Greek was the one generally employed. Wherever a Christian missionary went, he could preach his message in the knowledge that it would be understood.

Yet propitious though the times were, the way was not all smooth.[8] As the distinction between Church and Synagogue became too apparent to ignore, the former could no longer shelter beneath the toleration afforded to its parent. Moreover the developing Emperor-cult carried with it the possibility of a head-on clash between State and Church: this however would not appear to have been the cause of the first bitter encounter under Nero. According to the Roman historian Tacitus, the persecution of the Christians, in which Peter and Paul lost their lives, was undertaken deliberately to provide scapegoats and so lay the rumour that the Emperor himself had set fire to a district in the capital in order to obtain space for his building programme.

But all human efforts, all the lavish gifts of the Emperor, all the propitiation of the gods, did not banish the sinister belief that the fire was the result of an imperial order. Consequently, to be rid of the rumour, Nero fastened the guilt and inflicted the most exquisite tortures on a class hated for their abominations, called Christians by the populace. . . . Accordingly an arrest was first made of all who pleaded guilty; then, upon their information, an immense crowd was convicted, not so much of the crime of firing the city, as of hatred of mankind. Mockery of every sort was added to their deaths. Covered with the skins of beasts, they were torn by dogs and perished, or were nailed to crosses, or were doomed to the flames and burnt, to serve as nightly illuminations when daylight had expired. Nero even offered his gardens for the spectacle, and was exhibiting a show in the circus, while he mingled with the people in the dress of a charioteer or stood aloft on a car. Hence, even for criminals who deserve extreme and exemplary punishment, there arose a feeling of compassion; for it was not, as it seemed for the public good, but to glut one man's cruelty, that they were being destroyed.[9]

That Nero was able to pick on the Christians was in part due to the prevalent attitude; the educated classes were suspicious of this new religion, whose 'doctrine has but recently come to light',[10] and they looked askance at conversion as a breach of etiquette which was indicative of an unreasonable enthusiasm characteristic of the lower orders. If the apostolic writings provide evidence of the adherence of some of the well-born, the initial successes of Christianity were principally among the poor and the outcast, and it seemed to many to be essentially a revolutionary and working-class movement.

THE SOURCES

Evidence for the life and teaching of the Church in the Apostolic Age is largely, although not exclusively, contained within the New Testament. Amongst the documents that make up this collection, there are some that post-date the period, such, if Pauline authorship be denied, are the so-called Pastoral Epistles, i.e. I and II Timothy and Titus, while there are other writings outside the New Testament which antedate some of its contents, such as I Clement and, according to one critical view, the Didache.[1]

The Pauline corpus

In quantity as well as in intrinsic value, the letters of Paul represent a primary source. If April 3, AD 33, be accepted as a probable date for the crucifixion of Jesus and if Paul were converted some eighteen to twenty-four months later, then his career as a Christian may be said to have begun in the year AD 35. According to his own testimony,[2] after his conversion experience on the Damascus road,[3] this one-time persecutor of the Church retired to Arabia, probably for meditation, for an unspecified period of time. He next came back to Damascus, and after three years paid a visit to Jerusalem, and went on an evangelical mission to his native province of Cilicia – he was born at Tarsus, its capital – for some ten or so years. Antioch then became the centre of his operations and from this base he set out on his first missionary journey in or about AD 46; it is from this year onwards that his extant letters were written to the Christian communities he had founded to answer queries, give directions and supplement his verbal teaching. From Antioch, upon his return, he sent what is probably the first of his epistles, to the Galatians.[4] In AD 50, Paul began his second journey and during an eighteen-month stay at Corinth wrote I and II Thessalonians. From Ephesus in 55, while on his third mission, he sent I and II Corinthians, and from Corinth, the following year, his epistle to the Romans. There followed his final visit to Jerusalem, his arrest and eventual deportation to Rome where, in captivity, *c.* 60, he wrote Colossians, Philemon and Philippians. With this corpus may be included the epistle to the Ephesians, which many scholars regard as non-Pauline, issued between 75 and 80 by one of Paul's own disciples. The Epistle to the Hebrews on the other hand, while bearing the name of Paul in the English versions, has no direct connexion with him; upon this there is general agreement – but there is no certainty as to its real authorship, destination or date. From internal evidence it appears to have been sent either to or from Italy and was addressed to a community in need of encouragement at a time of trial. To place it between 60 and 90 is to set it within reasonable limits.

Acts

An account of Paul's missionary journeys is given in the Acts of the Apostles, which is the second part of a two-volume work, the first half being the gospel of Luke. There seem no adequate grounds for denying the identification of its author with 'Luke, the beloved physician',[5] who was the companion of Paul, and he would appear to have drawn in part for his record upon his own reminiscences, as represented by the so-called 'we-passages', which indicate participation in the events by the use of the first person plural.[6] Acts is the only book of its kind in the New Testament in that it alone tells the story of the progress of the Church from the first days in Jerusalem to its secure establishment in Rome some thirty years later. Its plan is stated in the opening verses where the ascending Christ says: 'ye shall be my witnesses both in Jerusalem, and in all Judaea and Samaria, and unto the uttermost parts of the earth'.[7] Nevertheless, just as the gospels are not biographies so Acts is not a straightforward account produced in accordance with the canons of modern historical study. Luke was not so much concerned to record exactly what happened as to justify the Gentile mission to both Christians who were uneasy about it and those pagans who were interested in it. The driving power of the Holy Spirit, the main stages, as he saw them, of the outward movement from the place of Jesus' execution and resurrection – these were his interests. If the work be the sequel to and continuation of the gospel, then Acts must be dated *c.* 85. This indicates that the gospels too, although devoted to Jesus of Nazareth, were documents of the Apostolic Age, providing material not only for the life of the Founder but also for the teaching of the Church at the time when they were compiled.

The General Epistles

The General or Catholic Epistles is the title given to the remaining seven letters in the New Testament – 'general' because they do not name an individual addressee, 'catholic' because they appear to have been written to the Church at large and not to particular churches.

James bears the name and is traditionally assigned to the brother of Jesus, who became leader of the Jerusalem community. This ascription is not impossible and, if correct, would date the work somewhere between 50 and 60. Essentially Hebraic in thought, this brief treatise seeks to supplement Paul's teaching about faith by insisting upon the necessity for works which are the fruit of faith.

According to the address of I Peter, the letter was written by the apostle to Christians suffering persecution in the north-west provinces of Asia Minor. If the responsibility for the polished Greek style be that of Silvanus, who is named as the secretary, there is no impossibility in this and the date would therefore be *c.* 64, immediately prior to the Neronian persecution.

I, II and III John are usually regarded as from the pen of the author of the fourth gospel and belong therefore to the end of the first century. They are devoted to matters of Church discipline and organization and heretical distortions of the gospel by certain schismatic teachers.

Jude purports to be by the brother of James and this little tract against heresy, being Jewish-Christian in character, may indeed be by the named author; it would therefore have been written between 60 and 85. Some scholars however, partly because the writer seems to look back to the days of the Apostles, as if to a period long past,[8] are of the opinion that this document emanates from the second century. A large part of it has been copied and included in II Peter, which was certainly not by the Apostle, and was probably produced several decades after the turn of the century.

There remains of the New Testament library one further work to be noted which, like Acts, belongs to a category of its own: this is the Book of Revelation. In style and content it is one of the class of apocalypses, represented in the Old Testament by Daniel, i.e. a series of visions of the future revealed to the writer. The name of the author is given as John and he is stated to have received his visions on the island of Patmos, which is some fifty miles from Miletus off the coast of Asia

Minor. Traditionally this John has been identified with John, the son of Zebedee, and as the author of the fourth gospel, but the objections to this are so weighty, being first formulated by Dionysius of Alexandria in the middle of the third century,[9] that it must be deemed to have little sound basis. During what persecution it was written, it is not possible to say: some have assigned it to the reign of Nero, others to the latter years of Domitian, others again to AD 110 when the Christians in Bithynia are known to have suffered under Pliny and his imperial master Trajan – a late first century date seems the most appropriate.

Of the twenty-seven books gathered together in the New Testament, twenty-four may be regarded, with some measure of confidence, as contemporary sources for first century Christianity, and this number may be increased rather than decreased. The historian cannot but be aware of the gaps in his material, but equally he must be grateful that, in comparison with other religions, so much of an early date survives to enable him to reconstruct the story of the spread and development of the early Church.

EXPANSION AND DEVELOPMENT

Almost every one of the documents that may be used to describe the steady expansion of the early Church contains an identical statement to the effect that Christianity has a twofold foundation. To Paul, Christians are those who have received a free gift from God in the form of 'eternal life in Christ Jesus our Lord',[1] but they are also those who are 'led by the Spirit'.[2] To Peter, Christians have undergone a new birth 'by the resurrection of Jesus Christ from the dead'[3] and they are enabled to preach the gospel 'by the Holy Ghost sent forth from heaven'.[4] To the author of Hebrews, Christians are both 'partakers of Christ'[5] and 'partakers of the Holy Ghost'.[6] These two missions, the one of Christ and the other of the Spirit, are associated in a statement of Paul which indicates that the latter depends upon and succeeds the former. 'When the fulness of the time came, God sent forth his Son, born of a woman, born under the law, that he might redeem them which were under the law, that we might receive the adoption of sons. And because ye are sons, God sent forth the Spirit of his Son into our hearts, crying, Abba, Father.'[7]

Two accounts are given of the beginning in time of this mission of the Spirit, one in Acts and one in the fourth gospel. According to Acts, after the ascension of Christ, the Apostles remained in Jerusalem until Pentecost, or the fiftieth day from the resurrection, when the Spirit descended upon them, accompanied by a visible manifestation in the form of tongues of fire.[8] According to John, it was on the evening of

Easter Day itself that Jesus breathed upon his followers and said, 'Receive ye the Holy Ghost'.[9] In both accounts the sequence of events is the same – resurrection, ascension and the gift of the Spirit – but while Acts spaces them out over a period of seven weeks, John confines them to one day, and from the point of view of exact dating it is the latter that would appear to be correct.[10]

Just as the life of Jesus was interpreted in terms of inaugurated eschatology, so this fresh experience of the divine action was understood to be a fulfilment, and, in the speech which Peter is reported to have delivered immediately after the descent of the Spirit, it is associated with the prophecy of Joel:

> And it shall be in the last days, saith God,
> I will pour forth of my Spirit upon all flesh . . .
> Yea and on my servants and on my handmaidens in those days
> Will I pour forth of my Spirit; and they shall prophesy.[11]

The burden of the apostolic message was therefore that the age of the fulfilment of the Old Testament prophecies had dawned; that this was taking place through the ministry and death of Jesus, who had been raised and exalted by God to be 'both Lord and Christ'.[12] The sign of his present power and glory was the Holy Spirit, now indwelling the Christian community. Those who responded to this proclamation were bidden to repent that they might receive the forgiveness of sins and become partakers of the same Spirit.[13]

The Church in Jerusalem

Although Jesus' disciples had been in the main Galileans and although there are some indications that Galilee was initially a Christian centre,[14] the sources give pride of place to Jerusalem as the headquarters of the primitive Church. There, under the twelve Apostles, their number preserved after the defection of Judas by the election of Matthias,[15] the little community began to grow, even winning some of the priestly caste to belief in Jesus as the Messiah.[16] It was not long however before they were faced with two major problems: their relationship on the one hand to the Jewish authorities and on the other to the Jewish faith and nation.

Those who had been in part responsible for Jesus' death were not likely to be any more sympathetic to his followers, especially as they insisted upon publicly proclaiming his resurrection and Messiahship. Acts accordingly records numerous attempts to silence the Apostles, in particular Peter and John, but when the efforts did not achieve the desired results a *laisser-faire* policy seems to have been adopted on the grounds that time alone would demonstrate the truth of the matter. While thus menaced from without, the Church was also undergoing a heart-searching within. The first Christians were orthodox Jews who continued to observe the law and to attend the synagogue and Temple. They were soon joined by a number of Greek proselytes and Greek-speaking Jews who had returned from foreign parts to live in the capital. These considered that they were not receiving proper treatment from their Aramaic-speaking brethren, in particular that their widows were not being given a fair share of the daily dole of food, organized under the auspices of the Christian society. This social difficulty foreshadowed the not so distant struggle between Jewish and Catholic Christianity.

To meet the situation, the Apostles appointed seven of the Hellenists to act as charity commissioners, but the activity of some of them did not stop there. It is evident that the Hellenists did not regard Temple worship as a necessary part of their new-found Christian faith, and one of them, Stephen, precipitated a crisis by a direct attack on the Jewish cultus. Whereas the Apostles were prepared to minimize the difference between their position and Judaism, and even to suggest that the execution of Jesus was the outcome of ignorance,[17] Stephen firmly asserted the distinction and had no hesitation in calling the Jewish leaders 'murderers'.[18] In the ensuing persecution the Apostles, whose essential orthodoxy was recognized, were unmolested, but the Hellenists, consequent upon the martyrdom of Stephen, were driven from Jerusalem.[19]

The Beginnings of the Gentile Mission

One of the original seven, Philip, reached Samaria where, possibly because the Samaritans and Hellenists were at one in rejecting the Temple cultus at Jerusalem, he succeeded in making a number of converts. In effect this was the beginning of the Christian mission, the first step towards realizing the catholicity or universality of the Church, for although the Samaritans accepted the authority of the Pentateuch, they were regarded as heretics and schismatics by the orthodox, being the descendants of intermarriages between Jews and the eighth-century colonists of North Israel. The recognition by Peter and John, who came especially from Jerusalem to investigate the situation, of the legitimacy of Philip's activity prepared the way for the preaching of the gospel to the Gentiles.[19] Equally important was the consent of Peter to associate with and to baptize the Gentile 'God-fearer', Cornelius, at Caesarea, an action for which he finally obtained the approval of the Jerusalem leaders.[20] It may be, though the dearth of evidence permits this to be no more than an hypothesis, that it was this experience that brought both Peter and James nearer to the Hellenists and explains the execution of the latter by Herod and the imprisonment and eventual departure from Jerusalem of the former, leaving the Jewish Christian community to regroup itself under the leadership of Jesus' brother, James.

Yet an internal crisis was steadily building up. The Jewish Christians were determined to preserve their orthodoxy; they were not opposed to the admission of Gentiles to the Church, but they were emphatic that they must be circumcised and must obey the law. They had before them the example of Jesus himself who had restricted his mission to Israel.[21] What they failed to appreciate, however, was that while Jesus considered that the call to Israel must come first, he believed that this would be succeeded by the incorporation of the Gentiles into the Kingdom of God. The one was preliminary to the other; there were to be two successive events, the first ushering in the eschatological action of God, in which was to be included the further gathering in of the Gentiles. The scattered Hellenists, reaching as far afield as Phoenicia, Cyprus and Antioch,[22] adopted this sequence, preaching first to the Jews and then to the pagans. The Hebrew Paul, at first violently anti-Christian and then converted on a persecuting mission to Damascus, was authorized by the growing Antiochene church to go with Barnabas on a preaching tour, and he similarly spoke first in the synagogues and only then to the Gentiles.[23] It was upon the completion of Paul's first missionary journey that the crisis came to a head.

Paul's missionary journeys

In AD 46, accompanied by his cousin, John Mark, the future evangelist, and Paul, Barnabas sailed from Seleucia for Cyprus.[24] Disembarking at Salamis, they went throughout the island, eventually reaching Paphos where their labours culminated in the conversion of Sergius Paulus, the pro-consul. They next took ship for the coast of Asia Minor, where, after Mark had left them, they made Antioch of Pisidia their centre. A recurring pattern of activity is now discernible. The missionaries first availed themselves of the hospitality of the synagogue to deliver their message and as a result of this, while winning over a number of the Jews and of the proselytes, they antagonized the rest of the congregation. Accordingly they addressed themselves directly to the Gentiles, until their opponents succeeded in having them expelled from the city. This sequence of events was repeated at Iconium, at Lystra and at Derbe, from whence they retraced their steps, encouraging the little Christian communities they had founded, and so returned to their base at Antioch.

News of their success having reached Judaea, certain Jewish Christians travelled to Antioch to insist on the need to circumcise all converts. As a consequence of the dissension that this produced, Paul and Barnabas were sent to Jerusalem to confer with the Apostles.[25] The debate is not reported in full, but from Paul's epistles it is possible to discover the main lines of the argument whereby he asserted his right not only to preach to the Gentiles but to accept them into the Church without requiring their adherence to the Jewish law.

It was Paul's contention that the Church was the true Israel and that the Jews, who had failed to understand that they had been chosen by God not primarily for the enjoyment of a privilege but for the performance of a service, had been replaced by the 'righteous remnant', the New Israel.[26] So the Christian community, composed of Jew and Gentile alike,[27] could appropriate the Jewish hope, and its members were 'Abraham's seed, heirs according to promise'.[28] Thus the divine purpose which ran through all the history of Israel, from the call of Abraham onwards, had entered upon the final stages of its fulfilment, which included the gathering in of the Gentiles. As regards the law, Paul, while not denying that it was holy, declared that it was not an end in itself. It was an interim dispensation to reveal the true nature of sin and convince man of his helplessness,[29] thus acting as a 'tutor to bring us unto Christ'.[30] It was therefore no longer authoritative, and loyalty to it, which might not unreasonably be expected of Jewish converts, was not to be demanded of those Gentiles responding to the proclamation of the gospel.

With the support of Peter and the concurrence of James, Paul and Barnabas were encouraged to continue their work and began their preparations for a second journey. The two missionaries however were unable to agree about the desirability of taking John Mark with them, Paul viewing him with some disfavour because of his previous defection. Barnabas therefore went with Mark to Cyprus, while Paul chose Silas and took the overland route[31] for the districts of Asia Minor that he had previously evangelized, visiting again Derbe and Lystra, and at the latter place he was joined by a recent convert named Timothy. Following a somewhat zigzag course, they came to Troas, where Luke would appear to have joined them, and they then crossed the Aegean to Philippi. Acts contains a graphic account of their activities in Greece, which need not be repeated here. Briefly it tells of their vicissitudes and successes at Thessalonica, Athens, and at Corinth, where Paul stayed eighteen months and where he met Aquila and Priscilla, Jewish refugees from Rome, expelled under the edict of Claudius, and how eventually he came via Ephesus and Caesarea back to Antioch.

On the third journey[32] Paul followed a similar route: overland to encourage and help the growing churches; a prolonged stay at Ephesus; a visit to Corinth, a return through Macedonia, and finally a sea voyage to Tyre and so up to Jerusalem. Paul intended this to be his final visit to the capital, since he wished to extend his campaign to the western Mediterranean, possibly as far as Spain, and with this in mind he had already written to enlist the support of the church of Rome. In this letter he also disclosed his reason for delaying his departure until he had been to Jerusalem.

The closing years of Paul's life

The decision of the Jerusalem council to afford him liberty of action in his mission to the Gentiles had issued in at best an uneasy truce. The extreme Jewish Christians could not accept his readiness to waive the demands of the law. These Judaizers gradually advanced to open opposition. Their envoys seem to have followed in Paul's footsteps and, upon his departure from a city, to have entered therein and to have sought both to discredit him in the eyes of the Christian community and to persuade them to adopt their version of the Christian faith. So they asserted that Paul had no real authority, not being one of Jesus' original followers, and that his own conduct proved this in that, unlike the other Apostles, he did not accept any means of livelihood from his converts but met his material needs by continuing his trade of tent-maker.[33] It is not surprising that in view of this hostile attitude, Paul's position should have begun to harden, so that he came to regard these men as preachers of 'a different gospel'.[34] He determined nevertheless to make a supreme effort to preserve the unity of Jew and Gentile within the one Church and to this end he organized amongst his converts a collection for the Jerusalem community.[35] This was to be more than a gesture of goodwill; it was to be a visible demonstration of the unity of all mankind in the New Israel – of Jew and Gentile alike.

Although welcomed by the Jerusalem church, Paul was required by James and his council to give proof of his personal loyalty to the law by joining publicly in certain rites in the Temple. There he was recognized by some Jews from the Province of Asia, who spread the false rumour that he had profaned the precincts by introducing the Ephesian Trophimus. Arrested by the Roman commandant to prevent his being lynched by the crowd, Paul successfully avoided being tried by the Sanhedrin and was taken in custody to Caesarea. After two years of indecision, a final attempt was made by the Jewish authorities to have his case transferred to their own court, and, to prevent certain condemnation, Paul exercised his right as a Roman citizen and appealed to the Emperor. His eventful voyage, including his shipwreck on the island of Malta, followed and he was placed under house arrest in Rome for two years.[36] Details of his fate are unknown. There is a tradition that he was acquitted and fulfilled his intention of going to Spain,[37] but this may well be no more than an assumption based upon what he had said in writing to the Romans. It is more likely that at the end of the two years either the Neronian persecution had broken out (AD 64) or that he was in any case condemned and executed forthwith.

With the death of Paul, the curtain falls on the detailed scene of Christian missionary endeavour. There is evidence that Peter went to Antioch, Corinth and Rome, being martyred in the last at approximately the same time as Paul. Titus, if the epistle to him preserves an accurate historical reminiscence, went to Crete, but no account remains of the many who carried on with the work of evangelization. Nevertheless the main features of the expansion are quite clear. From Jerusalem, and possibly Galilee, the Church spread first to Samaria and then further afield to Antioch. Thence it penetrated into Asia Minor and on to Macedonia and Greece. By the middle of the first century, it was strong in Rome, although who was responsible for its foundation there are no means of telling.

The fall of Jerusalem

Two years before the martyrdom of Peter and Paul, during the interregnum in the Roman procuratorship after the death of Festus and before the arrival of Albinus, Ananus, the Sadducean high priest, seized the opportunity to remove the Christian leader and had James stoned.[38] Two years after the martyrdom of Peter and Paul, the political and religious ferment in Palestine came to a head. In 64 Gessius Florus became procurator of Judaea and by 66 his tyrannical administration had stirred up a rebellion.[39] Unable to make headway against the Jewish uprising, Florus sought the assistance of Cestius Gallus, the governor of Syria, who, after some delay, advanced into Palestine with a strong force of legionaries and auxiliaries, but, although elsewhere successful, he withdrew from before Jerusalem. Nero accordingly entrusted Vespasian with the task of putting down the revolt, and in 67 he began a systematic occupation of all strong points throughout the country, until, upon the death of the Emperor and his own election to the purple, he transferred the command to his son Titus. On August 10, AD 70, the soldiers of Titus burnt the Temple and pillaged its treasures, including the seven-branched candlestick, which was to feature both in the eventual triumph at Rome and on the arch of Titus. By September 8, all resistance throughout the city had ceased and Jerusalem passed into the hands of the Romans.

Shortly before the city was finally invested, the Christian community, warned of the impending disaster by a prophecy, according to Eusebius, withdrew to Pella in Perea, on the east side of Jordan.[40] That this decision to withdraw, rendered all the more imperative if the Christians were familiar with the prophecy of destruction ascribed to Jesus,[41] was regarded by their fellow-countrymen as an act of apostasy, provides an intelligible explanation of the vigour with which they attacked these Jewish Christians shortly after the fall of Jerusalem, thus making absolute the divorce between Church and Synagogue. Seeking to establish a new uniformity in religion as a necessary basis for a new unity, the rabbis introduced into the synagogue service a formula which the Jewish Christians could not pronounce, to the effect that 'for the Nazarenes may there be no hope'.[42] They followed this by sending letters to all Jewish congregations in the Diaspora denouncing the practice and faith of Christianity.[43]

Repudiated by their compatriots, suspected by the Gentile Christians, their influence soon waned and with it the possible danger of the setting up of an hereditary Jerusalem caliphate, since the Church had been ruled by Jesus' brother, James, and he had been succeeded by a cousin of Jesus, Simeon.[44] Traces of Jewish Christianity are to be found in the following centuries, but the fall of Jerusalem reduced them to a position of complete insignificance for the future history of the Church. Nevertheless, in one particular the fall of Jerusalem and the structure of its Christian community may be said to have had a lasting effect. To appreciate this, we must turn from the expansion of the Church to its interior development.

The Church's interior development and structure

The first Christians did not think of the Church primarily as an organized society; to them it was the faithful Remnant consisting of the heirs to the divine promises; it was the New Israel and its members were therefore the elect or chosen of God; it was the Temple of the divine presence indwelt by the Spirit; it was the Body of Christ, a new creation transcending distinctions of race, class or sex. It was a divine-human organism, established by the direct action of God in history, and those who belonged to it were unconcerned about questions of constitutional order. Nevertheless, from the second century the Church possessed an ordained ministry, consisting of bishops, priests and deacons, the origins of which must be sought in the period under review. Unfortunately the evidence at the disposal of the historian is fragmentary and ambiguous; any and every account therefore partakes of that uncertainty which is inseparable from conjecture on the basis of insufficient material, and the facts to be gleaned from the relevant documents have been differently related.

From the gospels it is apparent that Jesus chose twelve men whose function was to act as his representatives,[45] and their number, corresponding to that of the patriarchs, suggests they were intended to be prince-rulers of the New Israel. Their complement was preserved, upon the defection of Judas, by the election of Matthias, chosen from among those who had been witnesses of the resurrection.[46] Matthias was in no sense a successor to Judas, but a replacement. The title 'apostle', which conveys the idea of one 'sent' with authority, was applied to these men, but also came to be extended to others, such as Paul,[47] who regarded himself as directly commissioned by Christ, or Barnabas, who had been separated for the specific task of missionary preaching by the local church at Antioch.[48]

In addition to the apostles, in both the confined and extended sense, there were also the seven appointed in Jerusalem as charity commissioners.[49] These were later regarded as the first deacons, but not only is the title not used in the passage which records their authorization but it is arguable that Luke was deliberately drawing a parallel between this incident and the appointing of the seventy elders by Moses;[50] in each account there is a 'murmuring', the selection of a specific number of men and a reference to the Spirit vouchsafed to them. If this typology were deliberate, then Luke was writing of the first elders or presbyters, who, in course of time, are found forming a council in Jerusalem under the presidency of James.[51] It is moreover recorded that the 'apostles', Paul and Barnabas, 'appointed for them elders in every church'[52] whither they had carried the gospel and these elders were on occasion called *episcopoi*, i.e. overseers or bishops.[53] So those active in the churches of Pauline foundation, under his plenary authority as an apostle, were subordinate missionaries, such as Timothy,[54] and overseers; to these must be added the deacons.

If Luke's account of the seven does not refer to deacons, then no hint of their origin survives. One may attempt to supply the lacuna conjecturally by noting that the Christian ministry is regarded as the organ of the continuing ministry of Christ in his Church. As Christ 'came not to be ministered unto, but to minister' (Lit. 'to be a deacon'),[55] so Paul could say: 'I glorify my ministry' (Lit. 'deaconing').[56] The wholeness of Christ's ministry, undifferentiated in him, was gradually divided between the three orders. Hence Paul addresses the Christians at Philippi 'with the bishops (or overseers) and deacons'.[57] Nevertheless, this statement may refer to functions rather than to distinct orders and indeed to sketch the history of the early ministry is to attempt to trace the process whereby the one hardened into the other.

It is at this point that the importance of the Jerusalem church needs to be emphasized. As already noted, the affairs of the Christian community in Jerusalem were controlled by a body of elders under James, the brother of Christ. This arrangement had affinities not only with the many local sanhedrins or councils, which however did not have a regular president, but more especially with the Jerusalem Sanhedrin under the high priest. The Jerusalem church itself was regarded in the apostolic age as the mother-church. Not only is this clearly indicated in Acts, but its pre-eminence is apparent from the Pauline epistles. It may well be that the fall of Jerusalem, the consequent virtual disappearance of the mother-church and the need to supply a substitute for its authority, issued in a reproduction of its organization in the Christian communities of the Middle East. If this be so, then Jewish Christianity made a lasting contribution to the developing structure of the Catholic Church, which was to be further refined and stabilized in the succeeding centuries.

BELIEFS

The first Christians conceived themselves to be charged with a message, which could be described as either 'the gospel of Christ'[1] or 'the gospel of God . . . concerning his Son'.[2] This message necessarily involved certain beliefs, but no attempt was made to systematize them. Christian missionaries did not begin by outlining a doctrine of God and then go on to consider the person of Christ, the activity of the Holy Spirit or the nature of the Church. They were not concerned to communicate a body of doctrine requiring assent, but to proclaim a fact to which they were witnesses, viz. that God had acted in Christ. Hence their belief in God was Christocentric. They could assert and teach that 'God is love', but they did so on the grounds that 'herein was the love of God manifested in us, that he hath sent his only begotten Son into the world, that we might live through him',[3] or that 'God commendeth his own love towards us, in that, while we were yet sinners, Christ died for us.'[4]

God

Nevertheless, the God whose action they proclaimed, whilst known to the Jews, in that he had 'of old time spoken unto the fathers in the prophets . . . and hath at the end of these days spoken unto us in his Son'[5] was virtually unknown to the pagans. The mission to the Gentiles involved the endeavour to convert the majority from polytheism to monotheism. In order to achieve this, the early Christian adopted both the positive approach of affirming that there is only one God, and the negative of denying the existence of the gods of heathenism. Thus on the one hand we read: 'there is no God but one';[6] 'there is one God';[7] and on the other hand, 'ye were in bondage to them which by nature are no gods';[8] 'though there be that are called gods, whether in heaven or on earth; as there are gods many, and lords many; yet to us there is one God, the Father, of whom are all things, and we unto him; and one Lord, Jesus Christ, through whom are all things, and we through him.'[9] But the one God had to be differentiated from the abstract absolute of certain of the philosophers. Greek thought in attempting to understand human life and God in relation to human life always starts from the cosmos; Hebrew thought, which in this particular is identical with Christian, starts from the 'living God' and seeks to understand human life in the cosmos from its vision of God. So the God of early Christian belief is the 'living God',[10] who 'speaks' to mankind,[11] chooses men,[12] makes a covenant with them,[13] judges,[14] raises the dead.[15] This God is not known by theoretical reflection but by self-revelation. The world of his creating is not an objective closed system: God cares for the world and is constantly active within it and has now acted supremely in Jesus Christ, whose action within history is identical with the action of God. At this point, following for the purposes of clarity and ease of exposition the logical progress that is the product of a later age, we turn from the doctrine of God to the understanding of the person of Christ, while recognizing the extent to which both were united in early Christian belief.

The work and person of Christ

Who is Christ? Christians in the Apostolic Age understood this question to mean primarily: what is his function? They answered it in terms of what they believed God had done in Christ, for he was to them the 'grace' of God, i.e. the medium of the divine gracious and merciful act. What God had done in Christ was expressed in varying ways by different writers. Paul drew his imagery from the institution of slavery, from the sacrificial system and from the law court. From slavery he took the idea of redemption or emancipation – the liberation of those in bondage. This term was also used in the Old Testament of the divine act of deliverance whereby Israel was set free from subservience to her Egyptian masters.[16] Paul used it to express his belief that through Christ the people of God had been delivered from enslavement to sin, to the demonic powers and to the law. From the cultus he took the idea of expiation – the covering or blotting out of sin that it might no longer be a barrier between God and man: so Christ is our passover that has been sacrificed,[17] in that God 'designed him to be the means of expiating sin by his sacrificial death.'[18] From the law court Paul took the idea of justification or acquittal, the passing of a verdict of not guilty. So man, guilty through his sinfulness, is justified in so far as he responds in faith to the divine act – and by 'faith' Paul meant total self-committal or the humble acceptance of what God has done. With these keywords of Pauline theology may be included also 'reconciliation' which conveys the idea of bringing together those that have been estranged; so 'God was in Christ reconciling the world unto himself.'[19] Redeemed, justified, reconciled, his sin expiated, man can now be elevated from the status of a slave to that of a son, becoming 'an heir through God'[20] of the promised salvation. This change of status is equivalent, for Paul, to an act of new creation. 'The old things are passed away; behold they are become new.'[21] The function of Christ is to make possible this transference from the old to the new condition; he has done so by himself passing through death to life by his crucifixion and resurrection. Physical death, to Paul, was the outward expression of spiritual death, itself the consequence of sin.[22] Christ's death was due to sin – not his own, but the sin of mankind – and this issued in death, but this death leads to life; 'the death that he died, he died unto sin once: but the life that he liveth, he liveth unto God.'[23] So liberated from the world's sin by his crucifixion, Christ was transferred into the new order of the resurrection life, and that life out of death is now available for all men.

As Paul drew on the cultus for his image of expiation, so too the author of Hebrews turned to the sacrificial system, and in particular to the ritual of the Day of Atonement, to describe the function of Christ. Regarding the heart of religion as worship, the writer sought to demonstrate the imperfections of the Jewish system and its fulfilment through Christ. It was imperfect on three grounds: the victims were unblemished simply because they were incapable of sin, whereas the true sacrifice could only be one who had faced and conquered the temptation to sin, so Jesus was in all points tempted like as we are, yet without sin.[24] In the second place, the animals were sacrificed unwillingly, whereas what was required was the offering of a truly dedicated will to God; so Christ was obedient to the Father's will, even unto death. Finally, the animal sacrifices were at a sub-human level, whereas the life offered needed to be that of one who had overcome sin in man's nature; so Christ, as the perfect victim and God-appointed high priest, has, through his resurrection and ascension, entered as man's forerunner into the divine presence and now appears 'before the face of God for us',[25] 'wherefore also he is able to save to the uttermost them that draw near unto God through him, seeing he ever liveth to make intercession for them.'[26] In this way, as Paul had vindicated the place of the law as a system of moral commands in the Old Testament, so the author showed the value of the law as a system of sacrifice which foreshadowed that which was to come through Christ.

The author of the fourth Gospel primarily interpreted the function of Christ in terms of revelation – the giving of light. This revelation was, in the first instance, a revelation of God: 'he that hath seen me hath seen the Father'.[27] In the second instance, it was a revelation of man as he should be according to the divine purpose. When 'the Word became flesh'[28] there took place 'the final concentration of the whole creative and revealing thought of God, which is also the meaning of the universe, in an individual who is what humanity was designed to be in the divine purpose.'[29] This revelation conveys saving knowledge, which is not just an intellectual activity. To 'know the Lord' is, according to the Old Testament, to trust in him, to enter into personal communion with him. So what John calls knowledge is virtually identical with what Paul calls faith. Yet this relationship of intimate unity is only possible because of the communication of new life through Christ,[30] and this in turn could only take place when the barrier of sin had been removed. Christ therefore was 'the Lamb of God, which taketh away the sin of the world',[31] voluntarily laying down his life that he might draw all men to himself.[32]

The question that the early Christians sought to answer – who is Christ? – was capable of bearing a second meaning: what is his nature? Even here the replies were formulated very much in terms of function. To Paul, Christ was indeed a man, who had been 'born of a woman',[33] but whereas to the first disciples the astounding paradox was that their leader Jesus, after being shamefully executed, had been exalted to the right hand of God, to Paul the paradox was that the Exalted One, proved by the resurrection to be the Son of God, should have taken flesh and died on Calvary. He who was 'in the form of God', that is, divine by nature, counted it not a prize to be on an equality with God, like Adam, 'but emptied himself, taking the form of a servant', that is, human nature, and 'humbled himself, becoming obedient even unto death, yea, the death of the cross'.[34] Christ was therefore a pre-existent being, the ground and origin of creation, since he, who is 'the image of the invisible God', made all things.[35] Paul further interpreted the relation between Father and Son in terms of function, by identifying Christ with certain of the intermediaries which had been introduced into later Hebrew thought between the transcendent God and the world. So the title 'image of God' was used in the Greek Old Testament of the Divine Wisdom,[36] who was pre-existent[37] and the artificer of creation,[38] and Paul could affirm that Christ was 'the power of God, and the wisdom of God'.[39] Equally, the author of Hebrews, using Wisdom terminology, stated that Christ was 'the effulgence of his glory and the very image of his substance',[40] while going on to declare his complete humanity in that he was 'made like unto his brethren' and became a partaker of flesh and blood.[41] John conceived of Jesus as the uttered Word of God, i.e., as the divine revelation and as the divine plan and purpose for the world, and coupled this with the belief that the Word became flesh, so that his message was of 'that which we have seen with our eyes, that which we beheld and our hands handled, concerning the Word of life.'[42] This pre-existent Word is indeed God, the unique Son of the Father, with whom he is one,[43] since they mutually indwell each other.[44] This Johannine teaching represents the summit of New Testament Christology, but it can nevertheless be said that 'behind all the theological interpretation we can discern the outline of the apostolic teaching, and beneath the whole structure of faith we can trace the foundation of the evangelic history of Jesus of Nazareth'.[45]

The Holy Spirit

One object of early Christian belief to which very little reference is made by the first three evangelists is the Holy Spirit; but this silence is readily explicable when it is recalled that the coming of the Spirit to the Church was believed to have been subsequent to the completion of Christ's mission. Such statements as are made do little more than reproduce the Old Testament understanding of the Spirit as the power of God in action. So the angel at the Annunciation says to Mary: 'The Holy Ghost shall come upon thee, and the power of the Most High shall overshadow thee.'[46] In Acts this 'impersonal' conception of the Spirit persists, so the Spirit can be 'poured out'[47] and just as the divine *ruach* could carry Elijah from place to place,[48] similarly the Spirit could transport Philip from the wilderness to Azotus.[49] Nevertheless, in this same document there is discernible a tendency to interpret this experience of the Spirit's activity in personal terms. 'It seemed good to the Holy Ghost, and to us' – this is the opening of the letter issued by the apostolic council.[50] Paul's first missionary journey was undertaken because 'the Holy Ghost said, Separate me Barnabas and Saul for the work whereunto I have called them.'[51]

The personal distinctness of the Spirit was also recognized by Paul in his writings, although the Christocentric character of his beliefs, which led him to speak of 'the Spirit of Christ'[52] has led some scholars to assume that he did not differentiate between Christ and the Spirit. Nevertheless, a close analysis of the relevant passages does indicate a difference of function. Thus while, for example, Paul ascribes intercessory activity both to the Spirit and to Christ,[53] in the one case he is speaking of the indwelling Spirit as the ground of prayer, and in the other of the ascended Christ interceding at the right hand of the Father; these activities are complementary but they are not the same. Again Paul affirms that in the believer dwell both Christ and the Spirit, but the latter does so as the creative source of the new life, of which the former is the content – the Spirit is the quickening cause, and the growth in Christlikeness, the conforming to the image of Christ, is the effect of his operation. Paul's advance in pneumatological belief upon his predecessors lay in his affirmation that the Spirit is not primarily to be connected with the extraordinary but with the ordinary daily life of the Christian. To Paul the whole of Christian existence is within the sphere of the Spirit's activity. Hence, as already quoted, the Spirit is the ground of prayer; he is the source of all spiritual gifts;[54] he guides and leads Christians;[55] he is indeed the earnest of the final redemption,[56] the pledge or guarantee that the work of salvation already begun will be brought to its consummation.

In all essentials this teaching is at one with that of the fourth evangelist. To him the Spirit is the one who comes forth or proceeds from the Father;[57] his mission succeeds that of the Son;[58] his task is to bear witness to Christ;[59] to guide men to Christ.[60] He therefore glorifies Jesus by revealing him to the believer as the only Way to the Father, and by leading him along this Way he initiates him into truth. Thus John understood Christianity to be a revelation given once and for all and yet ever renewing itself; the content of this revelation is the Incarnate Word, the agent of its renewal is the Spirit.

The Doctrine of the Church

Belief in the Spirit was intimately linked in the thought of the early Christians with their understanding of the Church. This is particularly noticeable in the Pauline image of the Temple of the divine presence. 'Know ye not that ye are a temple of God, and that the Spirit of God dwelleth in you?'[61] As God's presence had had its focal manifestation in the Holy of Holies, so now he was present in all believers who 'are builded together for a habitation of God in the Spirit.'[62] Hence, according to Peter, 'the Spirit of glory and the Spirit of God resteth upon you'[63] because Christians are 'living stones' in a spiritual Temple.[64] This presence was the consequence of the covenant status of the chosen people; in electing Israel God promised to be *with* them;[65] but now, through the new covenant, God dwells *in* his people.[66] Thus the Church was understood to be the Messianic Community or the New Israel, its members being 'Abraham's seed, heirs according to promise'.[67] It is indeed the *ecclesia* – a title no doubt adopted partly under the influence of Septuagint usage where it translates the Hebrew *qahal*, the congregation of God's people. Phrase after phrase is therefore borrowed from Jewish thought and applied to Christians as members of the Church: they are God's elect,[68] his holy people,[69] 'the circumcision',[70] 'an elect race, a royal priesthood, a holy nation, a people for God's own possession',[71] called not to privilege but to service as the instruments of God in his work of redemption. Consequently the Church can even be described as the Body of Christ.

To appreciate the meaning of this image – the Body of Christ – it is necessary to understand the Hebrew, as distinct from the Hellenic way of looking at things. The Hebrew, unlike the Greek, was not interested in things in themselves but only in things as they are called to be. He was not concerned with an object as such but with what it becomes in relation to its final reference according to the divine purpose. The meaning of an object therefore does not lie in its analytical and empirical reality but in the will that is expressed by it. Hence Jesus could say of a piece of bread: 'This is my body.' The bread does not cease to be bread, but it becomes what it is not, namely the instrument and organ of his presence, because through his sovereign word he has given it a new dimension. Similarly the Church is the Body of Christ because its true nature rests upon its relation to God's purpose. The Church is the organ of Christ's presence uniting his members to himself and in him to one another. So Christians are 'limbs of his body';[72] they are 'the body of Christ, and severally members thereof'.[73] Hebrew thought also provides the key to those few statements that declare that Christ is not so much the body as the head of the Church.[74] It would be anachronistic to understand this in terms of modern knowledge of the brain and the nervous system – factors of which the Hebrews were entirely ignorant – and so identify Christ with a *part* of the body, viz. that part which controls and directs. Rather 'head' in these passages would appear to be the equivalent of 'source', the thesis being that the life of the whole body and its continuing existence derives from Christ himself.

The various New Testament images of the Church tend to fuse together and this is particularly apparent in the concept of the Bride. Israel of old was seen as the Bride of Yahweh,[75] and, in course of time, the Messiah too was regarded as the Bridegroom. In the gospels Jesus is himself the bridegroom,[76] and so in Ephesians the Church, the New Israel, is presented as the Bride of Christ with whom he is one flesh or body.[77] Hence, in the apocalyptic vision of the seer of Revelation, 'the Spirit and the bride say, Come.'[78]

Christian belief in the Church has a twofold basis, the Christological and the Pneumatological, revealed by that which has been accomplished and that which is yet to be accomplished. From the Christological aspect the Church is static, built upon an unshakeable foundation, which is the action of Christ within the field of past history; from the Pneumatological the Church is dynamic, stretching out to its final destiny, through the present and future action of the Spirit. Hence the 'double polarity' of the Church: it *is* the Temple of the Presence; it *is* the Body of Christ; it *is* the Bride of Christ – yet the Temple has still to be built together, the Body has still to be built up, the Bride has still to become wholly one with her divine Bridegroom. There is thus a tension between the present blessings and the final consummation; between the Kingdom as a present reality and its complete realization at the end of all things. For early Christian belief there is no radical discontinuity between the present and the future; both are interpreted eschatologically; the teaching concerning the 'End' is therefore not an appendage but is central to the entire message, since Christians are those 'upon whom the ends of the ages are come.'[79] Nevertheless, there is an overplus of divine action still to take place.

The Last Things

The details of the Last Things were not greatly elaborated in the New Testament writings. Christians believed that they had a message for the present and that speculations concerning the exact minutiae of the future life were vain – even the author of Revelation, with his noble imagery, does not give an exact transcript of what lies ahead. The picture of the final consummation to emerge is therefore blurred and it is difficult to reduce it to a coherent pattern. Paul's expectation included belief in an imminent Second Coming, a final judgement, a resurrection of the righteous dead (possibly of all the dead), the transformation of those still alive and the ultimate establishment of God's universal rule.

Doubts and queries about the third of these items – the resurrection – led him to say more of this than of any of the others. As a former Pharisee, Paul already possessed a doctrine of the resurrection. Since the Hebrews, unlike the Greeks, refused to distinguish between body and soul – these being but two names for the same being seen from different points of view – they believed in the embodied nature of the resurrection life. The more spiritually-minded Pharisees rejected any crass notion of physical re-animation and understood resurrection to involve transformation or transfiguration. Paul accepted the same idea, and asserting that 'flesh and blood cannot inherit the kingdom of God'[80] and that Christ 'will transfigure the body belonging to our humble state, and give it a form like that of his own resplendent body, by the very power which enables him to make all things subject to himself',[81] he sought, by means of an analogy, to convey some idea of what resurrection of the body or person involved. He used the imagery of a seed being placed in the earth and eventually growing into a plant. The seed and the plant are in a sense identical, but between the two lies the critical point when the seed dies – Paul was ignorant of the fact that each seed contains a germ of life – and is transformed into a growing plant. The link between the two is the sovereign power of God: 'he gives it a body even as it pleased him.'[82] So, to apply the analogy, while the body of the believer is changed from flesh, which by its very nature decays, into glory, the personality, which has been displayed by the fleshly body, will by no means disappear. 'It is sown a natural body; it is raised a spiritual body'.[83] It was this assured belief, held on the grounds of the resurrection of Christ, that was to sustain the members of the Church in the centuries of persecution that lay ahead.

The formulation of belief

The need for some kind of doctrinal summary, comprising the essential content of belief or the real centre of the gospel must have been present from the first days of the Church. But although the early Christians may be said to have shared a common faith, they had no single formulary or creed, in the sense of an official and textually determined statement. Nevertheless, there are in the New Testament indications that there was a recurring pattern of belief. So the Thessalonians were instructed 'to hold the traditions which ye were taught',[84] and the Romans were reminded that they 'became obedient from the heart to that form of teaching whereunto ye were delivered.'[85]

The New Testament documents also provide evidence of the currency of quasi-credal affirmations and of liturgical tags and catch-phrases. These statements have sometimes one, sometimes two and sometimes three members. The one-member formulae were Christological, as is to be expected since Christians regarded the confession of Christ as the essential element in their faith. So we have 'Jesus is Lord'[86] or 'Jesus is the Christ'.[87] Occasionally this could be elaborated by the inclusion of relevant material from the history of redemption, e.g. 'Christ Jesus, that died, yea rather, that was raised from the dead, who is at the right hand of God, who also maketh intercession for us.'[88]

It was in conflict with paganism that belief in God required to be expressed, and hence the emergence of bipartite formulae, proclaiming faith in both Christ and God, e.g. 'To us there is one God, the Father, of whom are all things, and we unto him; and one Lord Jesus Christ, through whom are all things, and we through him.'[89] Yet this faith in God is really a function of faith in Christ and this is evident both from the description of God as Father, i.e. the Father of Jesus, in this quotation, and from the triadic scheme: 'The grace of the Lord Jesus Christ, and the love of God, and the communion of the Holy Ghost, be with you all.'[90] According to this passage, it is through the gracious activity of God in Christ that we know the love of God and belong to the fellowship of which the Spirit is the creative source. These simple and multiple forms existed and continued to exist side by side, while various factors worked upon the recognized body of teaching to crystallize it into conventional summaries. These factors included preaching and exorcism; the experience of bearing witness in persecution and the need to withstand false teaching or heresy, together with the practice of baptism and worship. It is to these two last items that attention must be next directed.

WORSHIP

Worship may be defined as the recognition of God's majesty and the acknowledgement of his sovereignty; it is reverential homage issuing in the adoration of and devotion to a personal God. To Christians, it is their response to the gracious activity of God in Christ. As such, worship is not just one element amongst many in the life of believers; it is rather an attitude or orientation that should characterize the whole of it. So, in the New Testament there is no essential distinction between worship and life: man's existence is not split into two areas, one where Christ is honoured and the other where man is more or less independent – everything should stand under the Lordship of Christ. Consequently cultic terms can be applied to daily life, and Paul, speaking to the Corinthians of the collection that they had made for the poor in Jerusalem, could describe it as 'the ministration of this liturgy',[1] and to the Philippians he could say: 'If I am poured out as a drink-offering upon the sacrifice and liturgy of your faith, I joy, and rejoice with you all.'[2] The same apostle could exhort the Romans to 'present your bodies a living sacrifice, holy, acceptable to God, which is your reasonable service.'[3]

Nevertheless, the first Christians did engage in specifically cultic acts, and the Jewish Christians attended the synagogue and joined in the Temple worship at Jerusalem. In so doing they had before them the example of Jesus, who went regularly to the synagogue on the sabbath and is recorded to have gone to Jerusalem for the Passover at the climax of his ministry. Similarly, contact with the synagogue was maintained, for example, by Stephen[4] and Paul, while Peter and John went to the Temple,[5] where Paul himself worshipped when he was in the city.[6] The expulsion of individuals and finally of all Christians from the synagogue and the destruction of the Temple were not themselves factors in providing specifically Christian cultic acts: these existed from the outset, side by side with the practice of Jewish worship, and took the form of baptism and the Lord's Supper, each of which is technically described as a sacrament by later theologians.

Sacraments

Sacraments may be understood both in terms of significance and of instrumentality. In terms of significance, the sacramental principle derives from belief as to the nature of Christ, i.e. that he is perfect God and perfect man in one person. As such he is unique, but at the same time he is representative of and embodies the true relation of the whole of mankind to God. The sacrament similarly takes the particular – a specific quantity of water in baptism or a particular piece of bread and some wine in the eucharist – in order to represent the true relationship of the whole to God. Thus the relation of specific acts of worship to life is that of the particular to the universal, that through the former the whole might be sanctified and recognized as subject to the divine sovereignty. In terms of instrumentality the sacramental principle derives from the Christian understanding of man, which itself rests upon the Hebrew conception. To the Hebrew man has not a body, he *is* a body. There is no rigid distinction between the physical and the spiritual, because body and soul are so intimately united that they cannot be distinguished; indeed they are more than united, for the body is regarded as the soul in its outward form. Man in his totality, therefore, is not a discarnate spirit but a spiritual-corporal entity. It was precisely because of this that God became man, for Christ came not to save the spiritual side of man, but the whole man. God in Christ therefore met man at man's level, i.e. at the level of his corporal existence, and God continues to meet man at this same level when such physical entities as water or bread and wine become the instruments of communion. The sacraments are the means whereby the fruits of Christ's saving activity are applied to the believer.

Baptism

Baptism is the first Christian sacrament, in the sense that it is the instrument whereby the individual is admitted to the fellowship of the Church. The Synoptic gospels record no command of Jesus, during his earthly ministry, that his disciples were to baptize. Matthew alone gives a logion of the risen and ascended Christ to this effect, but most scholars hesitate to accept this commission as original. Nevertheless, the first converts were baptized, and it is difficult to doubt that Jesus' followers, in requiring this rite, considered that they were acting in accordance with their Master's intention. Certainly they had numerous precedents to influence them: there were the lustrations practised by the Jews, the ritual baths of the Qumran community, proselyte baptism and the baptism of John and, above all, Jesus' own example in submitting to the last.

No complete description of a baptism in the Apostolic Age has been preserved. It clearly included the use of water, but whether the method adopted was sprinkling, as in many of the ablutions at Qumran,[7] or immersion, as was apparently the case with proselyte baptism, or by pouring, which is suggested by the meaning of the verb 'to baptize', i.e. to deluge or douse, it is difficult to determine. There is evidence that baptism in water was followed by the laying on of hands, a Jewish custom signifying identification[8] – the candidate thus being identified with the community by the action of its representative – but it is insufficient to allow any certain conclusion as to whether or not the laying on of hands was an invariable accompaniment of baptism. References to unction and to the putting on of Christ[9] have been understood of the anointing and clothing in white garments that were features of the ceremonial in the second century, but while these passages may reflect current practice, equally they may be only the basis from which the later unambiguously attested practice developed.

Baptism could be administered anywhere: in a wayside pool, as when Philip baptized the Ethiopian eunuch;[10] in a river, wherein Lydia would appear to have been initiated at Philippi,[11] or even in a prison, as was the case with the Philippian jailer.[12] If at first baptism immediately followed a response to the Christian message, it soon became customary to precede it by a period of instruction, and it is probable that the ethical teaching common to many of the New Testament epistles derived from an early pattern of catechetical teaching.

The meaning of baptism may be defined in different but complementary ways, depending upon the particular image of the Church that was consciously or subconsciously influencing the thought of any one writer. Thus if the Church is considered to be the Messianic Community, baptism is the means of initiation into it and is analogous with the rite of circumcision, whereby a proselyte became a member of the Israel of God and an heir to the promises. 'Ye,' wrote Paul to the Colossians, 'were also circumcised with a circumcision not made with hands, in the putting off of the body of the flesh, in the circumcision of Christ; having been buried with him in baptism.'[13] Christians are therefore those who have been 'sealed'[14] – 'seal' being a Jewish term for circumcision.

If the Church is regarded as the Temple of the divine presence, then baptism is the means of bringing the individual into immediate contact with the Holy Spirit. 'Know ye not that ye are a temple of God, and that the Spirit of God dwelleth in you?'[15] Consequently Christians are those who 'were once enlightened and tasted of the heavenly gift, and were made partakers of the Holy Ghost'.[16] When the Church is viewed as the Body of Christ, baptism is the means of incorporating the individual into that living organism: 'in one Spirit were we all baptized into one body.'[17] The believer thereby sacramentally dies and rises with Christ: 'all we who were baptized into Christ Jesus were baptized into his death. We were buried therefore with him through baptism into death: that like as Christ was raised from the dead through the glory of the Father, so we also might walk in newness of life.'[18] This death involves liberation from the forces of evil and it is followed by co-resurrection with Christ, for God has 'raised us up in him, and made us to sit with him in the heavenly places, in Christ Jesus'.[19]

As the Bride of Christ, the Church is the mother of believers and so baptism is the means of adopting and regenerating the individual. 'For ye are all sons of God, through faith, in Christ Jesus. For as many of you as were baptized into Christ did put on Christ';[20] hence 'except a man be born of water and the Spirit, he cannot enter into the kingdom of God'.[21] So too the candidate is enlightened or recreated;[22] the divine image, defaced by sin, is renewed; the remission of sin is conveyed[23] as the catechumen enters into the eschatological crisis of rebirth and regeneration.

The Eucharist

According to Acts the early Christians engaged in 'the breaking of bread';[24] according to Paul they assembled together 'to eat the Lord's supper'.[25] The thesis has been advanced that these titles designate two different acts, the first referring to simple fellowship meals, deriving from those that Jesus had with his disciples during his ministry, the second being a re-calling of the death of Christ, deriving from the Last Supper.[26] The New Testament evidence is insufficient to support this distinction and, if anything, suggests an identity. The sole pertinent information in this respect relating to the breaking of bread is that it was performed 'with gladness and singleness of heart'.[27] This 'gladness' is eschatological joy, being one of the qualities of the eschatological existence founded by the Spirit, for 'the kingdom of God is righteousness and peace and joy in the Holy Ghost'.[28] Eschatology is equally present in the records of the Last Supper, when the cup, according to the Marcan account, heralded the joy of the kingdom.[29] Thus both the breaking of bread and the Last Supper have the same eschatological keynote. It is, moreover, an arbitrary proceeding to treat the Last

Supper as an isolated incident, thus detaching it from the whole sequence of meals which Jesus is recorded to have eaten with his disciples both before and after his death and resurrection. It must take its place as one, albeit, whether or not a Passover,[30] probably the most important and therefore the most memorable of many meals. Hence when Paul affirmed the association between the cultic repast and the Last Supper, there is no reason to suppose that he was innovating or doing anything other than re-emphasizing a link which was familiar to all Christians.

Paul's account, which is the earliest to be written, reads as follows:

> The Lord Jesus in the night in which he was betrayed took bread; and when he had given thanks, he brake it, and said, This is my body, which is for you: this do in remembrance of me. In like manner also the cup, after supper, saying, This cup is the new covenant in my blood: this do, as oft as ye drink it, in remembrance of me.[31]

The command to 'do this' is found elsewhere only in Luke, being absent from Mark and Matthew, but in any case, it is doubtful if the words are to be interpreted as an injunction to perform the actions of breaking and distributing, since this is what any devout Jew would do every time he sat down at a communal meal. Rather the command, if a genuine tradition of the words of Jesus, is to the effect that, whenever this is done, it must be with a special intention, viz. 'in remembrance of me'.

From Paul's description of what took place at Corinth, it is apparent that the cultic meal was in effect a repetition of the Last Supper *in toto*, beginning with the breaking and distribution of the bread, followed by the several courses, and concluded by the blessing and distribution of the cup of wine. The failure of the Corinthian Christians to observe the decencies, their division into cliques, the refusal of the rich to share their food with the poor, together with the over-indulgence of some are amongst the reasons for the eventual removal of the meal proper from its central position in the celebration, thus bringing together the bread and the cup in the way that is customary in all later eucharistic liturgies. The meal continued as a separate observance, with its own grace at the outset and under the title of the *agape* or love-feast.[32]

In addition to the consumption of food, there is evidence that a homily was delivered,[33] that letters from leading Christians were read,[34] that a collection was taken for charitable purposes,[35] and that the worshippers exchanged a kiss of peace as a sign of their solidarity.[36] It is probable that petitions were made and intercessions offered and there may have been lections from the Old Testament. The meetings took place at night and, although it is impossible to determine their frequency in the earliest days, it soon became the practice to hold them once a week, early on Sunday morning, i.e. on the Lord's Day,[37] being the day of Christ's resurrection. The community assembled in the house of one of its members, presumably in the dining-room, and while in Jerusalem they tended to move from house to house;[38] elsewhere one private residence was recognized as the centre; so at Ephesus they gathered in the house of Aquila and Priscilla,[39] at Laodicea in that of Nymphas,[40] and at Colossae in Philemon's home.[41]

As with baptism, so with the eucharist, the meaning of the rite can be schematically presented in connexion with the various New Testament images of the Church. The old Israel celebrated the Passover once a year as the memorial of redemption from the bondage of Egypt, and on this annual occasion the individual Hebrew claimed his share in the covenant and the people re-engaged to keep the Law. The New Israel similarly engages itself afresh in the new covenant each time it celebrates the eucharist, which is the memorial of redemption from the bondage of sin, achieved by the sacrificial death of Christ, by whose blood the new covenant is ratified.[42] The eucharist is further a foretaste of the Messianic banquet, i.e. of the feast provided by the Messiah in the age to come.[43] The accounts of the feedings of the multitude in the gospels present them as anticipations of the Messianic banquet and as types of the eucharist, since the actions of Jesus on each occasion and at the Last Supper are closely paralleled.

When the Church is conceived to be the Temple of God and its members living stones and a holy priesthood, then the eucharist becomes a sacrificial meal – sacrificial in the sense that it is the means of entering into and sharing Christ's sacrifice. This is implicit in the words 'Do this in remembrance of me', although the translation 'remembrance' does less than justice to the underlying idea. 'Remembrance' implies the mental recollection of what is absent, but in the biblical perspective the word has rather the sense of re-calling, of making what is past present again so that it becomes operative by its effects here and now. The offering of the eucharist in the Church, therefore, is identified with the offering of Christ, not in the sense that his sacrifice is repeated, but that the eucharistic offering is the re-calling or re-presentation of his perfect oblation so that the sacrifice is present and operative by its effects.

In terms of the Body of Christ, the eucharist is the means whereby the unity between the head and its members is progressively actualized, 'seeing that we, who are many, are one loaf, one body: for we all partake of the one loaf.'[44] While as the Bride of Christ, the Church in the eucharist celebrates its wedding breakfast: 'Blessed are they who are bidden to the marriage supper of the Lamb.'[45] It is at the same time the means of providing sustenance for the newborn children of the heavenly

Father, and so the eucharistic food can be compared with the manna in the wilderness,[46] but it brings eternal life, since 'a man may eat thereof and not die'.[47]

Common to all these aspects of eucharistic theology is the joint historical and eschatological reference, which may be expressed in the form of a threefold significance. There is, first, the recollection of the historical fact of the death and rising again of Christ; there is, second, the experience of the contemporary fact of his invisible coming in the gathering; there is, third, the eschatological hope of his coming again at the final consummation. The eucharist is thus related to the action of the earthly Christ, to the abiding presence of Christ in the Church and to the end which the reigning Christ is to bring in. 'Looking back to an event of the past, it looks forward to the consummation of God's design; and in the present, at each celebration, it finds a creative meeting of the two.'[48]

It is this historical and eschatological character that distinguishes the Christian eucharist from any other cultic meal. Those of the Qumran community were little more than repasts in common, most nearly analogous to those of a monastic house. Those of the pagan confraternities were notable for a mystical-magical attitude which is foreign to the New Testament understanding of the eucharist, rooted as it was in historical and eschatological ideas.

Non-sacramental forms of worship

Within the New Testament there is little evidence of gatherings for worship other than at baptism and the Lord's Supper, and this has led to the conclusion that there were no assemblies of a non-sacramental kind. Nevertheless, it is reasonable to suppose that Christians did meet simply for prayer and bible study, and it could well be that Paul's description of worship at Corinth, in I Corinthians xiv, refers to a non-eucharistic assembly, since there is little in the account to connect it specifically with the Lord's Supper. Certain of the elements in the service are listed by Paul: 'when ye come together, each one hath a psalm, hath a teaching, hath a revelation, hath a tongue, hath an interpretation.'[49] Yet little can be gleaned from the Pauline letters of the order in which these elements were utilized, so that no clear structure emerges. On the contrary, there was considerable freedom for individual contributions to be made, although Paul himself was concerned to regulate the outbursts of enthusiasm and so avoid an impression of chaos. His two basic principles were that 'all things be done unto edifying' and that 'God is not a God of confusion, but of peace.'[50] While there was this controlled freedom, emanating from the activity of the Spirit, there was also a tendency to use fixed liturgical forms. These features included the Lord's Prayer,[51] benedictions[52] and doxologies[53] and the singing of hymns.[54]

Prayer

In addition to acts of public worship, the Christian also engaged in private prayer, following both the example and precept of Jesus who, before all his important decisions, spent time in prayer and is recorded to have spoken 'a parable unto them to the end that they ought always to pray, and not to faint.'[55]

To the Christian prayer was an encounter of personalities, a communing with a personal God. In this activity the believer experienced a greater freedom than hitherto, for he was no longer a slave to sin but an adopted son and able, through the Spirit of adoption, to approach God as Father.[56] Consequently prayer was considered to be not just a human activity, but one in which the Spirit participated; he 'helpeth our infirmity: for we know not how to pray as we ought: but the Spirit himself maketh intercession for us with groanings that cannot be uttered',[57] thus including the believer in the intercession of Christ at the right hand of the Father.

Christian prayer was not an attempt to influence God or to use him for the attainment of human ends, although one might legitimately bring one's needs to him, confident that 'if we ask anything according to his will, he heareth us.'[58] The objects of prayer were rather for the spread of the gospel,[59] for the salvation of the Jews,[60] for increase in love[61] and in the knowledge of God,[62] and for freedom from evil.[63] Intercession and thanksgiving played an important part, the latter emphasizing the extent to which prayer was a response to God's action in Christ.

The interior attitude of prayer was expressed by the exterior posture: in times of stress, agitation or humility, kneeling was customary;[64] when prayer was dominated by the thought of the risen and coming Lord, standing with the hands raised was natural,[65] and possibly the face was directed towards the East, in deliberate contrast with the Jewish practice of turning to Jerusalem, and in anticipation of the Parousia.[66] In this way the individual supplemented the corporate acts of the community of which, even in his private devotions, he was conscious of being a member.

SOCIAL LIFE

Those who sought to spread the Gospel in the Apostolic Age were concerned to enunciate a body of beliefs, an order of worship and also a pattern of conduct. Not only were a 'form of teaching'[1] and an account of the Last Supper, as the basis of their liturgical practice,[2] delivered to the converts, but in addition certain moral standards, whereby their everyday life was to be directed, so that they could be reminded that 'ye received of us how ye ought to walk'.[3]

Moral behaviour

The behaviour inculcated was governed by the experience of the new spiritual order already begun, so that every moral precept or exhortation presupposed either the action of God in Christ or the act of baptism whereby the fruits of the divine activity had been mediated to the believer. Hence Paul's plea to the Philippians for humility on their part is based upon the humiliation of Christ in being incarnate and in submitting to crucifixion.[4] Again, in his epistle to the Romans, he considers sin and grace; he starts from baptism and shows how it involves the death of the old self and the creation of the new; and then, on the basis of this common experience of believers, he exhorts them to resist sin, and concludes: 'sin shall not have dominion over you; for ye are not under law, but under grace.'[5]

The implications for conduct were worked out over the decades, reaching a more or less stereotyped form by AD 50 and being comprehended in a pattern of catechetical instruction with certain key-words to distinguish the principal items. Christians were to *abstain* from all lusts; they were to *put off*, i.e. renounce heathen idolatry and sin, and *put on* or clothe themselves with righteousness and virtue; they were to be *watchful* and, in particular, pray; they were to *subject* themselves in a graded series of social relations: wives submitting to husbands, children to parents, slaves to masters, and all to the civil power; they were to *withstand* temptation and persecution.[6]

God's decisive action had brought a new people into existence, which, like the Old Israel was to be holy – 'God called us to holiness.'[7] So Peter could assert that 'like as he which called you is holy, be ye yourselves also holy in all manner of living; because it is written, Ye shall be holy; for I am holy.'[8] Thus, again like the old Israel, the Church was summoned to be a neo-levitical community, a people apart, and Paul could apply this Old Testament text to its members: 'Come ye out from among them, and be ye separate.'[9] This was to perpetuate the social dualism characteristic of Judaism, which sought to protect its adherents from contact with the Gentiles: but the basis of the Christian distinction was no longer a racial one; it was essentially religious, between the worshippers of the one God through Jesus Christ and those who accepted polytheism. Yet as an earthly community the Church was set over against contemporary society. Christians 'have not here an abiding city, but we seek after the city which is to come',[10] being no more than 'sojourners and pilgrims'.[11] The Church was thus a concrete social entity, living in the midst of and yet distinct from the pagan society around it. But within the Church there were no distinctions: 'there can be neither Jew nor Greek, there can be neither bond nor free, there can be no male and female; for ye are all one in Christ Jesus.'[12] Since the conformity of Christians to the existing social pattern of the Empire was 'only incidental, while their real energy was devoted to filling these relationships with the personal meaning of love',[13] there was no attempt to set aside the system of slavery. Hence Paul could send the runaway slave Onesimus back to Philemon, his master, bearing a letter which requested that he might be received 'no longer as a bondservant, but more than a bondservant, a brother beloved'.[14]

Equally within the Church there was no division between sacred and secular activities, as long as the latter were devoted to the building up of the community. This is particularly noticeable in the early Christian understanding of work.

Labour

Working for a living was one of the areas common to men both inside and outside the Christian community, but this activity could be taken up into the new pattern of obedience in so far as it could be shown to be directed towards the goal of Christ. So the motives for work were, first, that the Christian might not be a burden on others;[15] second, that he might thereby obtain the wherewithal to help the needy;[16] and third, in order to make a good impression upon non-Christian workers and so commend the faith to them.[17] In this way, by working, the Christian was at the same time serving God: 'whatsoever ye do, work heartily, as unto the Lord, and not unto men; knowing that from the Lord ye shall receive the recompense of the inheritance.'[18] This Christian attitude differed markedly from that of the Greeks, to whom work was a servile activity, and of the Romans who also regarded work as beneath the dignity of a citizen. The Stoic ideal of brotherhood had removed some of the stigma of slavery and so of the work connected with it, but it was the Church above all that gave to labour a sense of purpose and direction.

Social categories

It was because of the general attitude of pagans to work that the

Christian community was frequently ridiculed in the second century on the grounds that its members were largely artisans. Christianity was indeed at first a working-class movement, and hence Paul's statement: 'behold your calling, brethren, how that not many wise after the flesh, not many mighty, not many noble, are called.'[19] So, among the early converts, there was a tanner, a seller of purple, a jailer, tent-makers[20] and household servants.[21] Nevertheless, there were some from the upper classes; these included a proconsul, 'of the chief women not a few' both at Thessalonica and Beroea, the ruler of a synagogue,[22] a certain number of men of means,[23] a doctor,[24] and even members of the imperial establishment.[25]

Food and clothing

Rich or poor, base or noble, there was no aspect of life outside the scope of the new faith, so that such matters as food and clothing came into its purview. It is possible to exaggerate the over-indulgence of pagans in the first century AD, and it would be over-hasty to accept the description of Trimalchio's feast, preserved in the *Satyricon* of Petronius, *c.* AD 60, as in any sense typical; nevertheless there is sufficient evidence to indicate the prevalence of a measure of gluttony, and it is against such a setting that the Christian insistence upon temperance, i.e. upon self-control, is to be appreciated.

Christians are not to be drunk with wine but rather filled with the Holy Spirit;[26] they are not to spend their time 'in revelling and drunkenness, nor in chambering and wantonness, nor in strife and jealousy.'[27] They are not to emulate those 'whose god is the belly'[28] 'for they that are such serve not our Lord Christ, but their own belly.'[29] Questions of food and drink are not indifferent, at least as to the quantity consumed 'for the Kingdom of God is not eating and drinking, but righteousness and peace and joy in the Holy Ghost.'[30] Similarly, in contradistinction to the costly styles of clothing affected by the well-to-do pagans, Christian wives were bidden to see that their coiffure, jewellery and dress were not 'the outward adorning of plaiting the hair, and of wearing jewels of gold, or of putting on apparel, but let it be the hidden man of the heart.'[31]

The records do not provide a detailed picture of Christian social life in the Apostolic Age – they tell us nothing of how they spent their leisure – but they do enunciate principles which were to be applied even more extensively as the centuries passed.

CHAPTER THREE

THE APOSTOLIC FATHERS AND THE SECOND CENTURY

The Background – Sources – Expansion and Development – Beliefs – Worship – Social Life

---

THE BACKGROUND

THE TURN of the first Christian Century witnessed no sudden transformation in the environment of the growing Church. The same religious and philosophical ideas, the same addiction to superstition, the same fascination of the mystery cults – all these continued to be characteristic of the thought world in which the Christian community had to make its way. Nevertheless, new emphases, new interpretations and developments of ideas and movements, nascent in the preceding decades, were coming to the fore.

Pagan religion

Scepticism concerning the ancient gods was still a powerful factor, which was given added potency by the translation, early in the second century, by Ennius of the *Sacred Histories* of Euhemerus, in which the Greek writer (*c.* 316 BC) had argued that the gods were no more than earthly kings and warriors, worshipped after their death for their benefactions or prowess. Yet the second century, as it progressed, was to witness something in the nature of a religious revival, typified by Plutarch, who though born under Claudius was active in the reigns of Trajan and Hadrian and rejected Euhemerism as atheistic.[1] It is this revival that explains the emergence into popularity of different gods, such as Asclepius whose worship became widespread in the age of the Antonines, temples being raised in his honour in every land where the Greek and Roman culture prevailed. The old oracular shrines slowly began to be patronized once again, and Lucian's account of the foundation of a new centre at Abonoteichos in Paphlagonia is witness to the eagerness with which these means of access to the supernatural were utilized.[2]

Yet this developing religious revival was not simply a return to the old gods; their distinctiveness had become blurred and they tended to lose their individuality in a form of a universalism whereby the several divine beings became identified. Thus in Apuleius' *Metamorphoses* the goddess addresses him:

> Though I am worshipped in many aspects, known by countless names, and propitiated with all manner of different rites, yet the whole round earth venerates me. The primeval Phrygians call me Pessinuntica, Mother of the gods; the Athenians, sprung from their own soil, call me Cecropian Artemis; for the islanders of Cyprus I am Paphian Aphrodite; for the archers of Crete I am Dictynna; for the trilingual Sicilians, Stygian Proserpine; and for the Eleusinians their ancient Mother of the Corn. Some know me as Juno, some as Bellona of the Battles; others as Hecate, others again as Rhamnubia, but both races of the Ethiopians, whose lands the morning sun first shines upon, and the Egyptians, who excel in ancient learning and worship me with ceremonies proper to my godhead, call me by my true name, namely, Queen Isis.[3]

Philosophy

The pagan religious revival tended to coalesce with the renewed interest in philosophy. Platonism came once again into favour, albeit a Platonism which had absorbed important Aristotelian and less important Stoic elements. While the professional philosopher still held to the system of one school, the cultured class was more eclectic in its approach. So Plutarch, while primarily a Platonist, accepted the moral teaching of Stoicism, and conversely Marcus Aurelius, while primarily a Stoic, accepted the ideas of Plato. Their philosophy continued to be, as in the first century, essentially a practical rather than a speculative discipline, purveyed by the cynics and by the sophists, whose rhetorical displays attracted and delighted their audiences and, at the same time, presented them with a way of life to be embraced, so that many of these discourses, notably those of Maximus of Tyre, expressed a remarkable mystic fervour and moral purpose.

Superstition and the mysteries

Despite the moral ideals propounded by the philosophers, most men continued to believe themselves to be the playthings of fate. Astrology was still regarded as authoritative, and even the Emperor Hadrian was prepared to forecast the events of the year each 1st of January.[4] Superstition of all kinds was rife: tales of werewolves and hobgoblins were the frequent subject of after-dinner conversations. There was, too, a growing belief in the activity of daemons. These half-divine, half-human beings had been introduced by Plato to safeguard the remote purity of God and to fill the interval between man and the Infinite. In the revived Platonism of the second century, these spirits were given considerable prominence, and were regarded, by Maximus of Tyre for example, as angelic ministers to succour weak mankind. But the religious revival of the period also favoured this belief, and Plutarch, following the teaching of Xenocrates, a contemporary of Plato, supported the view that some of the daemons were evil. By this means he hoped to preserve the ancient cults, despite their unsavoury features and the apparently immoral character of their deities. Each god, so it was asserted, has a corresponding daemon, and it is this latter that is responsible for the enormities perpetrated in the god's name. Thus man is subject to a host of bad spirits who lie in wait for the unwary.

To escape from all this, men turned as previously to the Mysteries, even more popular under Hadrian, whose phil-Hellenism encouraged the ready propagation of the Hellenized eastern cults. But again the spirit of eclecticism was at work and each individual sought to be initiated into as many Mysteries as possible in order to be sure that he had obtained the whole truth. So Apuleius records:

> In Greece I took part in very many initiations. I keep carefully certain symbols and memorials of them handed to me by the priests. What I say is nothing unusual or unknown. Those of you present who are initiated in the rites of Father Liber only, for instance, know what you keep concealed at home and worship far from all profane persons. But I, as I have said, learnt worship on worship, rites beyond number, and various ceremonies in my zeal for truth and in my dutifulness to the gods.[5]

The origins and characteristics of Gnosticism

Not only the Mysteries but also the various Gnostic schools, which proliferated and reached the zenith of their development in the second century, offered a way of escape from the wheel of fate and the predatory activities of evil spirits.

The difficult problem of the origins of Gnosticism requires for its resolution an answer to the question: was it a movement within Christianity which made use of non-Christian ideas or was it an independent movement which incorporated Christian beliefs into its system? The growing consensus of modern critical opinion favours the latter of these alternatives and sees Gnosticism as an eclectic phenomenon, being thus characteristic of the age, which arose out of a mixture of Hellenistic, Jewish, Oriental and Christian factors, and at the same time employed philosophical language as a terminology but not as a basic structure. It was therefore a patchwork of elements drawn from many sources and was essentially derivative and artificial. Emerging from and expressive of a climate of thought, it derived some substance from Christianity upon which it was parasitical and it was enabled, by its use or misuse of the apostolic writings, to develop its ideas and give them some compelling force.

Whereas Christianity, from one aspect, was the democratization of 'mystery', Gnosticism represented an attempt to reverse this situation by making the Christian mystery aristocratic. Its message of salvation therefore did not comprise the offer of a gift to all men but the realization of a right by some men; hence according to the *Gospel of Truth*, 'if one has knowledge, he gets what belongs to him and draws it to himself'.[6]

The basis of this claim is the myth that God has sown seeds of the divine substance in the world, created by a demiurge or lesser being; this fragmented material is scattered among the 'pneumatic' or spiritual men, who are by nature saved and are to be distinguished from the 'psychic', who have a latent capacity for knowledge, and the 'hylic' or earthly men, who will never be redeemed. Knowledge of this fact, i.e. of the possession of the divine spark or seed, brings salvation, and so this gnosis is awareness of status, which at the same time is presented in the form of cosmological and scientific information. The Gnostic message thus conveyed knowledge of the privileged position of certain men, and while not entirely deterministic, since the 'psychic' were capable of conversion, it was in the main a sanction and specious justification of a feeling of superiority on the part of those who considered themselves to be among the pneumatic.

The attraction of this 'good news' may be readily appreciated; it provided a way of escape from fate and from evil forces and it offered salvation without requiring the moral endeavour implicit in the Christian gospel, since 'it is not conduct of any kind which leads into the Pleroma, but the seed sent forth thence in a feeble, immature state, and here brought to perfection.'[7] As, therefore, the material cannot affect the spiritual, the gnostic may do what he likes, in the sure confidence of his ultimate ascension into eternity.

The specifically Christian element adopted into this system was that of Christ as the Saviour. He was presented as the channel of enlightenment: 'I have come to reveal to you that which is, that which has been, and that which will be, so that you may know the things which are seen and the things not seen and to reveal to you about the perfect Man'.[8]

Yet this Christ was very different from the one whose mission is recorded in the canonical gospels, in particular his human nature was regarded as no more than a semblance. This docetic strand, common to most of the Gnostic parties, had a multiple basis. The complete and enduring humanity of Christ was unacceptable to some because they held that God was either impassible and therefore could not be associated with the suffering of the Cross or immutable and therefore could not be one with human nature which is necessarily subject to change and growth. Others repudiated the human reality on the grounds that the material is incapable of salvation and that the soul is the true man. Others again objected to the view that the Messiah had suffered, interpreted the sinlessness of Christ to mean that he had had no contact with evil matter and affirmed that the Virgin Birth implied the passing of Christ through Mary like water through a pipe.

The Gnostics were essentially propagandists and, despite their claim to give an accurate description of man's nature and of his place in the universe, they were not greatly interested in ontology; their myths were no more than a rationalization or projection of their inner feelings and were intended to assure themselves and their converts that their status possessed universal significance. Consequently, the precise details of their systems were not of the first importance, nor did the adherents of the different groups regard themselves necessarily as rivals; indeed they were prepared to read one another's sacred books. A full account of the numerous schemes is therefore not required, especially as Gnosticism belongs more to the general history of religion in the period than to that of the Christian Church. But in so far as the latter was attacked and influenced by it and in part developed in reaction against it, a brief conspectus of its main types must be given.

The Gnostic Schools

According to the Fathers of the Church Gnosticism began with Simon Magus, with whom Peter clashed at Samaria;[9] Simon asserted that he was a manifestation of the Supreme God,[10] a claim repeated on his own behalf by his reputed successor Menander.[11] Later there are references to a number of groups, none of which proved a serious menace to the Church: the Nicolaitans, the Naasenes or Ophites, with whom are probably to be associated the Sethians, and the Cainites.[12] By the mid-second century three main schools had emerged: the Syrian, the Egyptian and the Pontic.

To the first belonged Saturninus, Tatian, a renegade Christian who founded the Encratites, and Bardesanes, who is said to have been initially a Valentinian – all these men are notable for the extreme ascetic form of their teaching.[13] It is, however, the second school, the Egyptian, which produced the most mature systems through the work of Basilides and Valentinus. The former, who lived in the time of Hadrian and Antoninus Pius (117–161) confined his labours to his native country,[14] but Valentinus stayed for some ten years in Rome (160–170) and would appear to have visited Cyprus also, and as a result of his activity he had both an oriental and an Italian school of followers. The Oriental party, which included Theodotus and Marcus,[15] did not differ over much from the Italian, led by Ptolemy and Heracleon. Ptolemy himself was the greatest systematic theologian of the party and it was the form established by him that Irenaeus sought to refute and of which, in so doing, he has preserved the most complete account.[16]

Valentinianism

According to the Ptolemaic system, at the head of all things is the Supreme Being, who is called Depth (Bythos); with him dwells his consort Thought (Ennoea), who is also named Silence (Sige) and Grace (Charis). These two beings united and produced the first pair of aeons or emanations from the divine nature, who are known as Mind (Nous) and Truth (Aletheia). They in turn begat Word (Logos) and Life (Zoe), who themselves produced Man (Anthropos) and Church (Ecclesia). In this way was completed the Ogdoad, the company of the eight highest aeons. From Word and Life proceeded a further five pairs, the Decad, and from Man and Church six pairs, the Dodecad. These thirty aeons together constitute the Pleroma or fullness of the Godhead.

Amongst all these beings Mind alone had complete knowledge of the Supreme, and his task was to reveal him to the others. But the last of the aeons, Wisdom (Sophia), desired to have the knowledge that had been vouchsafed to Mind alone, and this desire involved the attempt to pass beyond the limit of her individuality, the penalty for such action being expulsion from the Pleroma. Limit (Horos), the guardian of the boundaries, brought her to her senses, and, perceiving that the Father is ultimately unknowable, she cast out her desire, while Mind brought forth another pair, Christ and the Holy Spirit, to prevent any recurrence of the incident. The resultant harmony was so great that all combined to produce a final emanation, 'the perfect fruit of the Pleroma, Jesus, who is also called Saviour and Christ and Logos, after his origin, and All, because he is from all.'

So far the events described have been confined to the Pleroma, but now interest moves to the Kenoma, the region void of spiritual being, into which the passion of Wisdom had been cast. In pity for this fall,

Christ extended himself through Limit or Cross (Stauros) and gave her personal form with the name of Achamoth, which is to be derived from the Hebrew word for wisdom. Next Achamoth produced the demiurge and his six angels, thus bringing into existence a second and lower Ogdoad, which mirrors the superior, and the demiurge, in his turn, created the seven heavens, the lower world and man, in whom, unknown to their maker, Achamoth deposited a spiritual seed. It is this pneumatic element in man that yearns for redemption, and it was to liberate it from its bondage to matter that the Saviour descended from the Pleroma upon the psychic Christ at his baptism and brought the perfect knowledge that ensures salvation to those pneumatics who possess the seed, to those psychic who are capable of conversion, but not to the hylic who are doomed to perish.

This complicated system was supported by a detailed scriptural exegesis,[17] allegorical in character, of the gospels and the Pauline epistles, making little use of the Old Testament, which in any case was regarded as the record of the inferior demiurge. The eclectic nature of this myth scarcely needs comment, but its appeal to many Christians, whom the Gnostics regarded as belonging to the psychic and to whom they directed their main missionary endeavour, has to be appreciated. Christ occupies a position of central importance; his redemptive activity begins in eternity and is repeated on earth. The emanations were no stumbling block to those who believed in angels – all that the Valentinians had done was to make known their names and mutual relations. When they spoke of the divine origin of the soul, they claimed to be expounding the teaching of Paul who had spoken at Athens of the unknown God and had declared that 'we are his offspring'.[18] The only item to give pause was the repudiation of the Old Testament, but Paul again had said that it was delivered by angels,[19] and the Gnostic rejection was a convenient way out of the difficulties presented by the many immoral ideas contained within the Jewish sacred books. It is no wonder that Gnosticism, which incorporated so much that was current in the period and appealed to self-interest, offered a serious threat to the Church, and this threat was all the greater when it was wedded to careful organization, as was the case with the Pontic school or Marcionitism.

Marcionitism

Marcion was a wealthy shipowner of Sinope and the son of its bishop. Between 138 and 140 he came to Rome, contributing a large sum of money to the Church funds. Sharing the concern of many at the apparent contradictions of numerous passages in the Old Testament and statements in the apostolic writings, he approached the presbyters in 144 with a request for an explanation, and, when their reply failed to satisfy, he broke away from the Church, receiving back his original gift, and founded a new sect, which spread with such rapidity after his death *c.* 160 that by the end of the century Tertullian compared his followers, who had congregations under bishops and presbyters, to swarms of wasps building combs in false imitation of the bees.[20] Marcion's enthusiasm and ability were such that his movement continued for many centuries, there being a flourishing community in the East in the fifth century and survivors even into the Middle Ages.

Marcion set out what seemed to him a series of undeniable contradictions in a work entitled the *Antitheses*, which consisted of texts from the Old and New Testaments, side by side to bring out their variance. It was this opposition, of which he would not dispose by the only means to hand, viz. allegorical interpretation, that led him to affirm the existence of two gods: the one, an inferior being, the creator and God of the Jews; the other, the Supreme God, first revealed through Jesus Christ. To support his beliefs Marcion produced a canon of Christian scriptures, comprising ten of the Pauline epistles, with the omission of anything that seemed to favour Judaism, and a truncated text of Luke, leaving out similarly anything that did not agree with his theology.

In certain particulars Marcion's teaching differed from that of the principal Gnostic schools. His dualism was not that of one good and one evil god, but of a legalistically righteous demiurge, harshly and cruelly demanding obedience to his law, and of a forgiving Father, revealing himself in loving action instead of in hate and retribution. The Marcionite emphasis on faith too, in the sense of trust in God, seems to set him apart from the general Gnostic position. Nevertheless, his dualism was only a refinement of that commonly held and his advocacy of faith involved the prior mediation of gnosis of the Unknown Being who had given no evidence of his existence or love until the advent of Christ. If emanations play no part, docetism was primary and salvation accordingly was of the soul alone that it might be freed from its contact with evil matter. While of undoubted originality, Marcion can scarcely be set apart from the general Gnostic movement, and the shallowness of his ethical and religious judgement may be illustrated by his belief that Cain and the Sodomites were saved because they opposed the Creator God, while Abraham, Moses, etc., were doomed on the grounds of their service to Yahweh.

Pax Romana

While fighting on one front against the Gnostics, whose partial or, in the case of Marcionitism, considerable success was draining her manpower, the Church, on another front, found itself in conflict with the State. Within the empire the *Pax Romana* generally persisted. After the short reign of Nerva (96–8), Trajan (98–117) preserved internal peace and his Danubian wars were beyond the frontier. Hadrian (117–138) was pacific by nature and even surrendered some of his predecessor's conquests, the second and final Jewish revolt under Bar Cochba being one of the few disturbances during his reign. The rule of the Antonines began with Antoninus Pius (138–161), whose policy was also one of peace, although there were short outbreaks of violence in Britain and Egypt. Marcus Aurelius (161–180), however, was not only compelled to fight against the Parthians but in the Marcomannic wars had to withstand invasion by the German tribes into the empire itself. More stable times returned with his son, Commodus (180–192), the last of the Antonine house to wear the purple. But while this period of relative peace enabled the Church to increase its numbers, this very growth brought it more prominently to the notice of the authorities, with the consequent danger of suppression. Nevertheless the second century witnessed no systematic and official attempt to stamp out Christianity – such persecutions as did take place were often the outcome of local circumstances or even of personal pique and jealousy.

Persecution[21]

When Pliny arrived in Bithynia on 17th September, 111, he came as the special envoy of the Emperor Trajan, who had taken over the province from the senate so that he might restore it to some sort of order. The incompetent rule of the senatorial proconsuls, the rivalry of Nicomedia and Nicaea, each seeking to outdo the other in sumptuous but never completed public works, and the formation of many unauthorized associations had brought the district to the verge of ruin. One of the new governor's first acts was to issue an edict forbidding all clubs, for Trajan regarded them as disturbers of the peace and it was his view that 'whatever title we give them, and whatever our object in giving it, men who are banded together for a common end will all the same become a political association,[22] and so he would have 'all societies of this nature prohibited'.[23] When, on these grounds, the Emperor refused to sanction even a fire brigade, it was not to be expected that he would look with favour on the Church.

Pliny, whose practice it was to refer all major policy decisions to his master, had had no previous experience of Christians and so wrote for advice, at the same time giving an account of what he had done to date. As a consequence of information laid against them, a number of people had been brought before Pliny on the charge of being Christians. Some of them he had executed; others, who claimed Roman citizenship, he had despatched, according to the law, to Rome. The accusations multiplied and an anonymous notice, consisting of a list of names, was posted. Those who were thus accused were required to invoke the gods, offer incense to the Emperor's image and to curse Christ. The majority complied but since, upon investigation, Pliny could find them guilty of no obvious crime, for they declared that all they did was to meet on a fixed day to worship Christ, then later to eat together, he adjourned the proceedings to await the imperial ruling, while intimating that Christianity was responsible for the desertion of the temples and for the lack of sacrifices and asserting that 'this contagious superstition is not confined to the cities only, but has spread through the villages and rural districts; it seems possible, however, to check and cure it'.[24]

Trajan's reply was as follows:

> You have followed the correct course, my dear Pliny, in investigating the cases of those denounced to you as Christians. It is not possible to lay down any universal rule which can be applied as the fixed standard in all cases of this nature. No search should be made for these people; but if they are denounced and found guilty, they must be punished; with this proviso, that when the party denies that he is a Christian, and shall give proof that he is not, by worshipping the gods, he shall be pardoned for his penitence, even though he may have formerly incurred suspicion. But anonymously written accusations must not be admitted in evidence against anyone, for they form the worst precedent and are not in keeping with the spirit of the age.[25]

In this rescript, the Emperor laid down three principles; the first and last of which were undoubtedly to the advantage of the Church: there was to be no deliberate searching out of Christians; those who, when apprehended, recanted, were to be pardoned; anonymous accusations were forbidden. Trajan thus refrained from initiating any general persecution, although there is evidence of two other martyrdoms in his reign, that of Symeon, bishop of Jerusalem, and that of Ignatius, bishop of Antioch.[26]

Under Hadrian there is no record of anyone being executed for his Christian faith, with the possible exception of Telesphorus, bishop of Rome,[27] and the Emperor was prepared to go further than Trajan, as evidenced by his rescript of 125, addressed to the proconsul of Asia. In this, while acknowledging Christianity to be still unlawful, he forbade magistrates to proceed under the pressure of public tumults and imposed heavy penalties on false accusers.[28] This did not however close the door to those delators whose information was accurate and who could use it for personal ends as in the case of Ptolemy, under Antoninus Pius, an Emperor whose piety led the Senate to erect a monument in his honour 'on account of his zeal for public religious ceremonies'[29] and who, exemplifying the pagan religious revival, could be expected to have little sympathy for the Church. Ptolemy had converted a woman of some wealth and standing and she determined to be separated from her debauchee of a husband. He thereupon denounced her as a Christian, but baulked by her appeal to the Emperor to have time to arrange her affairs, he turned upon Ptolemy, who was thrown into prison and confessed himself to be a Christian. He was brought before Urbicus, prefect of the city, and immediately ordered to be executed, together with one Lucius, who objected to the proceedings and also admitted his adherence to the Christian faith; a second unnamed person did likewise.[30]

The martyrdom of Polycarp, in 155 or 156, was an example of the pressure of mob violence, to which Hadrian had been opposed. The occasion was the festival of the *Commune Asiae*, a notable anniversary of Caesar – worship of which Smyrna was a chief centre. There is good reason to suppose that the crowd, stirred by the ceremonies, turned against the Christians as known opponents of the imperial cult, and the Asiarch or High Priest, Philip, having tried in vain to induce the bishop to acknowledge Caesar as Lord, condoned the action of the mob by ordering Polycarp's execution.[31]

Personal jealousy and mob violence continued to be operative under Marcus Aurelius. According to Eusebius,[32] the lectures of Justin Martyr on the Christian faith in Rome had met with considerable success, to the anger of the Cynic Crescens, whom Justin had several times overthrown in discussion before an audience. Crescens took the easy way of dealing with this by laying information against Justin as a Christian, and in 163, after a trial before the prefect Q. Junius Rusticus – of which the *acta* or minutes have been preserved – Justin and his companions were put to death.[33]

At Lyons and Vienne on 1st August 177, there was held the annual festival of the Three Gauls, when sacrifices were offered to Rome and to the genius of the Emperor. Christians, some betrayed by their own servants, were arraigned before the governor and were thrown to the wild beasts for the amusement of the crowd in the amphitheatre. The letter containing an account of their sufferings reports that the authorities were concerned 'to make of the faithful a spectacle, and to form a procession for the benefit of the crowd'.[34]

The sporadic persecutions under Marcus Aurelius continued into the early years of his son Commodus, not as part of the latter's own policy, since he was indifferent, but as the aftermath of his father's. On 17th July 180, four months after the death of Marcus Aurelius, twelve men and women of Scili in Numidia were tried at Carthage and ordered to be beheaded.[35] Personal motives influenced Claudius Lucius

Herminianus in Cappadocia, during this period, his wife having been converted to Christianity, to 'treat the Christians with great cruelty'[36] thus indicating that the way in which a provincial governor exerted his *liberum arbitrium*, i.e. his discretionary powers as a magistrate, could make the difference between peace and oppression in any one area at any one time. This applies equally to Arrius Antoninus, the proconsul of Asia, whose repression induced all the faithful of the province to come in a body to his judgement seat, whereupon some of their number were executed, while to the others it was said: 'Wretches, if you must die, there are precipices and halters.'[37]

In the imperial capital itself, only the senator Apollonius was condemned to death, after trial before Perennis, prefect from 180–5,[38] since Commodus's mistress Marcia, a Christian, exercised a moderating influence and indeed, after procuring a list of confessors condemned to the Sardinian mines from bishop Victor, effected their release.[39]

Death, however, in a legalized form was an ever-present possibility for the Christians of the second century, and the influence of this element in their background upon their conduct and thought was by no means slight.

SOURCES

The material available for reconstructing the life and thought of the Church in the century succeeding the Apostolic Age, although insufficient to enable a complete account to be given, is by no means meagre in quantity. These sources, almost exclusively literary, fall into five groups: the writings of the Apostolic Fathers; those of the Apologists; the Acts of the Martyrs; apocryphal scriptures and heretical literature, to which last may be added the beginnings of anti-heretical polemic.

Apostolic Fathers

Under the heading of the 'Apostolic Fathers', a title first used in the seventeenth century, it is customary to include the writings of five or six authors, together with one anonymous treatise.[1] These documents are pastoral in character; their content and style relate them closely to the New Testament, especially to the epistles; they were written for special occasions, and it is these common characteristics and the fact that they all belong to the same period, for which the records are scanty, that justifies them being treated together, although they do not form a completely homogeneous group.

I Clement, a letter to the Christians of Corinth, was written by the third bishop of Rome, of whom little else is known, in the last quarter of the first century. News had reached the capital of dissensions which had issued in the repudiation by many of the authority of the local Church leaders. It was Clement's intention to settle the differences and to this end he contrasted the disturbed state of the Church with its past glories, deprecated discord and envy, with illustrations from the Old Testament of the evils inherent in them, and pleaded for discipline and love. So successful was this intervention that in the days of bishop Dionysius of Corinth (*c.* 170), this epistle was amongst the books being read, side by side with the Holy Scriptures, at the Sunday assemblies.[2]

Also ascribed to the same writer, but with no justification, is *II Clement*, which is not a letter but a homily, being the oldest Christian sermon extant. It is possibly to be dated *c.* 150 and may have emanated from either Corinth or Alexandria. It is general in character and treats of the moral combat in which the Christian has to engage as he faces the world.

By contrast the *Letters of Ignatius* of Antioch, written in the reign of Trajan (98–117) during his journey to Rome where he was to be thrown to the wild beasts, provide a vivid picture of Church life and organization, of Christian doctrine and of the character of their author. Of these seven epistles, four, to Ephesus, Magnesia, Tralles and Rome were penned at Smyrna, while those to Philadelphia, Smyrna and to its bishop Polycarp, were forwarded from Troas. They breathe an air of fervent devotion to Christ, of eagerness to die for his sake, of concern for Christian unity, and of hostility to any form of docetic teaching.

Polycarp, who had been Ignatius' host at Smyrna and had also been the recipient of a letter from him, was born *c.* AD 70, and is said, on good authority, to have been personally acquainted with the apostle John.[3] His *Epistle to the Philippians* probably consists of two letters, chapters 13 and possibly 14 being originally a covering note sent with a collection of the Ignatian letters (*c.* 110), and sections 1–12 written some twenty years later to denounce the heretic Marcion. Polycarp visited Rome to confer with bishop Anicetus, *c.* 154, and was martyred either on 23rd February 155 or 22nd February 156, a record of his last days having been preserved.

The *Epistle of Barnabas*, of unknown authorship and uncertain date, perhaps *c.* 130 and possibly of Alexandrian provenance, is in the main a controversial work against Judaism to which it is implacably hostile. The writer's view, that the Jews 'erred because an evil angel deluded them',[4] has a gnostic ring, but this did not prevent him from making use, in the second half of his work, of a Jewish document to express his moral teaching in the form of the antithesis between the 'Two Ways', the one of light, the other of darkness.

The same contrast between the 'Two Ways', albeit in terms of life and death, is to be found in the *Didache* and probably derives independently from the same lost Jewish source. The *Didache* or *Teaching of the Twelve Apostles* is a manual devoted to moral instruction and Church order, with sections on baptism, fasting and prayer, the 'Eucharist', and apostles and prophets. Ever since it was first published in 1883, this work has been the subject of debate; opinions have ranged from assigning it to as early as AD 60 to characterizing it as a Montanist document of the late second century or even as a forgery of the tenth. It would perhaps be nearest the mark to describe it as a comparatively primitive document written in all likelihood in Syria.

The *Shepherd* of Hermas, although numbered among the Apostolic Fathers, is an apocryphal apocalypse, consisting of a series of revelations granted to the author by two heavenly figures, the first an old woman, the second an angel in the guise of a shepherd. Hermas had been sold into slavery in early youth and was sent to Rome where he was bought by a certain Rhoda. According to the Muratorian fragment, he was the brother of Pius, bishop of Rome *c.* 140–50. His work is the fruit of sixty years of literary activity, the opening sections dating back to the first century and the later portions being completed during his brother's episcopate. Its main purpose is to preach repentance and in various ways it proclaims that a Christian who has fallen into serious sin after baptism may have one further chance of being restored by remorse and penitence. Its interest lies less in the principal idea than in the way it is worked out; Hermas's description of specific cases and of the different circumstances of the sinner provides a valuable account of the life of the Roman Church in the first half of the second century.

The Apologists

If the Apostolic Fathers were concerned with the inner life of the Church and the problems attendant upon it, the Apologists worked on the frontier of the Church and the world, seeking to defend the Christian faith from misrepresentation and attack, to commend it to the interested inquirer and to demonstrate the falsity of polytheism and the truth of monotheism. Nearly all the extant apologies are in the form of legal documents, petitioning the State authorities for careful investigation of what Christianity really was, and consequently they are chiefly directed to the first and third of these aims and are by way of being prolegomena to the second.

The earliest apologist was Quadratus who most likely presented his plea to Hadrian during the Emperor's stay in Asia Minor, either 123–4 or 129. While nothing remains of this save a brief fragment quoted by

Eusebius,[5] the whole of the next apologist's work, that of Aristides, has been recently recovered. A philosopher of Athens, probably active under Marcus Aurelius, Aristides does not reveal himself as an original thinker. His treatise, consisting of a series of categorical statements to the effect that Christianity is true, is clumsy with little attempt at reasoned argument, and shows him to have been the intellectual inferior of Justin Martyr who was the most considerable of the apologists.

Justin was born at Flavia Neapolis, formerly Sichem, in Palestine, of pagan parents. After familiarizing himself with the various philosophical schools, in particular the Stoic, the Peripatetic, the Pythagorean and the Platonic, and finding them unsatisfactory, he was converted to Christianity. He travelled as an itinerant teacher, setting up a school in Rome during the reign of Antoninus Pius and was eventually martyred *c.* 163. In his *First Apology*, Justin begins by refuting the accusations raised against Christians[6] and presents and justifies the contents of his religion, paying particular attention to worship and providing the fullest description extant from this period of baptism and the eucharist. The *Second Apology* is much shorter and is regarded by many as an appendix or postscript to the first. The *Dialogue with Trypho* (*c.* 160), based probably upon an actual disputation, gives an account of Justin's two-day conversation with a learned Jew and is valuable in that it is the sole example of a work intended to appeal to the members of the Old Israel and to present Jesus to them as the fulfiller of the Law.

Amongst Justin's pupils at Rome was Tatian, by birth a Syrian, who in 172–3 returned to his native East and founded a Gnostic sect known as the Encratites. Apart from his *Diatessaron*, which is a harmony of the four gospels, Tatian's one surviving work is his *Discourse to the Greeks*, notable for its vituperation and its savage invective against the pagan gods.

To Athenagoras of Athens are ascribed the *Supplication for the Christians*, *c.* 177, which rebuts the charges of atheism, Thyestian banquets and Oedipean incest, and *On the Resurrection*, which however may be a fourth-century work by another writer. Theophilus, bishop of Antioch, addressed his *Apology to Autolycus* shortly after 180 and covered similar ground to Athenagoras. The dialogue form reappears in the *Octavius* of Minucius Felix, which purports to record a discussion between three friends at Ostia. Possibly of African provenance, the author may have borrowed from Tertullian's *Apology*, 197, in which case it would belong to the early years of the third century and be contemporary with the *Epistle to Diognetus* which is an attractive argument for the superiority of Christianity to the beliefs of the Jews and heathen, its two final chapters deriving from another author, possibly Hippolytus.

The Acts of the Martyrs

While the apologies were destined for consumption outside the Church, the documents giving accounts of the deaths of the early martyrs were produced in the main to be read at the annual commemorations in their honour in the context of Christian worship. These *acta* were based either on the official minutes of the trial or upon descriptions given by eye-witnesses. To the latter category belongs the *Martyrdom of Polycarp*, *c.* 155, while to the former may be assigned the *Acts of St. Justin and his Companions*, between 163 and 167. The *Letter of the Churches at Lyons and Vienne* to the Churches in Asia and Phrygia, 177, describes a persecution in Gaul, while the *Acts of the Scillitan Martyrs* takes us to Carthage in 180.

Apocryphal Scriptures

Another genre of literature, devised for reading by the faithful during their leisure time and corresponding in some respects to the novels of a later era, was a group of apocryphal writings which both imitated the New Testament forms, being Gospels, Acts, Epistles and Apocalypses, and pretended to be the work of New Testament personages. In part these documents served to satisfy the curiosity about the activities of the apostles, stimulated by the Church's insistence upon their authority for anti-heretical purposes. In part the heretics themselves made use of this means to propagate their own interpretations of the Christian faith.

The apocryphal gospels relate in the main to those years in the life of Jesus for which there is no canonical record, i.e. to his childhood, together with his teaching after his resurrection. The *Book of James*, written in Greek towards the end of the second century, narrates the miraculous birth and infancy of the Virgin Mary. The *Gospel of Thomas*, of Syrian origin, contains legends of Jesus up to the age of twelve. It is to be distinguished from the recently recovered *Coptic Gospel of Thomas*, a Gnostic work, which does not concern itself with events but consists of a series of sayings and parabolic discourses. To the second half of the second century belongs the *Gospel of Peter*, of which only the parts concerning the crucifixion and resurrection have been preserved; it is a very free redaction of the four canonical Gospels and includes docetic elements.

Amongst the Acts, the first in point of time is probably the *Acts of Paul*, which incorporates the story of his association with Thecla. Next there is the *Acts of John*, written by a certain Lucius Charinius in Asia; the *Acts of Peter*, composed about 190, and the *Acts of Andrew* which is usually dated *c.* 260 but may have been issued before 200.

The *Epistle of the Apostles*, mid second century, is an imitation of the third class of New Testament writings, and consists of revelations made by the risen Lord to his apostles and concludes with an account of the ascension, while the *Apocalypse of Peter*, first half of the second century, belongs to the fourth class and records visions in which Jesus appears to his followers and describes the splendours of heaven and the terrors of hell.

How far any one of these books is consciously unorthodox is difficult to determine, since many of the 'heretical' ideas could well be no more than a reflection of popular belief in an age when orthodoxy was not yet clearly defined. But if doubt arises in certain instances, the heretical nature of our next class of literature is not in dispute.

Heretical literature

Until recently the writings of the second-century heretical schools were known only indirectly through the works of their orthodox opponents, who reproduced much of their thought in order to repudiate it. Only a few Gnostic texts such as the *Pistis Sophia*, conversations of the risen Christ with his disciples, from the third century, and the *Letter of Ptolemy to Flora*, transcribed by Epiphanius,[7] giving the Italian Valentinian criticism of the Mosaic law, together with the *Apocryphon of John*, *c*. 180, a revelation of the risen Saviour on the Mount of Olives, were preserved in their original form. But in 1945 or 1946, a large collection of Gnostic texts was discovered at Nag Hamadi on the east bank of the Nile, near the ancient Pachomian monastery at Chenoboskion. This collection comprises thirteen volumes, embodying a hundred or so treatises on some 1000 pages. These include the *Gospel of Truth*, possibly by Valentinian himself; a *Treatise on the Three Natures*, a *Letter of James* and the *Coptic Gospel of Thomas* referred to already. These works, of which only a few have so far been published, will be of the greatest importance for further research into Gnosticism. They contain, however, no representation of the writings of Marcion and his followers, and Marcion's *Antitheses* therefore can only be reconstructed from the extensive refutation of it composed by Tertullian. Montanism fares even worse, only a few of the oracles of its founder having been deemed worthy of recording by his opponents.

Anti-heretical literature

The number of anti-heretical writers in the second century, known chiefly through Eusebius, was great, but their works are almost all lost, apart from an occasional fragment. Only one important document of this type has survived, viz. Irenaeus's *Against Heresies*, and even this is known in full in a Latin translation of the Greek original. Irenaeus was the most outstanding of the second-century theologians and may be termed the Father of Church Dogmatics. Born in Asia Minor and a disciple of Polycarp,[8] he became a presbyter at Lyons in the reign of Marcus Aurelius, and succeeded Pothinus as bishop after the persecution of 177. Little is known of his life, apart from an embassy to Rome in connexion with the Montanist controversy and his intervention in the dispute about Easter. Irenaeus's work was not only destructive, in that he expounded the Gnostic systems in order to attack them, it was also constructive in that he sought to formulate the foundation principles of Christian theology, and gave a positive exposition of the Church's beliefs. A summary of this doctrine is contained in his other sole surviving work, the *Proof of the Apostolic Preaching*.

The Canon of Scripture

The Church's defence of its position was largely based upon the apostolic writings which during the second century assumed a position of authority as embodying a doctrinal norm. Thus the process was initiated whereby a canon of Christian Scriptures was acknowledged by the side of those sacred books inherited from Judaism. It had become the custom of the Church to read, during the course of worship, both from the Septuagint and from those Christian writings of which either the originals or copies were possessed, and this led to the inference that the latter were in some sense as authoritative as the former. Each local church had its collection, and the question inevitably arose, what should be included in our reading list? The answer would seem to have been determined by a combination of three main factors. First, whether or not the writing was deemed to have been by an apostle or by a close associate of an apostle. Second, whether or not it was accepted by the Church at large. Third, whether or not its contents were generally edifying. So lists or 'canons' were drawn up, the earliest known being that of the heretic Marcion *c.* AD 150, to be followed shortly, *c.* 170, by the Muratorian Canon, which, although mutilated, gives the major portion of the books accepted at that date at Rome. There was considerable agreement on the main contents of these lists, but there were differences of detail from centre to centre and also between East and West; the East, for instance, long hesitated to accept the Book of Revelation and the West the Epistle to the Hebrews.

Even before the final agreement on the list was reached in the fourth century, the *idea* of a canon was accepted and the apostolic writings were regarded as the main source of doctrine. It was this attitude that led to the defining of the canon, and not the eventual closure of the canon that generated this conception. Consequently when attention is directed later in this chapter, after outlining the development of the Church in this period, to the growth of Christian belief, the primacy of Scripture, i.e. of the Old Testament and the apostolic writings, must be recognized.

EXPANSION AND DEVELOPMENT

By the end of the Apostolic Age Christian communities were to be found in Palestine, Syria, Asia Minor, Greece and Italy. During the second century the new faith continued steadily but not spectacularly to spread. Although little headway was made in the land of its birth, in adjacent Syria, while evidence as to the countryside is lacking, the church at Antioch flourished and its pre-eminence in the district is revealed by Ignatius' reference to it as 'the church in Syria'.[1] Eastwards the gospel penetrated to Edessa; indeed *c.* 201, or possibly earlier, the royal house joined the Church. Mesopotamia and Persia too probably had their small groups. Asia Minor, on the foundation of Paul's labours, continued to be the Christian country *par excellence*, so that Pliny could state that 'the contagion of this superstition has spread not only through the free cities, but to the villages and rural districts'.[2]

In Greece, outside certain centres, such as Thessalonica and Corinth, the faith did not make great progress, although northwards along the Dalmatian coast a thriving congregation was established at Salona. In Italy, Rome continued to dominate the scene, but the second-century catacomb at Naples shows that it was not isolated. In Gaul, the letter reporting the persecution at Lyons and Vienne in 177 is the first evidence of the Christian mission. Since Gaul had close commercial relations with the eastern Mediterranean, the gospel may have been brought by traders from Asia Minor who voyaged up the Rhône – but when this took place and what persons were involved is now and probably will remain unknown. From Spain there is no information forthcoming, and in North Africa the first certain date is 180 when the Scillitan martyrs were executed. Intimate commercial connexions with Rome might suggest that the springboard of African evangelization was the imperial capital, but the evidence of close links between Asia Minor and North Africa indicates the possibility of the initiative having been taken by Christians from the East.

The early history of the Church in Egypt is similarly vague; not until the episcopate of Demetrius of Alexandria (188/9–231) does our information become precise, yet prior to that time there must have been numerous communities scattered between the Thebaid and the Delta, as indicated both by the biblical papyri and the activity of Egyptian

Christian Gnostics such as Basilides. Whether or not the origins of the Egyptian Church go back into the first century is a matter for surmise, which can only be turned into certainty by the discovery of fresh evidence.

Methods of evangelism

From this brief tour of the Mediterranean basin, it is apparent that Christianity was everywhere on the advance, but that its success was by no means remarkable. Its continued expansion was favoured by the same factors that had operated in the Apostolic Age and the methods of evangelism remained very much the same. There was no elaborate missionary machinery; the faith was spread rather by personal contact and example. Hence Justin could refer to many who have 'changed their violent and tyrannical disposition, being overcome either by the constancy which they have witnessed in the lives of their Christian neighbours, or by the extraordinary forbearance they have observed in their Christian fellow-travellers when defrauded, and by the honesty of those believers with whom they have transacted business'.[3] Others were converted because of their dissatisfaction with the alternatives; so Tatian records how he was admitted to the Mysteries, only to become nauseated with them. In this condition he came across the Scriptures and, according to his own report, 'I was led to put faith in them by the unpretentious cast of the language, the unartificial character of the writers, the foreknowledge displayed of future events, the excellent quality of the precepts, and the declaration of the government of the universe as centred in one Being'.[4] As for personal contact, the pagan Celsus could complain of workers in wool and leather and of fullers who laid hold of women and children to instruct them in the rudiments of the Christian faith.[5] Celsus himself was sufficiently representative of a wide body of pagans to inhibit the free spread of the Christian message. If there were factors favouring the Church, as it came more and more into the public view the climate of opinion was opposed to it.

Charges against Christians

The anti-Christian polemic arose in large measure from ignorance and misrepresentation. Believers were charged with atheism: 'why have they no altars, no temples, no images?'[6] They were held guilty of disloyalty, of treason and lack of patriotism, in that they refused to participate in the emperor cult, were known to be looking for another kingdom,[7] played no part in public life and were therefore no better than misanthropists. Their secret meetings, to which the unbaptized were not allowed entrance, were held to be occasions for immorality. Garbled accounts of the eucharist resulted in rumours that Christians practised cannibalism and incest. Hence according to the pagan in the *Octavius* of Minucius Felix: 'Now the story about the initiation of young novices is as much to be detested as it is well known. An infant covered over with meal, that it may deceive the unwary, is placed before him who is to be stained with their rites: this infant is slain by the young pupil, who has been urged on as if to harmless blows on the surface of the meal, with dark and secret wounds. Thirstily – O horror! – they lick up its blood; eagerly they divide its limbs. . . . On a solemn day they assemble at the feast, with all their children, sisters, brothers, people of every sex and of every age. There, after much feasting, when the fellowship has grown warm, and the fervour of incestuous lust has grown hot with drunkenness, a dog that has been tied to the chandelier is provoked, by throwing a small piece of offal beyond the length of the line by which it is attached, to rush and spring; and thus the conscious light being overturned and extinguished in the shameless darkness, the connexions of abominable lust involve them in the uncertainty of fate.'[8]

This unsavoury description is not just the product of hearsay; there were Gnostic groups which were prepared to condone such immorality on the grounds that the body is not the real self and that consequently what is done with it has no effect upon the divine spark. Thus Clement of Alexandria has given an account of the lewd assemblies of the Carpocratians which is all but identical with that which Octavius' pagan opponent provides of the Christian rites:

> These then are the doctrines of the excellent Carpocratians. These, so they say, and certain other enthusiasts for the same wickedness, gather together for feasts (I would not call their meeting an Agape), men and women together. After they have sated their appetites ('on repletion Cypris, the goddess of love, enters,' as it is said), then they overturn the lamps and so extinguish the light that the shame of their adulterous 'righteousness' is hidden, and they have intercourse where they will and with whom they will.[9]

Not all the charges against Christians issued from wrong identification or misinformed gossip. Unlike the multitude, which was little concerned with the truth or falsity of what they said, Celsus took pains to understand the new faith. In his *True Discourse*, published *c.* 178, he reveals that he had read the Bible and was acquainted with Church teaching and with the arguments employed by Christians. Even if the fictitious crimes already listed be left on one side, there still remained many points of attack that were developed by Celsus. Taking Jews and Christians together, Celsus asserted that their common authority was

Moses, whom he charged with sorcery and plagiarism. Jesus was the follower of Moses and was equally a magician. The God, worshipped by Jew and Christian alike, is an absurd being, in that he is subject to passion and was incapable of delivering his own Son from death. As for the Christian idea of an incarnation, this was inconceivable since it ascribed to the unchangeable deity a transformation into something on a lower plane. Moreover, fables were told about Jesus' virgin birth to hide the fact that he was a bastard. His lowly origin and shameful death show that he was not a son of God but a deceiver who paid the due penalty on the cross. Naturally his followers were only to be found among the uneducated and simple, and whatever was reasonable in their teaching was borrowed, without acknowledgement, from the wisdom of the Greeks.

Schism

Not only was the Church threatened from without but its inner life was in danger of dissolution, in part from the Christian Gnostics and in part as a result of the Montanist and Quartodeciman controversies.

The date at which Montanus first attracted notice is doubtful; according to Epiphanius[10] it was in 156–7, while according to Eusebius it was 172.[11] Montanus was a native of a Mysian village named Ardabau, on the borders of Phrygia, and is said to have been a convert from paganism, having previously held the position of a priest of Cybele.[12] If this be true, then he would appear to have transferred from that worship the fervid and ecstatic spirit which it nurtured, since he became famous for his transports in which he uttered strange sayings and as a consequence was regarded as a prophet. With him were associated two women, Maximilla and Priscilla, to whom the same authority was ascribed. The main impetus of the movement seems to have derived from these prophetesses, since Montanus vanished quickly from the scene. Maximilla is thought to have died *c.* 179 and Priscilla a few years later.

The basis of the Montanist teaching was the claim to a fuller revelation of the divine will, in virtue of their inspiration by the Spirit, than that possessed hitherto by the Church at large. The promises of Jesus at the Last Supper that he would send the Paraclete had now been fulfilled and the age of the Paraclete had dawned. Through Montanus and his companions the Paraclete was speaking directly; they were but the passive instruments of his activity. In this respect they were like those having the gift of tongues, only their message was intelligible. 'Behold,' said the Spirit through Montanus, 'the man is as a lyre, and I sweep over him as a plectrum. The man sleeps; I wake. Behold it is the

Lord who puts the hearts of men out of themselves and gives a heart to men'.[13]

To understand the rise of this movement it is necessary both to appreciate the part played by prophecy in the life of the Church and the extent to which the Montanists were reacting against the threat of Gnosticism. It is unnecessary to go back to the New Testament to examine the importance of prophets in the Christian community. The *Didache* can assert: 'thou shalt take therefore all first-fruits of the produce of winepress and threshing floor, of oxen and sheep, and give them to the prophets; for they are your high priests'.[14] Hermas was held in high honour as a prophet, as was also Ammia of Philadelphia;[15] nor were these isolated individuals. Justin in argument with Trypho points to the prophetic gifts manifested in the Church as evidence that the Christians are the chosen people[16] and Irenaeus gives a similar testimony.[17] This belief in the diffusion of the prophetic Spirit was not without its danger, as it gave an easy opening to charlatans and deceivers, but it also enabled the Montanists to obtain a hearing and their teaching spread rapidly. This teaching however was initially essentially orthodox and in three important particulars was quite clearly opposed to Gnosticism. While the Gnostics rejected the Old Testament, the Montanists 'receive themselves the whole of the Scriptures'.[18] Where the Gnostics were docetists the Montanists affirmed both the reality of Christ's body and the resurrection of the flesh. Finally, against the Gnostic repudiation of the primitive Christian eschatological hope, the adherents of the New Prophecy eagerly expected the future age, asserting that the New Jerusalem was about to descend at Pepuza, the home of Priscilla, and the millennial reign of Christ would begin. Unlike many of the Gnostic schools too the Montanists were rigorist, laying emphasis upon celibacy, condemning second marriages and prescribing long and severe fasts. It was this puritanical strain, together with the new certainty of the truth of the gospel, conveyed by this outpouring of the Spirit, that appealed to Tertullian and led to his adherence to the movement in the early years of the third century, its further spread being facilitated by its organization in terms of the threefold ministry, together with patriarchs and an ambiguous order known as the *koinonoi*.[19]

Montanism was condemned by the Church because it claimed to supersede the revelation contained in the gospels, because its doctrine of the Holy Spirit was extravagant and because it was a disruptive force at a time when there was a desperate need for unity. The tide steadily turned against it, although in the fourth century Epiphanius knew of Montanist churches still flourishing in Asia Minor and Jerome was aware of their continued existence in the highland fortress of Ancyra.[20]

Imperial laws were promulgated against them after the days of Constantine and although they disappeared some two hundred years after their foundation, their attitude continued to live on under other forms and names: faith in revelations of the Holy Spirit in the persons of men and women specially endowed with grace, passionate contempt for the world and complete surrender to the expectation of the Second Advent.

Quartodecimanism

The controversy concerning the date of the celebration of Easter did not assume the proportions of the Montanist debate and its threat to unity, although real, was considerably less. The problem was this: a considerable body of Asiatic Christians commemorated Easter upon the exact day of the Passover, the 14th Nisan, whatever the day of the week, whereas other churches observed it on the Sunday following the 14th Nisan. In 155 Polycarp discussed the matter in Rome with Anicetus and they agreed to differ. So the matter seems to have rested for some thirty-five years until *c.* 190 when Victor of Rome made an energetic attempt to secure uniformity since, because of the large Asiatic population in the capital, one part of the Church was still fasting when the other was feasting. Victor held a synod and sent out requests for others to meet. His view was accepted by the majority, but the synod of Asia under the leadership of Polycrates of Ephesus refused to conform, whereupon Victor cut the province off from communion with the church of Rome.[21] His action called forth strong protests from many bishops, including Irenaeus of Lyons, and it seems to have had little effect. The situation was further complicated by the charge of heresy, and while the Asian churches seem to have been entirely free from the taint, Blastus, who was active in Rome either shortly before or during the episcopate of Victor, apparently insisted not only upon the Quartodeciman dating but also on eating the Paschal lamb, and was therefore regarded as wanting to introduce Judaism secretly. In time the celebration of Easter upon the Sunday was adopted by all, the only question remaining was whether, in determining the date, the Jewish reckoning was to be followed, as was the custom at Antioch, or whether it should be calculated independently, as was done at Alexandria and Rome – this last method was the one eventually decided upon.

Monepiscopacy and apostolic succession

The preceding reference to Victor of Rome may serve to draw attention to two features of the Church's interior development and structure in the second century, viz. the growth of monepiscopacy in general and the position of the Roman bishop in particular. The most primitive structure of the Church may best be described as that of collegiate episcopacy, the oversight being exercised by a body of presbyters under a president who was *primus inter pares*. By the turn of the first Christian century however the president was beginning to assume a position of pre-eminence which is made abundantly clear in the Ignatian epistles.

In his letter to the Romans, Ignatius, who at the time of writing had had no successor at Antioch, referred to the church there as having 'God for its shepherd in my stead'.[22] Ignatius further congratulated the Magnesians because their presbyters had not taken advantage of the youth of their bishop Damas, 'but give place to him as one prudent in God'.[23] He could also tell the Smyrneans that 'it is not lawful apart from the bishop either to baptize or to hold a love-feast.'[24] Thus the constitution first apparent in Jerusalem, where the church was governed by a council under the presidency of James, was now becoming general for all local churches. This development was held to be in accordance with the mind of the apostles, so in the words of *I Clement*:

> Preaching everywhere in country and town, they appointed their first-fruits, when they had proved them by the Spirit, to be bishops and deacons unto them that should believe . . . and our Apostles knew through our Lord Jesus Christ that there would be strife over the name of the bishop's office. For this cause therefore, having received complete foreknowledge, they appointed the aforesaid persons, and afterwards they provided a continuance, that if they should fall asleep, other approved men should succeed to their ministration.[25]

The monepiscopacy, revealed in the letters of Ignatius, did not involve the separation of the bishop from his subordinates. Although Ignatius is emphatic that the position of the bishop must be recognized, he is also insistent upon the unity of the clergy as a whole: 'let all men respect the deacons as Jesus Christ, even as they should respect the bishop as being a type of the Father and the presbyters as the council of God and as the college of the Apostles. Apart from these there is not even the name of a church';[26] collectively one may speak of 'the council (sanhedrin) of the bishop'.[27] Yet the bishop was the focal point of the local church's unity and spiritual life and the guardian of the true teaching, and it was this above all that led to emphasis upon his function, gradually hardening into an office, in the second century when the unity of the Church was menaced by heresy and schism and hence the stress placed upon apostolic succession.

As a counter-claim to the Gnostic assertion that they possessed a secret tradition of esoteric wisdom handed down by a succession of private teachers, the orthodox writers laid emphasis upon the public tradition through the succession of official teachers in each church, the succession of its bishops. 'It behoves us', according to Irenaeus, 'to learn the truth from those who possess that succession of the Church which is from the apostles, and among whom exists that which is sound and blameless in conduct, as well as that which is unadulterated and incorrupt in speech'.[28] The emphasis was placed upon the bishop's official succession to his own dead predecessor in the same see, and back through that predecessor to his predecessor and so to the original apostolic founder of the local church. It was a succession from office-holder to office-holder and not a 'sacramental' succession of consecrated to consecrator. To validate this claim succession lists were drawn up and the pioneer in this undertaking would appear to have been Hegesippus who, *c.* 160, collected information relating to the bishops of Rome.[29]

The importance of the Roman church rested in part upon its prestige as the church of the imperial capital and in part upon its association with Peter and Paul. The activity of the two apostles, as it was understood in the second century, is made clear both by the succession lists and by Irenaeus' references. In the lists Peter and Paul are placed in a category by themselves and the succession of bishops begins after them; in Irenaeus' words the apostles 'founded and organized' or 'founded and built up' the community and then 'committed into the hands of Linus the office of the episcopate'.[30] The idea that Peter was the first bishop of Rome was not current in this period. Yet the pre-eminence of the church there is evident from numerous incidents, e.g. its intervention in the dispute at Corinth through the medium of *I Clement* and its attempt to resolve the Quartodeciman dispute through the initiative of Victor. Even in the second century there was primacy of honour accorded to Rome, which, however, fell short of a primacy of jurisdiction: this was to be asserted and made effective in the succeeding centuries.

BELIEFS

Faith, in the New Testament sense, is primarily the outcome of an encounter with the living Christ which issues in self-committal and trust; it is therefore to be distinguished from belief in certain propositions. This primitive understanding of faith tended to become obscured in the second century as the Church contended with heretical ideas and developed its own norms or standards of doctrine. The contents of this belief were expressed in a series of quasi-creedal formulae of which the following, from Irenaeus, may be taken as typical. According to him, the true tradition, handed down from the apostles, requires belief in one God, the Father Almighty, maker of heaven and earth and the sea and all things that are in them; and in one Christ Jesus, the Son of God, who became incarnate for our salvation; and in the Holy Spirit, who proclaimed through the prophets the saving dispensations, and the advents, and the birth from a Virgin, and the Passion, and the Resurrection from the dead, and the Ascension into heaven in the flesh of the beloved Christ Jesus, our Lord, and his manifestation from the heavens in the glory of the Father to sum up all things and to raise up anew all flesh of the whole human race.[1]

God

Belief in the oneness of God, accepted by the Church from Judaism, was strongly asserted against polytheism, Gnostic emanationism and Marcionite dualism. 'First of all,' says Hermas, 'believe that there is one God who created and established all things'.[2] Since God is one, the claims of all false gods are to be rejected. But God is also one as regards his essential nature, in the sense that he is indivisible; he does not consist, according to Athenagoras, of parts.[3]

As the maker of all things this one God is to be distinguished from matter, which is originate and perishable; 'out of things that are not he creates and has created things that are'.[4] He is, moreover, transcendent and, against Stoic pantheism, it was asserted that 'our God does not have his constitution in time. He alone is without beginning; he himself constitutes the source of the universe. God is spirit. He does not extend through matter, but is the author of material spirits and of the figures in matter. He is invisible and intangible'.[5] Against Old Testament anthropomorphism, on the other hand, it was affirmed that God is impassible,[6] i.e. that his will is determined from within and not swayed from without. This does not mean that God is inactive or uninterested in his creation; on the contrary, God's concern was expressed by belief in his providence, which was frequently referred to as his 'economy'.[7] This word was used originally of the duty of a steward to administer his master's estates; then of administration in general and so of God's administration of the world in particular; since his overruling providence was supremely manifest in the Incarnation, this too could be termed the 'economy'.

The work and person of Christ

Like the apostolic writers before them, the second century theologians sought to interpret the person of Christ in terms of his function. Since many of them were concerned to commend the faith to the educated pagan, they declared that Christianity is the true philosophy. Christ is the revelation of God and his function was to bring illumination.

'Through Jesus Christ, God has called us from darkness to light, from ignorance to the knowledge of his glorious name.'[8] Christ is thus the Teacher, who brings the perfect knowledge of God, previously lost through sin.

To regard the saving act of Christ as consisting in no more than illumination was insufficient to convey the full richness of the Christian experience, and side by side with this interpretation other aspects were being noted. Perhaps the most widely accepted of these was that which has been called the 'classical' theory – the belief that salvation consists in freedom from the power of evil spirits and that Christ's function or redeeming work is to be understood as a victory over Satan, over sin and over death. How this victory was won is a question that was not immediately faced, although Ignatius anticipated the idea of the deceit of the devil[9] that was to be elaborated later.

Irenaeus also gave currency to the Christus Victor theme, but his key concept may be summed up in the word 'recapitulation'. This means, in the first instance, 'going over the same ground again'. Christ placed himself in the same circumstances as Adam, but with the opposite result; where Adam yielded, Christ overcame. So the whole of his life was a single process of redemption, in which he shared all the experiences of men, sin only excepted, and finally through his resurrection rose triumphant over death.[10] But recapitulation has also, secondly, the sense of 'restoration into unity': God and man, divided by sin are in Christ made one. Finally recapitulation means 'summing up', and so Irenaeus declares Christ to have embodied in himself the whole of human history as purposed by God in his original creation. In addition to this, he further understood salvation in terms of divinization and he expresses this pithily in his statement that Christ 'out of his great love became what we are, that he might make us what he is himself'.[11]

It was also in terms of function that Christ's relation to the Father was understood. So Irenaeus' interpretation of Christ's work as recapitulation in the sense of bringing together that which had been disunited influenced his doctrine of the person of Christ, as evidenced by his statement:

> Unless man had overcome the enemy of man, the enemy would not have been justly vanquished. And again: unless it had been God who had freely given salvation, we could never have possessed it securely. And unless man had been joined to God, he could never have become a partaker of incorruptibility. For it was incumbent upon the Mediator between God and men, by his relationship to both, to bring both to friendship and concord, and present man to God, while he revealed God to man.[12]

From this it follows that the Mediator must be both God and man – an affirmation already implicit in the New Testament documents and in the Epistle to the Hebrews in particular.

In their approach to the problem of the relationship of the Father and the Son, the second-century writers were also content to use the Old Testament terminology pressed into service in the New Testament. So Justin Martyr ascribed to the Son the titles of almost every intermediary between God and man mentioned in the Old Testament.

> God begat in the beginning, before all creatures, a certain rational power from himself, who is called by the Holy Spirit now the Glory of the Lord, now the Son, again Wisdom, again an Angel, and then Lord and Word . . . for he can be called by all those names, since he ministers to the Father's will, and since he was begotten of the Father by an act of will.[13]

In similar biblical vein, Irenaeus, in opposition to the Gnostic reduction of the Son and the Spirit to mere emanations, referred to them as 'the two hands of God',[14] identifying the latter with Wisdom and the former with the Word. It was however more customary to see the Son both as the Wisdom and the Word of God, with especial emphasis laid upon the second, and statements relating to this fall into three main groups. First, there are those in which the Word or Logos is regarded as the interpretative revelation of God – thus in harmony with the presentation of Christianity as the true philosophy. So Justin declared that the 'power sent from the Father' is called 'the Word because he brings messages from the Father to men'.[15] The second set of statements are those in which the Word is regarded as the principle of rationality; so Justin again says: 'He is the Word of whom every race of men are partakers; and those who lived with the Word (i.e. rationally) are Christians, even though they have been thought atheists'.[16] Finally, there are those in which the Word is presented as the active expression of the Father's will; this is involved in Justin's further statements that Jesus gave brief and concise teaching for 'his Word is no sophist, but the power of God'.[17]

This use of the Logos concept had a twofold merit in the second-century situation: on the one hand it served as a bridge to introduce and make intelligible Christian belief to those whose background was that of Greek philosophy, and, on the other, it emphasized the unity of the Father and the Son. The imagery of the Logos was already familiar to Christians from the Old Testament, from the prologue to John and from the speculations of Philo, the Alexandrian Jewish thinker. But Logos was also employed by the Stoics who distinguished between the internal or immanent Word (*endiathetos*) and the expressed or uttered Word (*prophorikós*). Logos could thus mean both thought, or rather reason, and word. This dual connotation could be and was applied to the oneness of the pre-existing Son with the Father and to his manifestation in the world of space and time. So, according to Theophilus, the Word is 'eternally immanent (*endiathetos*) in God's bosom. For before anything came into being, he had him as his counsellor, being his own intelligence and thought. But when God willed to create all that he had planned, he begat and uttered (*prophorikon*) his Word, the first-begotten of all creation'.[18]

By speaking in this technical Stoic language, the Christians made themselves understood, while at the same time they went beyond the Stoic position by asserting the identity of the Word with the eternal Son who became man. They were also enabled by this means to emphasize the Word's essential unity with the Father. 'He came into being by distribution, not by severance. Whatever is severed is cut off from its original, but that which is distributed undergoes division in the economy without impoverishing the source from which it is derived. For just as from one torch many fires are lighted, but the light of the first torch is not lessened by the kindling of the many, so the Word issues from the Father's power without depriving his begetter of his Word. For example, I talk and you listen to me; but I, who converse with you, am not, by the conveyance of my word to you, made empty of my word'.[19]

While stressing the divine unity of the Father with his Word, the second-century writers also asserted their distinction, but in so doing they employed, not a Stoic, but an Aristotelian category. According to Aristotle, an individual is that which is one in number;[20] hence many individuals are many in number and the difference between them is a difference in number. In distinguishing the Father from his Word, therefore, Justin Martyr could declare that the latter is not distinct in name only from the former, as the light is from the sun, but is 'numerically distinct too',[21] and he also maintained that Christians must recognize the Son 'in the second place, and the prophetic Spirit in the third'.[22]

The Holy Spirit

The second-century Fathers were convinced that the Godhead is a triad, i.e. a collection of three objects – a term first used by Theophilus[23] – but their attention was concentrated upon the Father and his Word rather than upon the Holy Spirit, and this for two reasons. First, if the Godhead be not unitary, it is as simple to conceive of three Persons as of two, and so the trinitarian controversies centred in the question of the deity of Christ and his relation to the Father. Second, because the Spirit was operative in contemporary Christian experience, it was less easy to objectify him and to reflect upon his being and function than it was in relation to Christ who had appeared on earth at a particular point of time. Nevertheless the orthodox writers did not entirely neglect this doctrine and saw in the Holy Spirit the agent who links Christ's redemptive act in Palestine with the present day.[24] He is the one who inspired the prophets[25] and is 'an effluence of God, flowing from and returning to him like a beam of the sun'.[26] This implicit doctrine of the Spirit was not individualistic being connected with the understanding of the Church as the sphere of his operation.

The Church

Although the Church might appear to be diffused in a large number of local congregations, it was essentially one in the eyes of its members. It is therefore the 'catholic', i.e. universal and general Church,[27] and it is indwelt by the Spirit. 'Where the Church is, there is the Spirit of God; and where the Spirit of God is, there is the Church and every kind of grace.'[28] Consequently the Church stands over against the mass of mankind – Christians are indeed a 'third race',[29] there being three divisions of mankind into pagans, Jews and Christians.[30] Adopting the New Testament images for the Church, the second-century writers saw it as Abraham's seed, the New Israel,[31] and as 'the great and glorious Body of Christ'.[32] Influenced by their anti-heretical polemic, they drew most sharply a distinction between the Church and the world and between the one Church and the multifarious sects. God 'shall also judge those who give rise to schisms, who are destitute of the love of God, and who look to their own special advantage rather than to the unity of the Church'.[33] The Church alone is the repository of truth, preserves the apostolic doctrine, safeguarding, through its bishops, the tradition, and sure of deliverance at the final consummation.

The Last Things

Eschatology in the period under review had points of comparison and contrast with that formulated in the New Testament. The latter proclaims salvation as a present reality and while this emphasis is by no means lost in the second century there is discernible a growing tendency to concentrate upon the future consummation. The New Testament envisages the end as imminent, whereas this expectation gradually faded in the succeeding decades, apart from its sudden irruption in terms of Montanist ecstasy. The New Testament too is reticent about the future, in only a few passages is the veil, as it were, drawn aside; the second-century documents on the other hand contain not a little speculation about what is happening to those who have died and about what is to happen at the consummation.

Despite the prospect of his own near death, Ignatius was confident that salvation is a present possession and not merely an object of hope. 'From that time forward every sorcery and every spell was dissolved, the ignorance of wickedness vanished away, the ancient kingdom was pulled down, when God appeared in the likeness of man unto newness of everlasting life, and that which had been perfected in the counsels of God began to take effect. Thence all things were perturbed because the abolishing of death was taken in hand',[34] so 'the Gospel is the completion of immortality'.[35] According to *Barnabas*, Christ 'has renewed us by the remission of sins . . . he has accomplished a second fashioning in the last days' for 'having received the forgiveness of sins, and placed our trust in the name of the Lord, we have become new creatures, formed again from the beginning'.[36] To similar effect Justin asserts that Christ has spoiled Satan, that the outpouring of the Spirit, foretold by Joel, has taken place, that Jesus has liberated his people who, stripped of sin, are now 'the true high-priestly race of God' living under the new covenant – salvation is an accomplished fact.[37] The same note is sounded by Irenaeus that Christ has 'consummated the arranged plan of our salvation' and that 'by his advent he himself fulfilled all things and does fulfil in the Church the new covenant foretold by the law, onwards to the consummation',[38] and by the *Epistle to Diognetus* that Christians 'pass their days on earth, but they are citizens of heaven' and that by the coming of Christ God has 'conferred every blessing all at once upon us'.[39] If this realization did weaken, it was not entirely lost, in that it underlay the argument from prophecy, so dear to the Early Church, and was present in its sacramental life, to be reviewed in the next section.

The expectation of Christ's speedy return, so vivid in the New Testament, persisted but received less and less emphasis. While *Barnabas* could state that 'the Lord is near and his reward',[40] Irenaeus says nothing of his imminent coming. Christians were beginning to realize that the final consummation might be indefinitely postponed and so they systematized their beliefs in terms of the two advents of Christ and looked upon the present time as the interval between them. Justin devoted not a little attention to this and distinguished sharply between the first and the second advent. The former was indeed in fulfilment of prophecy, but there remained many that had not been literally accomplished, in particular those that spoke in terms of triumph and glory, and these were now applied to the Second Advent. 'Scripture,' says Justin to Trypho, 'compels you to admit that two advents of Christ were predicted to take place – one in which he would appear suffering and dishonoured and without comeliness; but the other in which he would come glorious'.[41] Such teaching was both a development of the primitive eschatology and an obscuring of one element, in that according to the New Testament the glory of Christ was revealed in his ministry and crucifixion and is therefore not just to be relegated to some future date.

The belief that the Parousia was not at hand stimulated interest in the intermediate state of the departed. Justin again was one of the first to consider this and gave his opinion that 'the souls of the pious remain in a better place, while the unjust are in a worse, waiting for the time of judgement'.[42] Connected with this speculation and to be included also amongst the details of the Last Things was the idea of a millennium, the reign of a thousand years when the righteous dead, risen to new life, will reign under their Messianic King. This theme, not uncommon in Hebrew literature, was first given expression in Revelation,[43] where it serves to allow the martyrs a period of privileged alleviation and a foretaste of future bliss. It was a belief accepted by Papias,[44] by Justin, who, however, acknowledged that 'many who belong to the pure and pious faith, and are true Christians, think otherwise',[45] and by Irenaeus.[46] Widespread though this chialism was, its acceptance by the Montanists brought it into discredit, but it continued to have a place in Christian belief in the form of the doctrines of purgatory and of the exemption of the saints from a period of waiting after death and of their immediate enjoyment of the bliss of heaven.

The generally accepted scheme of the Last Things, with the millennium left on one side, may be itemized under seven heads: (i) the Messianic woes, frequently understood as increased persecution; (ii) the coming of Anti-Christ; (iii) the Second Advent; (iv) the overthrow of Anti-Christ; (v) the resurrection; (vi) the Last Judgement; (vii) the world to come, with the righteous welcomed into heaven and the evil cast into hell. Of these details the fifth and seventh merit some close attention, since the one was given prominence in the writings of the period and the other was to undergo much development during the course of the centuries.

Greek reaction to the Christian belief in resurrection may be typified by Paul's Athenian audience of whom, according to Acts, 'when they heard of the resurrection of the dead, some mocked'.[47] Consequently, in presenting to the Greek world the gospel, in which the resurrection of Christ and that of the individual believer had an important part, Christians were at pains to enunciate and defend their conception. This conception, however, underwent a change, without those responsible being aware of it, in that the Pauline doctrine of transformation was replaced by one of reanimation. 'We expect,' states Justin, 'to receive again our own bodies, though they may be dead and cast into the earth'.[48] In the words of Tatian, 'even though fire destroy all traces of my flesh, the world receives the vaporized matter; and though dispersed through rivers and seas, or torn in pieces by wild beasts, I am laid up in the storehouse of a wealthy God. And although the poor and the godless know not what is stored up, yet the sovereign God, when he pleases, will restore the substance, that is visible to him alone, to its pristine condition'.[49] This in effect was to neglect Paul, or to misinterpret him, and to take the resurrection appearances of Christ, not as the unique events they are represented to be, but as illustrative of the destiny of his individual followers. Irenaeus' teaching may be taken as representative of the various arguments propounded in support of this belief. He contended that since man is a unity of body, soul and spirit, his salvation would be incomplete were it to exclude the physical frame; that since our bodies are temples of the Holy Spirit, it is blasphemous to assert that they will not be raised; that God would not be omnipotent were he unable to restore the body to life; that since the flesh is nourished in the Eucharist by the body and blood of Christ, it must be capable of incorruption, and that unless the flesh were to be redeemed, Christ would not have assumed it, indeed he gave 'his soul for our souls and his flesh for our flesh'.[50] The form taken by this doctrine was the result in part of the anti-docetic polemic and in part of its association with the idea of a millennium, the refashioned bodies having a new heaven and a new earth as the sphere of their thousand-year reign. When chialism was rejected, no corresponding readjustment of the resurrection belief was attempted and so it remained essentially materialistic.

In view of this materialism, it is not surprising to find that accounts of the torments of the damned were similarly conceived. According to the *Apocalypse of Peter*, the milk of those mothers who have killed their children is to congeal and turn into beasts who continually devour their progenitors; sorcerers will be hung on flaming whirling wheels and devils will torture slanderers with red-hot irons – here lay the seeds of the *Dies Irae* which was to dominate so much of Christian thinking about the future in the Middle Ages.

The formulation of belief

In the second century the situation as regards the crystallization of belief was very much the same as it was during the Apostolic Age, i.e. there was a common faith, often called the *regula fidei* and as such appealed to by Irenaeus,[51] but no single formulary. There were too quasi-creedal affirmations, of one, two and three membered forms existing side by side. So, to give an example from Justin of the Christological type of confession, there is reference to

Jesus,
Whom also we have recognized as
Christ the Son of God,
crucified,
and risen again,
and ascended to the heavens,
who will come again as judge of all men right back to Adam himself.[52]

The triadic form was also being encouraged by the use of interrogations at baptism, when a series of three questions were put to the convert to which he was required to give his assent. The framework of these questions was provided by the baptismal command in Matt. xxviii. 19, and the candidate was asked if he believed in the Father, in the Son and in the Holy Spirit.[53]

It is also within the second century that the origins of the Apostles' Creed are to be sought. This too is basically triadic, with the Christological member much inflated by additions. Since this creed is the formulary of the Roman church and since its main features are recognizable in third-century documents, the Christological insertion is to be dated within the period under review. The process of achieving a precise and definite formulation of belief was thus steadily advancing.

WORSHIP

The basic pattern of worship established in the Apostolic Age remained the same in the second century, although undergoing a steady elaboration. Baptism and the Eucharist were the twin poles of the Christian's cultic life, but, while references to them are not unplentiful, the observance of the *disciplina arcani* inhibited full descriptions of these rites.

Baptism

Baptism, by means of which a convert was initiated into the Church, was preceded by a period of instruction and fasting; so the *Didache* states that the rite is to take place 'having first declared all these things',[1] i.e. the moral teaching contained in the first six chapters of the document, and that the candidates are to fast 'for one or two days before'. To similar effect Justin refers to those who 'are persuaded and believe that what we teach and say is true, and undertake to be able to live accordingly, and are instructed to pray and to entreat God with fasting'.[2] According to the same source, the catechumens are then 'brought by us where there is water' – an almost identical phrase being used by Irenaeus[3] – since there was no special architectural provision for the rite; indeed, according to the *Acts of Peter*, the apostle on one occasion baptized the master of a ship in the Adriatic by sliding down a rope to the sea.[4] The *Didache* provides fuller details: baptism is to be in running water; if this be not obtainable, then other water is allowed, cold rather than warm; if only a small amount is available, then 'pour water thrice upon the head'. Baptism was in the threefold name of Father, Son and Spirit, and was followed by the clothing of the neophytes in white robes.[5]

As the century progressed, so the ceremonial was elaborated, at least in certain parts of the Eastern Church, if the *Odes of Solomon* be deemed to derive from that area. According to this collection of hymns, the candidate was apparently crowned with a garland, symbolizing the presence of Christ;[6] he was dressed in a special robe[7] and was signed with the sign of the cross.[8] The quotation of the first of these odes in the Gnostic *Pistis Sophia* suggests, however, that their orthodoxy was not unimpeachable and therefore these features may be those of Gnostic practice. That the Gnostics should have baptized, despite their depreciation of material things, seems initially somewhat illogical, nor did all their sects make use of it. There were some, according to Irenaeus, who 'reject all these practices and maintain that the mystery of the unspeakable and invisible power ought not to be performed by visible and corruptible creatures'.[9] Some however, to continue with the evidence of Irenaeus, 'construct a bridal chamber and perform a mystical initiation with certain secret expressions for the initiates. They call this rite "spiritual marriage" in imitation of the unions above. Others lead candidates to a place where water is, and in baptizing them use this formula: "Into the name of the unknown Father of all, into Truth the mother of all, into him who descended on Jesus, into Unity and Redemption and Fellowship with the powers" . . . But there are some of them who assert that it is superstitious to bring persons to the water, but mixing oil and water together, they pour this mixture on the heads of those who are to be initiated, with the use of some such expressions as we have already mentioned.' Elsewhere Irenaeus reports that the Carpocratians cauterized their disciples behind the lobe of the right ear.[10] The rationale at the basis of these actions was twofold: they drew a distinction between the water baptism of the earthly Jesus for the remission of sins and their rites with a view to the redemption effected by the heavenly Christ, and they asserted the necessity for an identifying mark to serve as a passport at their ascension through the spheres to the realm of blessedness. Gnostic 'baptism' was thus an effective sign of their followers' 'transformation', a key to the mysteries and a safe-conduct past all evil powers. This understanding is to be contrasted with the orthodox teaching about baptism.

The second-century Fathers believed that baptism was a means of conveying the Holy Spirit;[11] it provided weapons for spiritual combat;[12] it mediated the remission of sins[13] and illumination;[14] it initiated into the Chosen People and was therefore 'spiritual circumcision' in contradistinction to the carnal circumcision of the Old Israel;[15] it was a means of rebirth,[16] and was the 'seal' of eternal life.[17] This final term 'seal' was applied frequently to baptism during this period. The word was used of a mark to identify property, and owners branded their livestock with such a mark. Since therefore to be initiated is to be stamped with the indelible mark of the name of Christ, the candidates thereby becoming God's property, baptism was known as the 'seal'.

The Eucharist

The account of baptism by Justin Martyr, mentioned above, indicates that it culminated in a celebration of the Eucharist. He continues:

> Having ended the prayers, we salute one another with a kiss. There is then brought to the president of the brethren bread and a cup of wine mixed with water; and he, taking them, gives praise and glory to the Father of the universe, through the name of the Son and of the Holy Spirit, and offers thanks at considerable length for our being counted worthy to receive these things at his hands. And when he has concluded the prayers and thanksgivings, all the people present express their assent by saying Amen. This word Amen is the Hebrew for 'so be it'. And when the president has given thanks, and all the people have expressed their assent, those of us who are called deacons give to each of those present to partake of the bread and the wine mixed with water over which the thanksgiving was pronounced, and to those who are absent they carry away a portion.[18]

From other references a more or less clear picture emerges of the general structure of the Eucharist as it was celebrated in Rome in the mid second century. The community assembled each week, still in a private house, on the Sunday 'because it is the first day on which God, having wrought a change in the darkness and matter, made the world, and Jesus Christ our Saviour on the same day rose from the dead.'[19] The service began with readings from 'the memoirs of the apostles or the writings of the prophets'; this was followed by a sermon from the president; then all stood for intercessions. After the kiss of peace, bread and a cup of wine and water were brought to the bishop, who offered extempore prayers and thanksgivings[20] to which the people responded with the Amen. The deacons then administered the bread and the cup.

The close parallel between this and the actions of Jesus at the Last Supper is insisted upon by Justin and is sufficiently apparent to require no comment.

A certain parallelism too existed between the Gnostic eucharists and the Last Supper, although, as with baptism, modifications were introduced. Water was often used instead of wine, but the Marcosians had a mixed chalice with which they associated a complex ceremonial:

After preparing cups of mixed wine, Marcus greatly lengthens the prayer of invocation and makes them appear purple and red, so that the Grace from the powers above all may seem to pour drops of her blood into that cup through his invocation, and so that those who are present may have a strong desire to taste of that drink, by means of which the Grace may rain upon them. Again, he gives the women mixed cups and commands them to say the eucharistic prayer in his presence. When this has been done, he takes a cup larger than the one the woman has prayed over, and transfers the contents from the smaller one to his own, saying over it these words: 'May the Grace which is before all, inconceivable and ineffable, fill your "inner man" and increase knowledge of her in you, sowing in you the mustard seed in good earth.' After he has said these words, the large cup is filled from the small one so that it overflows.[21]

So the rite was connected with the Gnostic belief in the heavenly powers and with the presence of the spiritual seed in the pneumatic, and the orthodox understanding of the meaning of the eucharist was entirely transformed. Against such views Ignatius asserted that 'the eucharist is the flesh of our Saviour Jesus Christ, which suffered for our sins and which the Father in his goodness raised';[22] it is the bond of union between Christians and their Lord and between one another,[23] and is further 'the medicine of immortality'.[24] The same teaching was common to Justin and Irenaeus. The former writes:

And this food is called the eucharist, of which no one is allowed to partake but the man who believes that the things which we teach are true, and who has been washed with the washing that is for the remission of sins, and unto regeneration, and who is so living as Christ has enjoined. For not as common bread and common drink do we receive these; but in like manner as Jesus Christ our Saviour, having been made flesh by the word of God, had both flesh and blood for our salvation, so likewise have we been taught that the food which is blessed by the prayer of his word, and from which our blood and flesh by transmutation are nourished, is the flesh and blood of that Jesus who was made flesh.[25]

The latter states: 'as the bread, which is produced from the earth, when it receives the invocation of God, is no longer common bread, but the eucharist, consisting of two realities, earthly and heavenly, so also our bodies, when they receive the eucharist, are no longer corruptible, having the hope of the resurrection to eternity'.[26]

Also common to all the second-century writers was the belief that the Eucharist is a sacrifice, being the 'pure offering' of Malachi's prediction.[27] To Justin it is the bread and wine that constitute the offering, but in so far as they are presented 'for a memorial of the passion' and are identified by him with the body and blood of Christ, this is more than a mere mental recollection and suggests that the Eucharist is the offering of Christ's sacrifice on the cross. Irenaeus too saw the bread and the wine as offerings, primarily however as the first-fruits of the earth, but they are, too, the body and blood of Christ and may be described jointly as 'the oblation of the new covenant'.

The Agape

Side by side with the celebration of the Eucharist, it was customary to hold the agape or love-feast, the meal proper of the Last Supper. Ignatius, writing in the early years of the second century, distinguishes between the two but is insistent that both are to be under the supervision of the bishop.[28] A reference to this quasi-religious social gathering is possibly preserved in the *Didache*, but the relevant sections have been variously interpreted. Some critics contend that the account refers to a eucharist, which was not connected in any way with the death of Christ; others suggest that it was a non-sacramental meal preliminary to a eucharist proper; others again hold that it consists of model graces with which to open and close an agape. The passage reads as follows:

Give thanks in this manner. First for the cup. We thank thee, our Father, for the holy vine of David, thy servant, which thou didst make known to us through Jesus, thy servant. Glory be to thee for ever. And for the broken bread. We thank thee, our Father, for the life and knowledge which thou didst make known to us through Jesus, thy servant. Glory be to thee for ever. As this bread that is broken was scattered upon the mountains, and gathered together, and became one, so let thy Church be gathered together from the ends of the earth into thy kingdom: for thine is the glory, and the power through Jesus Christ for ever. . . . And, after you are filled, give thanks thus. We thank thee, Holy Father, for thy holy name, which thou hast made to dwell in our hearts, and for the knowledge, faith and immortality, which thou didst make known to us through Jesus, thy servant. Glory be to thee for ever. Thou, Almighty God, didst create all things for thy name's sake, and gavest meat and drink for men to enjoy, that they might give thanks unto thee, and to us didst vouchsafe spiritual meat and drink and life eternal, through thy servant. Above all we thank thee because thou art mighty. Glory be to thee for ever. Remember, Lord, thy Church, to deliver her from all evil, and to perfect her in thy love, and gather together from the four winds her that is sanctified into thy kingdom which thou didst prepare for her. For thine is the power and the glory for ever. Come grace, and let this world pass away. Hosanna to the God of David. If any is holy, let him come: if any is unholy let him repent. Maranatha. Amen.[29]

If this be indeed an agape, and this is probably the most likely explanation – the wording of the prayers having been influenced by contemporary eucharistic practice – then the order of procedure was, first, a thanksgiving over wine, perhaps in deliberate imitation of the non-eucharistic cup in the longer text of Luke,[30] followed by a breaking and blessing of bread, a typical Jewish way of beginning a repast that suggests that it became a feature of the observance before the Church was predominantly Gentile. The meal itself was concluded with the final grace.

Penance

In making provision for the bodily and spiritual health of its members, the Church was soon faced with the problem of post-baptismal sin. There were two possible courses to be adopted: the exercise of a rigorous control so that the sinner was excluded from the worship and life of the Church or the formation of a disciplinary system to school and receive back the repentant sinner. The author of Hebrews was in favour of the first method and had no hesitation in declaring of those who had fallen away that 'it is impossible to renew them again unto repentance'.[31] To similar effect Hermas approved of the statement that 'some teachers maintain that there is no other repentance than that which takes place when we descended into the water and received remission of our former sins'.[32] Nevertheless, the same writer was prepared to allow a special second opportunity for repentance for older Christians. This more realistic and charitable attitude was destined to prevail – although it was strongly opposed by the Montanists – and it, too, was not without its basis in the New Testament writings. *I John* is quite clear that Christians are not free from sin, but is also confident that 'if we confess our sins, he is faithful and righteous to forgive us our sins.'[33] *James* exhorts his readers to 'confess therefore your sins one to another'.[34] This injunction was repeated in the *Didache* to the effect that 'thou shalt confess thy transgressions in church, and shalt not come to thy prayer in an evil conscience', therefore, before the Eucharist, the faithful must 'confess your transgressions that our sacrifice may be pure'.[35] No details of this embryonic penitential discipline are forthcoming and it is not until the following century that information is available about practical arrangements.

Prayer and fasting

Since the bulk of Christian literature extant from this period is of an apologetic or polemical character, the subject of prayer has little or no mention in it. But in those works of a pastoral nature, in particular the writings of the Post-Apostolic Fathers, prayer as a necessary duty and privilege receives emphasis. 'Pray for all the saints', Polycarp exhorts the Philippians, 'pray also for kings and powers and princes, and for them that persecute and hate you, and for the enemies of the cross.'[36] 'Give thyself to prayer without ceasing,' Polycarp is told in his turn by Ignatius.[37] Hermas goes a little beyond this type of injunction in that he faces the problem of unanswered prayer and argues that it is the result either of the petitioner's sin or of his lack of patience.[38] The *Didache* recommends the use of the Lord's Prayer and directs that prayer is to be offered three times a day,[39] probably in imitation of the devotional habits of Daniel and the Psalmist.[40]

The authority of the Old Testament also ensured the practice of fasting, in conjunction with the example of Christ who after his baptism and before his public ministry fasted in the wilderness. The basis of this form of self-denial lay in the Hebrew conception of human nature as an ensouled body, i.e. as an indivisible whole. He might have spiritual and physical sides to his being, but these were but two different ways of regarding the one totality. Hence physical and spiritual react upon one another, and what the Christian does with his body is not indifferent as regards his spiritual health. Consequently fasting, or abstinence from food for a specific period of time, was as much a spiritual as a physical discipline. By it the Christian was enabled to practise mortification and self-denial; it was an exercise in self-control; it restrained the fleshly appetites and was a check to self-indulgence. Nevertheless the second-century writers were concerned to have it understood that fasting was not something merely negative. According to *Barnabas*, 'this is the fast that I have chosen, saith the Lord, not that a man should humble his soul, but that he should loose every band of iniquity, untie the fastenings of harsh agreements, restore to liberty them that are bruised, tear in pieces every unjust engagement, feed the hungry with thy bread, clothe the naked when thou seest him, bring the homeless into thine house.'[41] In similar vein, Hermas: 'Offer to God a fasting of the following kind: Do no evil in your life, and serve the Lord with a pure heart: keep his commandments, walking in his precepts, and let no evil desire arise in your heart; and believe in God.'[42] Hermas goes on to say that 'on the day on which you fast you will taste nothing but bread and water; and having reckoned up the price of the dishes of that day which you intended to have eaten, you will give it to a widow or an orphan, or to some person in want'.[43] So fasting was closely linked with alms-giving.

The basic principles of this charitable activity were enunciated in the New Testament, first by Christ in the words: 'Inasmuch as ye did it unto one of these my brethren, even these least, ye did it unto me.'[44] Second, by Paul who exhorted the Corinthians to give liberally to the collection for the Jerusalem poor and added: 'Ye know the grace of our Lord Jesus Christ, that, though he was rich, yet for your sakes he became poor, that ye through his poverty might become rich.'[45] This is not just an illustration of the need for charity but the very foundation of Christian giving. The response of the Christian in gratitude for his Lord's self-impoverishment must be self-giving, for giving to mankind is giving to Christ who gave himself for us.

In the second century fasting was expected on Wednesday and Friday in each week, i.e. on those days food was not taken before 3 in the afternoon. The choice of these two days was determined in opposition to the Jewish custom of fasting on Mondays and Thursdays,[46] and the Christians gave them the title 'station days',[47] which was derived from the word *statio* meaning a picket or military guard. So the idea was expressed that Christians by fasting were standing 'on watch' or keeping 'guard duty' by preparing themselves to welcome the Lord at his return.

SOCIAL LIFE

'Christians are distinguished from the rest of men neither by country nor by language nor by customs. For nowhere do they dwell in cities of their own; they do not use any strange form of speech or practise a singular mode of life. . . . While they dwell in both Greek and barbarian cities, each as his lot was cast, they follow the customs of the land in dress and food and other matters of living.'[1] If this statement from the *Epistle to Diognetus* were to be read out of context, it would suggest that the social dualism, characteristic of the Old Israel and emphasized as a pattern of life for the Church in the New Testament writings, had ceased to exist, and that Paul's injunction, based on the teaching of Isaiah – 'Come ye out from among them, and be ye separate'[2] – had been forgotten. But these are the words of an apologist, anxious to win the goodwill of a pagan audience, and moreover the passage continues to the effect that Christians 'show forth the remarkable and admittedly strange order of their own citizenship. They live in fatherlands of their own, but as aliens.' The author then proceeds to contrast the moral conduct of the faithful with that of the pagan society in which they lived.

Moral behaviour

The continuing emphasis upon right conduct is indeed set forth by the contrast between the Two Ways, described as the Way of Life or Light and the Way of Death or Darkness. In this moral teaching, certain of the key-words of the primitive catechetical instruction[3] recur: thus Christians are to be *subject* to God and 'to masters as the image of God';[4] they are to *watch*[5] and they are to *abstain* 'from fleshly and bodily lusts'.[6] In antithesis to the widespread pagan usage, they are not to practise abortion.[7] Perhaps what is most noticeable about this ethical teaching is its tendency to legalize Christian behaviour and to regulate it by a series of injunctions, thus turning conduct into obedience to a system of precepts rather than allowing it to remain a creative response to the encounter with God; the Christian way is in the process of becoming the observance of a set of rules. Rules indeed there were, some of them no doubt necessary, and certain methods of earning one's living were required to be given up upon conversion. Christians could no longer be augurs, enchanters or astrologers,[8] although there seems to have been no universal objection to service in the armed forces.[9]

Social categories

Initially a working-class movement, second-century Christianity still made its greatest impact upon the artisans and labourers of the Empire. If it could number amongst its adherents the Roman senator Apollonius and Marcia, the concubine of the emperor Commodus, those 'believing ones who are in the royal palace'[10] were probably imperial slaves, such as Euelpistus,[11] and indeed many of its leading figures were of the humblest origin. Hermas was sold into slavery in his youth, and Callistus was a slave of Carpophorus, who himself belonged to the household of Caesar.[12] If this elicited the scorn of the educated pagan, it was no bar to advancement in the Church, Callistus himself becoming eventually bishop of Rome. The Church accepted slavery without demur as an integral part of the social and economic fabric of the empire; but in terms of its own inner life it was a matter of indifference; so Ignatius wrote to Polycarp: 'Despise not slaves, whether male or female. Yet let them not be puffed up, but let them serve them more faithfully to the glory of God, that they may obtain a better freedom from God. Let them not desire to be set free at the public cost, lest they be found slaves of lust'.[13]

Food, clothing and leisure

Although the *Epistle to Diognetus* asserts that Christians do not differ from their pagan fellow-citizens in dress and food, this statement requires qualification in three respects. First, many Christians refused to eat the blood of animals, on the basis of the rule in Acts xv. 20, 29;[14] second, others abstained from meat that had been sacrificed to idols;[15] third, in relation to both food and dress, emphasis was placed upon restraint 'for all luxury is foolish and empty in the servants of God'.[16]

This restraint was especially noticeable in the Christian refusal to participate in many of the pagan festivals. Although some of them made use of the baths,[17] the majority abstained from all public shows. 'You do not visit exhibitions,' objects the pagan in the *Octavius*, 'you have no concern in public displays; you reject the public banquets, and abhor the sacred contests'.[18] Octavius acknowledges the truth of this charge and explains the motives that prompt this abstention; they are two-fold: on the one hand, most of the shows are inextricably bound up with honouring the pagan gods and, on the other, they purvey and stimulate immorality. 'For in the chariot races who does not shudder at the madness of the crowd brawling amongst itself? Or at the teaching of murder in the gladiatorial combats? In the theatre also the madness is not less, but the debauchery is more prolonged: for now a mimic either expounds or shows forth adulteries; now a nerveless player, while he feigns lust, suggests it; the same actor disgraces your gods by attributing to them adulteries, sighs, hatreds; the same provokes your tears with pretended sufferings, with vain gestures and expressions'.[19]

The second-century documents provide more information about how Christians were not to spend their leisure than of how they were expected to divert themselves. In the *Octavius* alone is the curtain lifted with its opening description of the three friends taking a walk from Rome to Ostia in order to paddle in the sea, and spending their time in improving conversation, admiring the view and watching some boys play at 'ducks and drakes'.

CHAPTER FOUR

THE CENTURY OF ADVANCE

The Background – Sources – Expansion and Development – Beliefs – Worship – Social Life

THE BACKGROUND

THE THIRD CENTURY was to witness two related phenomena: an accelerated expansion of the Church and an increasing struggle between it and the State. That the Church was to emerge victorious could scarcely have been foreseen by any but the most perspicacious in the opening decades when the impetus of the pagan religious revival of the second century continued to have its effect.

Pagan religion

The marriage of Septimius Severus to Julia Domna, daughter of the hereditary priest-prince of Emesa, encouraged the further spread of the eastern cults, and the emperor himself publicly avowed his adherence to Serapis by allowing his images to be assimilated to the likeness of the god. This devotion to Serapis was perpetuated by their son, Caracalla, who erected a temple to him on the Quirinal, and the climax of this orientalization was reached by Elagabalus when he sought to introduce the worship of the Syrian Baal, enthroning the black stone of Emesa in a shrine on the Palatine. This identification of the solar religion with one of its local forms was, however, too much for the Romans and was in part responsible for the opposition to Elagabalus that resulted in his assassination. Nevertheless official paganism was kept alive, Decius seeking to bring peace to a harried empire by demanding universal sacrifice and Aurelian attempting to revivify and unify paganism by erecting a temple to the Sun-God in Rome.

These, however, were isolated and, as it proved, ineffective acts. Whatever might take place at government level, paganism amongst the populace was to suffer a decline; after the year 235 very few dedications were made to the gods of the empire. Moreover in the financial stringency of the time, the Mysteries were proving too expensive, and although Mithraism was still strong, particularly in the army under the Severi and the Gordians, its exclusion of women reduced its appeal. Once popular cults were also losing their adherents, so that, for example, the worship of Saturn, so widespread in North Africa, appears to have ceased almost entirely between 240 and 275. Similarly in Egypt, to give a further instance, there is no direct evidence for sacrifice at Philae after 253, while the last inscription relating to the worship of Serapis at Aboukir is 247.

There is indeed every reason to accept the accuracy of the statement of Arnobius, written at the opening of the fourth century: 'the gods are neglected, and in the temples there is now a very thin attendance. Former ceremonies are exposed to derision, and the time-honoured rites of institutions once sacred have sunken before the superstitions of new religions'.[1] Here was both the opportunity for and the partial result of the advance of Christianity.

Philosophy

Just as the pagan religious revival of the second century persisted into the third, so the recrudescence of philosophical activity, which had found expression in Middle Platonism, continued to make its way. Julia Domna was again an important figure in its encouragement, since she set up a real literary salon on the Palatine and induced Philostratus to popularize the rhetoricians in his *Lives of the Sophists* and to stimulate others to follow their teaching by his *Life of Apollonius of Tyana*. But the third century was particularly remarkable in terms of philosophical advance for the work of Plotinus who virtually created Neo-Platonism.

Born at Lycopolis in 204, Plotinus studied at Alexandria under Ammonius Saccas and eventually established a school in Rome, where he died in 270. Plotinus sought to accomplish a twofold task: to give a complete account of reality and to provide guidance in the spiritual life. There is a striking similarity between aspects of his thought and that of Origen, which may be explained on the grounds that both were students of the same master, although not at the same time. It required however a popularizer for the complexity of Plotinus' ideas to be made generally intelligible and available; such was Porphyry (b. 232) who both edited the *Enneads* and wrote its author's biography. Porphyry was also the author of fifteen books against the Christians, in which he sought to refute their case, upon the basis of a critical examination of the Bible, and to bring such doctrines as that of the incarnation into disrepute. Undeniably a religious man, Porphyry's work, of which only fragments remain, was a powerful weapon against the faith, and the part that Neo-Platonism could play in propping up the failing paganism is to be seen further in the work of his pupil Iamblichus. Though the verdict of history was to be that they were supporting a lost cause, their philosophical synthesis was to prove of value as a medium of Christian theological expression, especially in the hands of an Augustine of Hippo.

The Empire

It would be more correct to speak of the *inquies* than of the *pax Romana* in the third century, which, until the reforms of Diocletian, witnessed an almost uninterrupted sequence of struggles both within and on the borders of the empire. It was a period of short reigns, with almost every emperor meeting a violent death, the majority by assassination;[2] it was characterized by a succession of civil wars, as one contender for the purple battled against another. Revolts were constantly breaking out in the different provinces, where financial suffering was fanned into open rebellion by ambitious governors, reaching such proportions that a Gallic empire was established by Postumus in 260, retaining its independence for some fourteen years, and the kingdom of Palmyra was able to extend its sovereignty over Asia Minor and Egypt until Zenobia's troops were eventually defeated by those of Aurelian in 271.

Along the northern frontiers scarcely a reign passed without the Germans or the Goths making incursions deep into imperial territory, while on the eastern borders first the Parthians and then the powerful Persians, under the Sassanids, made constant inroads – small wonder that several of the emperors fell in battle[3] and that one, Valerian, suffered the supreme ignominy of being captured and put to death. A series of weak emperors, with even the few able ones not surviving long enough to accomplish much, a tendency for each to reverse deliberately his predecessor's policy, the insubordination of large sections of the army, and the absence of any regular succession – all these were factors that contributed to the near ruin of the empire.

When Diocletian assumed the purple in 285, the glory that was Rome seemed to be fading rapidly; due however to his initiative and statesmanship the decline was stayed. Within a year of his accession, he had advanced Maximian to the rank of Augustus with responsibility for the West, while he remained superior in the East. For the next seven years the two Augusti were constantly on the move, repelling attacks and gradually resettling the empire, until in 293 Diocletian put into operation a new plan of government. The two Augusti were to continue in command, but each was to have a subordinate, Maximian having Constantius Chlorus as his Caesar in the West, and Diocletian having Galerius. By means of this tetrarchy there was secured a division of the cares of government without a division of the empire, and an opening was found for ambitious men who could become Caesars without recourse to rebellion. The years 293–9 were critical for the new rulers, with revolts in Britain and North Africa, an outbreak in Egypt, and Gothic and Persian invasions, but by the turn of the century stable government and general peace had been established. Then and only then did the tetrarchy turn to the question of the Church, persecution beginning in 303, just as a hundred years earlier Septimius Severus had held his hand against the Christians until he too was undisputed master of the Roman world after his victories over Pescennius Niger, over Clodius Albinus and finally over the Parthians. Indeed, while in the first two centuries the relative peace of the empire had fostered the extension of Christianity, the unrest of the third century favoured its intensive development, since as crisis followed crisis attention was diverted from it. Persecutions however there were, but divided by periods of freedom from molestation during which congregations rapidly increased in size.

Persecution

In the summer of the year 202 there began a persecution of the Church that was prosecuted with vigour in Egypt and North Africa. According to one report Septimius Severus had issued an edict forbidding Christians to make further converts;[4] it is however doubtful if such a law was ever promulgated and the outbreak is rather to be explained as a deliberate attack by the adherents of a local cult, confident of the approval of the emperor, who in the same year had made public his acceptance of Serapis. In this persecution Leonides, the father of Origen, suffered at Alexandria,[5] and Perpetua and her companions at Carthage.[6]

The persecution under Maximianus (235–8), when Pontianus, bishop of Rome, and Hippolytus were banished to the mines of Sardinia – a sentence equivalent to death – was less an attack on Christianity as a deliberate reaction to the reign of his predecessor, Alexander Severus (222–35), who had included a statue of Jesus in his pantheon.[7] Nevertheless, popular feeling was still sufficiently anti-Christian for earthquakes in Cappadocia and Pontus to be taken as the occasion for an attack on the Church, with the support of the governor Serenianus.[8] Even under such a friendly disposed ruler as Philip the Arabian (244–9), who received letters from Origen,[9] and was, though mistakenly, believed later to have been a Christian,[10] mob violence could easily break out. Dionysius of Alexander is witness to the ugly events, the work of a local agitator, that took place in 248.

First, then, they seized an old man named Metras, and bade him utter blasphemous words; when he refused to obey they belaboured his body with cudgels, stabbed his face and eyes with sharp reeds, and leading him to the suburbs stoned him.

Then they led a woman called Quinta, a believer, to the idol temple, and were for forcing her to worship. But when she turned away and showed her disgust, they bound her by the feet and dragged her through the whole city over the rough pavement, so that she was bruised by the big stones, beating her all the time; and bringing her to the same place they stoned her to death. Then with one accord they all rushed to the houses of the godly, and, falling each upon those whom they recognized as neighbours, they harried, spoiled and plundered them, appropriating the more valuable of their treasures, and scattering and burning in the streets the cheaper articles and such as were made of wood, until they gave the city the appearance of having been captured by enemies. But the brethren gave way and gradually retired, and, like those of whom Paul also testified, they took joyfully the spoiling of their possessions. And I know not if there be any – save, it may be, a single one who fell into their hands – who up to the present has denied the Lord.[11]

These were ominous signs that the comparative neglect of the Church was coming to an end, and, writing at the time, Origen uttered the warning: 'It is probable that the secure existence, so far as regards the world, enjoyed by believers at present, will come to an end, since those who calumniate Christianity in every way are again attributing the present frequency of rebellion to the multitude of believers, and to their not being persecuted by the authorities as in old times'.[12] Origen indeed foresaw that there would soon be 'persecutions no longer local as hitherto, but universal'.[13] His expectation was fulfilled early in 250 when Decius issued an edict commanding all citizens to sacrifice to the gods within a specified period.

This was the first persecution of an empire-wide scope initiated directly by the emperor himself and it was intended to be an attestation of loyalty. Measures were first taken against the leaders of the Church, and on 20th January Bishop Fabian of Rome was put to death, but the period of most decisive action was June, the anniversary of Decius' accession, when each citizen was required to offer sacrifice or incense and to be issued with a certificate of compliance by the local magistrates. After what Sulpicius Severus called 'the 38 years' peace',[14] there were many Christians, softened by their security, who were all too willing to obey. Some, who were called the *sacrificati*, brought their victims to the altar;[15] others, the *thurificati*, burnt incense before the emperor's image;[16] others again, the *libellatici*, obtained certificates by bribery[17] – these were to present the Church with a complex disciplinary problem. Yet a considerable number remained steadfast, headed by the martyrs, who died for their faith, and the confessors, who stood firm but were spared the final execution. Evidence is extant from all areas revealing a recurring pattern of events: some bishops were killed, e.g. Alexander of Jerusalem; others went into hiding and administered their dioceses by emissaries in order that the Church might not be leaderless, e.g. Cyprian of Carthage; others apostasized, e.g. Eudaemon of Smyrna. Many Christians confessed and were imprisoned, e.g. Origen who later died, upon his release, from the suffering inflicted upon him.

Towards the end of 250 the Gothic war occupied the full attention of the emperor; the persecution slackened to such an extent that the church of Rome, on 5th March 251, was able to appoint Cornelius as its bishop, having been without one for fifteen months, and the church of Carthage met in council on 1st April to discuss the disciplinary problems that had arisen. With the death of Decius in battle in the Dobrudja peace returned, but the outbreak of a plague, that was to ravage the empire for fifteen years and to be so intense that it reduced the population of Antioch alone by half,[18] led to a renewal of persecution under Gallus which however was soon arrested by the emperor's death in 253.

Preoccupied with the dangers to the empire from the Persians and from the Goths, Valerian, formerly chief lieutenant to Decius, took no action in the early years of his reign, but as defeat followed defeat he determined to renew the policy of his predecessors and in August 257 published an edict ordering the removal of all bishops from their sees and forbidding all assemblies for worship and access to cemeteries. Cyprian was forthwith required to go into enforced residence at Curubis and Dionysius was sent to Kephro in Libya.[19] A year later, in July 258, a second rescript was issued, which laid down that the recalcitrant clergy were to be forthwith punished; that laymen of high rank were to be deprived of their dignities and, if they persisted in the faith, were to be executed; matrons were to lose their property and to be banished and employees on the imperial estates were to be condemned to forced labour. Beginning in Rome with the martyrdom of Sixtus II and four of his deacons on 6th August, followed soon by that of the other three deacons, including Lawrence,[20] the persecution spread to Africa the following year where Cyprian was executed on 14th September,[21] to Spain where Fructuosus, bishop of Tarragona, and his two deacons were burned alive,[22] and to the East where, amongst others, Priscus Malchus and Alexander were condemned to the beasts at Caesarea in Palestine.[23] Respite came with the succession of Gallienus, upon the capture and death of Valerian at the hands of the Persians, and for the first time in its history Christianity, by a rescript of 261, obtained the position of a *religio licita*.[24] For forty years the Church was left free to go its way, until the final and most bloody onslaught upon it was unleashed by the edicts of Diocletian, of which the first was issued in 303.

The final attack

There can be little doubt that it was Galerius, Caesar in the East, who was largely responsible for the renewed policy of suppression. No sooner had he disposed of the Persian menace in 298 than he carried out a purge of the army of all Christian officers, who were either to sacrifice and thus give up their religion or be cashiered.[25] In the winter of 302–3 Diocletian and his Caesar were together at Nicomedia and there the latter pressed upon the former the need for a rigorous policy against the Church.[26] With reluctance Diocletian eventually agreed, on condition that no blood should be shed, and on 24th February, the day following the festival of the Terminalia, the order was issued for the destruction of all churches, the cessation of all worship and the burning of the Scriptures. Executions were not directly sanctioned, but the opportunity was provided since local officials were left free to treat those who refused to comply in any way they chose. A second edict commanded the clergy to be imprisoned; a third all clergy to sacrifice on pain of torture, and a fourth, in 304, all laity to sacrifice or to suffer for their refusal.[27]

In Gaul and Britain, under the direct authority of the Caesar Constantius Chlorus, the persecution was kept to a minimum; in Italy, Spain and Africa, which were dependent upon the western Augustus Maximian, the severity was as great as in the East where Galerius was the dominant figure, Diocletian more and more withdrawing into the background. The events at Abitina in North Africa may be taken as typical of many. In January 304, the magistrates and the military commander arrested forty-nine men, women and children as they celebrated the eucharist in the house of one Octavius Felix. They were transferred to Carthage and on 12th February they were brought before the proconsul Anulinus, charged 'as Christians who, contrary to the decisions of the Augusti and Caesars, had frequented the Lord's assembly'. Each was asked in turn why they had been present at an unlawful gathering and each replied in much the same words: 'As if a Christian could exist without the Lord's Supper, or the Lord's Supper without a Christian!' They were condemned to death and duly executed.[28]

On 1st May 305 Diocletian abdicated, to be followed by Maximian; Galerius succeeded as Augustus in the East, with Maxim Daia as his Caesar, and Constantius took over in the West, having Severus as his subordinate. This second tetrarchy was, from the outset, less stable than the first, since its members were by no means of one mind, and upon the death of Constantius at York on 25th July 306, divisions were not slow to reveal themselves. Severus was advanced to Augustus, with Constantius' son, Constantine, backed by his troops, as Caesar; but Maxentius, the son of Maximian, put forward his claims and secured South Italy and Africa. Within eighteen months the whole system of Diocletian had been discarded and six men were claiming each to be an Augustus: in the West, Constantine, Maxentius and his father, who had returned to public life; in the East, Galerius, his comrade-in-arms Licinius and Maxim Daia. Attention was thus diverted from the Church, but in 309 Maximian issued a new edict: pagan temples were to be rebuilt; all citizens were to be present at public sacrifices and taste the flesh of the victims; the articles on sale in the markets were to be sprinkled with libations and sacrificial blood.[29] The end however was in sight.

In 310, Maximian, unsuccessful against Constantine, committed suicide. The following year Galerius, suffering from a most painful disease, came to the weary conclusion that further measures against the Church were fruitless and accordingly issued an edict which grudgingly allowed toleration and at the same time demanded prayers for his recovery – he died however within a month.[30] Maxim Daia, reluctant to endorse this policy, then planned a general revival of paganism: priests were appointed in every city; those who had distinguished themselves in the public service were made provincial high-priests and false Acts of Pilate were circulated to discredit the Christian case. But the next year Maxentius was eliminated at the Milvian Bridge and Constantine, supreme in the West, was able to tell Maxim to cease all repressive measures. Maxim dared not disobey, but when his rivals, Constantine and Licinius, met at Milan, early in 313, and agreed upon general toleration, he realized the precariousness of his own political position and advanced against them, to die of disease eventually at Tarsus.

The peace of the Church

The Church had now emerged victorious, but another decade was to pass before the final settlement. The relationship between the two Augusti slowly deteriorated, until in 320 Licinius, who had never shared Constantine's sympathy for the Christians, began a persecution in the East which was brought to an end by his defeat at Chrysopolis in 324, his banishment and the establishing of Constantine as sole ruler of the Roman world.

Christians hailed the cessation of their suffering and the success of Constantine as a victory for God[31] and as a clear demonstration of his over-ruling providence. The long-protracted blood-bath had had the opposite effect to that intended by its instigators. While many Christians gave way – some, the *traditores*, handing over the Scriptures and others sacrificing quite willingly – the majority won the admiration of their previously hostile neighbours by their courage and endurance; indeed the government outran the public animosity so that 'these acts were abominated even by the unbelieving heathen',[32] many of whom, in the end, were prepared to protect the Christians by concealing and supporting them and by refusing to betray them.[33] Yet if the noble witness of the Church to the reality of its faith proved a defence against all aggression, not a little of the credit for the inauguration of a new period in its external history must be given to Constantine.

The genuineness of Constantine's conversion is a matter of dispute. According to Lactantius, Constantine was directed in a dream, before the battle of the Milvian Bridge, to mark his soldiers' shields with the sign of Christ.[34] Whatever is made of this account, it is evident that Constantine did attribute his victory to the God of the Christians and that from then on he favoured the Church and concerned himself with its problems. Nevertheless he was the ruler of subjects who were for the most part pagans, and hence a certain ambiguity in his actions – an ambiguity which has given rise to doubts about his conversion but which arose quite naturally from his position as a Christian emperor ruling a still pagan empire. Thus in 321 he made Sunday an obligatory holiday, but while the law was cast in a pagan form, referring to the day as *venerabilis dies solis*,[35] there can be little doubt that its inspiration was Christian. Granted this necessary ambiguity, the emperor's conduct is quite consistent with a genuine belief in Christianity, progressively deepening as the years passed after his triumph in 312. Christianity was well on the way to becoming the official religion of the Empire.

THE SOURCES

Christian writings surviving from the first and second centuries have two common characteristics: they are all written in Greek and they are relatively meagre in quantity. From the third century however the literature becomes more extensive and Latin is added to Greek as a language of theological utterance.

North African Latin writers

The pioneer in the creation of ecclesiastical Latin was Tertullian. Born *c.* 160 at Carthage, son of a centurion of the proconsular cohort, he practised law in Rome, returning to his native city after his conversion *c.* 193. Tertullian soon embarked upon a literary career in the service of the Church, but in 207 at the latest he went over to the Montanists, eventually heading a party of his own, the Tertullianists. His death is to be placed shortly after 220. The paucity of information about his life is to be contrasted with the amplitude of his writings, of which over thirty treatises have survived.

In his *To the Nations* and *Apology* (both 197), as well as in his *To Scapula* (212), Tertullian reveals himself in the line of the second-century apologists, but with a passion and a more incisive reasoning that sets him on a level of his own. These same qualities, which however at times predispose him to overbear rather than convince, are displayed again in his controversial works, from *The Prescription of Heretics* (*c.* 200) to his *Against Praxeas* (213). These are a mine of information concerning both heretical – which is equally true of *Against Marcion* (207–12) – and the opposing orthodox theological views. His *On Baptism* (*c.* 200) attacks heretical baptism but at the same time describes contemporary catholic practice being the sole pre-Nicene treatise on any of the sacraments. Tertullian's rigour, which made Montanism attractive to him, is expressed in a series of disciplinary, moral and ascetical works. In *The Shows* (197–200) he condemns all public games; in *Concerning Repentance* (203) he allows a single ecclesiastical penance to a baptized person who has committed grave sin, but in *On Modesty*, after his conversion to Montanism, he goes so far as to regard certain sins as unpardonable. In relation to fasting (*On Fasting*) and second marriage (*Monogamy*) his extremism is further apparent.

Tertullian was essentially an individualist with an original mind, combining Punic fervour with Roman practical sense; in theological thought he laid the basis of both the later Trinitarian and Christological formulations, while his writings played a dominant role in the creation of Old Christian Latin. The extent of his influence may be illustrated by the fact that, despite his defection to Montanism, Cyprian regarded him as his 'master', frequently reproducing his ideas.[1]

Although a life of Cyprian, by his deacon Pontius, survives, this is more a panegyric than a reliable historical account and indeed such information as is available relates only to his brief career as bishop of Carthage, from 248 to his martyrdom eleven years later. Since he exercised his ministry during the persecutions of Decius and Valerian, he lived in turbulent times with pastoral and disciplinary problems constantly thrusting themselves upon him, and his writings are directly related to this situation, being practical rather than theoretical. His letters, sixty-five from his own pen and sixteen addressed to him, all deal with matters of immediate concern. Of his treatises, *The Unity of the Church* springs out of the Novatianist schism, *Concerning the Lapsed* examines the effects of the persecution, while even his earlier *To Quirinus: Three Books of Testimonies*, a collection of scriptural proof texts, is polemical in intent. A man of action rather than ideas, seeking a midway between laxity and rigour, Cyprian nevertheless became a theological authority in the West up to the time of Augustine, being one of the most widely read of the Fathers.

Persecution was also the setting of *Against the Nations* by Arnobius of Sicca in Numidia, written under Diocletian to prove the sincerity of his conversion by defending Christianity against accusation and attacking the Greek myths on the grounds of immorality. Lactantius, also an African by birth, was his pupil and was sufficiently *persona grata* with Diocletian in the early years of his reign to be nominated by him as rhetorician at Nicomedia. Compelled to resign his chair in 303, Lactantius came back into the imperial service *c.* 317 when he was summoned by Constantine to act as tutor to his elder son Crispus. His principal work, the *Divine Institutes*, was the first attempt in Latin to give a comprehensive presentation of the Christian faith, while *On the Deaths of the Persecutors* is an invaluable source of the events under Diocletian and Maxim Daia. Often called the Christian Cicero for the elegance of his style, Lactantius' knowledge of Christian doctrine and literature was somewhat defective.

Writers in Rome

The speed with which Latin became the official language of the African Church was not matched in Rome. It was not until the middle of the century that Novatian used Latin and the letters of the bishops began to be no longer exclusively in Greek, as witness the epistles of Cornelius and Stephen. Hippolytus, the first author of any learning, still wrote in the language of the New Testament, but this was in part due to his eastern origin. Active in the capital during the first decades of the century, Hippolytus came into conflict with bishop Callistus (217–22) on questions of doctrine and discipline, and was elected anti-pope; his schism, of short duration, under Urban and Pontianus, came to an end when he and the latter were exiled to Sardinia under Maximinus Thrax, both dying in 235. Hippolytus was a prolific writer, notable more for the breadth than the depth of his knowledge and interests. Subordinationist in his doctrine of the Godhead, his theological ideas were less important than the information he provides about contemporary heresies and Church life. His *Refutations* (after 222) is one of the most important sources for the history of Gnosticism, while his *Apostolic Tradition* (217) is a mine of information on matters liturgical. His interest in chronology is represented by his treatise *On Easter* and his exegetical work by his *Commentary on Daniel.*

Novatian, a presbyter of high repute in Rome, was similar in two respects to Hippolytus: he also was an anti-pope and his understanding of the Logos was subordinationist, but his *On the Trinity* (250) remains an impressive witness to his clarity of thought and expression.

The first papal letters are also extant from this century, notable among them being that of Cornelius concerning Novatian and the two from Dionysius (259–60) to his namesake of Alexandria on Sabellianism and subordinationism.

The Alexandrians

The western mind was always more practical and less reflective than the eastern, and it is to Alexandria that we have to turn to find evidence of theological advance, where a catechetical school, given a certain official character by the bishop's recognition, was the centre of much activity. Pantaenus was the first recorded head, *c.* 180, but it is with his successor, Clement, that the literary tradition begins.

Clement was born of heathen parents, probably in Athens, about the year 150. After studying rhetoric and philosophy at the university, he was converted to Christianity and travelled in Southern Italy, Syria and Palestine, before settling in Alexandria and succeeding Pantaenus *c.* 200. He remained in charge until the persecution under Septimius Severus in 202, when he withdrew to Cappadocia, dying *c.* 215. Clement was the author of a trilogy, the first part of which, *Exhortation to the Greeks*, was intended to convert the reader; the second, *The Pedagogue*, to instruct in the Christian way of life, and the third, *The Miscellanies*, was a collection of diffuse material describing the ideal of a complete Christian, perfect in all spiritual knowledge. Convinced that 'the way of truth is one, but into it, as into a perennial river, streams flow from all sides',[2] Clement sought a synthesis of Christian thought and Greek philosophy. His work ensured the acceptance by the Church of scholarly thinking and research and paved the way for the greater achievement of his pupil Origen.

Origen (184–253), unlike Clement, was brought up as a Christian, his father, Leonides, being martyred under Severus. At the age of eighteen he took over the direction of the catechetical school, with his friend Heraclas acting as assistant to teach grammar, while he gave courses on philosophy, speculative theology and holy scripture. Despite a very heavy programme he attended the lectures of Ammonius Saccas, the Neo-Platonist. Following a life of extreme asceticism, Origen castrated himself in supposed literal obedience to Matt. xix. 12. His teaching career may be divided into two parts, the first being in Alexandria from 203 to 231, during which time he paid visits to Rome, Caesarea, Greece and Antioch. His settlement at Caesarea for the second period of his work from 231 until his death was forced upon him by his excommunication by a synod under bishop Demetrius. This was the outcome of a number of events that had steadily annoyed his ecclesiastical superior, although Eusebius states that jealousy of his reputation played its part. Demetrius held against him his self-mutilation, his presumption in preaching at Caesarea in 215, when he was not a presbyter, and his ordination, fifteen years later while on another visit to Palestine.[3] Setting up a school similar to that at Alexandria, Origen continued his work as an educator until his death as a consequence of the Decian persecution.

Origen's literary output was vast; indeed, according to Jerome, he was the author of no fewer than 2,000 books,[4] but many of these were short lectures, taken down as delivered by a team of stenographers, financed by one of his converts, a former Valentinian, Ambrose,[5] and only a small number survive of which many are in Latin translation. His main energy was devoted to the study of the Bible, and he was indeed the founder of biblical science. His *Hexapla* (a sixfold bible) was the first attempt to establish a critical text of the Old Testament and consisted of six parallel columns containing the Hebrew text, the same transliterated into Greek, together with the versions of Aquila, Symmachus, the Septuagint and Theodotion. This was the basis of his exegetical work, which comprises scholia, i.e. brief notes on difficult passages or words; homilies, i.e. popular lectures or sermons, and commentaries; of the last category there remain portions of his work on Matthew, John, Romans and the Song of Songs. His method of interpretation rested upon a belief in a threefold meaning corresponding to the division of man into body, soul and spirit: there was, first, the grammatical or historical meaning (= body), then the moral or anagogical meaning (= soul) and finally the mystical or allegorical (= spirit).

Origen was also the first systematic theologian, his *First Principles* (220–30) being an attempt to combine Christian pronouncements about God, the world and man in a closely-knit system of doctrine of a strictly scientific character. He also revealed himself as an apologist of no mean stature with his *Against Celsus*, while his *Discourse with Heraclides* shows him opposing a bishop's doubtful opinions regarding the trinitarian question.

Writing at a time when Christian belief was still imprecisely formulated, Origen exercised great freedom of speculation, but the influence of Neo-Platonism was greater upon him than he realized, and his allegorical exegesis, inherited in part from Alexandria and in particular from Philo, led him into a subjectivism that could easily issue in error, for which indeed he was to be attacked later by those who at the same time reveal their own indebtedness to this great thinker.

Other writers

The extent to which Origen provoked either great devotion or intense opposition may be illustrated from the work of two men, one of whom was his pupil. Gregory Thaumaturgus, at the age of twenty, attended Origen's lectures at Caesarea, 233–8, being converted and, soon afterwards, consecrated bishop of his native town of Neocaesarea. A practical man, with a zeal for the spread of the gospel, to such good effect that at his death in the reign of Aurelian only a few pagans were said to remain in Pontus, his writings are few. His *Panegyric on Origen*, a farewell discourse on leaving Caesarea, contains a valuable description of Origen's methods of instruction. His *Exposition of Faith* gives an exact statement of the dogma of the Trinity, and his *Canonical Epistle* considers moral problems raised by the invasion of Pontus and Bithynia by the Boradi and the Goths in 251.

Of Methodius, bishop of Philippi in Macedonia, little is known apart from his martyrdom in 311. His love of Plato is shown by his *Banquet*, which is in imitation of the *Symposium* and is in praise of virginity. His opposition to Origen took the form of a treatise *On the Resurrection*, in which he attacked the Alexandrian's teaching on the pre-existence of souls and affirmed the identity of the resurrection body with the earthly body.

Miscellanea

From the third century there are also extant a number of *acta martyrum* and the production of apocryphal works continued. The *Acts of Thomas* may have originated in the circle of Bardesanes at Edessa, having been written in Syriac. It tells of the apostle's mission to India where he converts Gundaphorus – a name historically attested – and eventually dies a martyr's death. The *Clementine Homilies* and *Recognitions* in their present form date from the fourth century, but may derive from a common document written in Syria in the early decades of the third, and recount the journeys of Peter, his controversies with Simon Magus and the conversion of Clement.

A further type of second-century writing, the Church Order, of which the *Didache* is an example, is also represented in the third by the *Didascalia*. This was composed in the first decades for a community in the northern part of Syria and consists of moral instructions and canonical regulations.

The Bible

The acceptance of the Old Testament and of the apostolic writings as the authoritative source of Christian doctrine ensured the preservation and circulation of the text of these. The work of Origen on the Greek version of the Old Testament has already been mentioned, but Latin translations were also required and Tertullian refers to the existence of a version of the whole Bible, although it possessed no official character.[6] But by 250 there was a Latin edition regarded as authoritative, as shown by Cyprian's consistent use of the same text throughout his works. Latin was thus tending to become in the West not only the language of theological writing but also that of holy writ.

EXPANSION AND DEVELOPMENT

In the expansion of Christianity, the third century was indeed a period of advance, but this advance was neither uniform nor sustained in all areas. In Palestine, where the Church had only a slender footing, its numbers remained small and were confined in the main to the Hellenistic towns. On the coast believers were amongst the floating population rather than of the inhabitants, so that, for example, few of the martyrs of Caesarea under Diocletian were citizens, the records mentioning one from Pontus, one from Tripolis, a third from Diospolis (Lydda), together with two Egyptians and a man from Gaza.[1] In Syria, on the other hand, the Christian population was by no means insignificant and Eusebius can speak of a 'countless number' being imprisoned as a consequence of Diocletian's second edict.[2] In Mesopotamia, too, numerous communities were in existence by the end of the century,[3] yet Asia Minor was still the land of the 'most populous churches',[4] Pontus being almost entirely Christian through the labours of Gregory Thaumaturgus, and Armenia Major becoming officially Christian through the efforts of Gregory the Illuminator.

Evidence is lacking to provide any clear picture of the advance in Greece, though the presence of bishops from Rhodes, Cos, Lemnos and Corcyra at Nicaea in 325 shows an extension of the faith from the mainland.[5] While to the north the first conversions in Moaesia and

Panonia are revealed by Eusebius' reference to their representatives at the dedication of the Constantinian buildings in Jerusalem in 335 as 'God's youthful stock'.[6]

In Italy the advance was more marked and so great was the increase in congregations in the capital that seven districts had to be organized and minor orders were created to assist the clergy. By AD 300 there were even as many as forty basilicas in Rome. Fifty years earlier, when Cornelius held a synod against Novatian, there were present some sixty Italian bishops, indicating a possible over-all total of at least a hundred in Southern Italy. In the north the number of Christians was not so great, but bishoprics were coming into existence, so that, e.g., the bishop of Aquileia was amongst those at Arles in 316. The attendance register of this synod also reveals the spread of Christianity in Gaul, since, although the majority of the Gallican delegates came from the Rhône valley and the south, there were also bishops from Bordeaux, Eauze, Mende and Bourges. Present too from England were the bishops of London, York and Lincoln, and the fact that the bishop of Cologne was there indicates the establishing of a few outposts of the faith in Germany.

The main advance in Spain is probably to be placed in the latter half of the century. Tertullian provides evidence of the existence of communities,[7] but no detailed information is forthcoming before Cyprian who mentions four centres – Leon, Astorga, Merida and Saragossa.[8] Yet by the Synod of Elvira, *c.* 303, although the majority of those who assisted came from Baetica, where the meeting took place, all the Spanish provinces were represented, save two. Moreover the extent of the secularization of the Church revealed by the canons indicates a considerable period of development.

A similar expansion can be traced in North Africa, and here again synodal attendance provides useful information. At one held under Agrippinus at Carthage *c.* 220 there were seventy-one African and Numidian bishops;[9] under Donatus, Cyprian's predecessor, ninety bishops assembled,[10] while Cyprian himself presided in 256 over eighty-seven bishops. But in the next fifty years their number seems to have almost doubled, so that by the outbreak of the Diocletian persecution some two hundred and fifty may be said to have been in office.

In Egypt likewise progress was being made, the leading towns in the nomes acquiring bishops of their own, so that there were Christians in all districts. The appearance of Coptic versions of the Bible, in the second half of the third century, shows that the foundations of a native Egyptian Church were being laid. The five towns of the Pentapolis too had each its congregation.[11]

Conversion

The steady and, in certain areas, the spectacular advance of Christianity is not patent of a simple explanation. The various factors – inclusiveness, moral ideals, fellowship and intellectual adaptability – that rendered it superior to its rivals gradually achieved their effect. Cyprian has given a valuable account of his own conversion which contrasts his attitude of mind prior to and after his adherence to Christianity. Describing his condition as a pagan, Cyprian writes:

> While I was still lying in darkness and gloomy night, wavering hither and thither, tossed about on the foam of this boastful age, and uncertain of my wandering steps . . . I used to regard it as difficult in respect of my character at that time, that a man should be capable of being born again. . . . 'How,' said I, 'is such a conversion possible, that there should be a sudden and rapid divestment of all which, either innate or hardened in us by the corruption of our material nature, or acquired by us, has become inveterate by long accustomed use? These things have become deeply and radically engrained within us. When does he learn thrift who has been used to liberal banquets and sumptuous feasts? And he who has been glittering in gold and purple, and has been celebrated for his costly attire, when does he reduce himself to ordinary and simple clothing?' . . . These were my frequent thoughts. For as I myself was held in bonds by the innumerable errors of my previous life, from which I did not believe that I could possibly be delivered, so I was disposed to acquiesce in my clinging vices; and because I despaired of better things, I used to indulge my sins as if they were actually parts of me, and indigenous to me.

Of his present state, after baptism, Cyprian has this to say:

> But after that, by the help of the water of new birth, the stain of former years had been washed away, and a light from above, serene and pure, had been infused into my reconciled heart . . . then, in a wondrous manner, doubtful things at once began to assure themselves to me, hidden things to be revealed, dark things to be enlightened, what before had seemed difficult began to suggest a means of accomplishment, what had been thought impossible to be capable of being achieved.[12]

The way to conversion was also eased by certain evangelists who were prepared to present the faith as a transformed popular religion. This would seem to have been the case in North Africa and there is direct evidence that this was the method of Gregory Thaumaturgus in Pontus.

> After the persecution (of Decius) was over, when it was permissible to address oneself to Christian worship with unrestricted zeal, he again returned to the city, and, by travelling over all the surrounding country, increased the people's ardour for worship in all the churches by holding a solemn commemoration in honour of those who had contended for the faith. Here one

brought bodies of martyrs, there another. So much so, that the assemblies went on for the space of a year, the people rejoicing in the celebration of festivals in honour of the martyrs. This also was one proof of his great wisdom, viz. that while he completely altered the direction of everyone's life in his own day, turning them into an entirely new course, and harnessing them firmly to faith and to the knowledge of God, he slightly lessened the strain upon those who had accepted the yoke of the faith, in order to let them enjoy good cheer in life. For as he saw that the raw and ignorant multitude adhered to idols on account of bodily pleasures, he permitted the people – so as to secure the most vital matters, i.e. the direction of their hearts to God instead of to a vain worship – he permitted them to enjoy themselves at the commemoration of the holy martyrs, to take their ease, and to amuse themselves, since life would become more serious and earnest naturally in process of time, as the Christian faith came to assume more control of it.[13]

Gregory thus substituted the cult of the martyrs for the old pagan local cults and in so doing achieved remarkable success.

Schism

Such compromise, though it may be justified by its results, ran counter to the rigorist strand in Christianity and it was precisely this that led to certain schisms in the third century, although other factors, including the personal, were also operative. Indeed jealousy would seem to have precipitated the first papal schism, when Callistus succeeded Zephyrinus in 217 to the acute annoyance of Hippolytus. Hippolytus charged Callistus with being a heretic and a follower of Sabellius and objected to his leniency in relaxing the treatment of penitents guilty of mortal sin.[14] But while these accusations reveal a zeal for orthodoxy and discipline, they were not the causes of the schism but rather the means whereby Hippolytus sought to defend himself after he had been consecrated as anti-pope. The schism moreover was neither extensive nor of long duration, coming to an end with Hippolytus' martyrdom in 235.

In the Novatian dispute personal feeling and disciplinary questions were again to the fore leading to a second papal schism which, unlike that of Hippolytus, had widespread ramifications. The Decian persecution presented the Church with a disciplinary problem of some complexity: what was to be done with those who had given way under the pressure? Three courses were possible: the punishment could be made to fit the crime, i.e. there could be a graded series of penalties dependent upon the gravity of the apostasy; the punishment could be remitted entirely, i.e. no disciplinary action of any kind need be taken; the punishment could be made absolute, i.e. no apostate should be allowed readmittance to the Church. Schism took place when three different groups each adopted one of these attitudes.

The first represents the policy of Cyprian, who, in hiding during the persecution, postponed any final decision until a council could be summoned. This met in the spring of 251 and decided that the *sacrificati* were to do penance and only be reconciled at the point of death; that the *libellatici* were to do penance for a shorter or longer period and then be reconciled; and that those who had entertained the idea of apostasy were to confess and undergo whatever suitable penance was imposed.[15]

The policy of leniency was adopted by a group of presbyters, who had originally opposed Cyprian's election, headed by Novatus with the assistance of the deacon Felicissimus.[16] These induced two heretical and three lapsed bishops to consecrate a certain Fortunatus as their leader.

The third party advocated extreme rigorism and was led by the Roman presbyter Novatian, whose zeal for strict discipline was encouraged by his personal disappointment at being passed over in the election of Cornelius, against whom he set himself up as a rival bishop.[17]

The situation now became more confused since Fortunatus sent envoys to Rome and Novatian despatched representatives to Carthage, where there were soon three claiming to be bishop – Cyprian, the lax Fortunatus and the strict Maximus who was a Novatianist.[18] Novatianism spread rapidly; in Gaul Marcianus of Arles declared himself in favour of it,[19] while in Asia Minor its adherents persisted into the sixth century.[20]

Persecution and its aftermath were also at the origin of two further schisms, the Donatist in Africa and the Melitian in Egypt, but while both those began under Diocletian their history belongs to the fourth century and is therefore left for later consideration.[21]

Church order

'It is not persecution alone that is to be feared,' according to Cyprian, 'the enemy is more to be feared and to be guarded against when he creeps on us secretly.'[22] Cyprian had in mind the schismatics, who 'have broken the Lord's peace with the madness of discord',[23] and against these he asserted the oneness of the Church with the episcopate as its centre of unity: 'the episcopate is one, each part of which is held by each one for the whole.'[24] He further declared: 'they are the Church who are a people united to the priest, and the flock which adheres to its pastor. Whence you ought to know that the bishop is in the Church, and the Church in the bishop; and if any one be not with the bishop, that he is not in the Church.'[25]

The functions of the bishop are clearly set out in the consecration prayer preserved in the *Apostolic Tradition*:

Grant unto this thy servant whom thou hast chosen for the episcopate to feed thy holy flock, and to exercise the high-priesthood before thee, without blame to serve thee day and night, unceasingly to propitiate thy countenance and to offer the gifts of thy Holy Church; endued with the high-priestly spirit to have power to forgive sins according to thy command, confer orders according to thy precept, and to loose every bond according to the authority thou didst give unto the apostles, and to be well-pleasing unto thee in meekness and cleanness of heart.[26]

Thus the bishop had 'to feed thy holy flock', i.e. concern himself with the spiritual welfare of his people, visiting the sick, looking after the poor, paying particular attention to the widows and orphans, and, to this end, administering the finances of the church where he exercised his oversight and dispensing the stipends of the clergy.[27] He had also 'to offer the gifts of thy Holy Church', i.e. to celebrate the sacraments and the eucharist in particular; he was in fact the primary liturgical minister and others undertook this duty only as his delegates. He had further 'to forgive sins', i.e. impose penance and convey absolution, and, in that he had to 'confer orders', he was the minister of ordination, although in the ordination of a presbyter other presbyters were associated with him.

Although the presbyterate was eventually to form the backbone of the Church, in that its members became the parish priests of the medieval and modern periods, in the first centuries its role was not clearly defined and indeed it is not easy to differentiate it from the episcopate, since with the sole exception of ordination, a presbyter could perform all the functions of a bishop: he did so however only with the latter's express permission. But the presbyters did have an important part to play in the government of the Church, forming a kind of council under episcopal presidency. So in the ordination prayer of the *Apostolic Tradition* the petition is made that the presbyter might be filled 'with the spirit of grace and counsel . . . and govern thy people with a pure heart'.[28] Presbyters were appointed by the bishop, after consultation with the existing clergy and people and after investigation of the character of the candidates.[29] The bishops too required the suffrage of the people, presbyters being 'appointed in the presence of all the assembly'.[30] Deacons equally had to be scrutinized 'with the calling together of the whole of the people, surely for this reason, that no unworthy person might creep into the ministry of the altar.'[31]

The deacon was the bishop's right-hand man, being the main channel of communication between him and the congregation.[32] He had to report who was sick so that visits could be paid;[33] he helped to administer church property;[34] he carried letters;[35] he ministered to the confessors in prison and supervised the burial of the martyrs.[36] All offerings were made through his hands and, at the eucharist, he carried the gifts to the altar.[37] So manifold were his duties that the limitation of the number of deacons to seven in any one city, which was the general although not universal rule on the basis of Acts vi – the account of the appointment of the Seven, believed, on uncertain grounds, to be the first deacons – meant that as congregations increased, it became more and more impossible for them to do all that was required. To meet this situation further orders, which came to be known as the minor orders, were created, but before this took place on any large scale there was already in existence a group of lectors or readers.

Minor Orders

At first the Church seems to have followed the practice of the Jewish synagogue according to which those in charge of the service could invite anyone to read the lessons: their choice however must have been severely limited by the minority of those present who were literate. References to the one who reads are to be found in the opening verses of Revelation[38] and in the description of Sunday worship given by Justin Martyr,[39] but the noun is not used until Tertullian[40] *c.* 203 and Hippolytus regards him as being appointed but not ordained.[41] But by the middle of the century the readers were beginning to form a definite order, so that Cyprian could refer to one Celerinus as 'having been added to our clergy'.[42] The lector was at first responsible for reading all the lessons and in the third century he was still the Gospeller.[43]

The subdeacon is first mentioned in the *Apostolic Tradition* and since its author was not concerned to innovate but to record practices that he believed to be of apostolic origin, the foundation of this order must go back to at least AD 170–80. According to Hippolytus, he is to 'serve the deacon', and he therefore shared many of his functions. Thus the subdeacon carried letters,[44] and, like the deacon, had to be 'alert on the bishop's behalf' to inform him of any that are sick.[45] In a list of the clergy at Rome given by Cornelius in 251 there are included seven deacons and seven subdeacons,[46] to each deacon therefore was attached one personal assistant.

Even the help of the subdeacon was insufficient to relieve the pressure upon the deacon and so under bishop Fabian of Rome (236–50) three more orders were instituted, viz. acolytes, doorkeepers and exorcists. Like the deacons, the acolytes carried letters,[47] distributed alms to the poor,[48] and administered to those condemned to the mines of Sigus under Valerian.[49] At Rome there were forty-two acolytes, there being therefore six allotted to each deacon. The exorcists[50] were those whose task it was to care for the energumens or demoniacs, i.e. the mentally deranged who were believed to be possessed by evil spirits. Their function was therefore a pastoral one, derived in part from the diaconate whose normal responsibility it was to visit the sick. As for the door-keepers, their title sufficiently indicates their function.

Widows and deaconesses

This inner structure of the Church was not initially a graded hierarchy, i.e. a series of offices through which an individual might advance from the bottom to the top. A deacon, for example, might remain a deacon all his life or he might become a bishop without the necessity of passing through the presbyterate. This was because the various orders were regarded as functions rather than as offices; for the harmonious conduct of the Church's life all were necessary, and one was not more important than another, since each was essential. But a process of clericalization began as the Church expanded and function was displaced by position. So in the middle of the third century in North Africa Cyprian sees the several orders as so many grades or steps; to move from one to another is held to be a promotion. Thus Cyprian can say of Celerinus, who has been made a reader, that he hopes he might advance to 'a further degree',[51] while of Anulinus, also appointed reader, he expresses the wish that he might 'merit higher degrees of clerical ordination'.[52] Thus the process was under way whereby the ministry would be set over against the Church and the idea of function would be subordinated to that of office and privilege.

The third century also witnessed the establishment of two orders for women: that of the widows and that of the deaconesses. There is no single period in the history of the early Church for which evidence of the importance of widows is lacking. Even in the small community of Joppa widows formed a recognized body,[53] while at Jerusalem they were held in such esteem that the dissatisfaction of a section of them could occupy the attention of the Apostles themselves.[54] They were however not an active order; rather they were an organized group of Church pensioners who were on the 'roll'[55] and were the recipients of special offerings at the eucharist.[56] In so far as they had any function at all it was that of intercession and so Hippolytus is emphatic that they are not ordained but are 'appointed for prayer and prayer is the duty of all'.[57] In the third century a change is to be noticed and the *Didascalia*, while affirming that they are recipients of charity[58] and are to spend their time in prayer,[59] also adds that they should work at wool to give to those in distress[60] and should visit the sick, laying their hands upon them.[61] According to the *Apostolic Church Ordinances*, there are to be three widows in each congregation, two to persevere in prayer for all those who are in temptation, and for the reception of revelations where such are necessary, but one to assist the women visited with sickness; she must be ready for service, discreet, communicating what is necessary to the presbyters, not avaricious, not given to much love of wine, so that she may be sober and capable of performing the night services, and other loving service if she will.[62]

The third of this trio is indistinguishable from a deaconess, save in name, and the description is based upon the characterization of a deacon given in I Timothy. This would suggest that an order of female deacons or deaconesses was recruited from the group of active widows, that it derived from the male diaconate in the same period as the creation of the minor orders and that it was concerned with a special ministry to women. So the *Didascalia* states that in the choice of deacons it is necessary to appoint 'a man for the performance of the most things that are required, but a woman for the ministry of women'.[63] The same document specifies her functions; she has to visit sick women in those heathen households where a deacon may not fittingly enter. She has to administer unction to women prior to their descent into the font. Finally she has to receive the female candidates after initiation and 'instruct them how the seal of baptism may be unbroken in chastity and holiness'.[64]

Deaconesses were an eastern creation, in part due to the seclusion of the female sex in certain oriental countries, and were unknown in the West before the fifth century, being accepted in Rome only as late as the eighth. But if conservative in this respect, Rome played an important part in the foundation of the minor orders which were shared out among the seven districts established by Fabian.

The parochial system

These ecclesiastical divisions, each one corresponding to two of the fourteen regions of Rome, point to the tentative beginnings of the parochial system. The word 'parish', which is the English equivalent of the Latin *paroecia* and of the Greek *paroikia*, originally meant a community of foreigners or sojourners. So in all the large cities of the Roman empire there were to be found 'parishes' of Jews, i.e. communities of foreigners who were not citizens in the strict sense of the term. In the first centuries of its history, Christianity was largely a city religion and the Christian community in each centre was a 'parish'. 'Parish' therefore referred to the community and not to the geographical area in which it lived. The increase in the numbers of Christians, which issued in the creation of the minor orders, also required the subdivision of the congregations, each group having its own building for worship, but all of them were still regarded as part of the one community or parish over which the bishop presided. Thus Rome might be organized into several ecclesiastical regions each with its own basilica, but it was still one parish under one bishop.

The situation began to change when the Church gradually established itself in the countryside and new centres of worship, at some distance from the old episcopal centre, were erected. The organization of these rural churches was not uniform throughout the empire. There were various possible arrangements and each was tried in different areas. It was possible to have itinerant or visiting presbyters who went out as delegates of the bishop and then returned to his seat. Such *periodeutai* or *circumeuntes* are mentioned in a letter of Phileas, bishop of Thmuis in Lower Egypt, written about 307.[65] Again it was possible to have resident presbyters, thus the district of Mareotis in Egypt had nineteen presbyters, each dependent upon the bishop of Alexandria.[66] This was also the situation in Upper Italy and Gaul. A third possibility was to have a bishop wherever there was a Christian community; this was the practice in North Africa and Southern Italy, while in Syria and parts of Asia Minor a category of second-class or 'country' bishops, the *chorepiscopoi*,[67] were instituted, limited in the exercise of their function, and under the jurisdiction of the bishop of the nearest large city. In this way a network of Christian centres was set up, each one being a means for further advance.

Councils

One of the modes of unification of these different churches was the meeting together of representatives to exchange ideas and, in some cases, reach a common decision. The first councils or synods known to history were the result of the Montanist controversy. Synods met in Asia and in Thrace to condemn these enthusiasts.[68] The paschal controversy was the occasion for the gathering of councils in Palestine, Pontus, Osrhoene, Asia, Gaul and Rome.[69] Reference has already been made to meetings in Africa in connexion with the Novatianist dispute; yet another is recorded in Antioch in 268 to consider the case of Paul of Samosata,[70] while *c.* 303 the Spanish clergy came to Elvira. None of these was a general or ecumenical council, but their decisions were communicated to all parts of the Church thus fostering its invisible unity.

The Roman primacy

By the end of the second century a primacy of honour but not of jurisdiction was being accorded to the bishops of Rome. In the third century this position was maintained and so, while there was an appeal to Dionysius of Rome by the opponents of Dionysius of Alexander, who believed him guilty of tritheism, the basis of this was not legal but the view that they were likely to receive support. From the fragmentary correspondence *c.* 260, it is evident that the one bishop did not claim nor the other acknowledge any authoritative jurisdiction.[71] Yet far-reaching claims had been made, not long previously, by Stephen in the course of his dispute about rebaptism with Cyprian.

It was Stephen who first used the Petrine text on behalf of the Roman pre-eminence. 'He contends,' reports Firmilian, 'that he holds the succession from Peter, on whom the foundations of the Church were laid.'[72] By his previous conduct Cyprian had made it clear that, much as he respected the bishop of Rome, he would admit no seniority. In 254 Cyprian had upheld the condemnation of Basilides of Leon and Martial of Lerida, who had lapsed in the persecution, despite Stephen's attempt to have them reinstated, and he further declared that Stephen, 'placed at a distance and ignorant of what had been done',[73] had been deceived. Later in the same year, Cyprian wrote to Stephen about the case of Marcianus of Arles, who had joined the Novatianists, reminding him, rather peremptorily, of his duty to intervene in the case, largely because of the nearness of Rome to Gaul.[74]

With the outbreak of the baptismal controversy, Cyprian set himself in direct opposition to Stephen, even removing certain passages from *On the Unity of the Church* which might mistakenly give rise to the view that he favoured the Roman primacy, and concurring in the verdict of the Carthaginian council of 256 that 'no one among us sets himself as a bishop of bishops, no one tyrannizes over his colleagues, nor terrorizes them in order to compel their assent, seeing that every bishop is free to exercise his power as he thinks best.'[75] To Cyprian the Petrine text was the charter of the whole episcopacy, which had been confided to Peter in the first instance, so that every bishop is his successor, enthroned as such in the apostle's chair. Stephen's counter-claim was prophetic of the future, for the later history of the Roman primacy is of the stages by which this claim was eventually accepted.

BELIEFS

In the closing years of the second and in the opening decades of the third century the Church was compelled to grapple with certain heretical movements of thought. Since previously Gnosticism was scarcely Christian and Montanism was initially orthodox this was the first encounter with large-scale heterodoxy arising from within the Christian community. These heresies were concerned with the relation of the Father and the Son; they raised acutely, therefore, the trinitarian question, and in seeking to define its position *vis-à-vis* this false teaching the Church was required to clarify its own ideas.

Dynamic Monarchianism

About the year 190 a Byzantine leather-worker named Theodotus came to Rome, teaching that Jesus was a mere man adopted as God's son at his baptism when the divine power descended upon him.[1] This doctrine is known severally as Psilanthropism (a mere man), Adoptionism (Jesus being the adopted Son of God) and Dynamic Monarchianism (Jesus having received the dynamis or power of God). Its supporters sought to safeguard the oneness of God by denying the divinity of Jesus. 'If,' they argued, 'the Father is one and the Son another, and if the Father is God and Christ God, then there is not one God, but two Gods are simultaneously brought forward, the Father and the Son.'[2] Theodotus, condemned by Victor (186–98), was succeeded by his namesake, a banker, and by Artemas or Artemon, and the last was prepared to contend that their views had been those of the entire Church up to the time of Zephyrinus (198–217) and that it was not until his episcopate that the official teaching had been altered. In truth the Adoptionists were really reviving a belief of the Ebionites, Jewish Christians, who had equally denied the divinity of Christ.[3]

The most notable exponent of this teaching in the East was Paul of Samosata, condemned by a council at Antioch in 268. Paul refused to divide the Godhead and declared that it was uni-personal. He acknowledged that God does possess a Word, but denied that this Word has any independent existence. He therefore asserted that Jesus was a mere man in whom God's Word, after acting upon Moses and the prophets, came to dwell in an exceptional degree as a divine power. This indwelling did not make Jesus personally God, nor did it give the Word personality, for the Word is a divine attribute imparted to the son of Mary as a quality. Yet because of this association, the life of Jesus was a continuous progress towards higher things, including moral perfection, so that he must be regarded as unique.[4]

This teaching did not commend itself widely since it so clearly denied the divinity of Christ, but the second heresy, which fully upheld his deity, won not a few adherents.

Modalistic Monarchianism

A twofold conviction, in the oneness of God and in the divinity of Christ, lay at the basis of the teaching of Noetus, the first of the modalistic monarchians. Noetus was a native of Smyrna and was twice interrogated by the council of presbyters before finally being excommunicated. 'He alleged that Christ was the Father himself, and that the Father himself was born, and suffered and died.'[5] He further declared: 'If therefore I acknowledge Christ to be God, he is the Father himself, if he is indeed God; and Christ suffered, being himself God; and consequently the Father suffered, for he was the Father himself'.[6] Hence the alternative title of Patripassianism that was given to this heresy. In effect this was a form of unitarianism which maintained that the distinction between the Father and the Son was not real but purely nominal, one single divine person bearing both names at different times. These ideas were brought to Rome by Epigonus, a disciple of Noetus, and supported by Cleomenes during the pontificate of Zephyrinus,[7] and they were attacked by Tertullian in his *Against Praxeas c.* 213. Praxeas could be a nickname, meaning 'busybody', and it has been applied to both Noetus and Epigonus, and even to bishop Callistus who seems to have been initially sympathetic. The position of 'Praxeas' represents an elaboration of that of Noetus in that the humanity of the incarnate Lord was identified as the Son and his divinity as the Father, 'so while it is the Son who suffers, the Father is his fellow-sufferer'.[8]

The naïveté of the modalism was transcended and the party was provided with a more philosophical platform by Sabellius, a presbyter of the Pentapolis, who reached Rome *c.* 215. There remains no contemporary account of his teaching but he would appear to have held that the divine being is one substance with three operations. God is thus a monad possessing internal powers of expansion, appearing in creation as Father, in redemption as Son and in sanctification as Holy Spirit, these three being not separate realities but aspects of a single reality. This expansion, whereby the three operations are brought into play, is balanced by a process of contraction whereby they are withdrawn again into the one.[9]

In the district of Sabellius' birth, the Pentapolis, modalism continued to be a powerful force, and *c.* 260 Dionysius of Alexandria sought to refute it in a number of letters in which he emphasized the distinction of Father, Son and Spirit to such an extent that his opponents considered him to be purveying tritheism, and attempted to enlist the aid of Dionysius of Rome against him. The bishop of Alexandria was charged with separating the Father and the Son, with denying the latter's eternity, with failing to describe him as *homoousios* (of one substance) with the Father, and with stating that he was a creature. In his defence, Dionysius, while acknowledging that certain of his illustrations were ill-chosen and capable of misinterpretation, affirmed that he did not separate Father, Son and Spirit; that he did acknowledge the Son's eternity, since God was always Father and therefore Christ was always Son; that he did not use *homoousios* because it was non-scriptural but he assented to the meaning intended by it, and that when he spoke of the Son as 'made' he understood thereby begotten and not created.[10] He summed up his teaching to the effect that 'we so expand the Monad into the Triad as not to divide it', i.e. Son and Spirit are not separated from the one divine essence – 'and again we so gather together the Triad as not to subtract from it' – as Sabellius did.[11]

It is possible that there was some misunderstanding between the two Dionysii because of a difference in their use of terms, but the approach of the one, from the aspect of the monarchy, was not identical with that of the other, from the aspect of the triplicity. Both were nevertheless concerned to present the right teaching previously elaborated, chiefly by Tertullian in the West and by Origen in the East.

Tertullian and western Trinitarianism

Tertullian asserted the relative unity of God, i.e. a unity allowing within itself a combination of distinct elements, by employing the term 'monarchy', used previously by the Apologists and similarly defined by him as 'unity of rule'. He was thus able to argue that this single divine rule does not cease to be real when it is exercised by more than one person, as when an emperor associates his son with himself in sovereignty.[12] Equally, with the Apologists, Tertullian upheld the distinction of Father, Son and Spirit by means of the Aristotelian definition of an individual as one in number,[13] and so could affirm that they are 'capable of being counted'.[14] From Aristotle he also adopted certain philosophical concepts of unity in order to safeguard the oneness of the three.

Aristotle expressed his understanding of different kinds of unity in terms of genus, species and substratum. A genus is a class of things or beings of the same type, having certain attributes in common, so a horse and a dog belong to the same animal genus. A species is a subdivision of a genus and is also a class of beings or things of the same type with common characteristics, so Socrates and Plato belong to the same human species. To these two correspond two types of unity: a unity of genus, so that a horse and a dog are one according to unity of genus, and a unity of species, so that Peter and Paul are one according to unity of species. The third unity, unity of substratum, is that whereby two entities are one because they have a common underlying element, e.g. oil and wine are one according to unity of substratum, because they have water as their basis.[15]

Tertullian was emphatic, as previously noted, that Father, Son and

Spirit are individuals – they can be counted; but since there is only one of each, they are also species and each is therefore an individual species. This is an advance upon his predecessors who tended to think of God as one person with his Word and Spirit immanent within him. From the aspect of its unity, the Godhead, according to Tertullian, is one according to unity of substratum, i.e. Father, Son and Spirit have one underlying substance which has no existence apart from them. This substance is the very being of deity of which the Father is the source, since the Son is begotten by him and the Spirit proceeds from him. This involves no division or separation but is the basis of the unity, just as there is unity between the root and its shoot, the sun and its light. 'I always maintain,' he said, 'one substance in three who cohere.'[16] Tertullian's formulation of the divine 'economy', i.e. of the interior organization and constructive integration of the Godhead, was expressed in his *Against Praxeas*:

> They are all of the one, namely by unity of substance, while none the less is guarded the mystery of that economy which disposes the unity into trinity, setting forth Father and Son and Spirit as three, three however not in quality but in sequence, not in substance but in aspect, not in power but in manifestation, seeing it is one God from whom those sequences and aspects and manifestations are reckoned out in the name of the Father and the Son and the Holy Spirit.[17]

The exact interpretation of this terminology is not easy and questions as to its legal or precise philosophical background have been raised. Briefly, in this extended sentence Tertullian sets three positive statements about the triplicity side by side with three negative statements about the unity. God is three in sequence, i.e. the Father is the source of the Godhead, being the first in sequence, since by him the Son is begotten and from him the Spirit proceeds. God is also three in aspect, i.e. as Father he is unbegotten, as Son begotten and as Spirit proceeding. God is likewise three in manifestation, i.e. as Father he is manifested as creator; as Son as redeemer and as Spirit as sanctifier. Yet God is not three in substance, i.e. the three divine persons are each what the others are, despite their being distinguishable; nor is God three in power, for his dominion and activity is not divided; nor finally is God three in quality, since the unity of the divine substance precludes the possibility of there being a plurality of degrees of the divine existence.

Tertullian's trinitarian doctrine eventually became the norm for the western Church, but there was one element in it, so far not specified, that did not commend itself and this was the 'stage' thesis of the Son's begetting. According to Tertullian, while the Word was always within the Father, he was not strictly Son until his extrapolation for the work of creation[18] – these two stages corresponding to the two meanings of Logos as immanent and expressed. Hippolytus, who shared the North African's beliefs, went even further and posited three stages: the Word immanent in the Father; the Word expressed for creation, and the Word incarnate when he completed himself as the true and perfect Son.[19]

Novatian, although his understanding of the Spirit was rudimentary, was in the line of Tertullian: 'the Father is manifested as the one God, true and eternal, from whom alone this power of divinity is emitted, and though transmitted to the Son and centred in him, it returns again to the Father through the community of substance'.[20] But Novatian would not tie the generation of the Son to creation, and affirmed that it was pre-temporal, thus freeing the western doctrine from the two- or three-stage theory of the Son's existence.

Origen and eastern Trinitarianism

Tertullian's pioneer work in the West was paralleled by that of Origen in the East, but while their views were in some respects identical, in others they differed. Like Tertullian, Origen stressed the triplicity, asserting, against the modalists, that Father, Son and Spirit are numerically distinct,[21] each being an *hypostasis*, i.e. an individual subsistence or existent. Indeed, Father and Son can be described as 'two things'[22] or 'two things in *hypostasis*'.[23] Yet they are not just three individuals, otherwise there would be three Gods, but three individual species, since each is unique and is not a specimen representative of a class. At the same time they are one, being one genus because the three belong to the same class, that of the Godhead, having certain attributes in common, and they are also one species because, being one God, they are not subdivisions of the one genus. Thus, Father, Son and Spirit are three individual species, or three *hypostaseis*, in so far as they are to be distinguished from one another, and they are one in so far as they have a common specific genus and may be said to be one in *ousia*.

As Novatian was to do after him, so Origen asserted the eternal generation of the Son, thus refuting the two-stage theory of the Word's existence found in Tertullian. Origen rejected the view that the eternal begetting of the Son could be compared in any way with a human act and declared that 'his generation is as eternal and everlasting as the brilliancy which is produced from the sun',[24] hence one cannot say 'there was when he was not'. But in company with Tertullian, Origen did regard the Father as the fountainhead of the divinity and on the basis of certain scriptural passages, which according to a modern critical view would be deemed to have little direct relevance, he uttered certain statements of an extreme subordinationist character that were to bear fruit in the Arian heresy of the following century. So he declared that the Son is transcended by the Father in as great a degree as he himself transcends the best of all other beings.[25] He could even call the Word a creature, in applying to him the Wisdom text of Prov. viii. 22: 'God created me in the beginning of his ways.' Origen's theological task was further complicated by the lack of an exact terminology with an accompanying failure to distinguish between derivation and creation. So he could speak of the Word as both *agenetos* and *genetos* and of the Spirit as *ageneton* and *geneton*; yet the one cannot just imply the negative of the other. Rather they are to be understood to mean that each is *agenetos* or uncreated because they belong to the triad of deity, but each is *genetos* or derivative because they are not the source or origin of deity which is derived from the Father, who begets the Son and from whom the Spirit proceeds.

Little evidence survives of eastern Trinitarianism in the latter half of the third century, but such as it is indicates Origen's enduring influence. Theognostus, head of the Alexandrian catechetical school, named the Son a creature but coupled this with the statement that he was derived from the Father's substance,[26] Gregory Thaumaturgus could speak of the Son as 'a creature or thing made',[27] but affirm in his creed that 'in the triad there is nothing created or servile'. The debate was to continue before full clarity had been achieved and adequate safeguards had been introduced.

The person and work of Christ

As with the doctrine of the Trinity, so with that of the person of Christ, Tertullian and Origen were the two outstanding contributors, although this subject, due to the exigencies of controversy, received less consideration than the former.

Tertullian, like the Apologists, interpreted the work of Christ in terms of illumination; he came as 'the enlightener and instructor of mankind'[28] and 'preached the new law and the new promise of the kingdom of heaven.'[29] Believing, however, that man consists of body and soul and that both are derived from one's parents, he held that man shared in the sin of Adam and participated in his death and that therefore 'our own death could not be annulled except by the Lord's passion, nor our life have been restored without his resurrection'.[30] But his understanding of Christ's function did not determine his Christology, which was rather the by-product of the trinitarian debate on the one hand and on the other of his attack upon the docetism of teachers such as Marcion. Hence Tertullian professed belief in Christ as 'the primordial first-begotten Word'[31] who truly lived and died in human flesh and therefore possessed two natures: Godhead and full humanity, consisting of body and soul.[32] But, as Tertullian realized, 'this provokes the inquiry, how the Word became flesh?'[33] i.e. what is the relationship between the two substances? This is the heart of the Christological problem, viz. how Christ can be God and man and yet one person. The answer was to take centuries to formulate, but Tertullian defined the three basic factors. He affirmed, first, that the Incarnate Lord is one Person; that, second, he has two natures, and that, third, these natures persist in their entirety unimpaired by their union with each other. So 'we observe a twofold quality, not confused but combined, Jesus in one Person, God and man', and 'there remain unimpaired the proper being of each substance'.[34] The resultant of the union of God and man in Christ is not a *tertium quid*, like electrum which is the product of the union of gold and silver, but one Person in whom may be recognized two natures. If Tertullian failed to resolve the problem, he ensured that all essential elements were kept in mind.

Novatian, who adopted much of Tertullian's thought, stating that Christ is both God and man, combining 'both substances' in himself,[35] was able to resolve the problem of the unity at the expense of the completeness of the humanity by describing the latter exclusively in terms of body or flesh. To him Christ was composed of flesh and the divine Word – a view that was to command a certain degree of acceptance, until it became a point of controversy through the teaching of Apollinaris of Laodicea in the fourth century.

Origen's understanding of the work of Christ was twofold in that he envisaged a Christianity suitable for the simple believer which was inferior to that open to the more mature. In New Testament terms he interpreted Christ's death as one of vicarious substitution; he is the one who has taken our sins upon himself and has offered the true sacrifice to the Father.[36] He has moreover overthrown the devil,[37] who has accepted his human soul as a ransom for mankind, only to be cheated of the victim he could not hold.[38] To the mature Christian, however, Origen could say: 'Happy are they who no longer need the Son of God as a physician who heals the soul, nor as a shepherd, nor as redemption, but as wisdom, and as word, and as righteousness.'[39] Thus the role of the Word is to illuminate men's souls, to purify and deify them. 'Discoursing in bodily form and announcing himself as flesh, he calls to himself those who are flesh that he may in the first place cause them to be transformed into the likeness of the Word who has been made flesh, and afterwards may exalt them so as to behold him as he was before he became flesh.'[40] This interpretation of Christ's work, together with his understanding of the origins of human life, directly influenced the Alexandrian's Christology.

Unlike Tertullian with his traducianist theory of the soul's beginning, Origen was a creationist and believed that all souls were made in eternity and fell into the material world as a consequence of individual sin.[41] Only Christ's pre-existent soul escaped this pre-cosmic Fall[42] and was thus able to provide the meeting point of the Son and human nature when the Word became flesh. Christ is therefore both God and man, there being not just a communion but a veritable union between the two natures, Jesus having been 'compounded, if I may so speak, both of God and of a mortal man'.[43] But since the purpose of the descent is the deification of man, the effect of the union is that the humanity is 'changed into God'[44] and the mature Christian, who is able to appreciate this, can say that 'although the Saviour was a man, he is now one no longer'.[45] Brilliant though Origen's speculation was, it went beyond anything that the majority of believers was prepared to accept and reaction to his views led, in the thought of Methodius of Olympus, to a Word-flesh Christology which replaced the Word-man belief of a Tertullian.

The Church

The various pressures that were leading to a clarification of trinitarian doctrine and, to a lesser extent, of Christology, also had their effect upon the doctrine of the Church. Indeed the extent to which outside influences could mould beliefs is very evident in the teaching of Tertullian. In his early career Tertullian, like Irenaeus, regarded the Church as the temple of the Spirit, the guardian of the apostolic revelation, with its doctrine guaranteed by the succession of bishops. This was a position he upheld strenuously against the Marcionites and other Gnostic sects. But upon his conversion to Montanism, he changed his ground, asserting that the Church is composed exclusively of spiritual men and that the episcopate was irrelevant.[46] Cyprian, on the other hand, in the face of schismatic movements, was concerned to defend and preserve the oneness of the Church and saw its unity as expressed and guaranteed by the consensus of its bishops. 'It is united and held together by the glue of the mutual cohesion of the bishops'.[47] Hence Church membership involves not only the acceptance of the teaching guaranteed by the episcopate, as in Irenaeus, but submission to the bishops themselves.[48] The schismatic is thus outside the Church, outside the sphere of the Spirit's operation, and no child of God, since 'he cannot have God for his Father who has not the Church for his mother'.[49]

Cyprian's practical approach to the doctrine of the Church, in the light of the disciplinary problems that were the aftermath of the Decian persecution, differed from the speculative theses of Clement and Origen in the East. While Clement sought to distinguish between the true Church and the gatherings of heretics, he also tended to set the invisible Church of the mature Christian over against the visible Church, consisting of saint and sinner alike.[50] Similarly Origen perceived a tension between the empirical Church on earth and the ideal,[51] but he was sufficiently aware of the Church as an organized community, with duly authorized ministers, not to sever the two entirely and so to regard the spiritually advanced as 'the eye' of the Body,[52] and indeed to interpret the phrase 'the resurrection of the body' of the whole Church,[53] if not the whole of humanity, which is to be raised up at the last day.

The Last Things

According to the pagan Celsus, the Christian doctrine of resurrection is 'such a hope as might be cherished by worms'.[54] Because of this pagan attack and in order to sustain the anti-docetic polemic, this particular article of belief continued to be given prominence in the writings of the third century.

Tertullian's view was identical with that of his immediate predecessors; he upheld not so much resurrection as reanimation. He could even argue that the sayings of Jesus about the hairs of the head being numbered and about there being weeping and gnashing of teeth demonstrated that at the resurrection we should have hair, eyes and teeth.[55] This same materialism is to be found in Cyprian with his quaint argument against cosmetics since they might prevent God's recognizing the individual at the resurrection.[56]

It is to be supposed that such a belief would not commend itself to the Alexandrians with their strong Platonic leaning. Clement was emphatic that the resurrection body is not one of flesh.[57] Origen too had no hesitation in siding with the pagans in their objections to physical reanimation. 'Neither we, nor the Holy Scriptures, assert that with the same bodies, without a change to a higher condition, shall the dead arise',[58] and 'we do not affirm that God will raise men from the dead with the same flesh and blood'.[59] Consequently, he advanced the same arguments that Justin, Athenagoras and Irenaeus had attempted to refute and himself contended that the body is like a river, which preserves a certain form although its matter is constantly changing and that there is therefore no abiding substance to be raised. Yet Origen did profess belief in the resurrection, but a resurrection of the body and not of the flesh. He argued that the resurrection body will have the same 'form' as the earthly body, but with its substance changed into something pure and ethereal.[60] Since this position does not safeguard the identity or continuity between the earthly and the risen body, Origen went further: 'as above the grain of wheat there arises a stalk, so a certain power is emplanted in the body which is not destroyed and from which the body is raised up.'[61] There is a seminal principle lodged in the tabernacle of the soul, a life-germ similar to that by which the ear of corn grows out of the seed.[62] This in effect is a doctrine of bio-spiritual evolution which has little in common with the miraculous divine act of which the New Testament speaks. It was accordingly attacked in its turn by Methodius.

To Origen the body was in a sense a prison-house of the soul, a Hellenistic view which was shared by Arnobius, who could say that 'we are confined in the shackles of this body', that Jesus, when he died, was 'freed from the body' and that Christians too may be confident that 'Almighty God will take care of us when we leave our bodies'.[63] Methodius would have none of this; to him the body was not a fetter to the soul and would not be precluded from the resurrection. On the contrary the corruption of the body is the result of sin, which death will bring to an end, and then God will refashion our bodies to dwell for a thousand years on a renewed earth. At the conclusion of this millennial reign, our bodies 'will be changed from a human and corruptible form into an angelic size and beauty . . . and shall pass to greater and better things, ascending into the very house of God above the heavens.'[64] In this way Methodius sought to harmonize the resurrection of the flesh, to which he believed he was committed by the scriptures, with the spiritual state of heaven. But the idea of the millennium which he utilized, on the basis of the Book of Revelation, was soon to disappear from Christian teaching, partly because of its acceptance by such groups as the Montanists, partly because of the objections raised against it by such as Dionysius of Alexandria.[65] Thus a belief widely accepted in the second century was beginning to vanish in the course of the third.

The same fading of the Parousia expectation also continued, although Hippolytus was prepared to calculate the date of the Second Advent. Belief in inaugurated eschatology was, however, kept alive. To Tertullian Christ has introduced a new generation into the promised land, into the possession of eternal life.[66] Cyprian declared that the devil had been 'detected and cast down by the advent of Christ'[67] and that believers are already 'placed in the heavenly camp'.[68] According to Clement Christ has permitted us 'to conduct a colony from earth to heaven'[69] but to Origen Christ has inflicted only the first blow on the power of the devil – others therefore are to follow.[70] That the belief in the accomplished act of Christ was kept alive was in part the outcome of the liturgical life of the Church, but before turning to this, attention

NEW TESTAMENT

1. Two of the earliest surviving fragments of the New Testament writings. These portions of papyrus, which date from before 150, come from St John's Gospel; they are in the John Rylands Library, Manchester.

2. Two Coptic ivory panels of the sixth century, representing the four evangelists.

3. St Peter. A bronze statue, now in the Vatican, possibly of the fifth century, representing the apostle holding the keys and raising his right hand in blessing.

4. St Paul. This ivory diptych, now in the Bargello at Florence, *c.* 380–400, represents on one leaf Adam as the lord of creation and on the other scenes from St Paul's ministry on the island of Malta: he is depicted teaching, shaking off the snake into a fire and receiving the sick (Acts 28, 1–10).

5. The baptism of Jesus by John in the Jordan, being the opening of his public ministry. This fifth-century mosaic in the Baptistry of the Orthodox at Ravenna has preserved Hellenistic conventions, the river being represented by the figure of a god.

6. The signs of the inbreaking Kingdom, being several of the miracles of Jesus on the Andrews diptych in the Victoria and Albert Museum, London. Reading downwards the scenes are: (a) The Feeding of the Five Thousand. (b) The Healing of the Blind Man. (c) The Paralytic. (d) The Raising of Lazarus. (e) The Wedding at Cana. (f) The Leper.

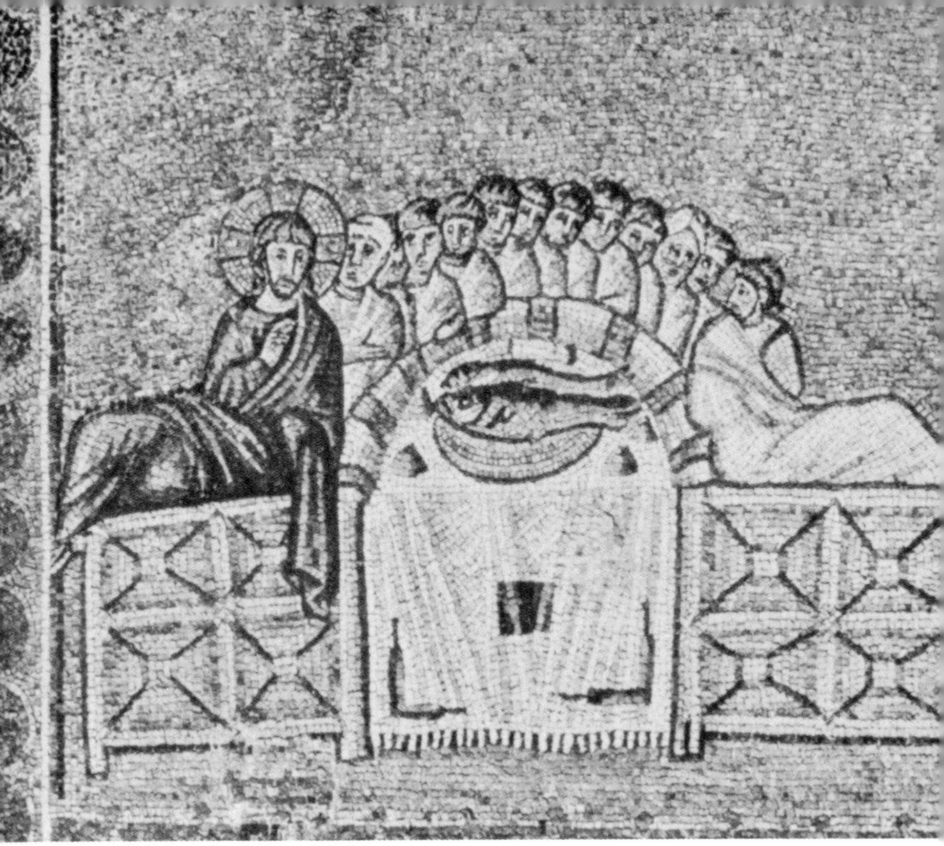

7. The Last Supper according to the stylized mosaic in S. Apollinare Nuovo, Ravenna, 520–30. Jesus and his disciples recline around the table on which there are fish, recalling both the miracle of the Five Thousand and the anagram, the initial letters of Jesus Christ, the Son of God, forming the Greek word ichthus, a fish.

9 (*right*). Jesus on the cross between the two thieves. A wooden panel from the doors of S. Sabina, Rome, *c.* 430.

8. The Via Crucis. On this panel from an ivory casket of the fifth century, now in the British Museum, London, Pilate washes his hands, Jesus bears the cross and Peter, beneath the cockerel, denies his master.

10. The Resurrection and Ascension. On this ivory panel, *c.* 400, now in the Bayerisches Nationalmuseum at Munich, the angel tells the women that Jesus is risen and Jesus himself is received into glory.

THE CHURCH IN THE ROMAN EMPIRE

11. The Emperors and the Church. (a) Nero (54–68), the first persecutor of the Christians. (b) Domitian (81–96), to whose reign the Book of Revelation and the First Epistle of Clement are usually assigned. (c) Septimius Severus (193–211), under whom Perpetua and Felicitas were martyred in Africa, and Leonides, the father of Origen, died in Alexandria. (d) Decius (249–51), whose edicts brought suffering to the Church in North Africa, where Cyprian went into hiding, and led to the arrest of Origen who later died from his treatment in prison. (e) Constantine the Great (sole ruler from 323–37), the first Christian emperor, who brought the persecutions to an end. (f) Julian the Apostate (361–3), who attempted to restore paganism. (g) Theodosius the Great (379–95), the last ruler of both parts of the empire and the one who finally overthrew Arianism.

12. The Martyrs. (a) St Laurence, deacon of Sixtus II, was roasted alive on a gridiron under Valerian on 10 August, 258. The instrument of his torture, together with a cupboard and gospel books, is shown on this mosaic from the tomb of Galla Placidia, 450. (b) St Menas, an Egyptian martyr who died under Diocletian at Cotyaeum in Phrygia, depicted on a sixth-century ivory box in the British Museum.

13. (*right*) Hippolytus (d. 235), the first anti-pope and a prolific writer, his works including the important liturgical text *The Apostolic Tradition*. On one side of the cathedra there is engraved a list of his books and on the other his table for the computation of Easter. Lateran Museum.

WORSHIP

14. Few direct representations of the rite of baptism survive, but the details of the often depicted baptism of Jesus by John were taken from contemporary liturgical practice. On this sarcophagus from S. Maria Antiqua, Rome, Jesus, in the form of a boy, stands in water to his ankles and John, the minister, lays his hand upon his head.

15. An Ampulla from Monza. This small flask contained holy oil and was brought by pilgrims. The ampullae were frequently decorated – this one represents the visit of the wise men – and often reproduced mosaics in the holy places which are now no longer extant.

16. An ivory panel, now in the FitzWilliam Museum, Cambridge, showing the Celebration of the Eucharist. Behind the bishop are five deacons and in front of him seven priests singing.

17. The Agape or Love Feast was in origin the meal of the Last Supper detached from the blessing of the bread beforehand and of the wine afterwards. In this fresco from the Capella Greca in the catacomb of Priscilla the eucharistic associations of the meal are indicated by the fish on the plates and by the baskets of fragments recalling the Feeding of the Five Thousand.

18. The normal posture for prayer was standing with arms outstretched in imitation of Jesus on the cross, as in this figure of an orans or praying woman from the catacomb of Domitilla, Rome. The accompanying doves symbolize the souls of the faithful departed with the olive branches of peace.

19. A sarcophagus from Ravenna. This stone coffin of the sixth century, splendidly decorated, represents the joys of Paradise, in the form of flowers, the cross of Christ, and the descending dove of the Spirit.

20. The descent into the catacomb of Domitilla, Rome, with several loculi or tombs in the walls.

21. The Crypt of the Popes in the catacomb of Callistus, Rome, where many of the bishops were buried. The memorial tablet was erected by Pope Damasus some hundred years after their deaths.

THE EARLY CHURCHES

22. The interior of S. Costanza, Rome, 324–6. This circular building was planned as a mausoleum by Constantine for his sister. It soon became the baptistery of the neighbouring basilica of St Agnese and was eventually adapted as a church. This centralized plan for a funerary building was to have a profound effect on the development of church architecture, particularly in the East.

23. The tomb mosaic of Valentia from Thabraca in North Africa, *c*. 400, depicting the main features of the basilica. The entrance is on the right beneath the gable end. The roof with clerestory windows runs along the top above the columns that support it and divide the interior into nave and aisles. The altar is set forward into the nave, while the apse is reached by several steps, its half dome completing the picture on the left.

24. The Baptistery at Dura Europos. A private house was adapted as a house-church soon after 232 and a room to the right of the entrance became the baptistery. The coffin-like font stood at one end under a baldachin. The remains of frescoes of the healing of the paralytic and the saving of Peter from the water appear in the upper zone of the wall and of the three Marys approaching the tub in the lower one.

25. The Baptistery of S. John Lateran. The first baptistery, dating from *c.* 310 was square; this was changed *c.* 350, to produce the so-called Constantinian baptistery which was circular. Under Sixtus III, 432–40, a porch was added and the circle altered into an octagon, the area of the font being demarcated by eight columns.

26. The sixth century quatrefoil font at Kelibia in North Africa. The shape recalls the cross and crucifixion; the trees and birds, in the mosaic, recall Paradise, and the catechumens hoping to regain in baptism what they had lost through Adam; the alpha and omega and the fish symbolize Christ.

27. The hexagonal font at Timgad, North Africa, the six sides recalling the sixth day of the week on which Jesus was crucified. Spaces for columns to bear a ciborium are to be noted.

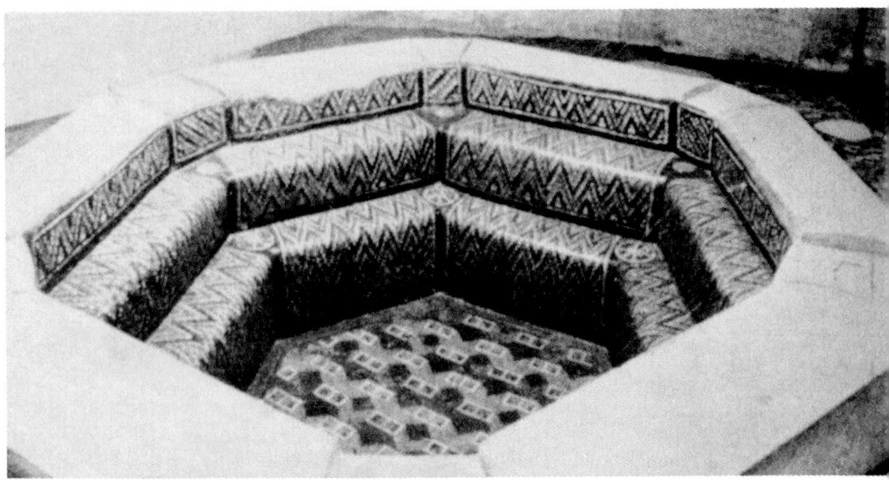

28. A sixth-century altar in S. Vitale, Ravenna.

29. The ivory cathedra or throne of Maximianus of Ravenna (546–54). The front bears the monogram of the bishop and figures of John the Baptist and the Evangelists; the sides biblical scenes.

30. An ambo or reading pulpit of the sixth century in SS. John and Paul, Ravenna.

31. Christ as founder and Lord of the Church. In this mosaic from the confessio in St Peter's, Rome, he raises his hand in blessing and holds a gospel book with the words: 'I am the Way, the Truth and the Life, Whoever believes in me shall live.'

must be paid to the continuing development of the creedal formulation of belief.

The formulation of belief

In seeking to describe the process whereby affirmations of Christian faith achieved a measure of fixity, it is important to distinguish between two types of creed, the one interrogatory and the other declaratory. The former was composed of a series of answers to the baptismal interrogations, i.e. to certain questions put to the candidate at the moment of his actual baptism. Hippolytus provides an example:

> And when he who is being baptized goes down to the water, let him who baptizes lay his hand on him saying thus, 'Dost thou believe in God the Father Almighty?' And he who is being baptized shall say, 'I believe.' Then, holding his hand placed upon his head, he shall baptize him once. And then he shall say, 'Dost thou believe in Christ Jesus, the Son of God, who was born by the Holy Spirit from the Virgin Mary, who was crucified under Pontius Pilate and died, and rose again on the third day living from the dead, and ascended into the heavens, and sat down on the right hand of the Father, and will come to judge the living and the dead?' And when he says 'I believe', he is baptized again. And again he shall say, 'Dost thou believe in the Holy Spirit, in the holy Church, and the resurrection of the flesh?' And he who is being baptized shall say, 'I believe.' And so he is baptized a third time.[71]

These triple interrogations were a feature of the late second century rite of baptism and became general in the third. So Cyprian can refer to 'the baptismal interrogations',[72] Firmilian of Caesarea to 'the customary and established words of the interrogations',[73] and Dionysius of Alexandria to 'the questions and answers'.[74]

The declaratory creed did not belong initially to the baptismal rite proper; it was rather the by-product and eventually the culmination of the developed catechumenate. Since this development is first evident in Rome in the second decade of the third century, it may be supposed that this centre was also a pioneer in the production of crystallized creedal forms, although many years were to elapse before anything like a formal and official text was accepted.

WORSHIP

The importance of worship as a factor serving to formulate and articulate belief has already been stressed in the previous section. During the third century the cultus became more elaborate and enriched, and while its basic patterns remained unchanged, as generation succeeded to generation these were supplemented in various ways.

Baptism

There remain two comparatively full accounts of baptism from the third century: the one in Tertullian's *De Baptismo* and the other in Hippolytus' *Apostolic Tradition.* Tertullian draws attention to the essential element with the statement: 'a man is dipped in water, and amidst the utterance of a few words is sprinkled and then rises again'.[1] This is the central core of the rite and around it were grouped a number of ancillary ceremonies and actions. Before the day, which was usually either what is now called Holy Saturday or Pentecost, the candidates were to prepare 'with repeated prayers, fasts and bendings of the knee, and vigils all the night through.'[2] Then, after the blessing of the water, the catechumens descended, being anointed immediately upon their ascent, and the bishop then laid his hand upon them for the reception of the Spirit. It is possible that between the unction and laying on of hands there was a signing with the sign of the cross.[3]

In North Africa, fifty years later, the practice remained much the same, according to the evidence of Cyprian who refers to the blessing of the water, to the interrogations, which correspond to Tertullian's 'utterance of a few words' and include the question: Dost thou believe in eternal life and remission of sins through the holy Church?[4] Cyprian also mentions the chrism, the laying on of hands and the signing with the cross.[5]

Hippolytus, describing the practice at Rome, details a more elaborate ritual.[6] The preparation is to take three years and is to include instruction, prayers and exorcisms. On the Thursday before Easter the candidates are to take a bath and are to fast on the Friday and the Saturday. On the final day they are brought before the bishop, who exorcises them and breathes in their faces for the expulsion of evil spirits. There follows a vigil for the reading of the scriptures and further instruction. At cockcrow, the water is blessed, clothes are removed and there is a renunciation of 'Satan, and all thy servants and all thy works', whereupon they are anointed with the Oil of Exorcism. Descending to the water, answers are given to the interrogations. Before putting on their clothes, the newly baptized receive the Oil of Thanksgiving; then the bishop lays his hand upon them, consecrated oil is poured on their heads and the kiss is exchanged. 'Thenceforth they shall pray together with the people' – indeed they forthwith participate in their first or baptismal eucharist. While the sequence of the ritual in North Africa and Rome was similar, in certain areas of the East a different order was observed. According to the *Didascalia* the ceremonies began with an anointing of the head only by the bishop with imposition of the hand; there followed an unction of the whole body by the minister, or by a woman when the candidates were female, and then came finally the baptism itself. There was therefore no anointing after baptism and the western post-baptismal acts all preceded the actual descent into the water.[7]

Although baptism was essentially a unified rite, comprising several elements, various circumstances contributed to break up this pattern. In cases of severe illness, it seemed reasonable to baptize the sick person, leaving his initiation to be completed later, if he recovered, by the bishop. This 'clinical' baptism was not regarded with favour and could be a bar to ordination, but it certainly existed.[8] A second type of emergency arose out of the persecutions; when the faithful were liable to be seized and executed, Christian parents, mindful of the welfare of their children, sought to have them included within the fellowship of the Church. Unable to secure the services of the bishop, for a variety of reasons, they would approach their presbyter who, fully appreciating the sincerity of their request and taking into account the abnormality of the times, was prepared to administer his part of the rite, leaving the concluding unction and laying on of hands for a more peaceful occasion. The spread of infant baptism, too, favoured a disintegration of the rite. Tertullian, in attempting to discourage it, reveals that infant initiation was in vogue in North Africa in his day;[9] Cyprian testifies that it was the practice to baptize infants within a few days of their birth.[10] Wherever this became widespread, unless there were a bishop to every local community – as was largely the case in North Africa – it became a physical impossibility for one to be present on every occasion when the rite was performed.

The matter came to a head after the Decian persecution when the Church had to cope with many baptized in schism who were desirous of joining the fellowship of orthodox believers. Carthage and Rome adopted different positions. Cyprian maintained that baptism outside the Church was no baptism and that the whole rite was to be performed for each returning schismatic.[11] Stephen of Rome argued that the laying on of hands was the essential element and was prepared not to repeat water-baptism.[12] His position was the one eventually to be accepted, but the controversy marked an important stage in the disintegration of the unified rite into two separate halves, later to be known as baptism and confirmation.

According to Tertullian, 'it makes no difference whether a man be washed in a sea or a pool, a stream or a fount, a lake or a trough'.[13] Nevertheless provision began to be made within the house-churches, the first such baptistery known being at Dura Europos on the Euphrates *c.* 232. The font, beneath a baldachin, is at one end of a rectangular room opening off the forecourt immediately to the right of the entrance.

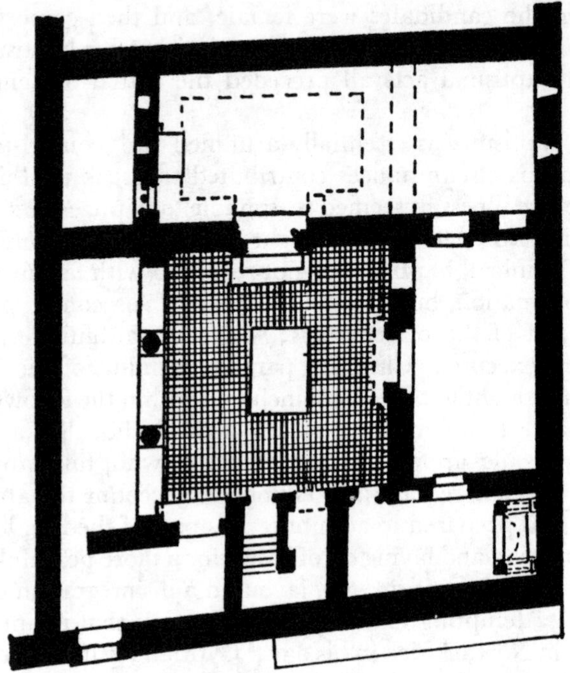

House-Church at Dura Europos

Both the shape of the font and the frescoes that decorate the walls indicate something of the meaning of baptism. The font is scarcely distinguishable from a sarcophagus, thus expressing the idea of burial with Christ in baptism. The subjects of the paintings include Christ walking on the water and the Samaritan woman at the well, each presenting the theme of God acting through the living waters. The scene of the women at the tomb proclaims the baptismal resurrection, while the figure of the Good Shepherd, who gives his life for the sheep, and so redeems man from sin and death, is contrasted with a painting of Adam and Eve and emphasizes that baptism is the means whereby one becomes a member of the flock of Christ and receives the 'seal' or identification mark of his ownership.

The Eucharist

If, apart from Justin Martyr's account, knowledge of the second-century eucharist is limited, in the third century the evidence becomes relatively more plentiful. From Tertullian it may be gathered that the faithful met in the early morning and also assembled on the annual festivals of the martyrs;[14] they further observed a year's mind of the departed.[15] There were readings from the law, the prophets, the epistles and gospels,[16] and psalms were sung.[17] Prayer was offered for the emperor, for all in authority, for peace and for the delay of the final consummation.[18] The kiss of peace was exchanged,[19] the words of institution were recited,[20] and the congregation uttered the 'Amen'.[21] Cyprian adds other details for North Africa: a sermon, the offertory of the people, the *sursum corda*, commemoration of the passion and resurrection, a mixed chalice administered by the deacons, and the celebration of a daily eucharist at Carthage.[22] At Alexandria there were similarly readings, psalms, the kiss of peace, the use of bread, wine and water, possibly the *Sanctus*, a commemoration of the passion and the fraction.[23]

Hippolytus again gives the most complete account of the celebration at Rome,[24] since he provides a model both for the consecration of a bishop and after baptism; he concentrates exclusively on the second half of the rite and says nothing of the synaxis. The eucharist proper begins with the kiss of peace, the bringing of the offerings and the exchange of a greeting. The *sursum corda* leads into a prayer of thanksgiving, at the end of which the bishop breaks the bread, and distributes the fragments while the presbyters and deacons administer the chalice. Although Hippolytus gives a text of the 'consecration' prayer, he does add: 'it is not necessary for anyone to recite the exact words that we have prescribed . . . but let each one pray according to his ability'.[25]

The rationale underlying the eucharistic action is in part defined by Hippolytus when he states that 'by thanksgiving the bishop shall make the bread into an image of the body of Christ, and the cup of wine mingled with water according to the likeness of the blood.'[26] This language, which is paralleled for example in Tertullian,[27] does not mean that the eucharistized bread and wine were regarded as mere symbols; in ancient thought the symbol is in some sense that which it represents or makes present, hence Cyprian can speak of Christ as our bread 'because he is the bread of us who touch his body'.[28] Only with the Alexandrians does a more Platonic and less realistic idea come to the fore, and, while using conventional phraseology, both Clement and Origen tend to concentrate upon the spiritual world behind the phenomenal. Origen in particular was prepared to regard the outward rite as suited to the simple Christian, while the more advanced were to find their nourishment in the Word alone.[29]

Like the second-century writers, those of the third regarded the eucharist as a sacrifice, but Cyprian was the first to expound anything like a theory of it. He declared that each eucharist must be a repetition of Jesus' actions at the Last Supper; the officiant 'truly discharges the office of Christ, who imitates that which Christ did.' As the Lord's representative, 'he then offers a true and full sacrifice in the Church to God the Father.' This sacrifice is a sacramental re-enactment of the oblation of Christ's person which he originally offered to the Father. Moreover, in the eucharistic offering there is a union effected between Christ and his followers and between the followers severally, so that the rite is the offering of the whole Church, Head and members.[30]

The eucharist was celebrated, as previously, in the ordinary house, although more frequently these were not private dwellings but community property, re-ordered to suit the liturgical needs. So at Dura Europos a room was created for the eucharist, *c.* 232, by removing an existing partition, while at Cirta, as late as 303, there was a house 'where the Christians customarily meet'.[31] But with the growth of congregations special buildings became necessary. The *Chronicle of Edessa* records that there was a *templum ecclesiae Christianorum* in the city that was destroyed by a flood in 202; in 258 Gregory Thaumaturgus built a church at Neocaesarea in Pontus, and twelve years later the emperor Aurelian ordered Paul of Samosata to surrender the 'church building' at Antioch to the orthodox party.[32] In the West, in Rome during the reign of Alexander Severus, there was a dispute between the Christians and the guild of *popinarii* concerning the ownership of a plot of land upon which the Christians intended to build a church and the guild a public house. The emperor decided in favour of the Christians on the grounds that the worship of God in any form was better than the license of a tavern.[33] At the time of the Diocletian persecution, in Gaul and Britain, Constantius 'lest he should have seemed to dissent from the injunctions of his superiors, permitted the demolition of churches – mere walls, and capable of being built again – but he preserved entire that true temple of God, which is the human body'.[34] Christian architecture was thus coming into being, and by the beginning of the fourth century there were, according to the report of Optatus of Milevis, more than forty basilicas in the capital;[35] indeed Eusebius could ask: 'how could one fully describe those assemblies thronged with countless men, and the multitudes that gathered together in every city, and the famed concourses in the places of prayer: by reason of which they were no longer satisfied with the buildings of olden times, and would erect from the foundations churches of spacious dimensions throughout all the cities?'[36]

Little or no trace has been preserved of these buildings and recourse must be had to the remains of the later Constantinian era to discover the features of the basilica which then became the predominant type of church building. Already, however, the development was sufficient to make the question of interior arrangement an important one, and so the *Didascalia* prescribes:

Appoint the places for the brethren with care and gravity. And for the presbyters let there be assigned a place in the eastern part of the house; and let the bishop's throne be set in their midst, and let the presbyters sit with him. And again, let the laymen sit in another part of the house toward the east. For so it should be, that in the eastern part of the house the presbyters sit with the bishop, and next the laymen, and then the women also. . . . But of the deacons, let one stand always by the oblations of the eucharist; and let another stand without by the door and observe them that come in.[37]

The Agape

The Meal proper of the Last Supper, dissociated from the eucharistic bread and cup, was by now a common quasi-religious gathering for the faithful. Accounts of and references to it are to be found in Tertullian, Cyprian and Hippolytus. If the reports of the first two be conflated to present a picture of North African practice, then it appears that the agape was known as the Lord's Supper, began with prayer over bread and a mingled cup, the food being provided by those attending. At the end hands were washed, lamps were lighted, psalms sung and there was a final grace.[38]

The blessing and lighting of the lamp in North Africa, an early form of the *lucernarium*, is also described in the *Ethiopian Church Order*, which here probably incorporates third-century material.

At Rome there is the blessing and breaking of the bread, but each one present blesses his or her own cup nor is there any concluding grace,[39] consequently it would be a mistake to suppose that there was a single stereotyped pattern for the agape. Once the meal ceased to be joined to the eucharist and became virtually a private party, although one to which the bishop or some other cleric was usually invited, it ceased in many areas to be under direct ecclesiastical control and so each host could, within limits, adopt any order he chose.

Admirable though the agape was in many respects, it was liable to abuse. Tertullian, turned Montanist, condemned the intemperance that had crept into its observance,[40] and Clement protested against the immodest revelry and the use of flutes[41] – yet centuries were to elapse before it was finally discontinued.

The Calendar

According to Cyprian, 'he who remembers that he has renounced the world knows no day of worldly appointment, neither does he who hopes for eternity from God calculate the seasons of earth any more'.[42] Such an attitude serves to explain the relatively late date of the development of an ecclesiastical calendar. The Church's Year, as it was to be arranged eventually, was the result of the fusion of two elements: the festivals of the martyrs, referred to by Tertullian, which were often local in character, and the festivals of Christ, which were universally accepted.

The central core of the pre-Nicene calendar was Sunday, the Lord's Day, the first day of the week. Being the day of Christ's resurrection, it was characterized by joy and was observed by a celebration of the eucharist. In addition to this weekly festival there were two annual feasts, the Pascha and Pentecost.

The Pascha, or Christian Passover, was a unitive festival, proclaiming jointly the cross and the resurrection. It was usual to prepare for it by a fast of two days, but in Egypt and Syria a six-day fast was observed,[43] and vigils, consisting of prayers, intercessions and readings took place.

Pentecost was the period of fifty days, succeeding the resurrection, and was one of universal rejoicing; 'we spend our time,' says Tertullian, 'in all exultation.'[44] This very meagre calendar perpetuated in part the eschatological outlook of the first Christians, and it was not until the conversion of Constantine, the consequent reconciliation of Church and State and a more sympathetic interest in the affairs of the world and so in time and history, that it underwent any extensive elaboration.

Penance

The embryonic penitential discipline of the first two centuries began to attain identifiable form in the opening decades of the third when it consisted of three elements: confession of sin, penitential exercises and absolution or reconciliation. The second and third of these were public and the first was a necessary part of seeking spiritual counsel, which might or might not issue in the need for disciplinary action. So, according to Origen:

> Look round carefully to find the proper person to whom to confess your sin. Prove your doctor first, the man to whom you must disclose the reason of your weakness, that he be one who knows how to sympathize with a sufferer, to weep with a mourner, one who understands words of sympathy. And then, if he, a man who has thus shown himself a learned and merciful doctor, tells you to do anything, do it; and if he judges your weakness to be of such a nature that it ought to be revealed to and treated in the assembly of the whole Church, so thereby perhaps both others can be edified and you yourself easily cured, do not hesitate to obey.[45]

For ordinary sins, prayer, alms-giving and mutual forgiveness were all that were necessary; public penance was reserved for the graver faults. The definition of these and agreement upon a policy towards them took many decades. In the last years of the second century, adultery, murder and idolatry seem to have been treated as irremissible.[46] Callistus of Rome pursued a more lenient policy, and the effect of his lead may be gauged later from Cyprian who reveals that, despite previous arguments on the subject, by his day sexual sins were regarded as remissible and that idolatry too, as a result of the Decian persecution, was included amongst those capable of forgiveness.[47] Rigorism was by no means past, but henceforth it was to be tempered by mercy.

Prayer and devotional practices

Recognition that most, if not all, sins could be forgiven was to have a profound effect upon Christian devotional life. If the Church is not a society of saints but a school for sinners, then post-baptismal training for heaven becomes necessary and ascetical theology will eventually develop.

Tertullian, uncompromisingly rigorist, remained severely practical in his teaching about prayer, emphasizing the need for praise, thanksgiving, confession and intercession. Cyprian, following in his footsteps, was equally direct, stressing the intimate connexion between prayer and daily life: 'that every one of us may be able to prepare himself, let him thus learn to pray, and know, from the character of the prayer, what he ought to be'.[48] The Alexandrians, however, under the influence of semi-Stoic theories of life as a progress, regarded this earthly existence as a training ground and so laid the foundation of an ascetical system.

Clement's teaching on prayer is extensive, but while he has more to say on the subject than any previous writer, he concentrates upon his 'gnostic' or ideal Christian rather than upon the normal believer. For Clement prayer is 'converse with God'; it is constant intercourse – 'his whole life is prayer'.[49] If it includes praise, thanksgiving, intercession and petition, it tends to exclude confession because the perfect Christian should have little need of it. In Origen this spirituality took on the features of an ascetical system, but his treatise devoted to prayer has little in the way of mystical language and is a guide to the proper disposition of the mind in preparation and an exposition of the four kinds of prayer listed in I Timothy ii. 1, viz. supplication, 'prayer', intercession and the giving of thanks.

Since much of the teaching on prayer was of a practical nature, attention was given to devotional activities that might accompany and assist it. Some – washing of hands and putting off of cloaks before and sitting down on a bed afterwards – were condemned as superstitious; others – standing with arms outstretched, like Christ on the cross, and facing the east – were recommended.[50] The sign of the cross was an habitual practice: 'in all our travels and movements, in all our comings-in and goings-out, in putting on our shoes, at the bath, at the table, in lighting our candles, in lying down, in sitting down, whatever employment occupies us, we mark our foreheads with the sign of the cross.'[51]

A further devotional practice to which several references are made is that of communicating from the reserved sacrament at home, it being the custom for the worshippers at the common eucharist each to take back with him his or her portion.[52]

While the individual's devotional life was free from regimentation, the attempt was made to recommend particular hours for prayer. In the *Apostolic Tradition* seven hours are listed – as soon as one wakes; at the third, sixth and ninth hours; before sleep; at midnight and finally at cockcrow.[53] The second, third and fourth of these corresponded with the main divisions of the day in the Roman world and were Christianized by relating the third hour to Christ's crucifixion, the sixth to the darkness and the ninth to the piercing with the lance. Prayer at waking and before sleeping were adopted very early in imitation of Jewish practice, but the origins of midnight and cockcrow are uncertain.

SOCIAL LIFE

Christianity made its first impact in the cities and, while the rural areas of North Africa and Egypt were steadily penetrated in the third century, elsewhere it continued to preserve its initial urban character. In the towns its main strength lay in the lower and middle classes, with but a minority in the upper strata, but this minority was on the increase. There were so many rich members of the Alexandrian Church that Clement devoted a special sermon to the question *Quis dives salvetur?* Origen mentions 'not only rich men, but persons of rank and delicate and high-born ladies who receive the teachers of Christianity'.[1] Valerian directed his second rescript against Christian senators and *equites Romanes*,[2] while the Council of Elvira refers to Christian *duum viri* and *flamens*.[3] But it was not until the conversion of Constantine that the upper class as a whole began to look with favour on the new faith.

Entrance into the Church for the working man was however by no means an easy option since it frequently involved his giving up his previous means of livelihood. The *Apostolic Tradition* gives a list of prohibited trades which was repeated and amplified over the centuries:

> Inquiry shall likewise be made about the professions and trades of those who are brought to be admitted to the faith. If a man is a pander, he must desist or be rejected. If a man is a sculptor or painter, he must be charged not to make idols; if he does not desist he must be rejected. If a man is an actor or pantomimist, he must desist or be rejected. A teacher of young

children had best desist, but if he has no other occupation, he may be permitted to continue. A charioteer likewise, who races or frequents races, must desist or be rejected. A gladiator or a trainer of gladiators, or a huntsman or anyone connected with these shows, or a public official in charge of gladiatorial exhibitions must desist or be rejected. A heathen priest or anyone who tends idols must desist or be rejected. A soldier of the civil authority must be taught not to kill men and to refuse to do so if commanded, and to refuse to take an oath; if he is unwilling to comply, he must be rejected. A military commander or civic magistrate that wears the purple must resign or be rejected. If a catechumen or a believer seeks to become a soldier, they must be rejected, for they have despised God. A harlot or licentious man or one who has castrated himself, or any other who does things not to be named, must be rejected, for they are defiled. A magician must not even be brought for examination. An enchanter, an astrologer, a diviner, a soothsayer, a user of magic verses, a juggler, a mountebank, an amulet-maker must desist or be rejected. A concubine, who is a slave and has reared her children and has been faithful to her master alone, may become a hearer; but if she has failed in these matters she must be rejected. If a man has a concubine, he must desist and marry legally; if he is unwilling he must be rejected.[4]

The objections to these methods of earning a living arose largely from their inevitable connexion with either idolatry or immorality. But the Church's proscription naturally produced the reaction that to give up one's work would mean starvation, hence the debate of which Tertullian has recorded the arguments and counter-arguments. Those required to cease their previous trades appealed to Paul who had said, 'As each has been found, so let him persevere',[5] and 'that each one work with his own hands for a living'.[6] They declared that while they might make idols, they did not worship them, and they pleaded: 'I shall be in need . . . I shall have no food . . . provision must be made for children and posterity'.[7] Nevertheless the Church set its face against many professions, but at the same time it recognized its responsibility to provide help for those who thereby lost their income. So Cyprian insisted upon a certain actor discontinuing his art, but added: 'If such a one alleges poverty and the necessity of small means, his necessity can be assisted among the rest who are maintained by the support of the Church, if he be content, that is, with very frugal but innocent food'.[8]

Food, clothing and leisure

Cyprian's emphasis upon 'innocent food' typifies the attitude of the Church to nourishment and clothing. Christians were to eat to live and not live to eat; they were not to be subject to the 'Belly-demon', and while they might consume a little wine they were to beware of this 'Bacchic fuel'.[9]

Since Christianity is concerned with the whole of life, there were no minutiae of everyday living too insignificant to be outside consideration. Hence Clement could devote page after page to describing and condemning pagan luxury and lack of temperance and advocating frugality and a plain diet for the faithful, even listing the kinds of food they may eat, e.g. olives, herbs, milk, cheese, fruit, cooked foods without sauces, and a little meat but boiled rather than roast.[10]

The same condemnation of extravagance extended to clothes. Tertullian could trace female ornament back to the fallen angels.[11] Clement had no doubt that 'our life ought to be anything but a pageant',[12] and Cyprian regarded ostentation in dress as fit only for prostitutes.[13] Complicated hair-styles were not tolerated and Christian men were expected not to shave but to preserve their natural beards.[14]

Leisure activity was to be characterized by a similar restraint. There was to be no gambling or dice-playing,[15] instead Christians were to gather together for meditation or sit at home and read the scriptures[16] while the women spun their wool.[17] Amphitheatres and theatres were forbidden; riotous parties were to be shunned. In the world but not of it, the Christian was to bear the mark of the cross of Christ by his self-denial. While still a persecuted minority, the Church was enabled to preserve in large measure these rigorous standards, partly through outside pressure, but once the Church had been opened to the world, with the conversion of the emperor, a constant struggle to preserve the ascetic ideal began.

CHAPTER FIVE

FROM NICAEA TO CONSTANTINOPLE

The Background – Sources – Expansion and Development – Beliefs – Worship – Social Life

THE BACKGROUND

Pagan religion

IF THE CONVERSION of Constantine placed Christianity in a favourable position, and indeed the Church was the recipient of many material benefits and assistance from the emperor, this did not mean that paganism was at an end. Constantine himself retained the office of *Pontifex Maximus*, as did his successors down to 383, and he protected the freedom of worship of his pagan subjects. Such measures as he promulgated with reference to the cults, as his prohibition of magic and of private auguries in 318 and 320,[1] were rather a purging of paganism than evidence of a policy of repression. Constantine indeed had to take cognizance of the fact that at least half his subjects were non-Christian, many through indifference and others, particularly the aristocratic and senatorial families, being hostile out of loyalty to their Roman heritage.

The increasing spate of conversions, however, began to sway the balance and Constantine's sons, in particular Constantius, moved slowly into deliberate opposition, and by a law of 356 all temples were to be closed and all sacrifices discontinued.[2]

The pagan reaction under Julian

The accession of Julian in 361 gave paganism a renewed lease of life. Brought up and baptized as a Christian, in his early twenties Julian did not so much lapse into paganism as be converted to it, his mystical spirit eagerly embracing the teaching of the Neo-Platonists. He became a devotee of the Sun and was in due course initiated into the Eleusinian Mysteries and into the cult of Mithra. It was not until he had assumed the purple that he made open profession of his pagan faith and offered daily sacrifice to the gods.

Julian's first move was to raise all prohibitions against the ancient cultus and proclaim toleration for everyone,[3] since his aim, in the words of Jerome, was to 'employ a gentle violence which strove to win and not to drive'.[4] But if he did not persecute Christians directly, he did attack Christianity. He restricted the magistracy and the major government posts to pagans and restored the army to heathenism by a combined policy of pressure and gifts. He discontinued the official observance of Sunday and forbade daylight funerals. It was his educational policy however which was liable in time to prove the most effective.

Paganism and the old culture were in Julian's mind inseparably bound together, and the means of spreading that culture lay to hand in the schools, of which there was at least one in each city. Julian shrewdly perceived that every school was a potential centre for pagan propaganda and, further, that if he could cut off the Christians from the higher culture of the day he might effectively if gradually check the Christian faith. His first educational decree of 12th May 362 was conservative and merely confirmed the existing privileges of all teachers. His second decree of 17th June required all intending teachers to undergo an examination and secure the approval of the local municipal council. Finally, towards the end of the same year he issued a rescript that all engaged in public education should be pagans: 'it is monstrous for men any longer to teach what they do not believe sound'.[5] The effect of this was to close classical culture to believers, for as Christian professors resigned, e.g. Victorinus at Rome and Proaeresius at Athens, the schools became hot-beds of pagan teaching and Christians avoided them.

The paganism that Julian intended to substitute for the Christianity he had renounced owed much to the latter. He appreciated its institutional, its moral and its theological aspects. He therefore sought to create a pagan 'Church', and under himself as *Pontifex Maximus* he appointed high priests in every province, corresponding to the Christian bishop, and by making their tenure life-long superseded the old system whereby leading laymen performed priestly functions for a year only. Each village was to have its priest, thus paralleling the parochial organization of Christianity. Julian also sought to regulate their lives and conduct, insisting that they were to be charitable, grave and chaste, and that they were not to frequent theatres or taverns nor associate with jockeys, actors or dancers. They were provided with funds to distribute to the poor; some were organized in communities on the lines of the Christian monasteries; fasting was approved, a sermon was introduced into the acts of worship and a psalter of pagan hymns was issued.[6] Undoubtedly this was the most effective side of Julian's scheme. He saw that the weakness of the old religion lay in its lack of organization and this he provided, but his attempt to co-ordinate the disconnected elements of pagan belief into a coherent theology was less successful. He sought to combine the mystical oriental religions, the theology of the Greek Mysteries, the Neo-Platonic philosophy and each separate and national cult into a pagan mythology which would provide the historical basis of his religion. The result of his efforts was to replace the gods by abstractions which made no appeal to the popular mind. Yet in certain areas the pagan mob was not averse to making the most of the opportunity afforded by the emperor's favour. In several towns of Syria, Phoenicia and Arabia churches were sacked or profaned. Some martyrdoms took place, such as those of the priest Basil at Ancyra and of Mark, bishop of Arethusa.[7] But these were prompted by no religious zeal, even the philosophers stood aloof, so that Julian complained bitterly to Arsacius, high-priest of Galatia, 'that Hellenism does not succeed as we wish is owing to its professors'.[8]

While at Antioch in the winter of 362–3, Julian began a literary polemic against Christianity, seeking to discredit the monotheism and anthropomorphisms of the Old Testament, objecting to the faith as a novelty and denying the divinity of Jesus. His labours were in vain, for leaving Antioch to engage the Persians in battle he died from a spear-thrust on 26th June, and with him any realistic hopes of stemming the tide of the advancing Christian faith.

Manichaeism

The religions of ancient Rome were not the only rivals to Christianity in the fourth century. Manichaeism, whose origins lay in the teaching of the Persian Mani, born 216, was also in the field – a religion that was unashamedly syncretistic, as evidenced by its founder's own statement:

> The writings, wisdom, apocalypses, parables and psalms of all previous religions, gathered from all parts, have come together in my religion, in the wisdom that I have revealed. As one river mixes with another and forms one great stream, so also the ancient books have been united to my writings and there has thus been formed one great wisdom, to which nought can be compared that has been preached to any previous generation.[9]

Manichaeism was essentially dualistic, with roots in Gnosticism, and professed to explain the origin of evil by a conflict between light, which was identified with spirit, and darkness, which was identified with matter. Organized carefully, with travelling missionaries, deacons, presbyters, seventy-two bishops and twelve apostles with a thirteenth representing Mani as head of all, it was fired with a proselytizing zeal and spread rapidly. Mani acknowledged Jesus, Zoroaster and Buddha as his predecessors, with the major importance given to the first, and his system rivalled that of the Catholic Church and attracted such adherents as Julian and the young Augustine.

Philosophy

With its claim to provide universal knowledge Manichaeism, from one aspect, presented itself as a philosophy, but the philosophical system of the fourth century was Neo-Platonism. From the time of Iamblichus onwards – he died *c.* 330 – Neo-Platonism had two main concerns. First, it sought to provide paganism with a coherent theology based upon the works of Plato and the 'Chaldaean Oracles' which were said to have been revealed by the gods through Julianus the theurgist. Second, it elaborated and attempted to bring out the logical implications of Plotinus' teaching in order to reduce it to a rigid system.

While this was the content of fourth-century philosophical thought, the form in which it was popularized was that of the Second Sophistic School which represented a fusion of two previously distinct tendencies in Greek letters – the Attic and the Asianic. The former was purist in style and restrained in thought, the latter was romanticist and inclined to vivid imagery. The Second Sophistic, which emerged in the second century under Hadrian and was revived in the fourth, possessed the Attic purity in grammar and the Asianic exuberance in rhetoric. It was this School that provided the Cappadocian Fathers with their mode of presenting Christian theological thought.

The Empire

From the time when Constantine became undisputed master in 324, the empire enjoyed a period of internal peace. Although two of his sons – Constantine II (337–40) and Constans (337–50) – came into conflict, the cares of government were eventually shared amicably between Constans and Constantius (337–61). The principal threat to Roman stability came from beyond the frontiers, from the Persians, who brought Julian (361–3) to his death, and from the northern tribes. Single rule was exercised by Jovian (363–4) and the empire was again divided into East and West under Valentinianus I (364–75) and Valens (364–78) and later still under Gratian (375–83) and Theodosius (379–95). Indeed the main threat to the *pax Romana* came from the Church itself, which was rent by schisms and doctrinal strife.

Church and State

The peace of the Church transformed the relationship between the government and Christianity. Whereas previously the emperor had been the enemy of the Church, he now became its patron and protector so that henceforth the history of the Church is not something apart but inextricably bound up with society and with imperial policy.

Constantine's victory was ascribed by the Christians to the divine aid and the emperor was acclaimed as a new David by the historian Eusebius.[10] This interpretation of Constantine's role meant that he was regarded as a God-given ruler and that his authority was not limited to the secular sphere. So Constantine concerned himself with the affairs of the Church, acting to preserve its unity whenever he saw it threatened. He therefore took measures against the Donatists in North Africa, a rigorist group which had cut itself off from the main body of believers because of their lenient treatment of the lapsed under Diocletian. Similarly he intervened in the Arian controversy and himself summoned the Council of Nicaea in an attempt to bring it to an end. The Church was quite content that he should do these things, its unity with the State being close and amicable.

When in 340 the empire was divided between Constans in the West and Constantius in the East, the same relationship continued as under their father. It was, however, a somewhat anomalous situation. Constans was a supporter of the Nicene orthodoxy, as were the majority of western Christians, while Constantius was more favourably disposed towards the Arian cause, as were the majority of eastern Christians. When Constantius became sole emperor in 350, his western subjects were naturally less happy about his position, and those in the East, who supported Athanasius in his defence of Nicaea, were equally disturbed. The pressure of these contemporary circumstances therefore led to a changed conception of Church-State relations which found its clearest expression in a letter of Hosius of Cordova to Constantius when he was ordered to communicate with the Arians in 355:

> Intrude not yourself into ecclesiastical matters, neither give commands concerning them; but learn from us. God has put into your hands the kingdom; to us he has entrusted the affairs of his Church; and, as he who would steal the empire from you would resist the ordinance of God, so likewise fear on your part lest by taking upon yourself the government of the Church, you become guilty of a great offence. It is written, 'Render unto Caesar the things that are Caesar's, and unto God the things that are God's.' Neither, therefore, is it permitted unto us to exercise an earthly rule, nor have you, Sire, any authority to burn incense.[11]

The dualist theory could not be more plainly enunciated. The emperor is declared to be, under God, responsible for secular affairs and the bishop for matters ecclesiastical; Church and State are regarded as two distinct spheres. This dualism may be further illustrated from the Priscillianite controversy.

Priscillian was a Spanish cleric whose teaching, as far as can be gathered from the few documents that survive, was a compound of extreme asceticism and certain heterodox views concerning the Trinity and the Person of Christ. Although condemned, if not by name by implication, by a council at Saragossa in 380, he was consecrated bishop of Avila through the efforts of the increasing number of his followers. Under the leadership of Ithacius of Ossonuba, his opponents appealed to Gratian who issued a rescript in condemnation of 'pretended – bishops and Manichaeans'. Priscillian made his way to Italy and succeeded in having this repealed. This reversal of the previous verdict laid his chief accuser, Ithacius, open to the charge of being a disturber of the peace and he fled to Gaul. There, Gratian having been murdered in 383, Ithacius appealed to Maximus and a synod was held at Bordeaux in the following year. Priscillian refused to acknowledge its authority and appealed to the emperor. In 383 he was brought to trial at Trier, found guilty of magic and executed, it being apparent that, although the charge was a civil one, he had been condemned for heresy.

The close relation of Church and State is evident throughout this series of events, but opposition to the whole proceedings, on dualist grounds, was voiced by Martin of Tours. Being present at the imperial court at Trier, he first attempted to dissuade Ithacius from pressing his charges and then extracted a promise from Maximus that no blood would be shed, arguing that secular judges should not try ecclesiastical causes. When his pleas proved vain, he refused to communicate with the Ithacians, but at last consented to do so when Maximus agreed to countermand an order to round up Priscillian's followers in Spain. In these events the precedent was set for the later handing over of heretics to be executed by the secular power, and the opposing view of Martin, that Church and State should occupy themselves with their own affairs, is clearly stated.[12] But Martin's dualism, while commendable in its simplicity and certainly applicable where a pagan State and the Christian Church are in opposition, is scarcely adequate where there is a Christian ruler. In such circumstances the distinction between the separate spheres becomes blurred and this was especially so in the fourth century. Further, if the ruler be a member of the Church, he is subject to its discipline and therefore liable to be reproved for misconduct. Such action was to be taken by Ambrose in his dealings with Theodosius after the Council of Constantinople.

THE SOURCES

Both in quality and quantity the patristic literature that was produced during the one and a quarter centuries that separated the Council of Nicaea in 325 from that of Chalcedon in 451 represents the summit of early Christian thought. The names of Athanasius, the Cappadocian Fathers, Hilary of Poitiers, Cyril of Jerusalem, Ambrose and Augustine are amongst the most illustrious of Christian antiquity, and any adequate account of their lives and work would require volumes; instead a brief survey of their most important works must suffice to illustrate both the richness and the contents of these sources.

The first Church historian

To Eusebius of Caesarea belongs the distinction of being the 'Father of Ecclesiastical History'. Born *c.* 263, Eusebius fled under Diocletian to Egypt, only to be imprisoned there. Elected to the see of Caesarea in 313, he soon became involved in the Arian controversy. Lacking in theological insight, although otherwise a scholar of great eminence, he tended to favour Arius and, while concurring in the findings of Nicaea, supported Eusebius of Nicomedia in his opposition to Athanasius. A great admirer of Constantine, he died shortly after his hero in 339 or 340.

Eusebius' *Chronicle*, which was published *c.* 303, gives short surveys of the history of the ancient peoples and prepared him for his *Church History* which extended from the birth of Christ to the defeat of Licinius in 324. Incorporating much earlier material, to which reference has been constantly made above in outlining the life of the pre-Nicene Church, his work was apologetic in aim in that it sought to furnish proof that the Church had been favoured and guided by God to its final victory. Apologetics were also the motive for his *Preparation for the Gospel* and *Proof for the Gospel*, the former defending Christianity against the pagans and the latter against the Jews. Eusebius' *Martyrs of Palestine* and his *Life of Constantine* both contain valuable historical material, but he also engaged in biblical exegesis with his *Commentaries* on the Psalms and Isaiah, and doctrinal controversy with his *Against Marcellus*, whose reactionary theology was to prove a source of embarrassment to the Nicene party, including Athanasius, whom he supported.

Athanasius

The story of Athanasius' life is in effect the history of the Arian controversy, which will be described below. Born in 295, he assisted at

Nicaea as deacon and secretary to his bishop Alexander, whom he succeeded in 328. His unremitting struggle with the Arians, who were often supported by the secular power, involved him in five exiles and in extensive literary labour to support his theological convictions. He died in 373, too soon to witness the final eclipse of the heresy he had combated throughout his life.

No trace of the Arian dispute is to be found in his earliest extant work *Against the Heathen* (*c.* 318), which consists of two parts, the first being a refutation of pagan mythologies, and the second, *The Incarnation of the Word*, being the classical exposition of the doctrine of redemption, issued in a Short and Long Recension. His three discourses, *Against the Arians* (probably 358), defends the Nicene doctrine of the eternal generation of the Son from the Father and the unity of essence of the two persons, and discusses the biblical passages used by the Arians to support their position. Shortly before writing these orations, Athanasius composed his *Apology against the Arians* which incorporates the proceedings and decrees of previous councils and is therefore a primary historical source. His *Letters* include four to Serapion which are important for the doctrine of the Spirit.

Athanasius was also closely associated with the monastic movement, writing on various aspects of asceticism and producing a *Life of Antony*, *c.* 357, whereby he both created a new type of biography and contributed to the spread of the monastic ideal in the West, where it was widely read in a Latin translation.

The Cappadocian Fathers

In the East Athanasius' doctrinal position was strongly supported by the Cappadocian trio, Basil the Great (*c.* 330–79), Gregory of Nyssa (d. 394) his brother, and their friend Gregory of Nazianzus (*c.* 330–*c.* 390).

Basil was one of ten children of Macrina and a famous rhetorician of Neocaesarea in Pontus. Educated at his native Caesarea, Constantinople and finally Athens, where he became the life-long friend of Gregory of Nazianzus, he returned home *c.* 356. After practising as a rhetorician, he was baptized, and then made a tour of Egypt, Palestine, Syria and Mesopotamia to obtain first-hand knowledge of the ascetic movement. So impressed was he that he adopted that way of life, being joined in his retirement by Gregory *c.* 350, the two of them working on the *Philokalia*, an anthology of Origen's works, and the two *Rules*, which were to regulate future Greek monasticism. He left his seclusion *c.* 364 at the request of Eusebius of Caesarea and was made priest, succeeding the metropolitan in 370. From his consecration onwards, Basil was indefatigable in his efforts to overthrow Arianism and restore Christian unity, fearlessly withstanding the emperor Valens, writing to Damasus of Rome, and upholding the Nicene cause in his preaching and writing.

Already in 363–5 Basil had issued *Against Eunomius*, in which the consubstantiality of the three divine persons is maintained, and in 375 he wrote *On the Holy Spirit* to the same effect. Not a few of his many letters were concerned with doctrinal questions; others touch on ascetical matters which received fuller treatment in his *Ascetica*. His homilies and sermons include the nine *On the Hexameron* and a series *On the Psalms*.

Where Basil was the man of action, his friend Gregory of Nazianzus was the master of oratory. Brought up on the family estates near to the town of which his father was bishop and from which he derived his title, he received his further education at the two Caesareas, at Alexandria and Athens. Joining Basil in his monastic retirement in Pontus, he answered an appeal from his father for help in his diocese and in 362 was forcibly ordained priest, withdrawing to Pontus in protest but soon coming back to his father's aid. When Basil founded new sees to consolidate his influence as metropolitan, diminished by the partition of Cappadocia, he induced his reluctant friend to become bishop of Sasima. Gregory, however, never obtained possession of his see and continued to assist his father, until the latter's death in 374. A year later he withdrew to Seleucia in Isauria to pursue the contemplative life. His peace was terminated in 379 when the catholic Theodosius succeeded the Arian Valens, and the Christians of Constantinople sought Gregory's help to reorganize the affairs of the Church. His position there was not a happy one for the Arians were constantly stirring up trouble, but his sermons and the saintliness of his life gradually made a deep impression and in 381, at the opening of the second Ecumenical Council, he was designated bishop of the city. When his election was disputed, he retired to his father's old diocese and then returned to his family estate to engage in ascetical exercises and writing until his death *c.* 390.

Gregory's literary remains consist of orations, poems and letters. The first group includes a number of theological utterances and several liturgical sermons; the second some dogmatic verse and an autobiographical study, and the third are mainly of a personal character. Master of style though he was, Gregory was no original thinker; that role was reserved for Basil's brother, Gregory of Nyssa.

Gregory at first occupied the post of a reader in the Church, but under the influence of his namesake he embraced the ascetic way of life, only to be made bishop of Nyssa in Cappadocia upon the insistence of his brother in 371. Deposed by Arian pressure in 376, he was reinstated after the death of Valens, was appointed visitor of Pontus by a synod in

379, became metropolitan of Sebaste for a short period, attended the Council of Constantinople in 381 and died some thirteen years later.

Amongst Gregory's dogmatic writings four are of particular note. *Against Eunomius*, previously believed to be a single work, consists of four treatises which represent a most important refutation of Arianism. His *Antirrheticus adversus Apollinarem* is also one of the most important works treating of that Christological heresy. His large *Catechesis* is a compendium of Christian doctrine, while his understanding of the resurrection receives full treatment in his dialogue dedicated to his sister Macrina. Allegorical interpretation characterizes his exegetical treatises; his ascetical writings have justly earned him the title of 'the Father of Mysticism'; his sermons and letters cover a variety of subjects, doctrinal and social.

Cyril of Jerusalem

While Gregory's *Catechesis* represents theological profundity, Cyril of Jerusalem's *Catechetical Lectures* represent simple and practical instructions for those about to be baptized. Cyril was consecrated in 348 by the Arian metropolitan of Caesarea, Acacius, with whom he soon came into conflict. He was twice deposed and exiled by synodal decree (357, 360) and his third exile, at the hands of Valens, lasted eleven years until 378. He was present at Constantinople in 381 and died four years later. His lectures, delivered in 350, consist of an introductory discourse and eighteen addresses, taken down in shorthand by one of the listeners, and include an exposition of the successive articles of the Jerusalem creed. The five *Mystagogical Lectures* treat of baptism, confirmation and the eucharist, and are ascribed by some to Cyril's successor John – as a source of the liturgy in Jerusalem in the fourth century they are invaluable.

Hilary of Poitiers

The main flowering of western Latin theology was reserved for the immediate post-Constantinopolitan period; before then, although many short treatises by a number of writers, have been preserved, such as *Against the Donatists* by Optatus of Milevis, first published in 365 and revised twenty years later, only one author can claim real distinction, and that is Hilary of Poitiers.

Hilary, born of pagan parents and converted in his early manhood, became bishop of Poitiers in 350. He was consecrated at a time when the Arian storm was gathering in the West and he was soon to suffer from it, his resistance to the Arian Saturninus of Arles issuing in his exile to Asia in 356. He employed his stay of three years to such good effect in defending and propagating the Nicene orthodoxy that the Arians eventually obtained his recall as 'the mischief-maker of the East'. Upon his return, he secured the condemnation of Saturninus in 361, and his influence became so great that it was felt even in Italy, whither he went in 364 to Milan to examine the orthodoxy of its bishop, Auxentius. Two years later Hilary died and has since been styled 'the Athanasius of the West', for his unceasing activities against the Arian heresy.

Hilary was a daring speculator in his theological thinking, as evidenced by his *On the Trinity*; he was too a pioneer, in that his *Commentary on Matthew* was the first of its kind in the West, while he was also the first Latin writer to compose hymns. *On the Synods* is an important source in that it includes a discussion of the various creeds issued by the several councils and a careful definition of all the disputed terms, a task he was well equipped to perform in that he not only knew Latin but was conversant with Greek.

Syrian writers

The oldest Syrian Church Father was Aphraates who has left twenty-three treatises, on ascetical subjects, written 337–45. But the classic writer of the Syrian Church was Ephraem, who was born at Nisibis *c.* 306, was made deacon in his early thirties, remaining one all his life, and withdrew before the Persians in 363 to settle at Edessa, dying there in 373. Lack of a critical edition of his works has prevented the examination they demand, but he left numerous treatises, orations and hymns.

Heretical writers

As is to be expected, the writings of orthodoxy have been preserved with greater care than those that were deemed heretical. Of Arius there are only three letters and a fragment of his *Banquet*, a long rhapsody of verse and prose. Of Marcellus there is a profession of faith, but not even the title of his treatise against Asterius, which led to his condemnation as a Sabellian, is known. That any of the dogmatic treatises of Apollinaris remain is due to the fact that they were mistakenly included in the works of orthodox writers, but few of them are of importance and, as is the case with the majority of those whom the Church condemned, his teaching is mainly to be ascertained from those works that attacked it.

Monastic writings

Reference has already been made to a number of ascetical treatises, e.g. by Basil and by Gregory of Nyssa, which convey something of the spirituality nurtured in the fourth century monastic movement. Few original documents, however, remain from the pens of the founders, apart from the very important *Rule of Pachomius*, which was to influence all subsequent monastic legislation, and a few letters from leading ascetics. Knowledge is derived rather from its admirers, such as Athanasius with his *Life of Antony*, Palladius with his *Lausiac History* and the *Sayings of the Fathers* compiled at the end of the fifth century.

Church Orders and liturgical documents

The class of Church Orders, of which a second-century example is the *Didache* and third-century one the *Didascalia*, is represented in the fourth by the *Apostolic Constitutions*. Its first six books are identical with the *Didascalia*, apart from alterations due to changed conditions. The first half of its seventh book is an enlargement of the *Didache*, and its second half a series of instructions on the teaching of catechumens and on baptism. The eighth book, which utilizes the *Apostolic Tradition* as a basis, contains the whole liturgy of a mass, together with regulations concerning confessors, virgins, widows, exorcists, presbyters, etc., and the last chapter is the eighty-five *Apostolic Canons*. The product of an Arian in Syria or Constantinople *c.* 380, this document preserves the largest collection of legislative and liturgical material from the early centuries of the Church's history.

Further liturgical material, in the form of prayers, is contained in the *Euchologion* of Serapion, bishop of Thmuis, *c.* 350. Eighteen of the prayers are connected with the eucharist, seven with baptism and confirmation, three with ordination and two with the blessing of oil and funerals. Knowledge of the Egyptian worship may also be obtained from the sixth-century *Der Balizeh* papyrus, which probably represents fourth-century practice, while a papyrus fragment of the Anaphora of St Mark would seem to describe the service used at the time of Athanasius.

EXPANSION AND DEVELOPMENT

The notable expansion of Christianity in the latter half of the third century continued apace in the fourth, favoured, as it now was, by Constantine and his successors. The efforts of the first Christian emperor were directed not only towards his own family, inspired by the hope of ensuring the dominion of his house and the stability of his realm with the help of his God, but also to his pagan subjects in general. Indeed he was prepared to style himself as bishop of those outside the Church,[1] and in this capacity he communicated with Sapor of Persia, saying: 'I am delighted to hear that the finest districts in Persia are also adorned with the presence of Christians'.[2] His favour however could be a mixed blessing and even Eusebius was led to deplore the number of interested conversions attendant upon it.[3] Nor did Constantine's personal faith immediately affect the nobility; the synthesis of Christianity and classical culture was still in its infancy and its adherents remained largely members of the middle and lower classes, as evidenced, for example, by the situation at Cyzicus under Julian. The town council, composed of the local gentry, sent a delegation to ask the emperor to order the restoration of the temples destroyed by the bishop Eleusis with the support of the workers in the mint and in the clothing factory.[4] In the East generally however, where civil government was coming to be based upon service and not upon birth, the social change that was then in process brought middle-class Christian men to the fore, and few of the leaders were pagan. But in the West the senate retained its ancient family composition much longer and their antagonism to Christianity was to reach its climax in the last decades of the century.

The Church too, except in North Africa and Egypt, was still mainly urban in character, the *pagani* or countryfolk remaining indifferent. Hence the efforts of a Martin of Tours to spread the faith outside the city walls. Martin was a Danubian peasant, born in 316, who after service in the army was converted to Christianity and eventually attached himself to Hilary of Poitiers, establishing the earliest monastic establishment in Gaul. In 372 he was consecrated bishop of Tours, then probably a place of only a few thousand inhabitants. Christianity appears to have been restricted chiefly to the city itself and Martin became an active and energetic missionary to the whole district. He led his monks in preaching, in destroying temples and in baptizing. He even extended his work to Auvergne, Paris, Saintonge and Vienne, so that the faith penetrated into areas which had hitherto scarcely heard of the gospel.[5] His efforts were seconded by his friend Vitricius of Rouen who evangelized the semi-nomads of the Flemish plain. Evidence of steady progress in similar areas comes from other parts of the empire, where it was sometimes the result not of deliberate policy but of seizing opportunities when presented. Thus Eulogius and Protogenes, exiled by Valens to Antinoe in the Thebaid, discovered that the population was mainly heathen and they thereupon devoted themselves to missionary work.[6] Similarly some monks, sent to an island in the marshes by Lucius, the Arian who attempted to seize the bishopric of Alexandria upon the death of Athanasius in 373, proceeded to convert the heathen inhabitants.[7] It was in ways such as these that Christianity secured a foothold outside the towns and so was better prepared to withstand the later shock of the barbarian invasions.

Some of the barbarians however were already converted before their entry into the empire. A tribe of Saracens in North Arabia, ruled by a Queen Mavia, was converted *c.* 374 and received the monk Moses as their bishop.[8] The Goths, established on the north bank of the Danube in the third century, heard of Christianity through the prisoners brought back from Cappadocia, and Theophilus of 'Gothia' attended Nicaea. Besides these Catholic Christians, there was also an Audian group, founded by Audius, a rigorist and schismatic, who had been exiled by Constantine to Scythia where his followers were ardent missionaries with monasteries that were models of religious discipline.[9] Many of them sought refuge in Mesopotamia in consequence of the persecution that followed the Gothic war of Valens *c.* 370. The third division of Gothic Christians, which was also to suffer persecution, was Arian and owed its creation to the labours of Ulfilas. Ulfilas was born about 311 among the already converted Goths and was consecrated bishop in 341 by Eusebius of Nicomedia. Seeking to evangelize his own people, he created a Gothic alphabet and translated the scriptures into his own language, winning many of the Visigoths to this form of Christianity.[10]

In Armenia, already officially Christian through the labours of Gregory the Illiminator, the fourth century was a period of quarrels between the Catholicos or head of the Church and the ruling house, as the former sought to reform the faith and reprimanded successive rulers for their disorderly lives. Under Nerses, who became patriarch in 364, the reformation progressed until he was poisoned by King Pap after ten years. Complete reformation of this Christian form of anti-Zoroastrianism had to await the work of Nerses' son, Chahak the Great.[11] In part the Armenian profession of Christianity was anti-Persian, where the ruling house remained faithful to the teachings of Zoroaster, and similarly the Persian attack on Christianity was anti-Roman, the Church being regarded as seeking to propagate a foreign religion belonging to the empire. From 338 to 383 Christianity was constantly afflicted, peace coming only with the end of the war with Rome.

Still further afield, beyond the boundaries of the empire, Christianity steadily advanced in the north into Georgia, in the south-east into Arabia and in the south as far as Abyssinia. The records of the last tell how a certain Tyrian philosopher named Meropius set off on a voyage down the Red Sea, accompanied by two young relatives. Touching at an African port for supplies, the whole ship's company was massacred except for the two youths. One of them, Aedisius, was made the king's cup-bearer, and the other, Frumentius, was entrusted with the care of the royal records. The latter, having acquired a position of some importance, undertook the spiritual care of Christian merchants visiting the city and built a church for them. Eventually he was allowed to go to Alexandria, *c.* 355, where Athanasius consecrated him bishop. News of this reached Constantius, who wrote to the prince of Axum bidding him send Frumentius back to Alexandria to receive better instruction from the Arian George. The bearer of this letter, Theophilus, was instrumental in furthering the spread of the gospel in Arabia, since he built three churches, one at Safar, one at Aden and a third at Ormuz near the entrance to the Persian Gulf. He even took the opportunity to visit his native Ceylon, where he found Christian congregations in existence.[12]

Despite the steady progression, within the empire much work remained to be done if the whole population was to be won for Christ, and that this was not achieved more speedily was in part the result of schism and doctrinal disputes that inevitably hindered the Church's expansion.

The Melitian schism

Two schisms arose out of the last Diocletian persecution: the first, that was the less serious threat to the unity of the Church, was the Melitian in Egypt; the second, which was to last for over a century, was the Donatist in North Africa.

In 305 Melitius, bishop of Lycopolis in Upper Egypt, proceeded to ordain clergy in dioceses other than his own and to seek the support of the presbyters of Alexandria during the absence of their bishop, Peter, who was in hiding as a consequence of the Diocletian persecution. It is possible that Melitius was prompted by a desire to ensure the continued life of the Church in the emergency, but more probable that he acted from personal ambition to achieve pre-eminence over the metropolitan authority of Alexandria. To this motive he added further, like Novatian before him, the rigorist plea when in 306 Peter issued an encyclical specifying graded penances for the lapsed. He was deposed by a synod at Alexandria, but his condemnation to the mines brought him the renown of a confessor, and upon his release in 311 he consecrated a number of bishops, so that by 325 his 'church' had twenty-eight of them.[13]

The Melitians seriously compromised their position when they joined the Arians against Athanasius and to discredit him brought forward certain charges in 331. They asserted that Athanasius had sent one of his presbyters to stop the services conducted by a certain Ischyras, that this envoy had found him in church celebrating the eucharist, had thrown down the altar, smashed the chalice and burnt the church-books, thus committing an act of sacrilege.[14] Athanasius was able to prove that Ischyras was not in orders, that on the occasion in question he was ill in bed and that there was not a single chalice in the village. Equally unfounded was the further accusation that Athanasius had murdered a Melitian bishop, Arsenius, and had cut off his hand for magical purposes – the hand being produced as an exhibit. Athanasius was able to produce Arsenius alive and unmaimed.[15] Such conduct and their Arian alliance alienated most Egyptians from the Melitians, especially as the monks, who were beginning to abound and were the objects of general admiration, were in the main orthodox and staunch supporters of the Nicene party. Nevertheless Melitianism managed to survive into the fifth century, although it at no time constituted a serious threat to Church unity.

The Donatist schism

Although the Donatist schism began with the consecration of Majorinus in 312 as bishop of Carthage in opposition to Caecilian, its origins are to be found in the reaction to Diocletian's rescript of 24th February 303, which required all sacred books to be handed over to the civil authorities. Some had complied quite readily; others had prevaricated, handing over either heretical works – such was the case with Mensurius of Carthage – or part of their library. The rigorist attitude to such conduct was to affirm that the *traditores* or handers-over were no longer members of the Church and that, if they were clergy, they had no right to exercise their former authority. This was first given expression at a small council of Numidian bishops who met at Cirta under the presidency of Secundus of Tigisis to consecrate a certain Silvanus. Secundus opened the proceedings by inquiring into the fitness of the assembled bishops, six of whom were charged as *traditores* and four admitted their guilt. One of the accused, however, Pupurius of Limata, counterattacked with a similar charge against the president and threatened to murder anyone who might oppose him. It was deemed politic to pursue the matter no further, and Silvanus, despite the protests of the local church, was duly consecrated.[16] Nevertheless sufficient had been said to make it plain that the question of traditor-bishops was likely to be a difficult one and matters came to a head with the death of Mensurius in 311.

Caecilian, Mensurius' leading deacon, was consecrated as his successor but immediately ran into opposition. The rigorists regarded him with disfavour both because he had supported Mensurius in a lenient policy towards the lapsed and because he was suspected of being unsympathetic in his treatment of certain confessors. They therefore invited Secundus to intervene and he came post-haste to Carthage with seventy Numidian bishops. They condemned Caecilian on the grounds that he had been consecrated by a *traditor*, Felix of Aptunga, and they elected a reader, Majorinus, in his stead. They then sent embassies announcing Majorinus' appointment to Rome, Spain and Gaul, and letters reporting their decisions to the African provinces. So the schism was inaugurated, Majorinus being soon succeeded by Donatus from whom the sect took its name.[17]

The next stage in the controversy began with the emperor's action, as patron and not as persecutor. Constantine ordered the restoration of all churches and lands recently confiscated and declared the clergy exempt from municipal levies. This was applied only to Caecilian and those in communion with him. The Donatists had no alternative than to appeal against this and asked that some Gallican bishops, who might be presumed to be neutral, should consider the matter.[18] The question was submitted to no less than five official investigations within the space of the next seven years 313–20. In October 313 a synod met at Rome and pronounced in favour of Caecilian.[19] The second enquiry was held in Carthage itself in February 314, when the allegations against Felix of Aptunga were examined and shown to have no substance.[20] The Donatists nevertheless appealed again to the emperor who summoned a council to Arles, where a representative gathering of western bishops met in August 314. Caecilian was once more vindicated and canon 13 recognized the validity of ordinations by a bishop even if he were a *traditor*, on the grounds that the character of the minister does not affect the essence of a sacrament. Despite these three adverse verdicts, the Donatists approached the emperor again, only to have Caecilian declared blameless at Milan in 316,[21] whereupon Constantine ordered the banishment of all the disaffected and the confiscation of their churches.[22] A further investigation at Thamugadi in 320 established that Silvanus, who had assisted in the consecration of Majorinus, was himself a *traditor*.[23] But Constantine was becoming weary of the wrangle and the following year he recalled his sentence of exile, leaving the case 'to the judgement of God'.[24] The period of toleration that followed, 321–47, only gave the Donatists the opportunity to grow from strength to strength, so that by the middle of the century they numbered as many as three hundred bishops.

In 347, in an attempt to reunite Catholic and Donatist, Constans sent two envoys to Africa, Paul and Macarius. When however they sought to enter Numidia, they were met with such hostility that they had to call troops to their aid. Force was met with force and Donatus of Bagi summoned the Circumcellions to assist him.[25] These Circumcellions, who were so named because they dwelt 'around the shrines' (*circum cellas*) living off the gifts of the worshippers, were peasants actuated by religious zeal and economic grievances. Wielding their clubs or 'Israels', they terrorized the countryside and were alternately favoured and disfavoured by the Donatist leaders depending upon the latters' need of their armed support. The battle with Macarius and his men went against them and the result was a policy of repression which continued until the accession of Julian in 361. His edict of toleration gave the Donatists an opportunity to bid for power and they rose again on a wave of popular religious fury. Their new leader Parmenian was opposed to violence, but in 372 the Donatists as a whole supported Firmus, a chieftain of the Jubaleni clan, in his revolt against the imperial authorities, and they suffered further repressive measures as a consequence, when the rebellion failed three years later. Yet they soon managed to reassert themselves and achieved a measure of predominance which was to continue until the efforts of Augustine against them at the turn of the century. Donatism was indeed a running sore in the side of the African Church, but it was confined to one area. Arianism set the whole of the empire afire, disrupting the Church's life at all levels.

Arianism – its origins

Arius was born in Libya, and after a theological education, possibly at the feet of Lucian of Antioch, was made deacon by Peter of Alexandria (300–311), only to be excommunicated for his association with the Melitians. He was restored under Achillas (311–12) and advanced to the priesthood in charge of the church of Baucalis. Attracting many adherents, Arius made a considerable impression by his teaching, a report of which was eventually given to his bishop Alexander. Deriving his ideas partly from Lucian and adopting the subordinationist elements in the thought of Origen, Arius began from the uniqueness of God, who is alone self-existent and immutable, and asserted that the Son cannot be God, since he derives his being from the Father, is mutable, as shown by the Gospels, and cannot have communicated to him the unique Godhead. He was prepared to say that 'the Son has a beginning',[26] that 'prior to his generation he did not exist',[27] and that 'there was when he was not', so that consequently 'he is called God in name only'.[28]

When, in August 323, Alexander examined his teaching, he readily appreciated that it reduced the Word to a demi-god, denied his true divinity and made him a creature. Arius then wrote to Eusebius of Caesarea to seek his support, not without good reason for the Church historian, also an heir to Origen's subordinationism, considered that the 'Father is prior to and pre-exists the Son'.[29] Arius further communicated with Eusebius of Nicomedia, a statesman-bishop who had the ear of Constantinia, the sister of Constantine and wife of Licinius. In September a synod of Alexandrian clergy condemned Arius' views, while another in Palestine obtained an undertaking from the Arians that they would refrain from public disputation. Alexander accepted this, but in October at a meeting in Bithynia under Eusebius of Nicomedia it was declared that the dissidents should be admitted to communion, and Alexander replied with a provincial synod in March 324 which anathematized the Arians. In September Arius himself rejected the uneasy peace, so that two months later the emperor decided to intervene, sending Hosius of Cordova as his envoy. Hosius satisfied himself of the justice of Alexander's position and in February 325 Arius was condemned by a synod at Antioch, although Eusebius of Caesarea refused to concur. The emperor forthwith determined to summon a general council to restore the threatened unity of the Church, and invited all bishops to Nicaea, placing the *cursus publicus* at their disposal for travel.[30]

The Council of Nicaea

On 20th May 325 the first ecumenical council assembled and the proceedings were opened by the emperor in person.[31] After discussion, Arius and his errors were condemned. A creed was then agreed upon which included the affirmation that the Son was of one substance (*homoousion*) with the Father, an unscriptural term that was held to express the true Christian belief and was strongly supported by Hosius and the Western bishops. To the creed was appended an anathema which rejected Arian teaching in very clear terms:

> As for those who say: 'There was a time when he was not', and 'before he was begotten he was not', and 'he was made from that which was not, or from another hypostasis or substance', or 'the Son of God is created, changeable and mutable', these the Catholic Church anathematizes'.[32]

This was the main concern of the Council, although it did not disperse until it had given consideration to the Melitian schism and to the date of Easter and had promulgated twenty disciplinary canons.

From Nicaea to Tyre

Although the controversy seemed to have been brought to an end by the findings of the council and the banishment of Arius to Illyricum, it was to continue for nearly half a century. The first stage, which centred in persons, lasted from 325 to 337 when Constantine died. During this period the Arian leaders sought by intrigue to engineer their own recall from exile and the banishment of their opponents. So in 328 Eusebius of Nicomedia was reinstated, while Eustathius of Antioch, a staunch supporter of Nicaea, was deposed.[33] Next, united with the Melitians, the Arians turned upon Athanasius, who had become bishop of Alexandria in 328, and a series of false charges were brought to discredit him. Although Athanasius was able to clear himself, Arius was recalled in 335 and in the same year a synod at Tyre, packed with Athanasius' opponents, ordered his deposition and secured the support of the emperor who banished him to Treves.

To the death of Constans

Upon Constantine's death, Athanasius was allowed to return to his see, but within two years he had been ousted by his irregularly consecrated rival, the Arian Gregory.[34] Athanasius withdrew to Rome and was exonerated of all charges by a synod under Julius in 340.[35]

The second stage of the controversy embraced the period of the joint rule to 350 of Constans in the West and Constantius in the East, the latter being sympathetic towards the Arians and the former to the Nicenes. The Arian policy was now to have the Nicene statement of faith replaced by another formulary, omitting the *homoousion*, and in this they were at one with the general body of eastern opinion, which was essentially conservative and, while accepting the Nicene condemnation of Arianism, disliked the term because it was unscriptural. This general consensus was expressed in the opening words of the encyclical drawn up at the Council of the Dedication at Antioch in 341:

> We are not followers of Arius: how, being bishops, could we bring ourselves to follow a priest? We have no other faith than that which has been transmitted from the beginning.[36]

The assembled bishops agreed upon a doctrinal formula, the so-called Second Creed of Antioch,[37] a rambling document which omitted the *homoousion* but was sufficiently orthodox to be acceptable to Hilary of Poitiers.[38]

It was at this point that Constans was induced to intervene under pressure from the western bishops, and he agreed to persuade his brother to call a general council in an attempt to close the growing rift between East and West. The council met at Sardica in 342, but the eastern representatives soon withdrew as they would not allow Athanasius to take part in a synod at which his own case was to be considered.[39] The westerns proclaimed Athanasius innocent and excommunicated the intruding eastern bishops, such as Gregory at Alexandria, but since these decisions were unacceptable to the orientals the council failed of its purpose and indeed only widened the breach. An uneasy equilibrium prevailed; embassies passed to and fro between East and West; some concessions were made: Athanasius was prepared to dissociate himself from Marcellus of Ancyra, an ardent Nicene but also a Sabellian, and the West concurred in the condemnation of Photinus of Sirmium, a disciple of Marcellus. In 346, Gregory having died, Constantius allowed Athanasius to return to his diocese, but the death of Constans, four years later, removed the restraining influence upon Constantius who, having become sole ruler, had no one to hinder the expression of his pro-Arian sympathies.

Constantius as sole ruler

The third stage of the controversy may be divided into two halves: the first, 350–6, witnessing the re-establishment of Arianism, the second, 357–61, its apparent triumph but inner disintegration. The West, under Constans, had hitherto remained firmly Nicene, but once Constantius was in command he moved steadily and relentlessly to bring the West to heel and to the acceptance of Arianism. In 353 at Arles the Gallican bishops were forced to sign a condemnation of Athanasius;[40] in 355 at Milan this condemnation was renewed and those who refused to assent, namely Lucifer of Cagliari, Eusebius of Vercelli and Dionysius of Milan, were exiled.[41] Of the outstanding champions of orthodoxy, there remained but four: Hilary, Liberius and Hosius in the West, and Athanasius in the East; each one of these was successively dealt with by the emperor.

Liberius, who had now been bishop of Rome for three years, was summoned to the court at Milan where he was required to subscribe against Athanasius and to communicate with the Arians on pain of exile. He refused and was banished to Beroea in Thrace.[42] Hosius was next so harried that, while refusing to repudiate Athanasius, he did communicate with the Arian party – an act he revoked before his death.[43] In 356 a council at Béziers deposed Hilary who, together with Rhodanius, bishop of Toulouse, was exiled to Asia.[44] The moment had now come to proceed against Athanasius in person. Already in 355 an imperial notary, named Diogenes, had tried to provoke a disturbance against him, but without success.[45] In January 356, the duke Syrianus arrived in Alexandria with a large contingent of troops; on the night of 8th February he invested the church of St Theonas where Athanasius was presiding at a vigil. The bishop was forced to flee and took refuge with the desert monks, remaining among them for six years.[46] Within twelve months a successor had been appointed in the person of George of Cappadocia, who unleashed a persecution against the supporters of Athanasius throughout Egypt. Arianism was everywhere triumphant, but now began the period of its inner collapse.

Arian divisions

By the mid-fifties Arianism had divided into three main groups. There were the real Arians, who differed from their predecessors in being frank rather than evasive and flatly declared that the Son is 'unlike' (*anomoios*) the Father. These Anomoeans were led by Aetius and Eunomius. The middle-of-the-road party, under Basil of Ancyra, were the Homoeousians, who asserted that the Son is 'of similar substance' (*homoiousios*) to the Father. Finally, there were the Homoeans, with Acacius at their head, who affirmed that the Son is 'like' (*homoios*) the Father.

The extreme Anomoeans succeeded in having their views endorsed at Sirmium in 357, and while their creed, condemned by Hilary as 'the blasphemy',[47] does not use the word 'unlike', it rejects both the *homoousion* and the *homoiousion* and stresses the Son's subordination to the Father. This document was received with general abhorrence; although Hosius had been forced to sign it, the West had no doubts as to its heretical nature, while in the East the conservatives at last perceived that Arianism, in its extreme form, reduced the Son of God to the rank of a creature and they would have none of it.

Basil of Ancyra gathered a council in his episcopal city and the assembled bishops issued a joint letter condemning Anomoeanism at length.[48] Indeed the emperor Constantius was won over to the Homoeousian position and proceeded to exile Aetius and Eunomius.[49] Both Hilary and Athanasius approved of the encyclical letter, realizing that Basil of Ancyra and his associates had moved much closer to orthodoxy. But it was not the turn of the Homoeans to gain the ascendancy.

The Homoeousians, encouraged by the attitude of the Nicene party, believed that the time was opportune to re-establish unity and to this end persuaded Constantius to call a general council. The Anomoeans, realizing that this might result in a coalition of the Semi-Arians and the orthodox, were able to arrange for the council to meet in two groups – the western bishops at Rimini and the easterns at Seleucia.[50] Further, knowing that a statement of faith would probably be issued, they arranged a preliminary committee meeting in the emperor's presence at which a formulary was produced to be a basis for discussion and possible approval. This was intended to be an ambiguous statement that would not harm the Anomoeans and yet would satisfy the emperor and the Semi-Arians. This 'Dated Creed', so-called because of the elaborate dating prefixed to it,[51] was mainly Homoean, affirming that the Son is 'like the Father who begat him'; but it appealed to the Anomoeans in that it condemned the use of *ousia*.

The council of Rimini opened at the beginning of the summer of 359, the council of Seleucia a little later in September. The majority of the western bishops refused to accept the Dated Creed and approved that of Nicaea,[52] while the easterns endorsed the creed of the Dedication Council of Antioch.[53] Each session then sent a deputation to wait upon Constantius and communicate their decisions to him. He however, by a combination of brow-beating and threats, induced the delegates to accept the Dated Creed, somewhat modified, so that the outcome was the confusion of the Homoeousians and the acceptance of a Homoean statement as the standard of orthodox belief. The Homoeans, under Acacius, followed up their success by packing the council of Constantinople, 360, which ratified the amended Dated Creed and deposed the leading Homoeousians.[54] The triumph of the Homoeans thus seemed assured, but political events, and in particular the death of Constantius, were soon to give a new turn to religious matters.

The Decline of Arianism

The toleration granted by Julian upon his accession allowed the exiled Nicene bishops to return to their sees. A series of local councils at Alexandria, in Italy,[55] Gaul and Spain,[56] endorsed the Nicene Creed, and Julian's anti-Christian policy served as a spur to close the ranks. But after the short-lived Jovinian, there came the elevation of Valentinian and Valens in 364, the one a Catholic in the West, the other a follower of the policy of Constantius in the East. Valentinian hesitated to cause unrest by a ruthless ejection of all Arian bishops, so that many, e.g. Auxentius of Milan, continued to remain in their sees. Valens was at first held back by the revolt of Procopius and the outbreak of the Gothic wars. Although he opposed the Homoeousians, condemning their proceedings at Lampsacus and refusing to allow them to meet at Tarsus,[57] he took no violent action. Despite an edict of 365 ordering cities to send away those bishops deposed by Constantius and restored under Julian,[58] Valens left the Church largely to itself, but little attempt was made to profit from this and indeed further divisions revealed themselves.

In Egypt the Tropici declared that the Holy Spirit is the creature of the Son. Derived from the Anomoeans and influenced by Aetius and Eunomius, these Pneumatomachi carried Arianism to its logical conclusion by excluding both Son and Spirit from the Godhead.[59] A denial of the divinity of the Spirit was also a prominent feature of the teaching of the Macedonians, such as Eustathius of Sebaste, Eleusis of Cyzicus and Marathonius,[60] all Homoeousian in origin and probably distinct from the Tropici.

Towards the end of 369 Valens returned to Constantinople with the Gothic threat all but ended. He immediately put in hand what amounted to a persecution of the Nicenes and others who would not accept unity on the basis of the Rimini-Constantinople creed. 'Banishments, expulsions, confiscations' are the words used by Gregory of Nazianzus to describe what took place.[61] Throughout Cappadocia, Syria and Egypt the pressure was inexorable, but the Goths brought relief when in 376 they once more raised their standards with such success that two years later they overwhelmed the Roman legions, killing Valens in the engagement. Deprived of official protection Arianism, in any of its forms, was soon to be eclipsed within the empire.

The year 378 was decisive for the future of orthodoxy. Not only did it mark the death of Valens but it was also the time when Gratian, hitherto indifferent to religious questions, came under the influence of Ambrose, the successor in 373 of the Arian Auxentius at Milan. Gratian was to take decisive action on behalf of the Nicene faith and to be seconded in the East by Theodosius, whom he associated with himself as ruler in the January of the year following. By an edict issued from Milan on 3rd August 379, Gratian proscribed all heresy, while Theodosius promulgated a similar law on 27th February 380 from Thessalonica.[62] Then in May 381 the second Ecumenical Council met in Constantinople and adopted a statement of faith, the 'Nicene' Creed, anathematized all heresies, and condemned Sabellianism, Eunomianism and Pneumatomachianism. The work of the council was furthered by other gatherings at Aquileia and Rome. Arianism was now crushed and its surviving adherents, split into rival groups, formed only obscure and powerless sects. It was only among the nations beyond the frontiers that it continued to exercise any influence.

The Meletian and Luciferian schisms

If the events of 381–2 brought the long-drawn-out Arian controversy to an end, they did not settle all the problems that had arisen during the course of it. Indeed the Meletian schism at Antioch, which was directly produced by it, was to continue until 414 and similarly the Luciferian schism was to persist into the early fifth century.

For the origins of the Meletian schism one must return to the year 328 when Eustathius of Antioch, a strong supporter of Nicaea, was deposed and banished by means of a court intrigue. His immediate successors, Euphronius and Flacillus (332–42) were not openly heretical, but were suspected to be such,[63] and a small group, under the presbyter Paulinus, refused to recognize them. About 360 Meletius was consecrated to the see and, although of Semi-Arian background, upheld the orthodox cause, so that he was eventually deposed and Euzoius established in his place.[64] The majority of the orthodox remained faithful to Meletius, but Paulinus' group, knowing of his Semi-Arian background, remained isolated.

Upon Julian's accession Meletius returned and in 362 a synod at Alexandria directed Paulinus and his flock to offer their communion to Meletius, as long as he would anathematize Arius and profess the Nicene faith. Meanwhile Lucifer arrived at Antioch and proceeded to consecrate Paulinus as bishop.[65] Athanasius had perforce to choose between Paulinus and Meletius and, hearing that the latter had entered into relations with the Homoeans, again recognized Paulinus. There were thus three bishops of Antioch: Euzoius accepted by the heretics, Paulinus accepted by Egypt and the West, and Meletius accepted by the remainder of the orthodox East.

In 378 Euzoius died and no successor was appointed, so that by 381 it seemed to the local clergy that the opportunity was favourable to bring the schism to an end, and they undertook to advance no claim to the bishopric on the death of either Meletius or Paulinus but to accept the survivor. Unfortunately when Meletius did die, while attending the Council of Constantinople, the other delegates refused to acknowledge Paulinus on the grounds that this would mean a capitulation to the West which persisted in recognizing him, and they elected Flavian. In 388 Paulinus died, but as he had previously consecrated one Evagrius to succeed him, the schism continued: Egypt and the West accepting him and the East in general acknowledging Flavian.[66]

In 391 both Flavian and Evagrius were summoned to the synod of Capua; the former however excused himself on account of his age and the latter, though present, was unable to press his case, it being referred to the jurisdiction of Theophilus of Alexandria. Flavian, who saw in this a move that might be prejudicial to himself, sought to have the matter settled through his influence at court and succeeded in securing his position. Evagrius was condemned, only to die shortly afterwards.[67] Flavian was then accepted by Theophilus and through him communion was re-established between Antioch and Rome. The strict Catholic group continued, bishopless, until it was finally reconciled in 414.

This Antiochene schism had been hindered not helped by Lucifer of Cagliari in Sardinia, who was himself the author of yet another schism. Lucifer would not agree to the mild treatment afforded to the returning

Arians, and renounced communion, on these grounds, with Athanasius.[68] Although he died in 371, his rigorist followers continued their isolation, being even more fanatical than their leader.

Monasticism

The doctrines of the Fathers are despised, the speculations of innovators hold sway in the Church . . . the wisdom of this world has the place of honour, having dispossessed the boasting of the Cross. The shepherds are driven out, in their place grievous wolves are brought in which harry the flock. Houses of prayer have none to assemble in them; the deserts are full of mourners.[69]

It was with these bitter words that Basil described the situation during his episcopate when the final overthrow of Arianism still lay in the future. He deplored the lack of respect for traditional Christian belief; he condemned the 'speculations of the innovators', i.e. of the Arians; he lamented the expulsion of orthodox bishops from their sees, and he drew attention – in his final phrase – to the monks of the desert, who frequently acted as hosts to those who sought refuge from persecution.

The ideal of a mortified life had never been absent from Christianity since its beginnings and in the second and third centuries many congregations possessed an inner group of virgins and ascetics. In the second half of the third century a number of men adopted a form of anchoritic life, chief amongst whom must be reckoned Antony.

Antony was born about 251 in the village of Comas in Middle Egypt of well-to-do Christian parents. Shortly after their death, when he was eighteen years old, he gave away all his inheritance, in response to the gospel message; 'Sell all that thou hast', and put himself under the tutelage of an old ascetic living on the outskirts of his village; there he worked with his hands, prayed and read the Bible. For thirty-five years, part of which time he lived in a tomb and part in a disused castle, he devoted himself to ascetic practices until his reputation for sanctity attracted such crowds that, seeking greater solitude, he fled further into the desert. Many, however, followed him and, building cells near his own, lived a semi-eremitical life under his guidance. Apart from two visits to Alexandria, one in 311 to strengthen those suffering persecution and one shortly before his death to oppose the Arians, he remained in comparative seclusion, dying on 17th January 356.[70]

While it is an over-simplification to regard Antony as the founder of Christian monasticism, there can be no doubt that the example of his life made it attractive to many who were disposed by the circumstances of the time to turn their backs on the world. The Peace of the Church virtually closed the list of martyrs, within the empire, and as their heirs the monks now came forward in great numbers. The increasing secularization of the Church, due to the incursion of time-savers and half-converted pagans, drove many to protest. The desert fathers indeed fled not so much from the world as from the world in the Church. There were of course other influences at work, e.g. the persecutions had driven many into the deserts where they discovered it possible to practise piety unhampered by the temptations of life in a pagan environment; again the economic situation, with the ever-increasing burden of taxation, led many to forsake the world that cost so much, but the main factor was the lowering of the ideal of Christian perfection inseparable from mass conversion. This meant that monasticism was at first, as it were, outside the Church – or at least outside the organized community life of the Church. Thus, in the period from Nicaea to Constantinople, while the movement was rooting itself firmly, it was only gradually that it won over leading Churchmen who could defend it against its detractors. A converted pagan, *c.* 360, is represented as asking: 'Explain to me now what is the congregation or sect of monks, and why it is an object of aversion, even amongst our own people?'[71] The support of an Athanasius and a Basil and, in the last decades of the century, of such influential figures as Jerome and Augustine, gradually turned the tide of opinion in favour of the 'athletes of God', but the progress, though in many respects spectacular, was not immediate.

Since monasticism, as typified by Antony, was initially a protest of individuals, it was at first eremitical in character. The kind of life adopted by Antony continued to flourish at Pispir, where he had lived in a castle, but its main centres were in the deserts of Nitria, with that of Scete as a close second.

Nitrian monasticism was inaugurated by Amoun, between 320 and 330.[72] The colony at Scete, a day's journey away, owed its inception to Macarius the Egyptian, a disciple of Antony, who settled there *c.* 330.[73] These monks had no common discipline but followed their own individual rules, which included long and severe fasts. The motive for this abstinence is indicated by Jerome: 'It is not that God, the Creator and Master of the universe, rejoices in the roaring of our bellies, the emptiness of our stomachs, or the ardent thirst of our lungs; but there is no other way of safeguarding chastity'.[73] They worked at palm mats, using a little of the money from their sale for their meagre diet and distributing the rest to the poor. They assembled for the eucharist on Saturdays and Sundays, returning to their solitude for prayer, manual labour and the learning of the scriptures.

The second type of Egyptian monasticism and that which was

destined to prevail widely was the cenobitic, a title composed from the Greek *koinos* and *bios* meaning common life, i.e. it involved living within an organized community. Here the pioneer was Pachomius.[74] He was born *c.* 292 of pagan parents in the Upper Thebaid. After service in the army, he was converted to Christianity and joined himself to a hermit named Palamon with whom he lived for seven years. In 323 Pachomius settled at Tabennesis and within a short time had around him some hundred or so followers whom he organized into a community with a common rule of life. This rule was a moderate one, encouraging work, allowing degrees of abstinence and demanding no vows. The Pachomian system spread with such rapidity that by the time of his death in 346 he had under his control nine monasteries for men and two for women. His successors, especially Theodore who presided over the communities for eighteen years, continued the development, Theodore himself being responsible for the foundation of at least four additional centres.

Another great figure of Egyptian monastic history was Schenoudi or Shenoute, who was born *c.* 333–4. As a young boy he went to live with his uncle Bgoul, the head of the White Monastery, where the rule was a stricter form of that of Pachomius. Schenoudi succeeded his uncle in 383 and continued as head until his death some eighty-three years later. His monastery was essentially a Coptic institution where the Sahidic dialect was in use. He seems to have attempted to combine the cenobitical and eremitical as he was accustomed to depart with some of his monks to cells in the desert from time to time.

The visits of pilgrims to Egypt, the popularity of Athanasius' *Life of Antony*, together with the same general causes that operated to originate monasticism, led to its adoption in countries other than that of its birth. In Palestine Hilarion was the prime instigator. Born *c.* 291 at Gaza, he was sent by his pagan parents to Alexandria to be educated. There he was converted, visited Antony and, returning home, practised the ascetic life. He soon became the centre of much attraction and founded several monasteries.[75] Traditionally monasticism is said to have been introduced into Mesopotamia by Eugenius, a disciple of Pachomius, but no historical truth can be attributed to this legend. It should be noticed however that whereas the tendency in Egypt was to abandon the eremitical life in favour of cenobitism, in Mesopotamia and Syria the opposite bias was at work.

It was Eustathius of Sebaste (born *c.* 300) who introduced monasticism into the districts of Cappadocia and Pontus, but his chief importance lies in his influence on Basil who, despite later doctrinal divergences, was at first his devoted disciple. It was in 357 that Basil went on a tour through Syria and Egypt to familiarize himself with the monastic ideal and practice at first hand. He was so impressed by what he saw[76] that upon his return he retired to Pontus and organized his first monastic community, drawing up rules which eventually became the norm for the Greek Church. He was opposed to the eremitical life and laid his emphasis upon the community. Although indebted to Pachomius, he went beyond him in refusing to allow any personal idiosyncrasies to interfere with the life of the monastery; nor would he permit excesses of austerity, saying that they made a man unfit for work, which was more important than fasting.[77]

Attention has so far been concentrated entirely upon eastern monasticism, and it is now necessary to consider its development in the West. Here Athanasius played a leading part. In 341 he came, in exile, to Italy accompanied by two Egyptian monks, and there he remained for several years, thus having time to inspire others with the example of the ascetic life. Details of its further advance are not plentiful, but about 360 a small book was published, entitled *The Conferences of Zaccheus and Apollonius*, possibly written by Firmicus Maternus, which is interesting both as an apologetic for the movement against its detractors and evidence of its growing popularity. Yet even by 383, when Jerome came to stay in Rome, there was little organized cenobitic life, although, near to Milan, Eusebius of Vercelli, who had met Athanasius in the capital, lived with his clergy under a common rule.[78]

The first monastery in Gaul would seem to have been that of Martin near Poitiers *c.* 360, and when he became bishop of Tours in 372 he established another close to the city at Marmoutiers. There he gathered eighty monks who lived in caves and huts, met only for services and meals and fasted rigorously. Work was discouraged, apart from the transcription of manuscripts, and in many respects this was an imitation of the simple Antonian monasticism in Egypt.

Western monasticism was therefore an adaptation of the eastern form made necessary by both a difference in climate and temperament. It was to nurture, particularly in Gaul, many future bishops and to play an important part in preserving Christian life from complete secularization and Christian culture from complete submergence in the centuries that lay ahead.

Church order

The movement to transform function into office proceeded apace in the fourth century – now no longer were the orders of the ministry regarded as possibly life-long spheres of service but rather as steps in a graded hierarchy. Illustrative of this is the consecration *per saltem* of Ambrose of Milan in 374. At the time of his election as bishop he had not even been baptized, but when he was compelled to accept the people's choice he underwent initiation and on successive days was made deacon, ordained priest and consecrated bishop.[79]

The official nature of the bishop's function was further emphasized by state recognition of his jurisdiction. From the earliest times the injunction of Paul not to take disputes between Christians before the civil magistrates had been observed. So in the third century the *Didascalia* gives very full instructions how a bishop is to hear a case, the form the interrogations are to take and how the dispute should be settled on a Monday to allow the contending parties to be at peace with each other by the next Sunday eucharist.[80] In 318 Constantine recognized the bishop's jurisdiction,[81] and in 333 the bishops were placed on an equal footing with the magistrates.[82] The kind of case that came to occupy more and more of the bishop's time may be illustrated by one that was heard by Ambrose in 378.

The brother of a certain bishop applied for the annulment of an agreement whereby the bishop had granted one of his family estates to their widowed sister on condition that it should pass on her death to the Church. The bishop was a decurion and it was contrary to the law for one in his position to sell or alienate his goods and property without the authorization of the prefect, since his hereditary membership of the curia involved heavy expenses which had to be met. The bishop's legal heir was his brother, who would succeed him as decurion and would have to bear the expense. The accused argued that by a law of 361 it was enacted that all clergy who were decurions, with the exception of those consecrated to the episcopacy, should forfeit their possessions upon ordination, so that as a bishop he retained full rights over his patrimony. The plaintiff replied that the law did not state that a bishop had the right to dispose of his property in such a way that it ceased to be available for the charges of the curia. Ambrose's decision was that the land in question should be given to the brother who was to make an annual payment to the sister; upon her decease, he could continue possession without obligation to further payment to the Church. The plaintiff thus received the land; the sister was assured of a fixed income and the defendant was relieved of a dissension in his family. Only the Church lost by this verdict and in Ambrose's view she could afford to dispense with temporal gains.[83]

Ecclesiastical divisions of territory

The development of the hierarchy of the Church was accompanied by a growth in organization whereby ecclesiastical divisions of territory were more precisely defined. In general these were modelled upon the administrative arrangements of the empire, although there were exceptions arising from different local situations.

The basic unit was the bishopric, which normally comprised the city where the bishop resided and the surrounding countryside and villages. The practice of having one bishop for each 'parish' or community persisted in Egypt and North Africa where many of the villages had each its own bishop. The Roman provinces formed the next series of units, each province being the concern of the bishop of the capital city, who was the metropolitan with jurisdiction over all the bishops in his area. So, for example, the Council of Nicaea confirmed the authority of the bishop of Alexandria over Egypt, Libya and the Pentapolis, and declared that the honour of the bishop of Jerusalem should be safeguarded while the rights of the metropolitan of Caesarea should not be impaired.[84] Nicaea further provided for a twice annual meeting of provincial councils.[85]

The grouping of the civil provinces into 'dioceses' also had its influence upon Church structure, promoting a parallel arrangement whereby the ecclesiastical provinces, each with its metropolitan, tended to come under a patriarch. The first step in this development was taken at Constantinople in 381 when the bishop of that city was declared to have the primacy of honour after the bishop of Rome because Constantinople is New Rome.[86]

Councils

The canons of Nicaea and Constantinople not only had a bearing on the development of territorial divisions, they also provided a nucleus for general ecclesiastical legislation. Hitherto the councils that had assembled had been local and their decisions were often unknown or not regarded as authoritative outside their own areas. The canons of Nicaea, the first *Ecumenical* Council, were accepted from the first and so the process of creating a body of canon law was begun. Moreover the meetings of these councils and the canons promulgated were to have a direct bearing on the question of the Roman primacy.

The Roman primacy

The position of the bishop of Rome under Constantine was not such as to enhance his prestige. The emperor largely ignored him, and by lending his ear to court-bishops and by creating a new capital he left a legacy that was injurious to the pope's position. Some recovery of authority was however achieved six years after Constantine's death when the council of Sardica gave legal recognition to certain of the pope's judicial powers. Canons 3 and 7 provide for appeals to be made to the bishop of Rome in certain cases. This was during the episcopate of Julius (337–52), and under his successor Liberius (352–66) a further step was taken to support the papal claims by the publication of the Liberian Catalogue in 354. This episcopal list, unlike the previous ones of eastern origin, which placed Peter and Paul in a category by themselves as the apostolic 'founders', omits Paul entirely and places Peter as the first bishop. This was to prove of assistance to Damasus (366–84) whose rule was a landmark in the history of the Roman primacy.

Damasus' election was at first disputed and a rival candidate, Ursinus, brought charges against him.[87] Damasus took the opportunity of these proceedings to present a petition to Gratian and his requests were formulated at a council in Rome in 383. It was asked that the emperor should confirm the privileges of the bishop of Rome and his fellows to try the cases of bishops still recalcitrant, so that no bishop might be brought before a secular judge; that such offenders, if living in Italy, should be compelled to appear at Rome or before judges appointed by the pope, and that, finally, any condemned bishop should be allowed the right of appeal either to the pope or to a synod of fifteen neighbouring bishops.[88] Gratian replied with the rescript *Ordinariorum sententiae*[89] to the effect that bishops in those provinces under the direct metropolitan control of Rome should be tried at Rome; that other bishops should be tried by their own metropolitans; that metropolitans should themselves be heard at Rome or by judges appointed by the pope; and that ordinary bishops could appeal to the pope or to a synod of fifteen neighbouring bishops. This was a significant step forward in the growth of papal authority, for while the emperor refrained from recognizing any inherent rights, he granted a new jurisdiction to the Roman see, so that in theory, if not yet in practice, the supremacy of the bishop of Rome in the West was largely asserted.

The Council of Constantinople in 381 itself acknowledged the primacy of honour of Rome, but the following year, in an attempt to counteract the growing importance of the new capital, a synod under Damasus reaffirmed the primacy, basing the claim on the promise of Christ to Peter. Moreover it further asserted that the three sees, recognized as pre-eminent at Nicaea, formed a Petrine hierarchy, with its *prima sedes* at Rome, its *secunda sedes* at Alexandria, believed to have been evangelized by Mark, Peter's disciple, and its *tertia sedes* at Antioch, where Peter had been active. Thus the attempt was made to offset the increasing ambition of Constantinople and at the same time to support the Roman claim to be the principal inheritor of the prerogatives of the prince of the apostles.

BELIEFS

The preceding survey of the expansion and development of the Church in the period from Nicaea to Constantinople, and in particular the account of the Arian controversy, has demonstrated that one question above all, in the sphere of beliefs, occupied the attention of Christian thinkers, and that was the relation of the Father and the Son. The trinitarian problem, already brought to the fore by the debates with the Dynamic and Modalistic Monarchians, was therefore still the centre of concern.

Arianism

Since the teaching of Arius provided the occasion for the further clarification of trinitarian belief, an understanding of his position becomes a necessary point of departure. Arius, by overstressing Origen's subordinationism to the neglect of his other equally important ideas, and by a process of theological rationalization, was able to by-pass the question of the relationship of Father and Son and to assert in effect that there was no direct relationship whatsoever. Holding to the absolute uniqueness, self-existence and immutability of God, he concluded that the Son could not be divine, since the Godhead cannot be shared, since the Son is not self-existent and since he is mutable, being represented in the gospels as subject to growth and change.[1] Hence Arius could assert 'that the Son had a beginning . . . that he is from nothing . . . that prior to his generation he did not exist'.[2] To describe the Son's cosmological role Arius adopted the Neoplatonic idea of an intermediary and, isolating the extrapolation stage of the Word's begetting found in such writers as Tertullian and Hippolytus, contended that the Son was made as the medium for the creation of the world which could not have endured direct contact with the Supreme God.[3] This was to declare the Son to be a creature and the Arians did not hesitate to say that 'he is called God in name only'.[4]

The attitude of Nicaea

The simplest way to reject Arianism was to state that the Son was fully divine. Hence the creed promulgated at Nicaea contains the statements that he is 'only-begotten, that is, from the substance of the Father, God from God, light from light, true God from true God, begotten not made, of one substance (*homoousion*) with the Father'. There can be little doubt that *homoousion* was here used to affirm that just as a human child is of the same substance or stuff as his father who begets him, so the Son of

God shares the same nature as his Father and is therefore fully divine. The bishops thus had a limited objective; they were not concerned to explain the relation of Father and Son; they were concerned to repudiate the teaching of Arius by declaring the Godhead of the Son and his equality with the Father, out of whose being he was derived and whose nature he therefore shared.

Yet the term *homoousion* had a second meaning; it could be interpreted, not only as 'of the same stuff', but also 'of one content', i.e. as numerical identity of substance. In this sense it had a bearing upon the question of the divine unity, and it was Athanasius' appreciation of this that led to a further advance.

Athanasius' Trinitarianism

Athanasius based his thinking upon the Christian experience of salvation, so that all his teaching was soteriologically determined. Hence he considered that 'the Word could never have divinized us if he were merely divine by participation and were not himself the essential Godhead'.[5] Athanasius was equally convinced of the oneness of God:

> There is then a Triad, holy and complete, confessed to be God in Father, Son and Holy Spirit, having nothing foreign or external mixed with it, nor composed of one that creates and one that is originated, but all creative; and it is consistent and in nature indivisible, and its activity is one. The Father does all things through the Word in the Holy Spirit. Thus the unity of the holy Triad is preserved.[6]

It was in this way that Athanasius rejected the Arian conception of the Son as a subordinate and inferior organ of creation. Yet while the Godhead is one, there are distinctions, as between the Father and the Son. 'They are two, because the Father is Father and not also Son, and the Son is Son and not also Father'.[7] The unity is understood to consist in oneness or identity of substance: 'the Son's divinity is the Father's divinity'.[8] The divine nature is indivisible – one cannot think of Father and Son as two parts forming one whole – but because the Godhead is indivisible and yet both are God, then they must be one identical substance, the same indivisible reality existing in two forms of presentation, since 'the Son is of course other than the Father as offspring, but as God he is one and the same'.[9]

Athanasius was also responsible for yet another step forward in that he extended his definition of the divine unity to include not only the Father and the Son who had occupied the centre of debate hitherto, but also the Holy Spirit. He was impelled to do this in the interests of the anti-heretical polemic, since the Tropici were taking the step of denying the Spirit's divinity. In 359 or 360 Athanasius expounded his theology of the Spirit in his letters to Serapion. Again he began from the experience of Christian life: 'If the Holy Spirit were a creature, we should have no participation in God through him.'[10] Athanasius' reasoning about the Spirit indeed followed the same path as his reasoning about the Son and issued in his affirmation of the consubstantiality of the Spirit with the Father and the Son.[11] The Spirit 'has the same oneness with the Son as the Son with the Father'.[12] The three are one because they have one identical and indivisible substance or essence.

The Cappadocian settlement

Athanasius' teaching was not fully understood nor accepted immediately throughout the East; that it was finally endorsed was the outcome of the efforts of Basil and the two Gregorys, although they themselves reflected the general lack of comprehension in that only slowly did they come to appreciate and expound the Athanasian position, adding to it at the same time certain refinements. This tardiness of advance is particularly noticeable in connexion with the *homoousion* of the Spirit, and Basil never reached the point of explicitly affirming his consubstantiality, contenting himself, in *On the Holy Spirit*, with reckoning him with and not below the Father and Son. Eventually, however, Gregory of Nazianzus was able to make an unambiguous declaration: 'Is the Spirit God? Yes, indeed. Then is he consubstantial? Of course, since he is God'.[13]

This acceptance of the consubstantiality of Father, Son and Spirit, in the sense of their identity of substance, enabled them to proclaim the unity of the Trinity. In so doing they upheld Origen's belief in a specific genus as the basis; the Godhead is therefore one *ousia* or substance. While thus safeguarding the oneness of God, the Cappadocians had further to explain how Father, Son and Spirit are to be distinguished. Granted that the three are one by identity of substance, what differentiates them to enable them to be spoken of as three? They sought a solution by saying that each *hypostasis*, or objective presentation of the one substance, is to be distinguished by certain individual characteristics or particularities (*idiotes*), which are in fact modes of existence (*tropoi hyparxeos*). The Father, Son and Spirit are not names representing substances but modes of being or relation.[14] The Father is ingenerate, the Son begotten and the Spirit proceeding.[15] These modes of subsistence refer to the relations between the divine persons and so express eternal processes continually operative within the divine being. Thus the distinction of the three is based upon their origin and mutual relations, and their individuality is the manner in which the identical substance is objectively presented in each several one. This meant the end of subordinationism. The Son and the Spirit are equal to the Father as touching their divinity because each is a presentation of an identical divine being. The only priority of the Father is a logical, not a temporal, one since the Son and the Spirit derive from him as their source; but this priority involves no superiority. 'The doctrine of the Trinity, as formulated by the Cappadocians, may be summed up in the phrase that God is one object in himself and three objects *to* himself. Further than that illuminating paradox it is difficult to see that human thought can go. It secures both the unity and the trinity'.[16]

The person of Christ

Although the Arian controversy was primarily a phase of the trinitarian debate, Christology was an important element in the earliest form of Arius' teaching. He agreed that Christ was the Word Incarnate and then argued that as, according to the gospels, he was capable of change, the Word must be regarded as mutable and therefore could not be equal with God. Arius held further that the Word had united himself to a human body without a rational soul. This was a Word-flesh Christology, which had been accepted previously by Novatian in the West and Methodius in the East. Hence according to the Anomaean Eudoxius: 'we believe . . . in one . . . Lord . . . who was made flesh but not man. For he did not take a human soul . . . He was not two natures, for he was not complete man, but God in place of a soul in flesh'.[17] This statement could equally well have been uttered by Athanasius, whose Christology was also of the Word-flesh kind and whose point of difference related not to the humanity but to the full divinity of the Word.

According to Athanasius, the Word 'prepared in the Virgin the body as a temple for himself, and personally appropriates this as an instrument, being made known in it and dwelling in it'; he was 'born and appeared in a human body'.[18] Athanasius was emphatic that the body is the Word's very own,[19] but there is little or no place in his thought for a rational human soul in the Incarnate Lord. It must be acknowledged that nowhere does he explicitly deny the existence of one and that it has been supposed by some that after 362 he did come to believe in a complete humanity,[20] but it seems most probable that he never abandoned the Word-flesh conception.

Apollinarianism

It is a measure of the development of doctrine that Athanasius was never regarded as unorthodox for his teaching on the person of Christ, while Apollinaris, who propounded essentially the same belief, was ultimately condemned as a heretic; but then Apollinaris, unlike Athanasius, did categorically deny the existence of a human soul in Christ, and so raised the whole question of the humanity of the Incarnate Word as Arius had raised that of his divinity.

Apollinaris, who became bishop of Laodicea in 361, was influenced in arriving at his position by three factors: his anti-Arianism; his objection to the Antiochene Christology of Diodore of Tarsus and his traducianist understanding of the origin of the individual soul. The Arians, as has been seen, rested their case in part on the mutability of Jesus. Apollinaris, who held that the soul or *nous* was the seat of sin and therefore of instability and changeability,[21] attempted to safeguard the immutability of the Word by denying that he assumed a human soul at the Incarnation. He was equally opposed to those who so stressed the full humanity of Jesus that they tended to divide the Incarnate Lord into two Sons.[22] He believed that to think of Christ as a man conjoined with God was in fact to create a duality and to separate the Godhead and the manhood, so denying the reality of redemption. If Jesus were an ordinary man indwelt by God then he could not be an object of worship nor could he bestow salvation.[23] He considered further that two principles of mind or volition cannot reside coincidentally or the one will contend with the other, and he therefore asserted an organic union between the Godhead and manhood by replacing the *nous* or mind by the pre-existent Word. 'The flesh,' he declared, 'is not something superadded to the Godhead for well-doing, but constitutes one reality or nature with it'.[24] Apollinaris thus believed that the Word was the life of the God-man, being the basis or source of all his energy even at the physical and biological levels. To him there is 'one nature composed of impassible divinity and passible flesh',[25] and his catch-phrase was 'one incarnate nature of the divine Word'.[26] That this made Jesus different from other man was acknowledged by Apollinaris without demur, since he accepted the traducianist view, that the human soul is passed on from one's parents, and was able to argue that the Virgin Birth precluded such a transmission since the divine spirit replaced the sperm.[27] No human soul could therefore be passed on and it was replaced by the Word himself.

The first murmurings against Apollinarianism were heard at the council of Alexandria in 362, but its implications were not immediately appreciated and it was not until 377 that formal condemnation was declared by a synod at Rome under Damasus,[28] and this was repeated at Constantinople in 381. The chief ground for rejecting Apollinaris' teaching was succinctly expressed by Gregory of Nazianzus:

If anyone has trusted in a man without a mind, he is indeed out of his mind and not worthy to be completely saved. For that which is unassumed is not healed; but that which has been united to God, that also is saved. . . . Let them not begrudge us complete salvation, nor equip the Saviour with only the bones and portraiture of a man.[29]

As a consequence of the debate occasioned by this heretical teaching, the Word-flesh Christology, which many, including Athanasius, had held previously, was discarded in favour of a Word-man Christology: Christ is completely divine (anti-Arian) and completely human (anti-Apollinarian). This only served to make more acute the problem of the unity of his person. How, once Apollinaris' thesis were rejected, were Christians to conceive of the relationship between the manhood and the Godhead? Attempts to answer this unleashed the series of Christological debates that were to continue for centuries, but Hilary of Poitiers had already made a valiant attempt to provide an answer. Convinced that Christ was true God and true man possessing a human soul,[30] he considered that the coexistence of the two within one person had been made possible by an act of kenosis. Starting from Phil. ii. 6ff., he declared that the Son of God emptied himself of the divine form in order to exist in the servant's form of man.[31] There was a self-renunciation or self-evacuation on the part of the Word of his divine glory. But Hilary's teaching had one serious flaw in that he maintained that the body of Christ, having been conceived by the Holy Spirit, was not really earthly but heavenly and was above all human weakness;[32] there was therefore a docetic element in his thought.

The work of Christ

Although the person of Christ has just been considered in isolation from his work, reference has been made to the fact that the Christology of Athanasius and Apollinaris was soteriologically determined. How then did Christians from Nicaea to Constantinople understand the work of Christ?

Athanasius drew principally upon the deification theory, previously expounded by Irenaeus and Origen. 'The Word became flesh that we might be deified'.[33] This deification he understood as the restoration of the divine image, marred by sin, through the coming of the Divine Image himself. 'None other could restore a corruptible being to incorruption but the Saviour who in the beginning made everything out of nothing. None other could re-create man according to the image, but he who is the Father's Image. None other could make a mortal being immortal, but he who is Life itself, our Lord Jesus Christ.'[34] By the union of the Godhead and manhood in Christ human corruptibility was overcome and man was made superior to death, entering upon a process of deification whereby he could attain his true end, not by being transformed into the Godhead but by receiving immortality and the final blessing of the divine vision. While this was the centre of Athanasius' thought about the atonement, he could also speak of adoption[35] and of Christ's death as a sacrifice for sin, whereby the debt was paid.[36] These same ideas, deification and the payment of a ransom, were common to the Cappadocians as exemplified by Gregory of Nyssa.

Gregory taught that the Word, at his Incarnation, mingled with himself a perishable nature so that that nature should be deified together with him.[37] He 'conjoined himself with our nature in order that by its conjunction with the Godhead it might become divine'.[38] So God took the initiative to achieve what man alone could not do. This same emphasis upon the divine grace appears in Gregory's elaboration of the Christus Victor theme along the lines adumbrated by Origen. He answered the question how the victory had been won by the idea of the deceit of the devil.

> The Godhead was hidden under the veil of our nature, that, as is done with greedy fish, the hook of the Godhead might be gulped down along with the bait of the flesh and thus, life being introduced into the house of death and light shining in the darkness, that which is contradictory to light and life might vanish away; for it is not in the nature of darkness to remain where light is present nor of death to exist where life is present.[39]

So the devil, unsuspecting, swallowed the bait, represented by the humanity of Christ, and was caught on the hook of his Godhead. Morally repugnant though this interpretation may be, it was a serious attempt to grapple with the problem of dualism which is bound up with this method of interpreting salvation, but it was not free from contemporary criticism at the hands of a Gregory of Nazianzus[40] and the anonymous author of *De Recta Fide*.[41]

The conception of Christ as victim and sacrifice, which was to dominate western thinking about the atonement, being expounded for example by Hilary of Poitiers,[42] was also a feature of eastern thought. Thus Eusebius of Caesarea understood Christ's death as a substitutionary sacrifice,[43] while Cyril of Jerusalem stressed the uniqueness of the cross[44] and Basil stated that 'he offered himself as a sacrifice and oblation to God on account of our sin'.[45]

The Church

Interpretations of Christ and his work inevitably affected the understanding of the Church. Athanasius' deification theme issued logically in the idea of the mystical body. 'Through participation in the same Christ we all become one Body, possessing the one Lord in ourselves.'[46] Similarly Gregory of Nyssa:

> Since we are all by participation conjoined with Christ's unique body, we become one single Body, viz. his. When we are all perfect and united with God, the whole Body of Christ will then be subjected to the quickening power. The subjection of this Body is called the subjection of the Son himself because he is identified with his Body, which is the Church.[47]

Nevertheless few eastern writers rose above the commonplace in ecclesiological doctrine, e.g. Cyril of Jerusalem,[48] but in the West the Donatist schism necessarily directed attention to it, and if full examination was to await the efforts of Augustine, Optatus of Milevis had already begun to consider it in 367. He discussed those marks of the Church – its oneness, holiness, apostolicity and catholicity – which were to be included in the 'Nicene' creed.[49]

The formulation of belief

Creedal formulae had hitherto developed in close connexion with the instruction of the catechumens and with the rite of baptism. By the fourth century, the Old Roman Creed, which was ultimately to evolve into the Apostles' Creed, as it is known today, in the seventh and eighth centuries in Burgundy, had already achieved a measure of fixity. Its text, which may be recovered from an apology which Marcellus of Ancyra presented to Julius at a synod in Rome in 340, reads as follows:

I believe
in God Almighty,
and in Christ Jesus, his only son our Lord,
who was born of the Holy Spirit and Mary the Virgin,
who, under Pontius Pilate, was crucified and buried,
and on the third day rose from the dead,
ascended into heaven and sitteth on the right hand of the Father,
whence he shall come to judge the living and the dead,
and in the Holy Spirit, the holy Church, the remission of sins,
the resurrection of the flesh,
life everlasting.[50]

In addition to these confessions, associated with baptism, the period from Nicaea to Constantinople witnessed the production of a multitude of conciliar creeds which, against the background of theological controversy, were intended to be tests of orthodoxy. Nicaea itself promulgated a creed, possibly of Jerusalem origin, which by the insertion of the *homoousion* was meant to exclude Arianism. From then on synod after synod tried its hand at producing statements of belief which reflected the views of the majority present and could therefore be Nicene, Anomean, Homoeousian or Homoean. The overthrow of Arianism made possible the promulgation of a formula that could be universally accepted and this was the 'Nicene' Creed approved and issued by the Council of Constantinople in 381. More theological than the baptismal creeds, this statement is the only one which the Church as a whole has ever received. Its original text reads:

> We believe in one God the Father Almighty, maker of heaven and earth, of all things visible and invisible;
>
> And in one Lord Jesus Christ, the only-begotten Son of God, begotten from the Father before all ages, light from light, true God from true God, begotten not made, of one substance with the Father, through whom all things were made, who for us men and for our salvation came down from heaven, and was incarnate from the Holy Spirit and the Virgin Mary and became man, and was crucified for us under Pontius Pilate, and suffered and was buried, and rose again on the third day according to the Scriptures, and ascended into heaven, and sits on the right hand of the Father, and will come again with glory to judge living and dead, of whose kingdom there will be no end:
>
> And in the Holy Spirit, the Lord and life-giver, who proceeds from the Father, who with the Father and the Son is co-worshipped and co-glorified, who spoke through the prophets; and in one, holy, catholic and apostolic Church. We confess one baptism for the remission of sins; we look forward to the resurrection of the dead and the life of the world to come. Amen.[51]

WORSHIP

In the year 326 or 327 Constantine wrote to Macarius, bishop of Jerusalem, concerning his projected church of the Holy Sepulchre, in the following terms:

> I desire, therefore, especially that you should be persuaded of that which I suppose is evident to all beside, namely, that I have no greater care than how I may best adorn with a splendid structure that sacred spot . . . a spot which has been accounted holy from the beginning in God's judgement, but which now appears holier still, since it has brought to light a clear assurance of our Saviour's passion. It will be well, therefore, for your sagacity to make such arrangements and provision of all things needful for the work, that not only the church itself as a whole may surpass all others whatsoever in beauty, but that the details of the building may be of such a kind that the fairest structures of any city in the empire may be excelled by this.[1]

This is only one of the many churches, in Palestine and elsewhere, for which the emperor was responsible, and the erection of these large and imposing buildings necessarily had an effect upon Christian worship. Whereas hitherto the gatherings of the faithful had preserved their domestic character, which went back ultimately to the Last Supper, henceforth the worship was *public* worship and that which had been suitable for a dining-room at Dura Europos or Cirta required adaptation if it were to be fitting for a great hall. Moreover the semi-converts who now thronged the churches were in need of instruction and so worship became more elaborate, not only to express the community's devotion but to impress the large congregations. A comparison therefore of the forms of worship in the fourth century with those existing previously reveals a development which, while preserving the basic patterns, seeks to make them more imposing and to bring out their meaning, with the concomitant risk of obscuring the primitive emphases. Elaboration there had been previously, in the second and third centuries, but the process was now accelerated in the period from Nicaea to Constantinople.

Baptism

Information concerning baptism during this period is contained in three documents: one from Egypt, the *Euchologion* of Serapion of Thmuis *c.* 350; one from Palestine, the *Mystagogical Lectures*, attributed to Cyril of Jerusalem *c.* 350; and one from Syria, the *Apostolic Constitutions c.* 375.

Serapion's Sacramentary contains prayers without rubrics but with headings to indicate where they are to be used. From these only the bare outline of the baptismal pattern is evident and consisted of the blessing of the water, a prayer for the candidates, acts of renunciation and adherence to Christ, baptism itself and a final unction with the sign of the cross.[2]

Cyril's exposition of the rite provides much fuller information and the meaning of the separate elements is also clearly defined. The candidates assembled in the vestibule of the baptistery and facing the West, the region of darkness, stretched out their hands and uttered the renunciation: 'I renounce thee, Satan, and all thy works, and all thy pomp, and all thy service'. Turning from West to East, the region of light, they made a brief confession of faith: 'I believe in the Father, and in the Son and in the Holy Spirit, and in one baptism of repentance'.[3] Passing into the dressing-room, they disrobed, as 'an image of putting off the old man with his deeds', so becoming imitators of Christ who hung naked on the cross and was borne naked to the tomb. Entering the inner chamber, they were anointed with exorcized oil to chase away all the invisible powers of the evil one.[4] They were next led to the font 'as

Christ was carried from the cross to the sepulchre', and made a second confession, descending three times into the water and ascending again, symbolizing the three days' burial of Christ.[5] Unction by the bishop followed: on the forehead that they might be delivered from shame; on the ears that they might be open to hear divine mysteries; on the nostrils that they might say: 'We are to God a sweet savour of Christ, in them that are saved'; lastly on the breast, that having put on the breast-plate of righteousness they might stand against the wiles of the devil.[6] Dressed in white robes, signifying that they had put off the covering of sin and put on the chaste garments of innocence,[7] and bearing each a lighted taper – 'the torches of the bridal train'[8] – they went in procession, singing: 'Blessed are those whose iniquities are forgiven, and whose sins are covered', to join in the baptismal eucharist.[9]

A similar pattern is observable in Book 7 of the *Apostolic Constitutions*. After the renunciation comes an act of adherence to Christ and the candidates are anointed 'for the remission of sins'. The blessing of the water precedes the actual baptism which is concluded with the chrism and saying the Lord's Prayer.[10]

The meaning of these ceremonies, both separately and as parts of one continuous rite, is consistent with the teaching of the preceding centuries. Baptism is a rebirth, a means of re-creation and of the forgiveness of sins and conveys the presence of the Holy Spirit – so Serapion. Cyril emphasizes that baptism is a dying and rising with Christ and drives away all evil spirits, but he is also insistent that it is not merely negative, a remission of sins only, which would equate it with John's baptism, but that it bestows the Holy Spirit who sanctifies the soul by his presence. The understanding of the editor of the *Apostolic Constitutions* is revealed by two prayers, the one for the blessing of the water, the other at the end of the rite:

> Look down from heaven and sanctify this water and give it grace and power, that so he that is to be baptized, according to the command of thy Christ, may be crucified with him, and may die with him, and may be buried with him and may rise with him to the adoption which is in him, that he may be dead to sin and live to righteousness.

> O God Almighty, the Father of thy Christ, thy only-begotten Son, give me an undefiled body, a pure heart, a watchful mind, an unerring knowledge, the influence of the Holy Spirit for the obtaining and assurance of the truth, through thy Christ, by whom be glory to thee in the Holy Spirit for ever. Amen.[11]

This understanding of baptism was also conveyed by the architecture that was now created to enshrine it, for buildings in the ancient world were intended to convey a meaning which transcended the visual pattern of the structure; each plan and elevation had its significance. The earliest baptisteries were quadrilateral, reproducing the form of contemporary pagan tombs and so declaring that baptism is the means of burial with Christ into death. Thus the baptistery at Nisibis, which was the work of the priest Akepsuma under the bishop Lolagesos in the year 359, was a simple cube with apse and porch, while the original

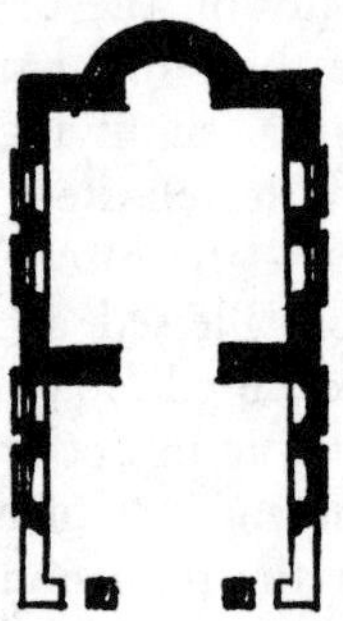

Baptistry at Nisibis

fourth-century one at Poitiers was also rectangular. Both these examples are freestanding buildings similar to separate tombs, but the baptistery could also be adjoined to the eucharistic hall, for when the Church emerged from the private house, it did not discard the additional rooms hitherto in use and so the baptistery in certain areas continued as a side-chamber. At Bethlehem the font was housed in a rectangular room opening off the south aisle; at Nesazio, near Pola, the baptistery was arranged along the north wall, being divided into three compartments with the basin in the central one.

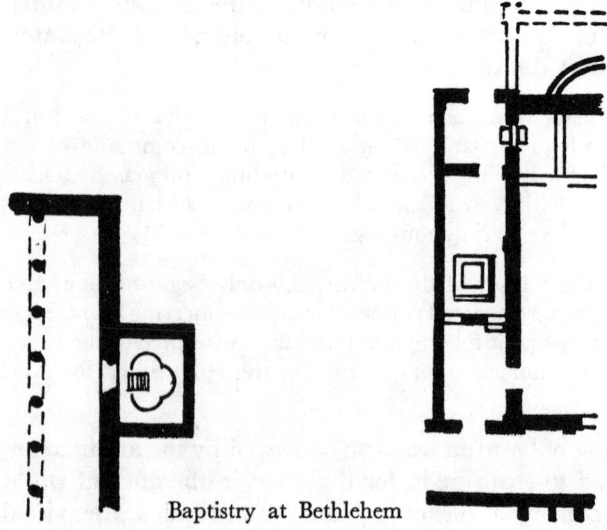

Baptistry at Bethlehem

Baptistry at Nesazio

The fonts too were rectangular, reproducing the shape of a sarcophagus or coffin, e.g. the one at Hippo from the first half of the fourth century. This last example is also surmounted by a baldachin on four columns and there are many other instances of this disposition which had its ideological content too. The dome was an image of heaven and so was placed over fonts, either as the roof of the baptistery itself or more closely as a ciborium, to express the belief that through baptism there is a dying and rising again that the candidates may become partakers of the Kingdom of God.

Since baptism was a unity of several elements, in certain centres, where finance was available, more than a single room with a font was

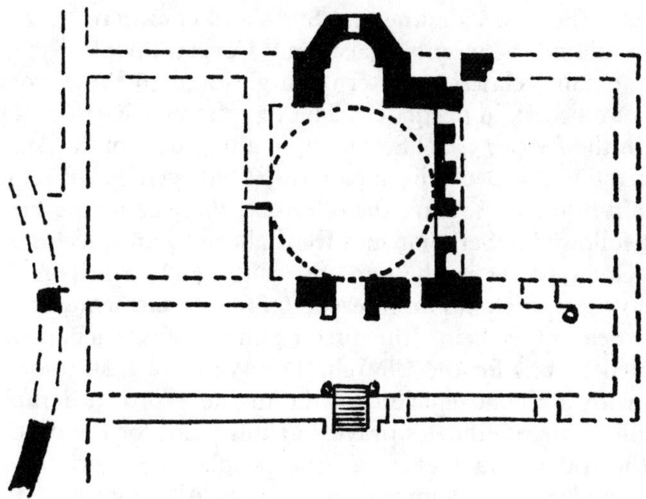

Baptistry at Jerusalem

erected. Cyril refers to the vestibule, and the baptistery attached to the Constantinian buildings at Jerusalem possessed a transverse entrance hall, with three rooms opening off it, the centre one containing the font, the second being possibly a dressing-room and the third for the concluding unction. Because of the close unity of baptism and episcopal confirmation, baptisteries were at first only erected in those cities where a bishop had his seat, and Gregory of Nazianzus reveals how many Christians advanced the long journey to the nearest font as reason for delaying baptism.[12] But the day of initiation – still largely confined to Holy Saturday or Pentecost – must have been an inspiring experience for those who took part, as the neophytes processed from the baptistery to the hall for the baptismal eucharist which brought the ceremonies to their culmination.

The Eucharist

If the development of the eucharist hitherto had been steady and unspectacular, various factors now combined to accelerate the process. Of primary importance was the acceptance in the West of Latin as its liturgical language. The immediate effect of this was to create a distinction between eastern and western liturgies. Further, within the areas differentiated by language, there also took place a rapid growth of local forms of worship, issuing in families of liturgies. So in the West there came into being, not immediately but over several centuries, Roman, Milanese, African, Spanish, Gallican and Celtic liturgies. In the East the forms in Egypt, some in Greek, some in Coptic, were not exactly the same as those in Palestine and Syria and elsewhere.

In the period between Nicaea and Constantinople the principal evidence extant relates to eastern liturgies and to those from Egypt, Palestine and Syria in particular. The Egyptian eucharistic rite may be studied in the *Euchologion* of Serapion, in a fragment of the Anaphora of St Mark and in the Der Balizeh papyrus,[13] but even between these there are certain differences. After the offertory, there came the Preface and Sanctus, followed in Serapion and Der Balizeh by an epiclesis or invocation, of God's power in the one and of the Holy Spirit in the other. Mark, however, includes an intercession for, or memento of, the living and the dead, this being the first example of a eucharistic prayer interrupted by one for the Church. The Words of Institution are next recited, with a second epiclesis of the divine Word in Serapion; this same, fuller source indicates prayers at this point for the dead and the living, the fraction, a blessing of the people, the distribution of the elements and a post-communion prayer. Already then the more primitive schema presented by Hippolytus is being elaborated; the simple prayer of thanksgiving has been expanded and fresh elements, such as intercessions, epicleses and blessings, are being introduced. The fragmentary nature of these documents does not allow an exact picture to be reproduced and the failure to mention certain features, e.g. the kiss of peace, does not mean that they were absent. From Cyril, however, a much more complete account can be obtained, although even his witness is selective.

Cyril begins with the Lavabo, i.e. the ritual cleansing of the priest's hands. There follows the Kiss of Peace, which is 'a sign of the blending of souls and the banishing of all remembrance of wrongs'. The Preface and Sanctus lead into an Epiclesis. Whether or not an Institution Narrative was read next is doubtful – Cyril does not refer to it and its absence from the East Syrian Liturgy of Addai and Mari shows that its presence was not universal. A commemoration of the living and the dead precedes the Our Father and the invitation to communion with the words: 'Holy things to the holy ones.' Cyril's account of the method of communion is not without its interest as an indication of fourth-century devotional practices:

> As you approach then, come not with your wrists extended or your fingers open, but make of your left hand a kind of throne by placing it under your right which is about to receive the King, and in the hollow of your hand receive the body of Christ, replying Amen. Carefully hallow your eyes with the touch of the holy body, and then partake of it, seeing to it that you lose no particle. . . . Then, after the communion of Christ's body, approach also the cup of his blood, not stretching forth your hands, but bending forward in an attitude of adoration and reverence, and saying Amen, be hallowed as well by the reception of the blood of Christ. And while the moisture thereof is still on your lips, touch it with your hands and hallow both your eyes and brow and other senses.

The liturgy of the *Apostolic Constitutions*, Book 8, once known as the Clementine Liturgy, is to be distinguished in several particulars from those reviewed so far. It is not the rite of any church, but is a literary production based upon Hippolytus' account and possibly upon the practice of some local community at Antioch or elsewhere. Further it is an Arian document, not orthodox, although the theology of the prayers does not affect the structure. Finally it does contain a synaxis, which is not described in any of the previous documents.

The synaxis, which is primitive in character, consists of five lections and then a series of litanies, the subjects being announced by a deacon with *Kyrie eleison* as the congregational response. This marks the first appearance of a litany in a fully developed form in a eucharistic rite, and it was to become a characteristic feature of all later eastern liturgies. After successive dismissals of the catechumens, the energumens, the competents or those in the last stage of their baptismal preparation, and lastly of the penitents, the Church prays for the world, the hierarchy, neophytes, the sick, travellers and young children.

The mass proper begins with the Kiss of Peace and Lavabo, thus reversing the sequence at Jerusalem, and deacons bring the gifts to the altar. The Preface leads into the first half of the Eucharistic Prayer, which is separated from the remainder by the Sanctus. The Words of Institution are followed by an anamnesis or recalling of Christ's passion, resurrection, ascension and second coming, this being the first eastern rite to contain one, and an Epiclesis. Intercession for the Church and mementoes for the living and the dead precede the Pax, a blessing given by the bishop and the invitation to communion in the words: 'Holy things to those who are holy'. Communion itself follows, the unconsumed elements are taken to the sacristy, and there is a post-communion-prayer, an episcopal blessing and the deacon says: 'Go in peace'. This is a much more involved pattern than those obtaining hitherto and the insertion of litanies, intercessions and blessings is already tending to overlay the primitive structure and at the same time to spell out more precisely the meaning of the action as it was then understood.

Consecration, primitively, had been a thanking of God over the elements; now there emerges in the East a theory, already adumbrated in the *Didascalia*, that the bread and the wine are transformed by the Holy Spirit. In Serapion it is the descent of the Word upon the elements that the one 'may become the body of the Word' and the other 'the blood of Truth'. Cyril of Jerusalem accepts the more general view in asserting the action of the Spirit with his statement: 'we call upon the merciful God to send forth his Holy Spirit upon the gifts lying before him; that he may make the bread the body of Christ and the wine the blood of Christ; for whatsoever the Holy Spirit has touched is sanctified and changed.' The *Apostolic Constitutions* pray that 'thou mayest send thy Holy Spirit upon this sacrifice . . . that he may make this bread the body of thy Christ'.

Parallel with this understanding of the causal efficacy of consecration came an affirmation of an actual change or conversion of the bread and wine, thus affecting the doctrine of the real presence. The idea that the elements are 'antitypes' or 'likenesses' of the body and blood persisted, these terms being used by both Serapion and the *Apostolic Constitutions*, but there was also a strong materialist theory coming to the fore that regarded the elements as being converted into the body and blood. Hence Cyril could use the words 'change' or 'convert', and Gregory of Nazianzus could speak of the priest's voice as a knife which cuts in two the Saviour's body and blood.[14] Gregory of Nyssa likewise referred to the transelementation of the species in the course of an argument to explain how Christ's body and blood could be consumed repeatedly without diminution. His answer is that whereas bread and wine consumed by Christ on earth were transformed into his body and blood by digestion, now in the eucharist the bread and wine are instantaneously changed into his body and blood.[15]

The conception of an antitype was also used in connexion with the sacrificial aspect of the eucharist. Gregory of Nazianzus regarded the eucharist as an outward sacrifice that represents as antitype Christ's offering on the cross.[16] Cyril was more realistic in his phraseology, describing it as 'the sacrifice of propitiation', and saying that we offer 'Christ, sacrificed for our sins, propitiating our merciful God' – hence the inclusion of mementoes of the living and dead in the canon, 'for all who stand in need of succour we all supplicate and offer this sacrifice'.

The architectural setting of worship

The elaboration of the eucharist matched its comparatively new architectural setting, and while few traces remain of pre-Constantinian buildings from his reign onwards there date many fine structures. Nevertheless, not all congregations could afford to undertake a special building programme and so houses continued to be adapted for use. Such, belonging to the first third of the fourth century, was the church at Kirk-Bizzeh. This consisted of a closed courtyard with porticoes out of which, on the north side, two doors led into the room for worship, two storeys high. The sanctuary, at the east end, had a triumphal arch, and opposite to this was the horse-shoe-shaped ambon with cathedra, typical of many Syrian basilicas. The small room to the south of the sanctuary was a martyrium, established some time after the house had

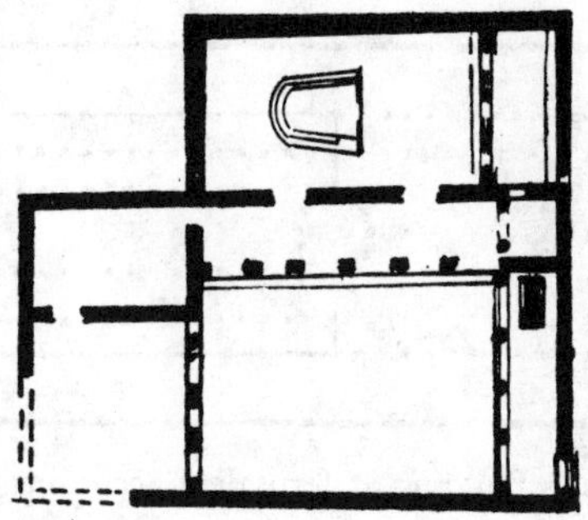

House-Church at Kirk-Bizzeh

been arranged for liturgical use. In most centres, however, the form adopted for the enlarged eucharistic room was that of the basilica, which was modified and adapted to Christian usage from existing pagan edifices.

The Christian basilica was a large hall, its horizontal perspective being emphasized by parallel colonnades which seemed to converge on the altar standing towards one end on the middle axis. This was the focal point of the building, added attention being given to it by a ciborium, and around it priesthood and laity assembled for the celebration, each section of the community having its prescribed place. In the centre of the semi-circular apse, roofed by a half dome, the bishop had his throne or *cathedra*, with his presbyters on a bench on either side and his deacons around the altar, which could stand as far as a third of the way down the hall and was fenced off by a chancel or balustrade of marble.

The hall was divided by parallel rows of columns into aisles, of which there was always an odd number. The centre one, the nave, corresponded to the apse in width and was equivalent to the sum of the side aisles where there were two. The columns supported long architraves which in turn bore the weight of the clerestory, on top of which the timbered gable roof rested, a flat ceiling hiding the tangle of rafters and thus maintaining the horizontal lines of the building. The upper wall, rising above the lean-to roofs of the side aisles, allowed the daylight direct admission into the naves through windows which usually corresponded to the spaces between the columns.

The exterior appearance was very bare, being of undressed brick. There was, however, frequently a porch, which could become a portico on four sides thus forming an atrium or open court.

Besides these congregational buildings, the fourth century also witnessed the erection of memorial edifices and here the initiative seems to have been aken by Constantine himself, who was anxious to make the

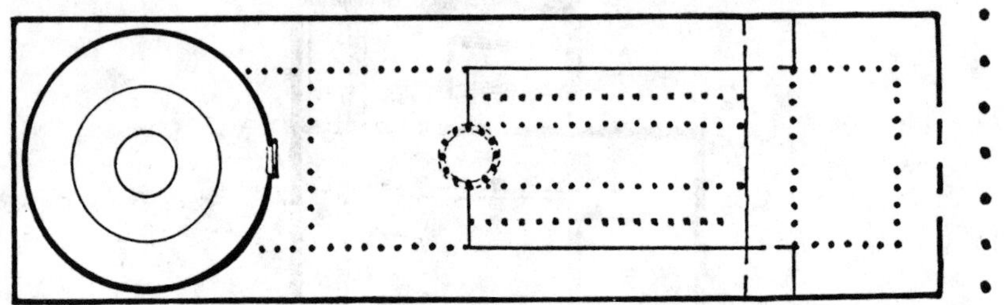

Constantine's Building at Jerusalem according to Eusebius

Holy Land a centre of pilgrimage and a means of fostering the unity of Christendom, menaced as it was by the Arian heresy. The architectural complex which was completed at Jerusalem in accordance with his instructions to the bishop Macarius consisted of a series of buildings set out axially in a long line running from east to west. A great entrance at the former extremity led from the street into an atrium, a forecourt surrounded by colonnades. Out of this opened a five-aisled basilica, later called the Martyrium; it was floored with marble slabs of various colours and had its panelled ceiling overlaid with gold. The sanctuary end of the Martyrium was somewhat unusual and probably consisted of a dome, borne on twelve columns, half of it projecting beyond the west wall and half inside. This marked the place where the empress Helena had discovered what was believed to be the true cross. Beyond this building, still moving in a direct line westwards, was a second atrium, also surrounded by colonnades, which contained, a little to one side, a small hill, the site of the crucifixion. Beyond was the Anastasis or church of the resurrection containing the tomb; at first this may have been an enclosure open to the sky, but it soon took the form of a rotunda with a wooden dome.

The Anastasis was circular, and so was S. Costanza, erected by Constantine at Rome, 324–6, to contain the huge porphyry sarcophagus for his sister; but memorial buildings could also be octagonal – such was the Imbomon or church of the Ascension, built on the summit of the Mount of Olives *c.* 375 by the Roman matron Poemenia, or even cruciform, like the martyrium of Babylas completed at Antioch in 381. These buildings belong to what is known as the central type of architecture and at first they were employed exclusively for memorial edifices to enclose the tomb of a saint or to mark a place hallowed by association with Christ. In time their plan was to have a considerable effect upon that of the congregational halls.

Within the churches the main item of furniture was the altar, which continued to have the form and shape of a dining-table and during the fourth century was generally of wood, as evidenced by Augustine who recounts how, during the Donatist troubles, bishop Maximianus was almost beaten to death by boards from a destroyed altar. Occasionally, when a rich patron could be found, more precious materials were used. Constantine presented S. Peter's with a silver altar 'inlaid with gold, decorated with green and white jewels and jacinths on all sides, the number of the jewels being 400, the weight 350 lb'.[17] Since the altar was relatively small compared with the size of the room, further attention was directed to it by surmounting it with a ciborium; this was carried on four pillars which bore in the East a cupola and in the West more usually a conical or pyramidal roof. The first one to which there is reference was that given by Constantine to the Lateran. It was probably carried on four marble columns and weighed 2025 lb. Facing the nave was a seated figure of Christ, 5 feet high and weighing 120 lb., flanked by two apostles, each 5 feet tall and 90 lb. in weight; along the sides were disposed the remaining apostles and at the rear, facing the apse, was another seated Christ with two angels, weighing 105 lb. each and holding rods; the whole structure was of pure gold.

Next in importance to the altar as an article of furniture was the bishop's seat, usually known as the throne in the East and the cathedra in the West. This kind of chair was common in the early days of the empire and was later adopted by rhetoricians and philosophers, the bishops readily transferring to the basilica the seat from which many had given lessons in the schools. Frequently made of perishable material, such as wood or ivory, few early examples remain. It was from this place that the bishop delivered his sermons, facing the congregation across the altar in front of him. Readings from the Scriptures, however, took place from a special desk no doubt taken over from the synagogue.

This 'desk' soon assumed the shape of a pulpit, and as it was ascended (*anabaino*) by a flight of stairs it was given the name *ambon*. Its position was not immediately standardized, although it was usually connected with the cancelli or balustrades that demarcated the sanctuary. Transennae of open work marble, with geometrical designs, were common throughout the fourth century.

The congregation could occupy the nave and side aisles or, as in some churches, the aisles only. The sexes were strictly separated, with either the men in front and the women behind, or the men on the right and the women on the left. Seating was negligible, since the worshippers were expected to stand for most of the service, but some few benches were provided for the aged and infirm.[18]

The impression of the buildings was enhanced by mosaic decoration which not only provided colour and light but also, by its choice of subjects, served to instruct the worshippers. In S. Costanza there remain some few early examples of this burgeoning Christian monumental art. In one of the large lateral niches Jesus is represented seated upon the globe of the world, in the midst of ten palms, symbolizing heaven, giving the keys to Peter. The corresponding mosaic shows Christ on a mountain, from which flow the four streams of paradise; the two chief apostles approach him and Peter receives the new law.

The Calendar

The didactic intent which in part influenced the production of these decorations was also evident in the much more developed calendar. Whereas previously there had been few festivals and their predominating note had been eschatological, there now took place an elaboration and an historicization which was the outcome of a changed outlook consequent upon the reconciliation between Christianity and the State, following the conversion of Constantine. The purpose of the new liturgical cycle was to set the facts of the gospel before the many nominal Christians who flocked into the Church. This is clearly shown by the institution of Christmas Day on December 25th to commemorate Christ's nativity. The date was chosen deliberately and principally to draw the converts away from the pagan solemnities associated with the day since the establishing of the *Natalis Solis Invicti* by Aurelian in 274. It appears to have been accepted in Rome *c.* 336. Even before then Lent was beginning to be observed, its origins lying in the season of preparation for baptism. The instruction of the catechumens was now spread over a period of six weeks and this time of fasting was also applied to the Church as a whole in order to assert the claims of Christian self-renunciation upon the lives of the nominal believers. The observance of a forty-day Lent, related to the forty days of Jesus in the wilderness, is apparent in Egypt before 330, and a letter of Athanasius to Serapion, written from Rome in 340, refers to 'all the world' fasting during these weeks.[19]

The development of the final period of Lent into Holy Week was largely the work of one man and one local church, viz. Cyril at Jerusalem. In order to organize the devotions of the pilgrims around the sacred sites, many of which were being embellished with memorial edifices, and to set forth to the local inhabitants as well the death and resurrection of Jesus as the pattern of Christian living, Cyril devised a series of Holy Week services closely linked with the topography of Jerusalem. So on Palm Sunday there was a procession from the Mount of Olives to the Anastasis; on Tuesday there was a service in the Eleona, built by the empress Helena, to hear a reading of Jesus' discourse there to his disciples. On Maundy Thursday there was a celebration of the eucharist in the afternoon recalling the Last Supper. On Good Friday, amongst many activities, there was a veneration of the cross in the atrium close to the hill of the crucifixion. On Holy Saturday night a vigil, including baptisms, culminated in the Easter eucharist at dawn. So each day was connected with an event in the final week of Jesus' life.[20] Other developments were obvious extensions of this practice and outlook. Given the commemoration of the resurrection on Easter Day, then forty days later, following the Lukan chronology, came the Feast of the Ascension and ten days after that Pentecost, recalling the descent of the Spirit. Gradually the whole year was being organized to set forth the facts of the ministry and the meaning of the gospel.

SOCIAL LIFE

The opening remarks of Basil of Caesarea, in his third homily on the Hexameron, refer to the many artisans in his congregation, and he adds the humorous comment: 'I must make my address short in order not to keep them too long from their work.' Here is direct evidence that the working class continued to provide a substantial proportion of the membership of the Church, and indeed the Church recognized this, as well as the importance of the middle class, by insisting that they taught their children a trade or profession.[1] The young were bidden to work hard and save money so that they might buy their own tools and cease to be a burden on others, 'for certainly he is a happy man who is able to support himself'.[2]

The surviving epitaphs, relatively abundant from the fourth and fifth centuries, indicate the diversity of trades and professions now adopted by Christians. We read of a barley-seller, a blacksmith, stone masons, grave-diggers, of two cloakroom attendants at the Baths of Caracalla on the Via Appia at Rome. The tombstone of the barber Leopardus, now in the Lateran museum, depicts a mirror, scissors and two razors. There were, further, soldiers, archivists, bailiffs, schoolmasters and doctors.[3] All means of livelihood connected with idolatry continued closed to the Christian, the list of prohibited vocations, given in the *Apostolic Tradition*, being reproduced and expanded in the *Apostolic Constitutions*.[4] To these must also be added the practice of money-lending. Canon 17 of Nicaea requires any cleric who has taken interest to be deprived of his office and many of the Fathers, both eastern and western, repeat this condemnation of usury.[5]

Food, clothing and leisure

The puritanical outlook of the pre-Nicene Church in regard to living conditions, which reached its zenith in the practices of the Desert Fathers, was also re-emphasized in the teaching of the fourth century. 'Let the body be nourished,' says Cyril of Jerusalem, 'with food that it may live and serve without hindrance; not, however, that it may be given up to luxuries.'[6] Gregory of Nazianzus held up his sister Gorgonia as an example of how a Christian married woman should approach the question of clothes.

> She was never adorned with gold wrought into artistic forms of surpassing beauty, nor flaxen tresses, fully or partially displayed, nor spiral curls, nor dishonouring designs of men who construct erections on the honourable head, nor costly folds of flowing and transparent robes, nor graces of brilliant stones, which colour the neighbouring air, and cast a glow upon the form; nor the arts and witcheries of the painter, nor that cheap beauty of the infernal creator who works against the Divine, hiding with his treacherous pigments the creation of God, and putting it to shame with his honour, and setting before eager eyes the imitation of an harlot instead of the form of God, so that this bastard beauty may steal away that image which should be kept for God and for the world to come. But though she was aware of the many and various external ornaments of women, yet none of them was more precious to her than her own character, and the brilliancy stored up within. One red tint was dear to her, the blush of modesty; one white one, the sign of temperance: but pigments and pencillings, and living pictures and flowing lines of beauty, she left to women of the stage and of the streets, and to all who think it a shame and a reproach to be ashamed.[7]

Indeed so strong was the ascetic tone that the Christian living in the world was to take the solitary as his model, so Basil to Gregory:

> The tunic should not be fastened to the body by a girdle, the belt not

going above the flank like a woman's, nor left slack so that the tunic flows loose like an idler's. . . . The one end of dress is that it should be a sufficient covering, alike in winter and summer. As to colour, avoid brightness; in material, the soft and delicate. To aim at bright colours in dress is like women's beautifying when they colour cheeks and hair with hues other than their own. The tunic ought to be thick enough not to want other help to keep the wearer warm. The shoes should be cheap but serviceable. In a word, what one has to regard in dress is the necessary. So too as to food; for a man in good health bread will suffice and water will quench thirst; such dishes of vegetables may be added as conduce to the strengthening of the body for the discharge of its functions. One ought not to eat with any exhibition of savage gluttony, but in everything that concerns our pleasure to maintain moderation, quiet and self-control. . . . Before meat let grace be said, in recognition alike of the gifts which God gives now, and which he keeps in store for time to come. Say grace after meat in gratitude for gifts given and petition for gifts promised. Let there be one fixed hour for taking food, always the same in regular course, that of all the four and twenty hours of the day and night barely this one may be spent upon the body.[8]

Yet things could be carried too far, and the Council of Gangara condemned those women who 'under pretence of asceticism' either wore men's clothes or cut off their hair. At the opposite extreme were those men who wore striking and even effeminate dress and were over-nice in their toilet, they too were equally censured:

Do not adorn yourself in such a manner as may entice another woman to you. . . . Do not permit the hair of your head to grow too long, but rather cut it short; lest by nicely combing your hair and wearing it long and anointing yourself you draw upon yourself such ensnared or ensnaring women. Neither wear over-fine garments to seduce any; nor, with an evil subtility, affect over-fine stockings or shoes for your feet, but only such as suit the measures of decency and usefulness. Do not put gold rings on your fingers; for all these ornaments are signs of lasciviousness. . . . It is not lawful for a man of God to permit the hair of your head to grow long, and to bush it up together, nor to allow it to spread about, nor to puff it up, nor by combing and plaiting to make it curl and shine.[9]

As regards their leisure time, Christians were to avoid 'indecent spectacles' such as theatres and public sports;[10] they were not to 'club together for drinking entertainments',[11] nor were they to enter taverns.[12] They were discouraged from being gadders abroad, from rambling about the streets, and were exhorted to rest at home and read the Scriptures. This did not, however, involve absolute seclusion; hospitality was advocated, Gorgonia being again extolled upon this score:

Who opened her house to those who live according to God with a more graceful and bountiful welcome? And which is greater still, who bade them welcome with such modesty and godly greetings? Further, who showed a mind more moved in sufferings? Whose soul was more sympathetic to those in trouble? Whose hand more liberal to those in want? I should not hesitate to honour her with the words of Job: Her door was opened to all comers; the stranger did not lodge in the street. She was eyes to the blind, feet to the lame, a mother to the orphan. Why should I say more of her compassion to widows, than that its fruit which she obtained was never to be called widow herself? Her house was a common abode to all the needy of her family; and her good no less common to all in need than their own belonged to each.[13]

Christians were also encouraged to engage in good works and Basil was praised for providing 'bowls of soup and meat' during a famine.[14] Basil too was among those who established hospitals for the sick, and his letters reveal him defending his foundation to the provincial governor, petitioning the prefect's accountant to exempt it from taxation and commending the chorpepiscopus who managed it for him to an official.[15] It was in this way, by both precept and practice, that the Church sought to baptize the whole of daily life into Christianity, attempting also to make worship the centre of that life, by increasing the number of acts of public devotions and by encouraging the practice of communicating at home from the reserved sacrament during the week.[16]

CHAPTER SIX

FURTHER ADVANCE

The Background – Sources – Expansion and Development – Beliefs – Worship – Social Life – Conclusion

THE BACKGROUND

Paganism

THE CLOSING decades of the fourth century were to witness a final pagan revival in the West, where the senate, now that Constantinople had displaced Rome, assumed once again a conspicuous role. As guardian of the Roman heritage, including the state religion, the senators sought to defend the dying paganism, and taking advantage of the toleration prevailing under Julian's successors, Praetextatus, as *praefectus urbis*, restored the last known pagan religious monument to be dedicated by an official, viz. the *Porticus Deorum Consentium* in 367 or 368.[1] Gratian, however, under the influence of Ambrose did not assume the title of *pontifex maximus*, and in 382 withdrew the funds that had supported the public cult and removed the altar of Victory from the Curia. The pagan caucus in the senate led by Symmachus, carried on a struggle throughout the next decade to have the altar restored, but the offensive against paganism was renewed by Theodosius, who issued a series of laws prohibiting pagan worship throughout the empire.[2]

The defection of the West under Eugenius in 392 gave the pagan cause a last chance, and the revival, led by Flavianus, resulted in widespread lapses from Christianity. Processions in honour of the Magna Mater and of Isis were seen again in the streets of Rome and the attempt was made to restore many of the ancient cults. With Theodosius' victory on 6th September 394 the pagan renaissance collapsed and the unsuccessful struggle for a lost cause came to an end. Arcadius in the East and Honorius in the West promulgated laws prohibiting sacrifice and temple worship[3] – henceforth the only religion was to be Christianity.

Church and State

The extent to which the Church was now assuming a dominating role may be gauged from the relations between Ambrose of Milan and the emperor Theodosius. In the year 388 the Christians of Callinicum, a small town on the Euphrates, burnt down a Jewish synagogue and some monks had also fired a church belonging to a group of Valentinian Gnostics. Theodosius ordered the local bishop to rebuild the synagogue at his own expense and the monks to be punished for their disorderly conduct. Ambrose then saw fit to intervene, arguing that this was in effect a condemnation of the bishop to martyrdom, since this was the only way he could avoid the apostasy he would certainly commit were he to obey the imperial command. When Theodosius directed that the cost of the rebuilding was to be borne by the State, Ambrose was still not satisfied, declaring that in a Christian State public money should not be spent on non-Christian worship, and as for the plea that the State must maintain order, religion was more important than even that. The bishop followed this with a sermon, directly aimed at the emperor who was in the congregation, and indeed he was prepared to forbid him communion if he did not withdraw his decision. Theodosius gave way and the civil authority thus bowed to that of the Church.[4]

The second clash between Ambrose and the emperor arose in connexion with happenings at Thessalonica in 390. A charioteer, idolized by the populace, attempted to rape a Gothic officer by the name of Butheric and was cast into prison. Riots took place and Butheric was killed. Theodosius sent orders for a secret massacre; soldiers were to surround the amphitheatre when the people gathered to see the games and were then to slaughter the spectators. Although the emperor relented and sent a revocation of his order, it arrived too late and seven thousand were butchered. Ambrose accordingly excommunicated him and it was only after a penance lasting several months that Theodosius was restored to communion.[5] In this incident many have seen the beginning of the road to Canossa, where in 1070 Henry IV was humiliated before Gregory VII, and of the claim of the medieval popes to the right to depose emperors.

The Empire

The *pax Romana* which had so facilitated the spread of Christianity in its early years was soon to become a memory rather than a present reality. Its disruption was the outcome both of internal conflicts and external pressures. The empire of the late fourth century was in many respects like a fortress surrounded by turbulent seas; as its defences were weakened from within, so it became less able to withstand the wave upon wave of barbarian invasions that no longer broke against it but broke over it.

Back in 376 a decisive step had been taken when Valens allowed the Visigoths, hard pressed by the Huns, to cross the Danube and settle in Moesia and Thrace. The external enemy was thereby provided with a base within the fortifications themselves, and their revolts, issuing in Valens' death in 378, were to continue, although temporarily brought to an end by Theodosius in 382. Internal struggles next dominate the scene when, the following year, Gratian was murdered and the usurper Maximus, allowing Valentinian II to keep Italy, Africa and West Illyricum, ruled the provinces beyond the Alps. In 387 he invaded Italy and Theodosius was compelled to march against him, securing victory at Siscia in Pannonia. Peace was short-lived: in 392 Arbogastes, commander of the forces in Gaul, had Valentinian assassinated and appointed Eugenius as puppet emperor; both were to die in 394 when Theodosius was again victorious.

Upon Theodosius' death in 395, the empire was divided between his two sons, the ten-year-old Honorius in the West, dominated by the Vandal Stilicho, who was Master-General of the Roman armies, and the weak Arcadius in the East, who was successively under the influence of Rufinus and of the eunuch Eutropius. Into the tortuous and fascinating story of the moves and counter-moves of the strong men behind the two thrones it is not necessary to go; it is necessary to emphasize how these rivalries steadily weakened the power of the empire. It was this that in part encouraged the Visigoths to move once more. In 395, under Alaric, they entered Macedonia and penetrated into southern Greece, only to be halted by Stilicho. In the same year hordes of trans-Caucasian Huns poured through the Caspian gates and brought desolation as far south as Syria. In 398 there was a revolt in Africa under Gildo which once again occupied the attention of Stilicho. Three years later he was again in the field, this time against Alaric who had crossed the Alps into Italy. In 405 the Vandals under Radegast swept south as far as Florence and then retreated into Gaul. At the same time there was a revolt of the legions in Britain and their leader, Constantine, brought his forces across the channel into Gaul, adding, in 408, Spain to the territories under his control. The murder of Stilicho in the same year removed the one general capable of out-manœuvring Alaric, who thereupon invested Rome itself: this was the first of three sieges, the final one in 410 issuing in the fall of the eternal city and the ravaging of Italy to its southernmost tip.

Meanwhile, in 409, the Vandals had poured down from Gaul into Spain, and, next, the Visigoths, now led by Ataulf upon the death of Alaric, entered Gaul. The dismemberment of the western empire was now proceeding apace, further assisted by a fresh revolt in Africa under Heraclian. When Honorius died in 423 he left to his son Valentinian III a realm almost as disunited as it had been before the *pax Romana* was established.

In the East, where the eight-year-old Theodosius II had succeeded his father Aracadius in 408 the situation was more propitious for the preservation of imperial rule. While the northern tribes made incursions into Asia Minor and elsewhere, their eyes were mainly fixed upon the West, and as a consequence of this movement the eastern empire, with its greater wealth and more strongly organized defences, was able to withstand attacks and to allow itself, as it were, to be by-passed and so to survive. Marcian (450–7) and Leo I (457–74) were both reforming emperors and secured peace, while Zeno (474–91) created an army of native troops, as distinct from barbarian mercenaries, and so paved the way for the victories of Justinian (527–65). But the final extinction of the West was in sight.

First came the loss of Africa. There the imperial commander Boniface was suspected of treason and, in his own defence, seems to have invited the Vandals in Spain to cross the straits of Gibraltar. In 429 Genseric, at the head of a large army, descended upon the province and within ten years was master of the country, ruling over an independent Vandal kingdom. Next came the incursions of the Huns under Attila, who had previously attacked the East (441–50), but in 450 led his hordes into Gaul. Defeated at the battle of the Catalaunian plain by Aetius, he invaded Italy, only to turn back eventually as his troops were thinned by famine and disease and harried by the imperial forces. Jealous of Aetius' success, Valentinian foolishly had him killed and himself suffered the same fate as an act of revenge in 455. Calamity now followed upon calamity, as the Vandals sailed from Africa and sacked Rome and one short-lived emperor followed another: Maximus (455), Avitus (455–6), Marjorian (457–61), Severus (461–5), Athemius (467–72), Olybrius (472), Glycerius (473–4) and Julius Nepos (474–5). Finally Romulus Augustulus (475–6) resigned the purple to Zeno, thus bringing the western empire to its inglorious end. It is a testimony to the strength of the Church that it survived all this turbulence and destruction and emerged in the West as the one unifying and civilizing influence, gradually converting the Semi-Arian Goths and Vandals to orthodoxy and spreading the faith among the pagan Franks and Burgundians who now lived within the bounds of the old Roman empire.

SOURCES

If the Golden Age of patristic literature began with the first ecumenical council, by the second, in 381, it was in no way diminished in quality but, if anything, was going from strength to strength. The names of John Chrysostom, Jerome, Ambrose and Augustine, if they stood alone, would be sufficient to render any one period illustrious, and they were but four of the many outstanding scholars and men of original genius that now devoted their pens to the Christian cause.

Church historians

In the field of ecclesiastical history the model remained the work of the pioneer Eusebius of Caesarea, and indeed his literary heirs were concerned either to translate, if they were Latins, or to continue his narrative from the point at which he had left it. Rufinus of Aquileia (*c.* 345–410) produced a Latin version and abridgement, bringing the narrative up to AD 395, possibly on the basis of a work already completed by Eusebius' second successor Gelasius. A further continuation of Eusebius, covering the years from 305 to 439, was produced by Socrates (born *c.* 380) at Constantinople and his work was drawn upon by Sozomen, who *c.* 450 gave an account of the period 324–425. This valuable source material can be supplemented and checked at various points from the work of many imitators, such as Thedoret of Cyrus (*c.* 393–466).

Antiochene and Syrian writers

Equally important as a source for the history of theological ideas are two of the writings of Epiphanius, who was born *c.* 315 near Gaza, presided over a monastery for some thirty years and became bishop of Salamis in Cyprus in 367, occupying this see for thirty-six years until his death. His *Ancoratus*, 374, is a compendium of the doctrines of the Church and his *Medicine Chest* or *Haereses*, 374–7, describes eighty heresies. Very much a traditionalist, he was opposed to Greek learning and for this reason took part in the struggle against Origenism which began in the last decade of the fourth century. In particular he disliked Origen's method of allegorical interpretation and in this respect had affinity with the Antiochene School of theology which favoured a more literal exegesis. One of the most outstanding products of this school was Theodore of Mopsuestia, who studied under the sophist Libanius and, after a period of monastic retirement, was appointed to his bishopric in Cilicia in 392. His commentaries reveal a remarkable critical acumen and his *Catechetical Lectures* are important evidence for the liturgies of baptism and the eucharist. He numbered among his friends John Chrysostom and among his pupils Nestorius, and posthumously – he died in 428 – suffered the fate of the latter in being condemned, possibly unjustly, for Christological heresy.

John Chrysostom

The life of Theodore's friend requires a more complete account, for while John was rather a popularizer than an original thinker, his career illustrates the relations of Church and State in the East, where the former came to be dominated by the latter, and the contrast with the situation in the West, as evidenced by the exchanges between Ambrose and Theodosius, where the Church came to dominate the State. John's episcopate also reveals the rivalry between Alexandria and Constantinople, which played not an unimportant part in the Church history of the early fifth century.

John was born between 344 and 354 at Antioch[1] and since his father, an army officer, died when he was young, he was brought up by his mother Anthusa. Educated in philosophy by Andragathius and in rhetoric by Libanius, he at first embraced the vocation of a lawyer, but under the influence of the bishop Meletius he became ardent in his Christian faith and withdrew into monastic retirement. In 381 he was ordained deacon by Meletius and in 386 priest by Flavian, and for the next twelve years he entranced the congregations of Antioch with his preaching; so intently did they hang upon his words – which earned him the title of Chrysostom, i.e. Golden-Mouth – that pickpockets were able to ply a busy trade. To this period belong his ninety homilies on Matthew and his eighty-eight on John, together with studies of other Old and New Testament books, and *On the Priesthood.*

In 397 Nectarius, bishop of Constantinople, died, and the following year John was appointed to succeed him. From the first he gave offence to all: his uncompromising denunciation of vice affected the clergy as well as the rich; his refusal to parade in pomp, his ascetic practices, his profuse almsgiving, his selling of some marbles bought for one of the churches in order to provide a hospital for sick strangers – all earned him unpopularity. Entirely fearless, he fulminated against iniquity wherever he perceived it; when the eunuch Eutropius fled to his church for sanctuary, he braved the emperor Arcadius to his face. He was not, however, wholly absorbed by the claims of moral reformation amongst his clergy and his flock. He managed to enlist many bishops in a successful attempt to end the schism at Antioch by the recognition of Flavian; he obtained from the emperor fresh decrees against paganism and he sent missionaries to labour among the Goths. But the storm was gathering that was eventually to sweep him from his post. In AD 400 a synod of twenty-two bishops met at Constantinople and various charges were brought against one of them. John appointed a commission of three bishops to go into the matter, and when they were hindered by intrigue in the performance of their task he went in person to Ephesus in 401 to settle the affair. He forthwith deposed at least six bishops – with good reason – and this necessarily increased the number of his enemies. On his return to the capital he found that plots against him were rife and that his character was being slandered; most dangerous of all, it was being asserted that he had used treasonable language against the empress Eudoxia and she determined upon his downfall. Theophilus of Alexandria, known as the 'weathercock', was also anxious to have him removed, for as his saintly character enhanced the prestige of Constantinople so that of Alexandria declined.

In 402 Theophilus was himself summoned to the capital to give an account of his proceedings against the 'Tall Brothers'. These four men had presided over a monastery at Nitria and had been ousted by Theophilus because they would not be subservient to him. Thinking attack the best means of defence, Theophilus first sent Epiphanius to charge John with heresy – a task which the aged prelate found himself unable to fulfil – and then came in person as accuser. In August 403, he held a synod at Chalcedon, known as the Synod of the Oak from the name of the villa that housed it. This body, completely under Theophilus' control, declared John deposed. Their decision was accepted by the emperor and, to avoid bloodshed, John surrendered to his officers and was led into exile, but an earthquake that shook the palace a few days later induced the superstitious Eudoxia to ask for, and secure, his recall. John was hesitant to re-enter the city because of a canon of the Council of Antioch in 341 which decreed that a bishop deposed by one synod could not return to his see unless reinstated by a second and larger one; but popular impatience was irresistible and he was led back in triumph.

Some two months later, in September 403, a statue of the empress was erected close to the cathedral; at its dedication the usual ceremonies lasted several days, with games and dancing and other amusements which reached such a pitch that the cathedral services were disturbed. John's disapproval was taken by Eudoxia to be a personal affront and she communicated with Theophilus in a further attempt to have him removed. The bishop of Alexandria would not visit the capital again, but through his envoys invoked the canon of Antioch. The validity of this canon was not universally acknowledged and the legality of the sentence passed by the Synod of the Oak was highly doubtful, but the emperor forthwith ordered John to cease performing his ecclesiastical functions. He refused, and on Holy Saturday, 404, when he was baptizing the catechumens, soldiers broke in and drove the faithful from the church. A few weeks later the bishop was exiled and was hastily transported to Cucusus in Lesser Armenia. His quiet surrender and withdrawal did not prevent violence; his followers rioted, burning the senate, the forum and the cathedral. John himself, after three years of peace, was ordered to Pityus and died as result of his harsh treatment on the journey, an example to everyone of the fate that awaited those who opposed the imperial will.

Nestorius

Nestorius, who was also formed by the Antiochene school and like John was to incur the hostility of another bishop of Alexandria, Cyril, was of Persian descent. In 428 he was appointed to Constantinople and it was his preaching there that led to a violent Christological controversy, to be considered below, and to his deposition by the third ecumenical council at Ephesus in 431. After four years in a monastery, where he had spent his early manhood, near Antioch, he was banished to Oasis in Upper Egypt. Since his works were condemned to be burned by Theodosius II in 435 only fragments remain, apart from a few sermons and the *Bazaar of Heraclides* which is a defence of his teaching written in his latter years.

Cyril of Alexandria

Nestorius' implacable opponent was Cyril, nephew to and successor, in 412, of Theophilus of Alexandria. Present at the Synod of the Oak, jealous of the prestige of his see and therefore predisposed to be antagonistic to the bishops of the capital, ruthless against his opponents and determined to uphold what he believed to be the true Christian doctrine, Cyril entered the fray against Nestorius in 429 and was gratified to witness the success of his campaign. He died in 444, leaving a voluminous literary legacy, consisting of many commentaries, sermons and letters and a series of dogmatic treatises concerned principally before 428 with Arianism and after 428 with Nestorianism.

Western writers – Ambrose

In the West, Ambrose was the great anti-Arian champion, in succession to Hilary of Poitiers. Born at Treves in 339, his father being Praetorian Prefect of the Gauls, Ambrose was brought up in Rome by his early-widowed mother. Trained in all the branches of a liberal education, especially in grammar, jurisprudence and rhetoric, he became a lawyer and achieved such distinction that by the age of thirty he was appointed governor of the province of Liguria and Aemilia, with the rank of pro-consul. In 374 he presided at the election of a new bishop of Milan, following the death of the Arian Auxentius and, despite his protests, was himself invested with the honour. He immediately distributed his possessions to the poor and devoted himself wholeheartedly to his new task, spending long hours in study, fasting each day until evening, taking communion daily, having open house to all his flock and spending much of the night in meditation and writing. He was so successful in the ordering of his diocese that Arianism practically ceased to exist.

One of the most notable features of Ambrose's character was his sturdy and fearless independence; this has already been exemplified by his relations with Theodosius described above and it was equally evident in his dealings with the Arian Justina, mother of Valentinian II. Upon the murder of Gratian, Justina approached Ambrose to intercede with Maximus; the bishop journeyed to Treves where circumstances compelled him to stay for several months. His dauntlessness is shown by his refusal to communicate with either Maximus, because of his guilt, or those clergy who had brought about the execution of those charged with Priscillianism. His embassy was not without success in that it delayed Maximus sufficiently to allow Valentinian's generals to seize the alpine passes, and it further earned the young emperor's gratitude who, at Ambrose's instigation, refused the request of Symmachus to have the altar of Victory restored to the senate house. Justina was not so grateful and used her position to further Arianism. In 385 she demanded that a church at Milan should be handed over to the Arians; Ambrose refused and soldiers were sent to take over the property; the populace almost became out of hand, but Ambrose was able to control them and Justina, realizing she was playing with fire, withdrew the troops. The next year the attack was renewed when a decree was published permitting all Arians freedom to hold religious assemblies, death being the penalty for those who withstood them. Again Ambrose stood fast, again soldiers were sent, and again the court climbed down. The death of Justina shortly afterwards meant that the Arian cause had lost its leading supporter in the West and that Ambrose's policy had triumphed.

Despite a most active episcopate, Ambrose found time to write many books; for Gratian he produced *On the Faith*, which defended the Son's divinity, and *On the Holy Spirit*, which owed much to the treatises of Basil and Didymus the Blind on the same theme. His lectures *On the Mysteries* and *On the Sacraments*, apparently taken down in shorthand and then revised, give important information about the Milanese rites of baptism and the eucharist. His orations and letters are products of fine literary workmanship and *On the Duties of the Ministers*, modelled upon Cicero's work of the same title, is a compendium of Christian ethics. Ambrose's principal concern was practical religion; he had the

Christian life constantly in view and both wrote and taught, not for the scholar, but for the ordinary believer. Nevertheless many of the ideas that Augustine was to develop so brilliantly found a beginning in the thought of Ambrose, his master.

Augustine

The possession of Augustine's *Confessions* (397–401), of his *Retractions* (427) in which he gave an account of his literary productions, of over four hundred sermons and more than two hundred letters, gives an insight into their author's mind and a detailed knowledge of his life that is almost unique. Born at Thagaste in 354, the son of a pagan municipal officer and his Christian wife, Monica, Augustine was enrolled among the catechumens at birth, but his initiation was to be delayed for many years. Continuing his youthful studies at Madaura, he went to Carthage in 371, where he attached himself to the Manichees and entered into a union with a woman whom he never married and who bore him a son (d. 390). Setting up as a teacher of rhetoric, Augustine removed to Rome in 383, despite his mother's protests, and, although at first associating with the Manichees, he entered upon a phase of agnosticism. In the following year he was appointed professor of rhetoric at Milan and there he came under the influence of Ambrose. From him he learned of the allegorical exegesis of the Old Testament, which served to remove the Manichean objections to it, and he was introduced to Neo-Platonic thought, which enabled him to understand God as a purely spiritual substance, to regard evil as a negation and to see the Plotinian conception of the *Nous* fulfilled in the Logos of the Fourth Gospel. He now turned to the letters of Paul, was impressed by accounts of the desert monks, and, in the autumn of 385, resigned his post and retired to Cassiciacum, a friend's estate near the city, to prepare for baptism. On Holy Saturday 387 he was baptized to the great joy of his mother who had recently joined him from Africa. A few months later he set out for home, but upon his mother's death at Ostia he stayed in Rome for a further year, reaching Thagaste in 388 and setting up a small monastic community. In 391 bishop Valerius of Hippo prevailed upon him to become priest; four years later he was consecrated as Valerius' coadjutor bishop and succeeded him soon afterwards.

Augustine's episcopate was largely occupied with controversy; until 400 he was on the offensive against Manicheism; for the next twelve years he concerned himself with the Donatist schism, and from then he was occupied with the Pelagian heresy. He died in 430 at the age of seventy-six, in the third month of the siege of Hippo by the Vandals under Genseric; thus while he was the contemporary and interpreter of the fall of Rome, in his *City of God*, he was spared the knowledge of the devastation of his home country and of the bitter Arian persecutions that were to follow the triumph of the Vandals.

According to his own account,[2] by the year 427 Augustine had written ninety-three literary works and two hundred and thirty-two books, apart from his sermons and letters. Only ten of the works he discusses have been lost, and it is difficult, if one is not to be exhaustive, to pick out any particular ones as more important than others. His chief dogmatic work was *On the Trinity* and took twenty years, 399–419, to complete. Amongst his anti-Donatist treatises mention may be made of *On Baptism* (400–1), and in the anti-Pelagian corpus there is *On the Spirit and the Letter* (412). *On Christian Learning* stands at the head of his work on biblical scholarship. The *City of God*, published in instalments from 413 to 426, is an apology for Christianity and gives the first outlines of a theology of history. It was prompted by the pagan charge that the fall of Rome was due to the Christian encouragement of disregard for the pagans' gods, and it presented the thesis that the ancient cultus provided neither earthly happiness nor the pledge of eternal life and that world history comprises the struggle between faith and unbelief.

Jerome

Amongst Augustine's most distinguished correspondents was Jerome who is justly famous in his own right as the one responsible for the Vulgate or Latin version of the Bible. Sophronius Eusebius Hieronymus was born at Stridon in Dalmatia between 340 and 350. His parents were Christians in easy circumstances and he was sent to Rome, where he studied the Latin classics under Donatus, whose grammar was the torment of schoolboys down to the Reformation; he also devoted himself to rhetoric and logic and pursued an eclectic course in philosophy. The licentious life of the capital was not without its attractions and he was guilty of certain moral lapses, but these did not prevent his attendance at worship nor mitigate his eagerness to learn of the heroes of the Church by visiting their resting-places in the catacombs. Shortly after his baptism, he went to Treves, one of the best universities in the West, where he first developed an interest in theology. *c.* 372 he returned home, but spent most of his time at nearby Aquileia, with a circle of like-minded friends, including Rufinus. He then set off on a journey through the Middle East, visiting Thrace, Bithynia, Pontus, Galatia, Cappadocia and Cilicia. In the late summer of 373 he reached Antioch where he was laid low by a fever that was ravaging the city; upon his recovery he withdrew into the wilderness of Chalcis there to practise the ascetic life in solitude; during this time he learned Hebrew. In 379 he was ordained priest and then left for Constantinople where he attended the lectures of Gregory of Nazianzus and entered into friendly relations with Gregory of Nyssa.

At the invitation of Damasus he went to Rome to attend a council on the subject of the Antiochene schism, 382; while this meeting does not appear to have had any appreciable effect, Jerome's stay at Rome was of great importance for his future career, for he was requested by Damasus to prepare a text of the scriptures; this work, which was later to bear fruit in the so-called Vulgate, was to occupy him for several decades. The popularity which he enjoyed initially began to fade as he was unscathing in his criticism of all that fell short of the highest Christian ideal, enthusiastic in his respect for Origen and vigorously independent. The wealthy Christian ladies, who all but doted upon him, were unable to protect him against his enemies, and although at first he had been mentioned as a possible successor to Damasus, he considered it politic to leave upon his patron's death.

Visiting Antioch and then the holy places in Palestine, Jerome went on to Alexandria, next to the desert monks and finally settled at Bethlehem in the autumn of 386. In a few years a community of monks had gathered around him, as well as one for women which was directed by Paula, a Roman matron who had followed him to the holy land. Here Jerome pursued his studies for the next thirty-four years, translating, writing, teaching theology to his monks and opening a school for the children of the neighbourhood. The record of his life becomes mainly the record of his literary activities, as he lived pen in hand. He began a revision of the text of the whole Old Testament according to Origen's *Hexapla*, also taking account of the Hebrew original. He produced translations of the works of Origen, of several monastic rules, and of certain of the works of Eusebius of Caesarea. He wrote numerous commentaries on the Bible, together with homilies and letters, the last revealing his mordant wit; fiery and tempestuous, bitingly sarcastic, he was ready to engage in controversy at the slightest provocation. His part in the Origenist and Pelagian struggles will be considered below; together with his attacks upon Helvidius, Jovinian and Vigilantius.

Jerome's declining years were a period of privation and loss; often ill, with failing eyesight, he had to cope with fugitives from Rome, with threats from marauding bands, with the burning of his monasteries by Pelagians, and with the deaths, one after another, of his faithful friends; he himself died on 30th September 419 or 420.

Papal writings

Jerome's letters were addressed to all parts of the empire and his correspondents included two bishops of Rome, Damasus and Innocent. Papal letters extant from this period have a bearing both upon the claim to primacy and upon contemporary doctrinal issues. There are examples surviving from the hands of Siricius (384–99), Anastasius I (399–402), Innocent I (402–17), Zosimus (417–8), Boniface I (418–22), Caelestine I (422–32), Sixtus III (432–40) and Leo the Great (440–61). Epistle 28 of the last is his famous *Tome* which gives a classical formulation of Christological doctrine and was accepted by the Council of Chalcedon. Leo has also left a number of sermons delivered on the feasts of Christ and containing references to theological questions.

Christian poets

Beside the writers of theological treatises and letters must be placed Christian poets who began to practise their art in the fourth century. Whereas, apart from Gregory of Nazianzus, the Greek East produced no important poets, the West included, amongst many who were versifiers, Prudentius and Paulinus of Nola. The first was born in 348 at Calahorra, was twice consul of a Spanish province, held high office under Theodosius I and died after 405. Some ten thousand lines of his verse remain, containing hymns for Christmas and Epiphany, a defence of the Trinity, an attack upon the pagan Symmachus and praises of the martyrs. Paulinus was born in 353 at Bordeaux, became governor of Campania in 379, visited Spain and retired to Nola where he was elected bishop in 409, dying in 431. His thirty-five poems may lack creative power, but they contain useful information about Church life in the late fourth century. As a composer of hymns, reference should be made again to Ambrose who made use of Greek church tunes for his musical settings.

Monastic authors

Many of the authors referred to above produced treatises and letters that bear upon the monastic movement. Jerome, for example, wrote extensively on the ascetic life and translated the rules of Pachomius, Theodore and Orisisius. Augustine was responsible for a rule of his own and wrote *On the Work of Monks c.* 400 to insist that they earned their own living by manual labour. Two men, however, stand out in this sphere: Evagrius of Pontus and John Cassian.

Evagrius (346–99) was ordained deacon by Gregory of Nazianzus but left Constantinople for Nitria in 382. There he wrote a series of works on spirituality which have only gradually been recovered. His studies of prayer, of the capital sins and his maxims reveal him as the great architect of the contemplative way. It seems probable that John Cassian met him during his visit to Egypt and certainly Cassian's own writings on monasticism reveal the influence of Evagrian ideas. Cassian was born *c.* 360 in Scythia Minor and was trained in a monastery at Bethlehem. He next visited Egypt and *c.* 400 came to Constantinople where John Chrysostom ordained him deacon. After the fall of his patron, Cassian moved to Rome and then *c.* 415 founded at Marseilles two monasteries, one for men and one for women. Here he wrote his three main works: the *Institutes* in 425, which he describes as concerned with 'what belongs to the outer man and the customs of Caenobia', i.e. the life and system of a monastery; the *Conferences*, 426, whose subject was 'the training of the inner man and the perfection of the heart', and finally, in 430, *On the Incarnation against Nestorius*. In his last years he was accused of Semi-Pelagianism but died in peace in 435.

EXPANSION AND DEVELOPMENT

The failure of Eugenius and the triumph of Theodosius, together with the laws promulgated by the latter and his sons, meant that the pagan cults no longer had any legal status. Christianity was the sole religion recognized throughout the empire. But the execution of the government policy depended upon the enthusiasm of local officials and this was by no means uniform. Nevertheless there were many who were eager and willing to stamp out the vestiges of paganism, such were the counts Jovius and Gaudentius in Africa, 399,[1] such too was Theophilus, bishop of Alexandria. In city after city, Christians, assisted by a detachment of soldiers, attacked and destroyed the ancient temples, the most famous to suffer this fate being the Serapeum at Alexandria.[2] In other centres temples were not razed but were transformed into Christian churches, e.g. the basilica of Junius Bassus on the Esquiline became the church of St Andrew in 470, while the Parthenon was eventually dedicated to all the martyrs under Boniface IV (608–15). The result of this activity was a shift in the Christian polemic against the pagan temples; whereas previously they had been condemned as the abodes of demons, now they were held up to ridicule as houses of trickery, secret passages and hollow statues, thus enabling the priests to speak through the idols' mouths, being exposed to view.[3] But by no means all pagan edifices disappeared: in the sixth century the towns of Borium and Angila in Libya had a temple of Jupiter Ammon and one of Alexander of Macedon,[4] and Benedict in 529 found one dedicated to Apollo on Monte Cassino, whither the countryfolk brought their offerings and at which they performed sacrifice.[5]

Indicative of the declining paganism was the dwindling of the stream of Christian apologetic literature. Augustine's *City of God* was one of the last great works to belong to this category, defending the faith of responsibility for the fall of Rome, and by the middle of the fifth century the anti-pagan writings had all but ceased; educated men were now in the main Christian, and the non-Christian barbarians required other methods.

The conversion of the barbarians

Missionary activity now increased. Ambrose corresponded with Queen Fritigil of the Marcomanni[6] and encouraged missions in the Tyrol. Vigilius of Trent (*c.* 385–405) co-operated with him and sent his representatives into the Alpine districts, some of them suffering martyrdom as a result of their endeavours.[7] Niceta of Remesiana evangelized the Goths in Dacia and the Bessian brigands in his neighbourhood.[8] In the East John Chrysostom organized work among the heathen Goths[9] and, even in exile, established mission stations in Cilicia and Phoenicia.[10] In North Africa Augustine sought out the non-Christian in his diocese, wrote many letters presenting the faith to pagans and devised a graded catechetical instruction suited to the different educational backgrounds of the converts.[11]

This activity was in the main confined to the empire and indeed, at least in the north, missionary work beyond the frontiers was slight. The tribes that now pressed down into northern Greece, Italy, France and Spain were converted after their entry rather than before. This conversion, which is difficult to chronicle because of defective evidence,[12] had two distinct stages as regards the majority of the invaders: first they were converted to Arianism and, second, often much later, they were brought over to Catholicism. The first to be won to the Arian form of Christianity were the Visigoths during their settlement in Moesia, 382–95. Their fellow Ostrogoths, in the Crimea, were still pagan in 406 but, probably through the efforts of Goths from Constantinople, they were won over while in Pannonia, 456–72. Gothic missionaries also had success with the Rugi, a little before 482, while they occupied Lower Austria. The Rugi, in their turn, probably evangelized the Lombards, 488–505, who followed them into Lower Austria. The Gepids were converted between 440 and 472, while the Burgundians were much earlier, adopting Arianism between 412 and 436, when in Germania Prima. A little before them the Vandals, having reached Spain, became Arians, 409–17.

Of these various groups, three stubbornly refused to give up the heresy they had embraced, being eventually overthrown by force: the Vandals, now in North Africa, in 534, and the Ostrogoths in 554 by the Byzantines, and the Gepids in 572 by the Lombards. The remainder made the transition from Arianism to Catholicism from the sixth century onwards, sometimes as the result of patient orthodox teaching, sometimes, as in Spain, as a result of armed struggle. In 516 the Burgundians were converted to Catholicism; the Visigoths, their king Recared influenced by the teaching of Martin of Braga and Leander of Seville, rejected their former beliefs at Toledo in 587; a restoration under Witteric in 603 ended with his assassination seven years later. The Lombards, who invaded Italy in 568, were also Arian, but the continued loyalty and solidarity of the orthodox population and the lack of unity between the Arian churches, each limited to its particular tribe or kingdom, led to its final disappearance by the end of the seventh century, after a period of wavering. So Agilulf, who died in 616, was an Arian while his wife Theudelinda was a Catholic; Adaloald (616–21) shared his mother's orthodoxy, but his successor Arioald (626–36) reverted to Arianism, although his wife Gundiperga was orthodox. Liutprand (712–44), probably the greatest of their leaders, also rejected Arianism and from then onwards the movement failed to win any serious support.

The Franks were one of the few tribes that did not follow the path from paganism through Arianism to orthodoxy. Occupying Belgium and the Rhine lands, they moved down into France in the last decades of the fifth century. Clovis, who became king in 482, married the Burgundian Clotilda, a Catholic, and for diverse reasons himself adhered to the orthodox Christian faith, being baptized on Christmas Day, 496.[13] As the founder of what was to become the most important of the kingdoms which in the West succeeded the Roman empire, including amongst his descendants Charles the Great who ruled over the Carolingian empire, Clovis was an essential link in preserving a large area of the old Roman domain for the Christian faith.

That the Church, so closely identified with the Roman State in its declining years, did not go down in the general ruin was in part an index of growing strength and vitality; it was also in part due to the fact that many of the invading tribes did not so much wish to destroy Rome as to succeed to its splendour. So, according to Ataulf, who led the Visigoths from Italy into Gaul:

> At first I longed to obliterate the Roman name and to convert all Roman soil into an empire of the Goths. . . . But I have been taught by much experience that the unbridled license of the Goths will never admit of their obeying laws, and without laws a republic is not a republic. I have therefore chosen the safer course of aspiring to the glory of restoring and increasing the Roman name by Gothic vigour; and I hope to be handed down to posterity as the initiator of Roman restoration.[14]

In this restoration the Church was regarded as having a necessary place.

Extension to East and South

The termination of the war with Rome and the accession of Sapor III brought peace to the Church in Persia and indeed it enjoyed some measure of royal favour. By 410 Christianity was so well organized that a council could be held at Seleucia, which accepted the creed and canons of Nicaea, and its findings were approved by the king. Ten years later a brief persecution broke out, to be followed by a further period of freedom for the Church from molestation, although it was disturbed by Nestorian and Monophysite disputes and progressively fell into decadence.

In Armenia, under Sahag *c.* 402, the Church achieved some autonomy since he was responsible for the creation of a national literature by his encouragement of the monk Mesrop or Machtots to devise an alphabet. The Bible and select works of the Greek fathers were translated and independent theological treatises followed. Persecution at the hands of the Persians ensued in 454 and although the Church survived, it embraced Monophysitism at a council in 491 and became cut off from its westerly neighbours.

Further east the faith penetrated steadily. On the borders of Arabia amongst the nomadic tribes Euthymius was responsible for converting a whole group,[15] while Simeon, the pillar-saint, exercised a wide influence.[16] By the time of Chalcedon in 451 nineteen bishops from Arabia were able to be present, and towards the end of the fifth century a law of Zeno prescribed the setting up of bishoprics in all new and restored towns.[17] Even further east, Christian communities were being established, a monastery being founded on the Bahrein islands in the Persian Gulf *c.* 390[18] and others in Ceylon.

To the south Christianity made progress in Axum and towards the end of the fifth century the mission of the nine monks to Abyssinia took place, each one establishing a monastery in the district he evangelized.

Schisms and disputes – Donatism

As previously, however, progress, both extensively and intensively, was hampered by disputes and schisms. In North Africa the Donatist schism persisted;[19] by the Council of Constantinople in 381 the dissidents were once more in the ascendant under Parmenian, who was to die in 391. So secure did they feel that they could even indulge in their own internal schisms – the Maximianists opposing Primian, Parmenian's successor. Then, through the prompting and example of Optatus of Thamugadi they gave support to another anti-Roman revolt led by Gildo, a younger brother of the previous rebel Firmus. The Donatists did not fare so well after the overthrow of Gildo in 398 as they had done after the suppression of Firmus, and indeed the next twelve years were to witness their virtual eclipse, although not their final extinction. The State, more and more menaced by the invasions of the Germanic tribes, determined to have no further truck with a movement whose loyalty was suspect and the Catholics launched an energetic counter-attack under the competent direction of Aurelius of Carthage and Augustine of Hippo.

To each Donatist stronghold an able Catholic opponent was consecrated and they availed themselves of imperial legislation to crush them wherever possible. Their efforts were backed by a series of councils and by a voluminous literary offensive in which Augustine played a leading role. At first the Donatists gave as good as they received and Petilian of Constantine wrote forcibly in their defence. The situation, however, steadily deteriorated, violence becoming widespread, until the Catholics determined upon open persecution. The development of Augustine's own thought to this point has been outlined by him in a letter to the Donatist Vicentius:

> At first it was my view that no one should be led by force into the unity of Christ, that action should be confined to words, combat to discussion and victory to the exercise of reason and that furthermore we were concerned with false Catholics and not with out-and-out heretics. That was my view. It has had to give way before that of my contradictors, not before their words but before the facts they have adduced. In the first place, they opposed me with the history of my native town Thagaste, which at one time belonged entirely to the Donatist party and which, since then, has been brought over to the Catholic unity through fear of the imperial laws: it is now so hostile to your party of hatred and death that it seems always to have been a stranger to it. Further I have been presented with the examples of many other towns. . . .

Augustine goes on to cite the violence of the Donatists as further grounds for seeking the intervention of the imperial authorities.[20] So in 405 Honorius promounced the Donatists to be heretics and their property forfeit, but though the policy of suppression was pursued with vigour, they were still undefeated in 410 when an imperial 'mediator' was despatched to Africa in the person of the count Marcellinus. Under his authority a conference was called to Carthage, where eventually 286 Catholic and 284 Donatist bishops met on 1st June 411. The result was a renewed ban on Donatism whose assemblies were forbidden, property confiscated and clergy exiled. As a consequence many came over to the opposing allegiance, but throughout the seventeen years that remained of Roman rule in Africa, 412–29, the struggle continued, nor was there any sign of its final end when Augustine died in 430. Indeed there are traces of Donatism still active in the seventh century, and its final disappearance coincided with the destruction of Catholicism when both were swept away by Islam, each greatly weakened by their fruitless struggle and by their persecution at the hands of the Arian Vandals.

Disputes with Helvidius, Jovinian and Vigilantius

More restricted and less disastrous in their consequences, though some would consider their doctrinal and devotional results undesirable, were the controversies in which the names of Helvidius, Jovinian and Vigilantius figured together with that of Jerome who was their chief opponent. Each of these debates reveals Jerome's championship of extreme asceticism and the reluctance of his adversaries to accept the ascetic ideal as supreme.

Helvidius denied the widely held belief in the perpetual virginity of the Virgin Mary. He argued that references in the gospels to Jesus' 'brothers' and 'sisters' indicated that Mary and Joseph had subsequent issue and that his view was supported by Tertullian, as indeed it was.[21] Jerome, writing in 383, argued, somewhat speciously, that those mentioned were either children of Joseph by a former marriage or cousins of Jesus, being the children of Mary's sister.[22] Siricius, bishop of Rome (384–99) had also occasion to condemn a similar denial of the perpetual virginity in a letter he addressed to Anysius of Thessalonica against Bonosus of Sardica.

Siricius was also concerned with the Jovinian controversy, issuing *c.* 390 an encyclical on the subject, and in 393 Jerome too wrote books against his teaching. Jovinian maintained that 'a virgin is no better as such than a wife in the sight of God', that abstinence is no better than thankful partaking of food, that the baptized cannot sin and that there is no gradation of rewards in heaven. Jerome took up Jovinian's first proposition that the contemporary holding up of virginity was a reflection of the ideas of Marcion, Mani and the Encratites. Augustine too entered the lists in 401 with his *De Sancta Virginitate* in which he praised the virginal state against Jovinian.

An exaggerated estimate of virginity was also assailed by Vigilantius, another protagonist of Jerome of whom more personal details are known. He was born *c.* 370 at Calagurris on the road from Aquitaine to Spain. Taken into the service of Sulpicius Severus, he was ordained and stayed some time at Bethlehem with Jerome. Back in Gaul he produced a treatise in 406 which was the object of Jerome's abusive onslaught. In addition to his censure upon virginity, Vigilantius objected to the worship of relics, to vigils and to the sending of alms to the Jerusalem church. He was so persuasive that his own bishop, Exuperius of Toulouse, was in favour of his views and it was in order to refute them that Jerome wrote his *Adversus Vigilantium.*

The Origenist controversy

Jerome had a further reason for disliking Vigilantius; he had been spreading reports that the Bethlehem scholar was a strong supporter of the views of Origen,[23] and whereas this was true of Jerome in his early years, by the turn of the century he was deep in the Origenist controversy and had changed his admiration for opposition.

Origen's many-sided genius had encouraged him to engage in much speculative thought, which tended to be disregarded by his followers and was to be seized upon by his later detractors. Opposition to his teaching was slight until Epiphanius of Salamis, eager to unmask all heretics, declared him to be one in his *Ancoratus*, 374. At first there was little reaction to this condemnation, and in Palestine Origen was widely respected, at Jerusalem by its bishop John and the presbyter Rufinus and at Bethlehem by Jerome. In 393 Aterbius, an envoy of Epiphanius, came to demand the anathematization of Origenistic errors by Jerome and Rufinus; the former, making a complete *volte face*, hastened to comply,[24] the latter refused even to see Aterbius. Shortly before Easter, in the same year, Epiphanius himself came and, being invited by the bishop to preach, delivered a sermon which was virtually a personal attack upon John for favouring the teaching of Origen.[25] Epiphanius then withdrew to Bethlehem, where he induced Jerome and his monks to break off communion with John. Since Jerome, although a presbyter, through 'modesty and humility'[26] would not celebrate the eucharist, Epiphanius next seized Jerome's younger brother Paulinianus and ordained him priest. This irregularity in defiance of John and in John's own diocese brought about a rupture between the two bishops and their adherents, which was not eased by a violent pamphlet by Jerome, *Contra Iohannem Hierosolymitanum* in 396. An uneasy reconciliation was brought about in 397 by the intervention of Theophilus of Alexandria, John recognizing Paulinianus and Jerome undertaking to harass his bishop no further.

Now that the dispute appeared to be settled, Rufinus set out for Italy and in 398 he issued a translation of Origen's *De Principiis*, omitting what seemed to him unorthodox and including, in his preface, a statement to the effect that Jerome was the authority on Origen. Jerome, furious at once more incurring the suspicion of heterodoxy, produced his own literal rendering of the *De Principiis* and sent it to Rome with letters repudiating any sympathy with Origen's thought. Marcella, his firm friend, then induced the new bishop Anastasius (399–401) to condemn Origenism and to summon Rufinus to answer for his opinions. Rufinus had, however, returned to his native Aquileia and, incensed by all that was happening, published his *Apologia adv. Hieronymum* (400), Jerome answering with his Apology against Rufinus (402). Rufinus now had the good sense to hold his peace, but Jerome was not content and even after Rufinus' death in 411 continued to pursue his memory, referring to him as the 'Grunter'[27] a nickname taken from a currently popular burlesque entitled 'The Porker's Last Will and Testament'.

Meanwhile Theophilus of Alexandria had changed sides; initially an Origenist, in the year 400 he found it politic to repudiate his former position, since this enabled him to take issue with the Nitrian monks, strong Origenists, whom he wished to control. The expulsion of the 'Tall Brothers' and their appeal to Chrysostom embroiled the bishop of Constantinople in the controversy which resulted, as previously recorded, in his exile and death. Yet the Origenist dispute was not ended; echoes of it resound throughout the fifth and sixth centuries until in 543 under Justinian the Alexandrian scholar's errors were listed and duly condemned at a council.

Pelagianism

The next controversy, which was to disturb all parts of the Church, not being confined to the East,[28] was one in which Jerome again had a part to play, although its inception was in the West and its pursuance was the concern of the North African Church and of Augustine in particular. Pelagius, who was born in the fifties of the fourth century, was British in origin and was resident in Rome during the final years of the pontificate of Damasus. He was primarily a moralist rather than a theologian, seeking to raise the ethical tone of the Church by advocating ascetic conduct, not in isolated monasteries, but in the world. He was prompted by a genuine missionary zeal to uplift the level of Christian life. His stress therefore was upon good works and upon man's freedom to perform them. He sought to develop interior perfection which he believed could be obtained by the exercise of the unaided personal will. Pelagius' teaching and example fired many with enthusiasm, and Augustine himself could not but acknowledge the virtue of his followers:

> These are not people to be easily despised; they live chastely and are praiseworthy for their good deeds; they do not believe in a false Christ, like the Manichees and many other heretics – they adore him in his true nature,

equal and co-eternal with the Father and truly made man; they believe in his first coming and they hope for his future advent.[29]

Nevertheless, the logical outcome of the Pelagian position was a disparagement of divine grace, a belief that human nature is not corrupted and a rejection of the practice of infant baptism. Man, to Pelagius, is the captain of his soul; his salvation is his own to make or mar.

On the approach of Alaric and his Goths, Pelagius and his close supporter Caelestius left Rome for Sicily. They next moved on to Carthage, Pelagius only making a brief stay before leaving for Palestine, while Caelestius remained and sought ordination, only to be faced with a charge of heresy.[30] The accusations against him, were, in Augustine's words, that he taught that

> Adam was created subject to death, and that he must have died, whether he had sinned or not; that Adam's sin hurt only himself and not the human race; that the Law no less than the Gospel leads us to the Kingdom; that there were sinless men before the coming of Christ; that new-born infants are in the same condition as Adam was before he fell . . . that a man is able to live without sin if he likes; that infants, even if they die unbaptized, have eternal life; that rich men, even if they are baptized, unless they renounce and give up all, have, whatever good they may seem to have done, nothing of it reckoned to them, neither can they possess the Kingdom of God.[31]

Caelestius was condemned by a council at Carthage and, in his turn, left for the East. Augustine forthwith took up his pen and the first of a long series of anti-Pelagian treatises was issued in 412: *de Peccatorum Meritis ac Remissione et de Baptismo Parvulorum*, to be followed, amongst others, by *De Spiritu et Littera*.

In Palestine Jerome was soon involved: disliking Pelagius for his reception by John of Jerusalem and erroneously convinced that Origenist ideas were at the basis of the new teaching,[32] he began his *Dialogue against the Pelagians*. At this juncture he was joined by Orosius, who having fled from Spain before the Arian Visigoths had come to Hippo in 414 and was sent on to Bethlehem by Augustine as his envoy. On 28th July 415 Orosius attended a meeting of the Diocesan Synod at Jerusalem and launched an attack upon Pelagius, but without success.[33] However, two Gallican bishops, Heros of Arles and Lazarus of Aix, were induced to press charges and on 20th December thirteen bishops assembled at Diospolis (the ancient Lydda) under Eulogius of Caesarea.[34] In the absence of his accusers, Pelagius was able to prevaricate to such effect that he was acquitted.

The North Africans were aghast at the result and in 416 the bishops of Proconsular Africa, gathered at Carthage, and those of Numidia, at Milevum, renewed their condemnation and appealed to Innocent at Rome, who concurred in the sentence of excommunication against Pelagius.[35] No sooner had Innocent done this than he died, and his successor Zosimus accepted statements of faith from Caelestius in person and from Pelagius by letter, found them orthodox and wrote to the Africans to condemn them for over-hasty action.[36] Again the Africans met in November 417[37] to renew their decision, following this with an approach to the emperor Honorius who agreed to banish Pelagius and Caelestius, whereupon Zosimus hastened to fall in with this decision. This sentence, however, did not terminate the dispute; nineteen Italian bishops held out and under Julian of Eclanum continued to support the Pelagian cause, even when exiled themselves.

In Gaul the monk Leporius[38] and in Britain Agricola, son of Bishop Severian, propagated the same opinions. Leporius was eventually won over by Augustine himself,[39] while the Britons required the mission of Germanus of Auxerre to bring them back to orthodoxy.[40]

Semi-Pelagianism

In the further writings against Pelagius produced by Augustine from 419 onwards, the bishop pressed his position to such extremes that he formulated a doctrine of predestination and a denial of free will which appeared to exempt man from all responsibility for his actions and to issue in an amoral determinism. It was against this unbalanced and exaggerated later Augustinian view that protests were now made.

In 426 the monks of Adrumetum were disturbed by Augustine's apparent annihilation of free will,[41] and at Carthage, the following year, the monk Vitalis argued that the first movement of faith may be a free act of the individual which is then met by the divine grace.[42] But it was in South Gaul that the main opposition arose from such monks as John Cassian and Vincent of Lerins, who would have nothing to do with Pelagianism but who regarded Augustine as having gone too far; they asserted that grace was not necessarily either prevenient or irresistible. The bishop of Hippo once more took up his pen with *de Praedestinatione Sanctorum* and *de Dono Perseverantiae*, and was seconded in Gaul itself by the efforts of Prosper of Aquitaine. The dispute was mainly literary, including the *Commonitorium* of Vincent of Lerins in 434, the *Praedestinatus* of Arnobius Junior in 440 and the *de Gratia Dei* of Faustus of Riez in 474 in defence of Semi-Pelagianism, and the works of Fulgentius of Ruspe (467–533) who reiterated the extreme Augustinian position. The final settlement of the question took place at the Council of Orange in 529, under the influence of Caesarius of Arles, when the fundamental teaching of Augustine was accepted but his more extreme speculations, and in particular his predestinarianism, were dismissed.[43]

Christological controversies – Nestorianism

While debate concerning the doctrine of man was continuing, the series of Christological controversies, begun with the Apollinarian dispute, was also in progress. The theological intricacies of these may be left for later consideration when the beliefs of the period are outlined; here an account must be given of the course of events produced by these discussions.

On 10th April 428 Nestorius was consecrated bishop of Constantinople. The pupil of Theodore of Mopsuestia, himself the purveyor of the teaching of Diodore of Tarsus, Nestorius shared the Antiochene emphasis upon the distinct reality of the two natures in Christ. Strongly anti-Apollinarian, they all spoke of the manhood as '*a* man' and were thus in difficulties in establishing a true unity within the one person of Christ. It was this stress upon the humanity that led Nestorius to object to the use of the title *Theotokos* of the Virgin Mary, i.e. he refused to style her Mother of God, since to him that which was born was the manhood. To the Alexandrians, with their stress upon the oneness of Christ's person, this seemed to deny the unity of the God-man and, under their bishop Cyril, they proceeded to counter-attack. On Easter Day 429, Cyril preached a sermon in which he declared that the abandoning of the title *Theotokos* meant the repudiation of the faith of Nicaea, and he published an encyclical letter to that effect.[44] Meanwhile copies of Nestorius' sermons had reached Rome and the bishop Caelestine wrote to Cyril to ask if they were genuine, whereupon Cyril addressed Nestorius directly in his first letter which urged him to accept the use of *Theotokos*,[45] and he followed this, early in 430, with a second and more peremptory missive. In August Caelestine, having received full documentation from Cyril, held a synod which condemned the teaching of Nestorius, giving him ten days to recant upon receipt of the sentence, the execution of which was placed in Cyril's hands.[46] In November Cyril assembled his own synod, which drew up a further letter together with twelve anathemas which were despatched, along with Caelestine's epistle, to Constantinople. When the envoys carrying these arrived in December, they discovered that the emperor had, a fortnight previously, issued the mandate for a General Council to meet at Ephesus by Pentecost 431.

The parties that eventually assembled for what was to be regarded as the third Ecumenical Council were six in number. First there was Nestorius and his friends; second there came Cyril with some fifty suffragan bishops. He was supported by Juvenal of Jerusalem, with some fifteen bishops, who was motivated by a desire to be free of the domination of the bishop of Antioch, and Memnon of Ephesus, with some hundred Asiatics, who wished to be independent of the authority of Constantinople. The three papal legates, who were to arrive late, were solidly behind Cyril, but John of Antioch and his forty or so companions, who had difficulties on the journey which delayed them a fortnight, were more friendly disposed towards Nestorius. This sympathy for Nestorius on the part of the Orientals had been aroused by the twelve anathemas which seemed to them one-sided and smacking of Apollinarianism. Without waiting for the late-comers, Cyril opened the council which soon decreed the deposition of Nestorius, in which the papal legates concurred. John of Antioch and his associates, however, refused to accept the legality of the proceedings and immediately held a session upon their own, when they pronounced the deposition of Cyril and Memnon and excommunicated all who would not repudiate the Twelve Anathemas.[47] Appeal was made by both sides to the emperor who at first ordered the deposition of all three bishops – Cyril, Nestorius, and Memnon – and then accepted the majority decision by allowing Cyril to return home, sending Nestorius back to his monastery near Antioch and having Maximian consecrated as his successor at Constantinople.[48] This left, however, the Egyptians and the Orientals unreconciled and it was not until eighteen months later, through the efforts of John of Antioch's envoy Paul, that reunion was achieved. In 436 Nestorius was banished to the Great Oasis on the borders of Upper Egypt[49] and died *c.* 451. But this was not the end of Nestorianism; within thirty years of Nestorius' death it had become the official faith of the Persian Church. This Church sought to obtain its independence and freedom from suspicion of favouring their fellow Christians within the empire by adopting the Nestorian Christology, chiefly under the influence of Barsumas (420–96) who became bishop of Nisibis. It thus secured its protection from the State by assuring the king that its religion was not the religion of his enemies the Romans.[50]

Eutychianism

Reaction to Nestorianism, on the part of certain individuals, was not satisfied with its condemnation; pushing the Alexandrian position to extremes, they now declared that Christ had only one nature, his humanity having been absorbed by his Godhead like a drop of honey dispersed and swallowed up in the sea. The principal upholder of this view was Eutyches, head of a monastery at Constantinople and he was attacked at a council in 448, held in the capital and presided over by its new bishop Flavian. Eutyches declared: 'I recognize that before the union of the divinity and the humanity there were two natures, but after the union I recognize only one nature.'[51] The condemnation of Eutyches by this council had no immediate effect because he had the ear of the emperor through his godson Chrysaphius, who was the favourite of Theodosius II. Indeed, so sure was Eutyches of his position that he appealed to Leo of Rome for support and agreed with the emperor's plan to summon a council to settle the affair.

The council at Ephesus was carefully packed and its procedure so regulated that its conclusions were decided before it even met. A majority in favour of Eutyches was ensured either by not inviting his opponents or by allowing their presence without power to vote. The Roman delegates were not permitted to speak and the missives from Leo were left unread. Not content with upholding Eutyches, Dioscorus of Alexandria seized the opportunity to direct a blow at the rival see of Constantinople and insisted upon the deposition of Flavian, who was so mobbed that he died within three days.[52] This was followed by sentences of deposition against Flavian's supporters, including Theodoret of Cyrus and Domnus of Antioch.

As long as Theodosius was on the throne nothing could be done to alter the findings of this council, soon known as the 'Robber Synod' or *Latrocinium*. Leo received and made numerous appeals; Valentinian III interceded with Theodosius, but without success. Then on 28th July 450 Theodosius died after a fall from his horse; as he left no issue, he was succeeded by his sister Pulcheria who thereupon, to share the burden of responsibility, married Marcian the senator, both of them being supporters of the orthodox position. Without delay Chrysaphius was put to death and Eutyches under restraint, and the exiles, including Theodoret, were recalled.[53] In the light of these events Leo was less eager for another council, since the faith had been secured and the West was menaced by Attila. But Pulcheria and Marcian had no hesitation and on 8th October 451 the first session of the Council of Chalcedon began and concluded with the deposition of Dioscorus and his supporters.[54] In subsequent sessions Eutyches was condemned, various documents were approved, including Cyril's first and second letters to Nestorius and Leo's *Tome*, and a *Definition of Faith* was issued to affirm the agreed orthodox doctrine of the person of Christ.

Monophysitism

To many eastern Christians the Chalcedonian Definition, while acceptable because of its condemnation of Eutychianism, was unacceptable because of its acknowledgement that Christ has two natures, since this was understood to be a reaffirmation of Nestorianism. The followers of the Cyrilline theology believed that his views had been displaced and, accepting his formula 'one incarnate nature', they withstood the emperor's attempt to impose the Definition. These Monophysites, as they were called, were in part influenced by political motives, the Egyptians in particular resenting imperial pressure. The struggle was protracted: in 476 the usurper Basiliscus issued his *Encyclical* condemning Chalcedon and in 482 Zeno published his *Henoticon* or *Instrument of Union*[55] which again favoured the Monophysites, and the result was a schism between East and West that lasted thirty-five years. The accession of Justinian in 527 brought to the throne a man ardent for uniformity and an upholder of the Chalcedonian faith; the result of his policy, however, was a final separation between the Chalcedonians and the Monophysites.

Monasticism

Amidst the external tumults of the barbarian invasions and the internal struggles of doctrinal dispute, the Church managed to preserve its identity thanks not a little to the fostering of its spiritual life by the developing monastic movement. Supported by such illustrious names as Basil, Jerome and Augustine, its progress was phenomenal: although Pachomius only began his work in 323, by the turn of the century there were over seven thousand Pachomian monks and houses were being founded in all parts of the empire and beyond its frontiers. The movement, however, could be a mixed blessing: whereas in the main the ascetics were strong supporters of orthodoxy, they could be turbulent and be used in power politics by such unscrupulous clerics as Dioscorus of Alexandria. They needed control; their spirituality wanted guidance and they required regulation. Chalcedon provided the first, Evagrius the second and Basil in the East and Cassian and Benedict in the West the third.

Canon 4 of the Council of Chalcedon subjected the monasteries to episcopal control:

> Let those who truly and sincerely lead the monastic life be counted worthy of becoming honour; but, forasmuch as certain persons using the pretext of monasticism bring confusion both upon the churches and into political affairs by going about promiscuously in the cities, and at the same time seeking to establish monasteries for themselves; it is decreed that no one anywhere build or found a monastery or oratory contrary to the will of the bishop of the city; and that the monks in every city and district shall be subject to the bishop, and embrace a quiet course of life, and give themselves only to fasting and prayer, remaining permanently in the places in which

they were set apart; and they shall meddle neither in ecclesiastical nor in secular affairs, nor leave their own monasteries to take part in such; unless, indeed, they should at any time through urgent necessity be appointed thereto by the bishop of the city. And no slave shall be received into any monastery to become a monk against the will of his master. And if any one shall transgress this our judgment, we have decreed that he shall be excommunicated, that the name of God be not blasphemed. But the bishop of the city must make the needful provision for the monasteries.

Already, before this canon, the Church had acted to suppress ascetic aberrations in the form of the Messalians who had been condemned by the Council of Ephesus in 431. The title Messalian derives from Aramaic and means 'praying folk', the Greek equivalent, also in use, being Euchites; they were also known as the Adelphians after their first leader, attacked by Flavian of Antioch in 376, and Lampetians after the first priest ordained *c.* 458. Previously condemned at Side in 388 or 390, they emanated from Mesopotamia and were mendicant ascetics, believing that each soul is attached to an individual demon who can only be expelled by constant prayer. Quietist in practice, they also refused to work.[56]

The pioneer in developing a science of the spiritual life was Evagrius of Pontus, a citizen of Ibora, who after ordination to a readership by Basil and to the diaconate by Gregory of Nazianzus became archdeacon of Constantinople and attended the council of 381. He eventually embraced the monastic life and withdrew to Cellia, north of Nitria, where he lived for fourteen years until his death in 399.[57] In his writings he defined the goal of the Christian life and the means to attain it. He described the way of prayer; he analysed the virtues and the vices; he classified evil and laid the foundation of the later concept of the seven deadly sins; he gave advice on how to overcome temptation; he saw the Christian life as the ascending of a ladder with its several rungs clearly labelled.

Evagrian spirituality, with its Origenistic basis, was made familiar to the West by the work of John Cassian, the founder of monasteries at Marseilles *c.* 415 and the author of two widely influential books on the monastic life, the *Institutes* and the *Conferences*, which enunciated the ascetic ideal that was to dominate European thought for centuries. The essence of the calling, as Cassian saw it, is expressed in a brief address to one who had just entered upon the novitiate.

You ought in the first instance to learn the actual reason for the renunciation of the world. Renunciation is nothing but the evidence of the cross and of mortification. And so you must know that today you are dead to this world, and that, as the apostle says, you are crucified to this world and this world to you. Consider, therefore, the demands of the cross under the sign of which you ought henceforth to live in this life; because *you* no longer live, but *he* lives in you who was crucified for you. We must therefore pass our time in this life in that fashion and form in which he was crucified for us on the cross so that we may have all our wishes and desires not subservient to our own lusts but fastened to his mortification. For so shall we fulfil the command of the Lord which says: 'He that taketh not up his cross and followeth me is not worthy of me.' But perhaps you will say: How can a man carry his cross continually? Or, how can anyone who is alive be crucified? Hear briefly how this is.

The fear of the Lord is our cross. As then one who is crucified no longer has the power of moving or turning his limbs in any direction, so we ought also to affix our wishes and desires – not in accordance with what is pleasant and delightful to us now – but in accordance with the law of the Lord, where it constrains us. For in this way we can have all our desires and carnal affections mortified.

Take heed to continue even to the end in that state of nakedness in which you make profession in the sight of God and of his angels. For not he who begins these things, but he who endures in them to the end shall be saved. The beginning of our salvation and the safeguard of it is the fear of the Lord. For through this those who are trained in the way of perfection can gain a start in conversion as well as purification from vices and security in virtue. And when this has gained an entrance into a man's heart it produces a contempt of things and begets a forgetfulness of kinsfolk and a horror of the world itself. But by the contempt for the loss of all possessions humility is gained.

That you may the more easily arrive at this, you must observe three things. As the Psalmist says, 'I was like a deaf man and heard not, and as one that is dumb and does not open his mouth; and I became as a man that heareth not, and in whose mouth there are no reproofs.' So you also should walk as one that is deaf and blind. You should be like a blind man and not see anything of those things which you find to be unedifying. If you hear anyone disobedient or disparaging another, you should not be led astray by such example to imitate him, but 'like a deaf man' as if you had never heard it, you should pass it all by. If insults are offered to you or wrong done, be immovable, and as far as answer in retaliation is concerned be silent 'as one that is dumb'.

But cultivate above everything else this fourth thing which adorns and graces the three things of which I have just spoken; namely, make yourself, as the apostle says, a fool in this world that you may become wise, exercising no judgements of your own on any of those matters that are commanded you, but always showing obedience, judging that alone to be holy which is God's law or the decision of your superiors declares to be such. For built upon such a system of instruction, you may continue for ever under this discipline, and not fall away from this monastery in consequence of any temptations or devices of the enemy.[58]

Some seven years before Cassian began his work at Marseilles, monasticism in Gaul had received a further impetus from the founding of a house on the island of Lerins by Honoratus and his brother Venantius. This became a nursery of scholars and bishops, Honoratus himself becoming bishop of Arles in 426 to be succeeded in the same see by yet another Lerins monk Caesarius, 502–42.

If however Lerins had most influence upon the affairs of the Church, Cassian played a leading part in relations to its spirituality, since his writings became prescribed reading for the Benedictine monks. Born *c.* 480 at Nursia, Benedict spent his early years in Rome and then, after a time as a hermit in the district of Subiaco, eventually established a monastery on Monte Cassino, some eighty miles to the south of the capital, and remained there as abbot until his death in the middle decades of the sixth century. In Benedict Western monasticism found its great organizer and legislator. In Benedict's Rule, intended not only for his own community, but as a model for general imitation, counsel was replaced by command, generalization by detailed direction, and exhortation by administrative procedure to preserve and inculcate the ideal. Benedict expected his monks to read their Cassian, but he did not rest content with this and sought to foster sanctity by habit-forming rules approved and maintained by authority. He devised a constitution for the monastery which left no doubt as to who was in authority and he endeavoured to avoid failure by legislating for every possible situation. In contrast to the individualism of the hermits and the large measure of personal preference allowed by Pachomius, Benedict, like Basil, legislated for a community life free from excesses. The monks were to live as a family under the government of the abbot to whom they were to promise utter obedience. They were to observe poverty, chastity and stability, i.e. they were not to pass from house to house. They had to share in the agricultural and domestic work, read and learn the psalms. Their timetable was regulated by the performance of the divine office – Vigils at 2.0 a.m., Lauds at dawn, Prime at six, Terce at nine, Sext at noon, None at three, Vespers at four-thirty and Compline at six. This was the system, partly through its intrinsic merit and partly through the influence of such men as Gregory the Great, that was gradually adopted throughout Europe, replacing even the vigorous Celtic monasticism that had flourished in comparative isolation on the extreme confines of the western empire.[59]

Meanwhile in North Africa the movement had progressed through the efforts of Augustine. Upon his return home, he had gathered about him a group of men who were prepared to give up all their worldly goods. When later he became bishop of Hippo he established a monastery where he lived with his clergy. Many laity were attracted and from these Augustine recruited further members for the ranks of his clergy.

The guidance that he gave this and other communities formed the basis of the later *Rule of St Augustine*.

In the East the Basilian rules continued to dominate the scene, but the East was also remarkable for its individual ascetics, amongst whom Simeon Stylites is probably the most noteworthy. Born *c.* 389 at Sisan on the borders of Syria and Cilicia, Simeon entered the monastery at Teleda early in 403. Determined to pursue the eremetical life, he moved

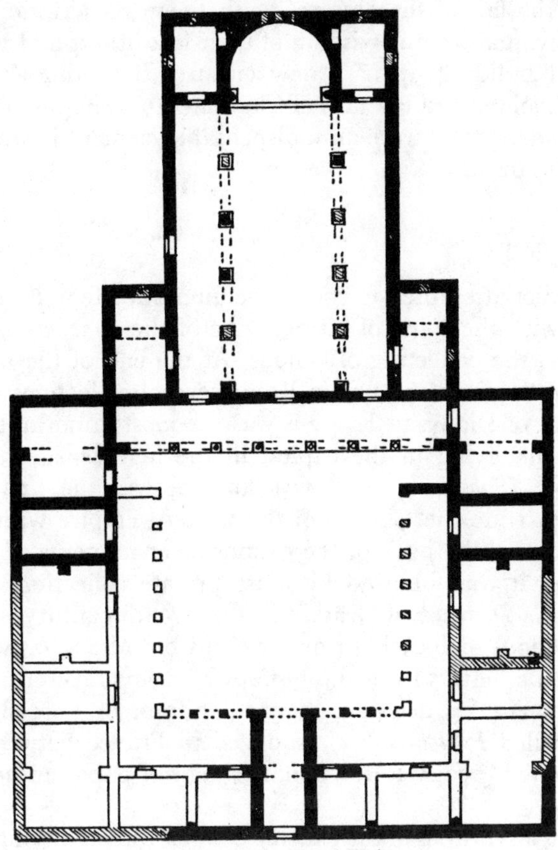

Monastery at ed-Deir

to the village of Telanissus, near Antioch, in 412, and since the fame of his sanctity brought hordes of pilgrims to seek his counsel and since their admiration was so great and so forcible in its demonstration – they tried to tear off pieces of his clothes to bear away as relics – Simeon had constructed a stone column on which he lived for thirty-seven years, from 422 to his death in 458, being the first of a number of ascetics who spent their days either on pillars, the stylites, or in trees, the dendrites.[60]

That the inner life of the Church was not irreparably disrupted by disputes and by external pressures was due in no small measure to these 'athletes of God'. Moreover, relatively secure and self-supporting within their monasteries, each with its well, its mill and its kitchen garden, its chapel, courtyard and surrounding rooms, e.g. the sixth-century monastery at ed-Deir, they were able to preserve a pattern of life and learning throughout the period of economic anarchy that began in the West with the fall of the empire. With their transcriptions and their libraries they guarded the wisdom of their forefathers and thus enabled the gradual building up of a new culture. If at times they need a Benedict of Aniane or a Bernard of Clairvaux to recall them to the ideals of their founders, they were an indispensable element in the continuity of the Christian faith.

Canon Law

When Benedict attempted to codify the monastic life in his rule, he was in keeping with the spirit of his age, one of the characteristic features of which was the collecting of canons. At the end of the fifth and the beginning of the sixth century in Rome several collections were made, of which that of Dionysius Exiguus was the most important – he was a Scythian monk living in the capital in the first decades of the sixth century. The *Dionysiana*, as it was known, was the first important attempt to provide the Church of the western empire with a uniform system of law, on the basis of the canons or enactments of the various councils, and it was followed by more private collections which culminated in the *Decretum* of Gratian in the twelfth century.

The collections included not only canons but also what were known as decretals, i.e. letters from the bishops of Rome answering questions referred to them for decision. A compendium of Forged Decretals, sometimes called *Pseudo-Isidore*, produced in France between 841 and 851, contributed greatly to the enhancement of papal authority in the Middle Ages.

In the East a synthesis of the existing canons and an attempt to supply their *lacunae* was undertaken by Justinian. John of Constantinople (565–77), a former Antiochene lawyer, produced one of the first eastern collections and characteristic of these was their close association of civil and ecclesiastical laws.

Church order

The ferment of events that issued in the disappearance of the western empire was not without its effect upon the role of the bishop; there were indeed four factors that influenced it considerably. First, the imperial policy of centralization, which was to preserve unity and prevent anarchy, resulted in the sapping of local initiative. Second, the episcopal exercise of the power of jurisdiction, granted by the civil power, and of the right of intercession with imperial officials increased. Third, legacies and grants of property made bishops responsible for many large estates. Finally, the urban civilization of the empire was replaced, after the incursion of the barbarians, by a predominantly rural system, which had the social effect of sweeping away absentee city-dwelling landowners and their substitution by local proprietors living upon their own estates. As a consequence of these changes prominent men were drawn to the episcopate as the sole sphere within which they could find adequate scope for their talents and they became more and more the leaders of the entire local community in civil no less than in ecclesiastical affairs. Their importance was further enhanced and they acquired a position of pre-eminence in the countryside because of their possession of large estates. Here indeed lay the origins of the later system of feudal prelacy. Thus the function of a bishop became more general than that of the chief local minister of religion.

Inevitably the bishop had to become something of an administrator, but in order to find time for the more essential pastoral duties many delegated these tasks to others, and so Chrysostom at Constantinople appointed one Domitian as his *oikonomos* or steward.[61] Chrysostom himself continued to keep a very close check on all matters and regularly examined the accounts book.[62] Augustine, by contrast, was impatient about such things and when the yearly statement of income and expenditure was read he scarcely troubled to listen.[63] Indeed to the mother of one of the richest heirs in Rome he wrote that the care of Church property was something that he endured but did not desire.[64] He much preferred, as did many of his episcopal colleagues, to observe the dictum expressed by Ambrose to Vigilius of Trent: 'The first things is to know the congregation which has been entrusted to you by God'.[65] Hence the time spent in visiting the sick, praying with them and laying hands upon them; hence also the care of the widow and orphan, the setting up of hospitals and the great extension of works of charity.

With the bishop so occupied it was natural that the presbyter should come to have more and more duties laid upon him. Now began the movement that was to create the parish priest of the Middle Ages. The country churches, which were initially mission stations served by clergy sent from the city, were provided in the sixth century, in Gaul in particular, each with its own resident staff. The oratories or chapels built upon estates by rich landowners for themselves and their tenants also become independent centres of worship, with separate endowments, provided in many instances by the proprietors who had erected them, and they reserved the right to nominate the priests, thus initiating the practice of private patronage. It was not until Charlemagne however that the policy was pursued of having a church and priest for every village with their own territorial districts.

While the presbyter was increasing in importance the minor orders, and with them the diaconate, tended to decrease. By the sixth century the reader had practically ceased to have function whatsoever, due to the reduction in the number of the lessons and to the taking over by others of the readings. The subdiaconate became primarily a liturgical office and by the fifth century, when the spurious canons of the Fourth Council of Carthage were compiled at Arles, his ordination comprised the reception of an empty pattern and chalice from the bishop and of a towel and ewer from the archdeacon and it is further stated that his task is to prepare the sacred vessels and to give them to the deacon 'in time of divine service'.[66] The doorkeeper, with the end of the *disciplina arcani*, became a verger and was required to provide for the cleaning and lighting of the church and sanctuary.[67] The acolytes' duties were restricted to the liturgy, while those of the exorcists passed to other clerics and there is no mention of them save in the rituals of ordination. The diaconate too became increasingly no more than a liturgical office, with the archdeacon alone continuing to exercise anything in the nature of a full ministry within the administrative machine of the developed diocese.

The Roman primacy

The disruption of the western empire which so affected the role of the diocesan bishop also influenced that of the bishop of Rome, for as organized government broke down the pope emerged as the one stable and dominant figure acknowledged by all. The eighty years from the Council of Constantinople to the death of Leo the Great witnessed the final stages of the growth of the Roman primacy.

The importance of political events in influencing the position of the pope may be clearly seen in the pontificate of Innocent I (402–17), for when Alaric sacked Rome, Honorius having withdrawn to Ravenna and many of the leading citizens having fled or been killed, Innocent it was who was looked up to as the greatest man in the capital. Already, however, he had been exerting his authority over the western Church; so in his letters to Vitricius of Rouen and Exuperius of Toulouse Innocent encouraged them to refer matters of dispute to the apostolic see.[68] In writing to Decentius of Eugubium he asserted that no churches had been founded in the West save those for which Peter or his

"the disruption of western empire which so affected the role of the diocesan bishops also influenced that of the bishop of Rome; for as organized government broke down the pope emerged as the one stable and dominant figure acknowledged by all."

successors had provided bishops and that therefore all should follow the Roman lead.[69] In his relations with Africa about the Pelagian controversy Innocent was prepared to affirm that he was acting in the place of Peter.[70]

Zosimus (417–18) added nothing to these claims, but Boniface I (418–22) was more outspoken in his correspondence relating to the consecration of Perigenes as bishop of Corinth, a matter which concerned him because of his nominal jurisdiction over Illyricum. In his first letter Boniface declared that the Roman see is the see of Peter and that Peter lives on in his see. In his second he wrote of the Roman see that 'this church is, as it were, a head over the members; and if anyone is separate from it he is an alien to the Christian religion as having failed to remain in the body'. In the third he insisted that while 'bishops hold one and the same episcopal office', they should 'recognize those to whom for the sake of ecclesiastical discipline they are bound to be in subjection'.[71]

Of all the western churches that of Africa continued longest its steady independence, acknowledging the primacy of honour of Rome but refusing to bow to its jurisdiction. The relationship is best studied in connexion with the sordid case of Apiarius which reached its climax under Caelestine (422–32) but had begun under Zosimus. Apiarius was a priest of Sicca Veneria in Proconsular Africa; he had been deposed and excommunicated for serious offences by his diocesan Urbanus. Apiarius made his way to Rome where Zosimus took up his case, threatened Urbanus with deposition if he did not retract and sent the discredited priest back to Africa with three of his own legates. Meanwhile the African bishops had met at Carthage in 418 and had passed canons forbidding appeals outside the country. The legates arrived and demanded that bishops should have the right of appeal to Rome, that they should be forbidden to go often to court, that priests and deacons should have the right of appeal to neighbouring bishops and that Urbanus should cancel his proceedings or be excommunicated. Zosimus supported his demands by reference to the canons of Sardica, though quoting them as Nicene. The Africans declared that the canons were not in their copies of the proceedings of Nicaea and sent to the East for another transcript. Apiarius then confessed his errors, the action of Urbanus was confirmed, and having received a copy of the Nicene minutes, which did not include the canons, the Africans regarded the matter as closed. It was reopened for its final stage under Caelestine.

Apiarius began work at Tabraca where he repeated his offences, was again excommunicated and again appealed to Rome. Caelestine restored him to communion without hearing his accusers and despatched him back to Africa in the company of his legate. *c.* 426 a further council met at Carthage, before which Apiarius broke down and confessed, whereupon the African bishops reported what had taken place and at the same time asserted their right to decide their own judicial affairs and, while acknowledging the primacy of Rome, repudiated any powers of jurisdiction.[72] But the end of African independence was in sight; with the collapse of synodal organization, upon which the African Church so much depended, before the Vandals, there was no rival to the pope and his good offices, together with his decisions, were gratefully received.

Under Leo the Great (440–61) the primacy of Rome was finally established and it was he who provided it with a theory or dogmatic basis which was to be upheld for centuries. Leo's conception is to be found in five sermons delivered to an audience of some two hundred bishops assembled to celebrate the anniversary of his consecration.[73] He interpreted the Petrine text to mean that supreme authority was bestowed by Jesus upon Peter. Next he held Peter to have been the first bishop of Rome, and his authority to have been perpetuated in his successors. He further conceived of this authority as enhanced by a mystical presence of Peter in the Roman see. He therefore drew the consequences that the authority of all bishops, other than the pope, is derived not immediately from Christ but mediately through Peter and that it is limited to their own dioceses, whereas his was a *plenitudo potestatis* over the whole Church. These claims, never accepted in the East, were readily admitted in the West in return for papal assistance. In Italy they were approved without question; in Spain under the Visigoths the bishops were eager to have the pope's help; in Gaul, backed by Valentinian III, the papal authority was acknowledged: Leo was supreme throughout the West.

It has been said with some cynicism but with some truth that the Roman Church was the ghost of the Roman Empire sitting on the grave thereof; and indeed much of the prestige of the old civil power passed, at its defeat, to the bishop of Rome as the head of the western Church throughout what are usually called the Dark and the Middle Ages.

BELIEFS

In the period from Nicaea to Constantinople it was the doctrine of the Trinity that received the most attention; but even before the second ecumenical council had met there were signs, in the teaching of Apollinaris, that concern about the Christological problem was now coming to the fore, and it was soon to be the centre of debate. Nevertheless theological thought about the Godhead did not stand still: in the

East the Cappadocian teaching was further refined; in the West Augustine clarified belief.

The Trinity

According to the Cappadocians God, from the point of view of internal analysis, is one Being, but, from the point of view of external presentation, he is three Objects. This subtle formulation of the trinitarian belief was in part misunderstood in the sixth and seventh centuries, but through the efforts of an anonymous writer, known as Pseudo-Cyril, whose work was incorporated by John of Damascus in his *de Fide Orthodoxa*, the original meaning of the Cappadocian settlement was recovered and became the standard of belief for Eastern Orthodoxy. But Pseudo-Cyril not only helped to preserve his predecessors' insights, he also pressed into service a further term to safeguard the unity in trinity. This term summed up one aspect of the biblical record of which little notice in relation to the doctrine of the Godhead had been previously taken in the East. In John's Gospel Jesus says: 'I am in the Father, and the Father in me',[1] thus the divine Persons are, as it were, coexstensive; Pseudo-Cyril expressed this by the word *perichoresis* or coinherence. So if one begins with the three objective presentations of the Godhead, there is no danger of lapsing into tritheism because the doctrine of coinherence or circuminsession, as the Latins were to call it, necessarily involves identity of being.

Augustine and the West

The eastern doctrine of the Trinity filtered through to the West partly by means of the writings of Ambrose, who was familiar with the Cappadocian teaching and in particular with that of Basil. So he held that there are three divine persons: these three are one since each possesses in all its fullness the same one indivisible substance of Godhead. Each of these persons has a property or peculiarity whereby he is distinguished from the others, notwithstanding the sameness of essence – the property of the Father is to beget, that of the Son to be begotten and that of the Spirit to proceed.[2] This was not independent speculation nor was it completely identical with the eastern belief, as Ambrose's pupil, Augustine, fully realized: 'for the sake of speaking of things ineffable, that in some way we may be able to express what we are in no way able to express fully, our Greek friends have spoken of one essence and three substances, but the Latins of one essence or substance and three persons'. Either position is legitimate for 'the transcendence of the Godhead surpasses the power of ordinary speech'.[3]

Augustine's own contribution to the doctrine of the Trinity was twofold. Previously, in the West, where a unity of substratum had been accepted, it has been customary to regard the Father as the substratum, i.e. the Godhead common to the three persons was identified with the Father, since it was from him that both the Son and the Spirit derived their own Godhead. Hence, according to Tertullian, 'the Father is the entire substance, but the Son is a derivation or portion of the whole'.[4] Augustine, however, did not identify the Godhead with the Father but with the substratum common to all three, while at the same time declaring that it had no existence apart from the three. 'We say "three persons of the same essence" or "three persons, one essence"; but we do not say "three persons out of the same essence", as though therein essence were one thing and person another'.[5]

Augustine's second contribution lay in the use of analogies drawn from the structure of human nature on the grounds that some faint traces of the Trinity are discernible within it since it was created in the image of God. In so doing Augustine owed something to Marius Victorinus, the Neo-Platonic philosopher converted to Christianity, for Victorinus drew an analogy between the Trinity and the unity of the soul, in which existence (*esse*), life (*vita*) and intelligence (*intelligentia*) though distinct, are still united by their relation to each other.[6] Augustine preferred the analogies of memory (*memoria*), internal vision (*interna visio*) or knowledge (*notitia*) or understanding (*intelligentia, intellectus*) and will (*voluntas*) or love (*amor*).[7] These he put forward, not as an explanation, but as an aid to comprehension, for he would have agreed with Gregory of Nazianzus that 'it is difficult to conceive God, but to define him in words is an impossibility'.[8]

The person of Christ

The problem of the Trinity, as has been emphasized, is that of unity in multiplicity; the problem of Christology is precisely the same. From New Testament times Christians believed three propositions about Christ: that he is God, that he is man and that he is one person. By the end of the fourth century the first two of these had been explicated. As a consequence of the Arian controversy the divinity of Christ was declared to be full and entire, while the outcome of the Apollinarian debate was the affirmation of his complete humanity. This, however, only made more acute the problem of the unity of the Godhead and manhood in one person – the Christological debates turned upon the resolution of this.

As with the doctrine of the Trinity, so with Christology, contemporary philosophical ideas of unity were employed and three of these require particular notice. First there is the union of composition or juxtaposition, the resultant being an aggregate of the component parts, and examples, provided by Aristotle, are 'a faggot held together by a band and pieces of wood held together by glue'.[9] Second there is the Aristotelian union of predominance, the resultant being one of the original constituents, namely the one of the greater power or action; the lesser part does not completely disappear but only remains as a qualitative or quantitative accident of the other. So 'a drop of wine is not mixed with ten thousand gallons of water for the form of the wine is dissolved and changes into the whole of the water'.[10] The wine does not therefore completely disappear but all that remains is its volume or bulk as a quantitative accident. Third there is the Stoic union of predominance, the resultant being a mutual coextension, even if there is considerable disparity between the combining elements. 'There is nothing to hinder a drop of wine being mixed with the whole sea,' they said; 'thus one drop will by mixture extend through the whole world'.[11]

In seeking to define the unity of Christ's person, the Nestorians adopted the union of juxtaposition, the Eutychians the Aristotelian union of predominance, while the orthodox position was more nearly that of the Stoics.

It may be doubted whether or not Nestorius was guilty of Nestorianism, and for clarity it is necessary to distinguish between the views attributed to him and his actual teaching. Nestorius made use of the term juxtaposition or conjunction and this was understood as a union of composition to the effect that the Godhead and manhood existed side by side in a kind of partnership. To many, and to the Alexandrian school in particular, this was no real union but a splitting of the one person into two: God and a man. Nestorius did indeed make statements that were both provocative and ambiguous. He could assert: 'I hold the natures apart but unite the worship';[12] he objected to the use of the title *Theotokos* of Mary thus suggesting that he did not think Christ to be one person since, if he were, the Godhead must be deemed to have experienced the processes of birth in union with the manhood. To some it seemed that he was reviving the heresy of Paul of Samosata; to others that he was endorsing the teaching of Diodore of Tarsus who spoke of Christ as a man conjoined with God. Cyril of Alexandria, Nestorius' implacable opponent, indicated clearly his interpretation in the third and seventh anathemas he appended to his third letter, when he referred to the natures being connected 'by a mere association in dignity or authority or rule' and condemned the view that Jesus 'as a man, was energized by God the Word'.

In his *Bazaar of Heraclides*, written some twenty years after the main controversy, Nestorius sought to answer his critics and expound his position more fully. Indeed from this document it is evident that the union of which he conceived was not one of composition but is rather to be described as a prosopic union. *Prosopon* means the external aspect or self-manifestation of an individual. Each person therefore has his own *prosopon*, but it is possible for him to extend his self-manifestation by means of other things, e.g. a man who uses a paint-brush to express himself is including it within his *prosopon*. So God the Word used the manhood for his self-manifestation and the manhood therefore became part of his *prosopon*. Hence Nestorius could say: 'the two natures were united by their union in a single prosopon'.[13] He further illustrated his view by drawing a parallel between the creation of Adam from the dust of the earth and the creation of the Second Adam in the womb of the Virgin. At the first creation God formed an animal mechanism and then breathed into it a living soul; at this moment of vivification God and Adam were united. This act performed, God withdrew himself, and Adam became a separate entity. At the second creation, God again formed an animal mechanism and vivified it, yet on this occasion he did not withdraw himself but remained permanently as at the moment of vivification. Thus while there never was a separate man Jesus, there was a potentially separate man, since God could have withdrawn himself and so maintained an exact parallel with the creation of Adam. As a result of this divine act, God the Word now entered upon a period of existence within the world of space and time during which he manifested himself through the manhood, i.e. he made use of a potentially separate man as his *prosopon*. While thus adequately defending himself against the charge of teaching 'two Sons', Nestorius did not produce any adequate solution to the problem. All that he was saying in effect was that Christ was a single object of presentation – which no one would wish to deny: the real problem was what constituted his person.

Reaction to 'Nestorianism' went to the opposite extreme in the confused teaching of Eutyches. On the basis of the Aristotelian union of predominance he asserted that there was in Christ only one nature, the humanity having been absorbed by the divinity, 'like the sea receiving a drop of honey, for immediately the drop, as it mixes with the sea's water, vanishes'.[14] Nevertheless, he was prepared to go on: 'what we assert is not the destruction of the assumed nature but its change to the substance of divinity'[15] – so the humanity becomes only an accident or property. Cyril of Alexandria also accepted a union of predominance, but in the Stoic sense; he was emphatic that there was no 'confusion' and he used the analogy of the live coal in Isaiah's vision: the coal being penetrated by the fire, but each retaining its distinctive identity.[16] Like all the orthodox Fathers, Cyril believed in 'one person' and 'two natures', although in his vocabulary he employed the term 'nature' for 'person' and the expressions 'natural property or quality' for 'nature'. Hence he was prepared to express his belief in words he held to be Athanasian but which in fact emanated from Apollinaris: 'one nature, and that incarnate, of the divine Word'.[17] The point of departure in his thinking was always the pre-existent Word; at the incarnation he did not cease to be what he was but added to it by taking human nature; so that both before and after the incarnation he was the same person, the difference being that now he has two natures. There was thus no division but a real and hypostatic or personal union because the human nature was his own and had no separate existence apart from him. He who had existed outside flesh had now become 'embodied'. 'After the union one nature is understood, viz. the enfleshed nature of the Word'.[18]

Cyril's teaching was endorsed in the West by Leo, whose *Tome* was to become one of the basic documents of Chalcedon. Like Cyril Leo affirmed that the person of Jesus Christ is identical with that of the divine Word: 'he who, abiding in the form of God, made man, was also made man in the form of a servant'. Further, Leo emphasized that the divine and human natures were not impaired by the union: 'just as God is not changed by compassion, so the manhood is not absorbed by dignity . . . each form, in communion with the other, performs the functions that is proper to it'. Hence, finally, the *communicatio idiomatum* is to be accepted, viz. the interchangeability of Christ's human and divine attributes, experiences, etc., in view of the unity of his person. 'By reason then of this unity of person to be understood in both natures the Son of Man is said to have come down from heaven when the Son of God took flesh from the Virgin that bore him; and again the Son of God is said to have been crucified and buried, although he suffered these things not in the Godhead itself, wherein the Only-begotten is co-eternal and consubstantial with the Father, but in the weakness of human nature.'[19]

At Chalcedon the positive beliefs of the schools of Alexandria and Antioch and of the Western theologians were accepted.

Following, then, the holy Fathers, we all unanimously teach that our Lord Jesus Christ is to us one and the same Son, the same perfect in Godhead, the same perfect in manhood; truly God and truly man; the same (consisting) of a rational soul and a body; of the same substance as the Father as to his Godhead, and the same of one substance with us as to his manhood; like us in all things, except for sin; begotten of his Father before the ages as to his Godhead, and in these last days, the same, for us and for our salvation, of Mary *Theotokos* as to his manhood; one and the same Christ, Son, Lord, only-begotten, made known in two natures (which exist) without confusion, without change, without division, without separation; the difference of the natures being in no way taken away because of the union, but rather the properties of each nature being preserved, and (both) concurring into one person and one hypostasis – not parted or divided into two persons, but one and the same Son and only-begotten, the divine Word, the Lord Jesus Christ.[20]

So at Chalcedon the unity of Christ's person was affirmed and the principle of 'recognizing' the natures was established. The Godhead and the manhood, in Cyril's phrase, are 'two, though only in contemplation'. In the one person are 'shewn forth' and therefore are 'to be recognized' both natures, but it must never be forgotten that they 'concur into one person'.

Unfortunately, the Council's findings were not universally accepted, largely due to a lack of agreement as to the meaning of the terms used. The representatives of the extreme Alexandrian tradition, following Cyril's terminology, who came to be known as Monophysites or believers in one nature only, understood 'nature' to mean 'person', and therefore when they read the Council's Definition, with its reference to Christ 'made known in two natures', they regarded this as affirming that in Christ there are two persons, which was in effect the Nestorian error. The debate was long and protracted and was unfortunate in that both sides were in fundamental agreement without being aware of it. Such men among the Monophysites as Timothy of Alexandria (457–77), Philoxenus of Mabbogh (died 523) and Severus of Antioch (exiled from his see in 518) condemned both Nestorianism and Eutychianism and upheld the belief that Christ was the divine Word who had united to himself a complete manhood and that he is now one incarnate nature (= person). Yet the debate had also a valuable outcome in that it led to a clarification of belief, culminating in the work of Leontius of Byzantium who died *c.* 534.

The orthodox formulation was to the effect that Christ was one person (*hypostasis*) with two natures (*physeis*), Godhead and manhood, the latter being generally regarded as impersonal (*anhypostatos*) to rule out Nestorianism. This expression raised the problem as to how there could be a nature without an *hypostasis* or personal basis? Did not the affirmation that in Christ there were two natures necessarily involve there being two persons (*hypostaseis*)? Leontius sought an answer by beginning, like Cyril, from the pre-existence of the Son of God; before the incarnation there was already in eternity a person, the second person of the Trinity. At the incarnation that person created for himself a human nature and, uniting himself to it in the process of creating it, made it his very own. Consequently he was both human and divine; but his humanity never had any existence prior to its being united with the Godhead; it was not the human nature of a distinct human person or *hypostasis* but his very own. Thus the one person of the God-man was the pre-existent Son of God and his humanity became personal in him: it was, to use Leontius' term, not impersonal but in-personal, not *anhypostatos* but *enhypostatos*.[21] This teaching was endorsed by the fifth Ecumenical Council at Constantinople in 553. It was also included by John of Damascus in his *De Fide Orthodoxa* in the following terms: 'He took on himself the first fruits of our flesh, and these not as having a separate existence or as being formerly an individual, and thus assumed by him, but as existing in his own person (*hypostasis*). For the person (*hypostasis*) of the divine Word itself became the person (*hypostasis*) of the flesh'.[22]

This belief, that in Christ there are two natures, had as its corollaries the idea that he had two operations, divine and human, and two wills. These conclusions were, however, not drawn until the opposite had been urged in the Monergist, i.e. one energy or operation, and the Monothelite, i.e. one will, controversies. So at the sixth Ecumenical Council at Constantinople in 680–1 it was laid down in its Definition of Faith that in Christ there are 'two natural wills and two natural operations without division, without change, without separation, without confusion, according to the teaching of the holy Fathers. And these two natural wills are not contrary the one to the other, but his human will follows and that not as resisting or reluctant but rather as subject to his divine and omnipotent will'.

This belief in two wills, it was held, did not lead to a split personality since, in the words of John of Damascus, the human will 'wills of its own free will those things which the divine will willeth it to will'.[23] This involved the recognition of a single activity of redemption, the two natures and wills concurring into the one person of the God-man – belief in the person of Christ had achieved its classic expression.

The Church

Classic expression was also given to the doctrine of the Church in the period after 381 by Augustine of Hippo, who, in opposition to the Donatists, clarified this article of belief. Following Optatus of Milevis, Augustine stressed and defined the four marks of the Church – oneness, holiness, catholicity and apostolicity. To him there is and can be only one Church[24] and what is outside that unity is outside the Body of Christ. The Church is the unity of faith[25] and it is the unity of charity or love.[26] Heresy denies the one and schism is the antithesis of the other. 'Who can truthfully say that he has the love of Christ when he does not embrace his unity?'[27] The principle of this unity is the Holy Spirit, as he is also the author of its holiness, which is however potential rather than actual. The Church is constantly working for the sanctification of souls[28] but it consists of an admixture of good and bad alike and will remain so until the final consummation. This affirmation of the Church as a *corpus permixtum* was in opposition to the Donatist view of sanctity here and now, and similarly Augustine's assertion of the Church's catholicity, in the sense of its universality, was anti-Donatist, the schismatics being confined to North Africa. Further, the term catholic not only means that the Church is spread over the entire world but also that it teaches the whole truth and not a part of the truth like the heretics.[29] Finally the Church is apostolic in that it can trace its succession back to the apostles,[30] the individual members being in communion with the apostolic sees and with Rome in particular.

The most characteristic expression used by Augustine of the Church is that it is the Body of Christ, and he considered that Christ has a triple mode of existence:[31] as the eternal Word, as the God-man and as the Church. The Church is *totus Christus*: 'he is our Head and we are his Body'[32] – 'the Head and the Body are one Christ'.[33] But Augustine was also prepared to distinguish between the Visible and the Invisible Church, the former consisting of good and evil, the latter of the elect, some of whom are within and some outside the Visible Church. He did not appreciate that his idea of predestination, sharpened by the Pelagian debate, was at variance with any idea of the Church as of divine ordinance and institution.

Man

In the development of the doctrine of man Augustine was again the leading figure in the West, although he was strongly influenced by the teaching of Ambrose. The problem that presented itself to Christian thinkers and had to be faced in the course of the Pelagian controversy is neatly summed up by Gregory of Nazianzus: 'It is necessary both that we should be our own masters and also that our salvation should be of God'.[34] In effect Pelagius and his followers overstressed the first item of this paradox, while Augustine and his disciples exaggerated the second.

According to Ambrose, man's primal state was one of supernatural blessedness[35] from which he fell through pride.[36] The solidarity of the race with Adam involved all mankind in his sin: 'In Adam I fell; in Adam I was cast out of Paradise; in Adam I died'.[37] Hence the corrupting force of sin has been transmitted to all. Ambrose further stressed both free-will and grace: 'in everything the Lord's power co-operates with man's efforts',[38] yet grace is bestowed 'simply according to the will of the giver'.[39]

Pelagius, with his summons to moral endeavour, insisted upon man's freedom of choice; he rejected the idea that he has any bias towards evil as a consequence of the fall, and while acknowledging the necessity of grace, he understood by it free-will together with the revelation, through reason, of God's law and the teaching and example of Christ.

Augustine, who was convinced that 'without God's help we cannot by free-will overcome the temptations of this life',[40] endorsed Ambrose's view of man's original perfection; he was emphatic that the fall was man's responsibility and that it had issued in the ruin of the entire race which thereby became a *massa damnata*.[41] He went beyond Ambrose in asserting that original sin involves original guilt[42] and he affirmed that while we have retained free-will we have lost all freedom and cannot avoid sin. The necessity of grace follows from this: there must be prevenient grace, i.e. God must be the initiator of all that is good in thought, argument or will: there must be co-operating grace, i.e. God must assist the will once it has been moved. Augustine did not rest here: he also held that God's grace is irresistible and that it acts only upon those whom God has chosen. He was therefore led to the position of maintaining a predestination to election and a predestination to damnation – concepts that were not to commend themselves to all.

In the East a more optimistic view of man's present condition prevailed. By refusing to accept that mankind is a *massa damnata*, the easterns were able to hold the concepts of grace and free-will in a more balanced tension. So Theodore of Mopsuestia rejected the view that we participate in Adam's guilt, while accepting the idea that we inherit the corruption of sin.[43] 'There is need,' according to Theodoret, 'of both our efforts and the divine aid'.[44]

The work of Christ

This developing interest in the doctrine of man inevitably affected the understanding of the work of Christ, since what Christ has done must be defined in part by one's interpretation of the human condition into which he came and which it was his purpose to set right.

In the West, where the sense of law and order was strong, Christians tended to place their emphasis upon the practical rather than the speculative, on simple definitions rather than upon complex formulations. Sin, to them, was a crime against God requiring satisfaction. Man is unable to offer the necessary satisfaction and is therefore under the divine condemnation from which there is no escape, unless God himself intervenes and both vindicates his law and pays the debt. So, according to Jerome, Christ 'endured in our stead the penalty we ought to have suffered for our crimes.'[45] Hence to the westerns the main stress must be laid upon Calvary, on the meritorious death when the blood was freely given as the price of reconciliation to God. Christ, in Augustine's words, 'is both Victor and Victim, and therefore Victor because Victim'.[46] The work of Christ consists in bringing forgiveness to sinful man through the vicarious and sacrificial death of the God-man.

In the East the differing approaches of the schools of Antioch and Alexandria, patent in their Christological beliefs, are again to be noted. The former regarded man's state of mutability and corruption as the result of his disobedience to the divine will. To restore stability and order, a new stage in the history of the universe was needed, involving the creation of a new man who would live in perfect obedience to God. Since fallen man cannot achieve this alone, God must intervene and both create and unite to himself the new man, thus re-establishing man in moral obedience to his will. At the Incarnation the Son of God did unite man to himself, and having consummated his lifelong obedience upon the cross, triumphed over corruption and death through his resurrection.

If the West emphasized the cross and the Antiochenes the resurrection, the Alexandrians concentrated upon the incarnation. To this school of thought which had previously found expression in Ignatius, Irenaeus, Clement, Origen and Athanasius, with differing physical, metaphysical and mystical overtones, the primary consequence of sin was the corruption of human nature with the corresponding loss of immortality. Christ's work was therefore to restore incorruption and for this the reunification of God and man was necessary. In Christ God and man were made one, and so the divine image, defaced but not effaced by the fall, could be restored after the original. So Cyril of Alexandria: 'The Only-begotten made himself like us, that is complete man, in order to deliver our earthly body from the corruption which had invaded it.'[47]

Last Things

A pessimistic estimate of man, especially in the West after Augustine, also affected the Christian hope, and while the expectation of the Parousia faded ideas of judgement and hell became more vivid.

If Ambrosiaster could interpret the collapse of Rome as a sign of the approaching end of the world,[48] Augustine himself was prepared to say that the Second Coming would be 'at the most seasonable time'[49] without any indication of its date or of its immediacy; the urgent expectant note of the New Testament was no longer sounded. By contrast greater emphasis was placed upon the Last Judgement, while acknowledging that the divine judgement is a permanent feature of history and that the Great Assize will be therefore the consummation of a continuing process.[50] The darkness of that 'day of doom'[51] was to settle upon the medieval mind and to engross it with the fear of eternal perdition.

Belief in the resurrection remained largely one of physical reanimation, the identity of the earthly body with the resurrection body being stressed, for example, by Jerome.[52] But in the thought of Gregory of Nyssa the attempt was made to refine this materialism.[53] Nevertheless even this belief gave rise to some concern. At the beginning of the fifth century many Christians feared that the resurrection might only lead to their dying again, that although they would rise they might undergo, like Lazarus, a second death, and they required reassurance not only by the words of such men as John Chrysostom[54] and Augustine[55] but also by the insertion of the words 'life everlasting' in the creedal formulae.

Formulation of Belief

The reference to 'life everlasting' is not found in the text of the Old Roman Creed to be derived from Rufinus' *Commentarius in symbolum apostolorum*, *c.* 400, but it was soon to be included. This process of additions and slight alterations was to continue for several centuries before this ancient baptismal formula attained its final shape, still used to this day with the title of the Apostles' Creed. The birthplace of the *textus receptus* would appear to have been south-west France at some date in the late sixth or seventh centuries.

To this creed and to the 'Nicene' symbol there was also added a third which was to be accepted as authoritative in the West – the so-called Athanasian Creed or *Quicunque vult.* This semi-liturgical document was probably of Gallican origin and dates from the end of the fifth century. It comprises a statement of the necessary antitheses in relation to both Trinitarian and Christological teaching. It sought not so much to explain as to safeguard the essential elements of belief that had been progressively defined throughout the patristic period.

WORSHIP

The theological differences, already noted, for example between East and West or between Antioch and Alexandria, are but one series of illustrations of the multiplicity in unity that characterized the Early Church. These first centuries demonstrate, if demonstration be necessary, that it is possible to have unity without uniformity. But this was true not only of theological formulations; it was also applicable to forms of worship. If there was an overall similarity of pattern, there was also differentiation in terms of local usage, so that baptism was not administered in Milan in exactly the same way as it was in Antioch, while the eucharistic rites began to assume certain regional peculiarities which led to the creation of whole families of liturgies.

Baptism

In speaking of the rite of baptism it is possible to make three generalizations: first, the same essential elements are to be found in all areas; second, there can be a difference from centre to centre in the order or sequence of these elements; third, there are a number of ancillary ceremonies which differ from local church to local church.

The common elements can be listed as follows: (i) Removal of clothes; (ii) Unction; (iii) Renunciation; (iv) Blessing of Font; (v) Declaration of Faith; (vi) Baptism in Water; (vii) Putting on White Robes.

The most notable difference in the order of these concerns the unction. In the West this is both a prebaptismal act and also the outward sign, sometimes together with the laying on of hands, of the signing or confirmation after the immersion in water. In the regions of Edessa and Nisibis, however, there was no postbaptismal unction whatsoever.[1] The position of the renunciation too was not everywhere the same: in North Africa it took place in the church before the procession to the baptistery,[2] and similarly at Nisibis it was the first of the baptismal acts,[3] while in Milan and Rome it followed the preliminary unction.[4] Usually the renunciation preceded the declaration of faith, but in Syria, according to Theodore of Mopsuestia, the affirmation of belief took place before the baptismal ceremonies proper began.

Amongst ancillary ceremonies, there was the washing of the feet, as at Milan also after the second unction[5] – a practice not found at Rome but observed at Hippo on Maundy Thursday;[6] the placing of a stole of linen over the head after the signing in Syria[7] and the Effeta or opening of the ears at Rome and Milan.

Two baptismal orders may now be taken to illustrate the interconnexion of the elements, the one from the West as described by Ambrose of Milan and the other from the East as described by Theodore of Mopsuestia.

At Milan on Easter Eve the candidates assembled and had their ears and nostrils touched – the Effeta – to symbolize the opening of the faculties to the fruitful reception of the sacraments. Next 'thou wast anointed as Christ's athlete, as about to wrestle in the fight of this world'. The renunciations were twofold, of the devil and his works, of the world and its pleasures, and may have been followed by the *sputatio* or spitting in the devil's face. After the consecration of the font, the candidates entered it and made their baptismal profession. The bishop then anointed their heads and began the pedilavium. Finally, vested in white robes they received the 'spiritual seal' and went in procession to the altar.

According to the account of Theodore of Mopsuestia, the candidates, after a profession of faith, uttered a renunciation and a declaration of adherence to Christ. They were then signed with the chrism on the forehead and this meant 'that you have been stamped as a lamb of Christ and as a soldier of the heavenly king'. Linen was next spread over the heads because this was what freedmen were accustomed to do and therefore was a sign that baptism had set the candidates free from sin. Upon removal of the clothes a second unction of the whole body was performed and the descent into the water, previously blessed, took place. White garments were donned and after a final signing on the forehead, the neophytes were ready to 'draw near unto an immortal food'.

From the extant rites and from the commentaries upon them it is possible to reconstruct the baptismal theology of this period which continues that of the preceding centuries. Baptism draws the individual out of isolation into unity; 'Through the second birth and through the Holy Spirit all of us become one body of Christ.'[8] Baptism further restores the divine image marred by sin: 'made partners of the Holy Spirit, we are being restored to the primitive beauty of our nature; the image which we bore at the first is engraved afresh upon our spiritual life, for Christ is formed in us through the Spirit.'[9] Hence baptism is also the means to the remission of sins: 'baptism washes away all, entirely all, our sins, whether of deed, word or thought, whether sins original or added, whether knowingly or unknowingly contracted.'[10] This emphasis upon the rite as a sin-washing accords with the pessimistic concept of man and, as a corollary of this, man's subservience to the devil is also stressed and so baptism is seen as a setting free from demonic powers. Speaking of the unction Narsai says that 'by its firmness it makes the body firm and the faculties of the soul, and they go forth confidently to wage war against the evil one.'[11] Still predominant however were the themes of death and burial and of rebirth. 'When thou dippest,' says Ambrose, 'thou takest on the likeness of death and burial; thou receivest the sacrament of the cross.'[12] According to Chrysostom, 'what the womb is to the embryo, the water is to the believer, for in the water he is fashioned and formed.'[13]

Expressed in architectural terms these beliefs produced the quadrilateral fonts like sarcophagi: 'The appearance of the font is somewhat

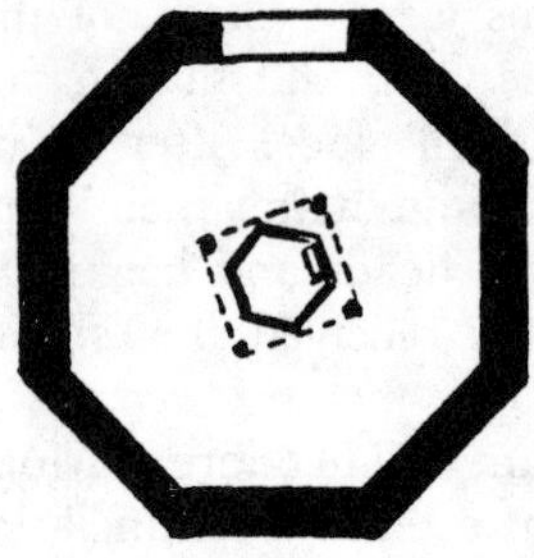

Octagonal Baptistry at Hemmaberge

like that of a tomb in shape.'[14] They also produced hexagons, e.g. at Timgad, since Christ was crucified in the sixth day of the week, and octagons, e.g. at Poitiers, since he rose on the eighth day, i.e. the first day of a new week. They further issued in the cruciform and quatrefoil fonts, for, as Chrysostom expressed it, 'baptism is a cross. What the cross was to Christ and what his burial was, that baptism was to us'[15] – hence the shapes at Salona and Milos.

The same shapes, with the identical ideological content, were used for the baptisteries. The octagon was widespread in Italy and in countries under its influence, e.g. at Ravenna, Parenzo, Melas and Hemmaberge. The hexagon may be seen at Zara in Dalmatia; the

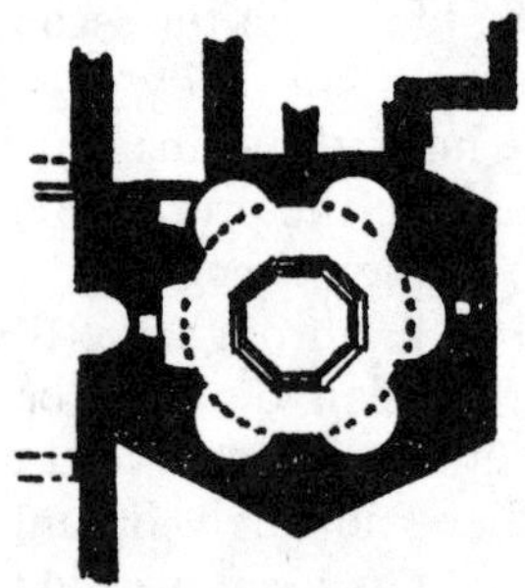

Hexagonal Baptistry at Zara

circular plan at Nocera and Djemila. In those areas such as Greece, Syria and Palestine, where the square tomb was and continued to be the norm, the baptistery likewise continued to be a quadrilateral, either free-standing or in the form of a room adjacent to the church. Quatrefoil and trefoil baptisteries, e.g. at Tigzirt and Apollonia I, also reproduced the characteristic features of local tombs and martyria. So belief, practice and architecture were welded into one.

Although the central act of baptism, the immersion in water, requires no more than a font in a single chamber, quite evidently in view of the complexity of the rite it was open to Christians to produce a series of rooms, each corresponding to one element in the whole. Indeed, entire suites of rooms were erected, but in the absence of inscriptions or

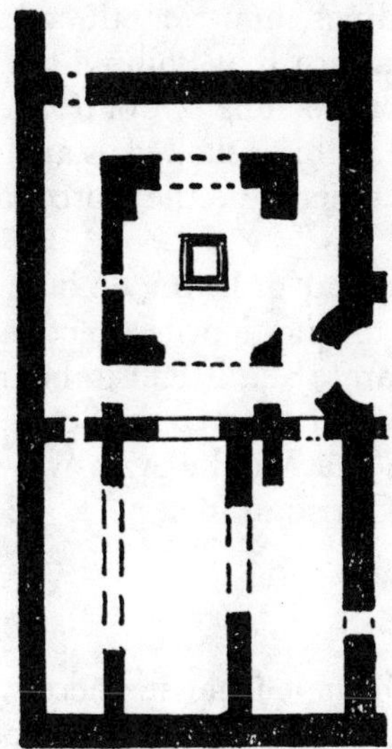

Baptismal rooms at Gul Bagtsche

distinctive furniture it is all but impossible to determine their exact use. At Gul Bgatsche in Turkey, leading off the narthex, there is a square room with three others opening off it; these last could be changing-rooms; one could have been a *chrismarion*, i.e. the place where the bishop administered the chrism, but certain identification is out of the

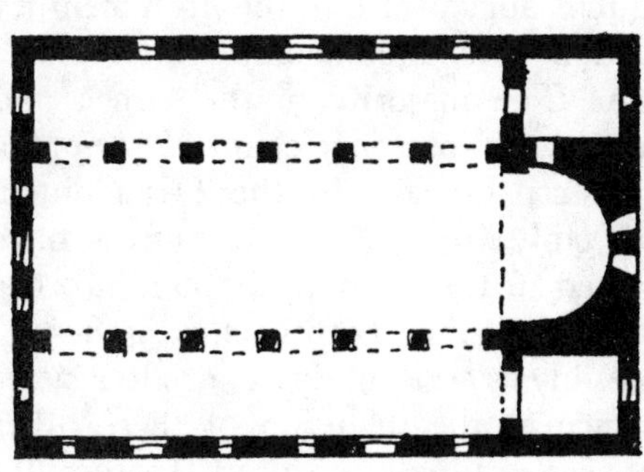

Basilica at Mshabbak

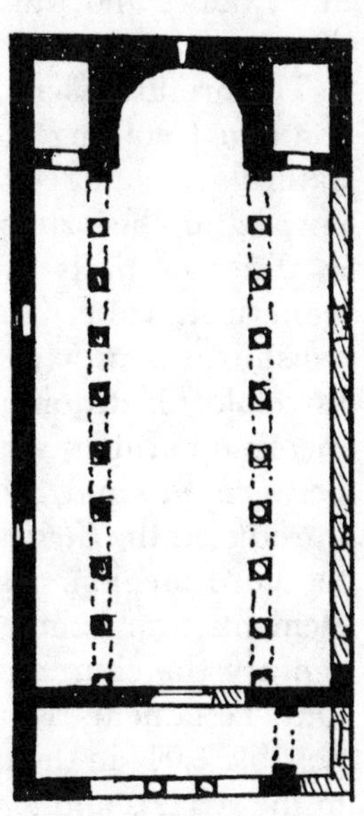

Basilica at Midjleyyā

question. In other buildings, however, the arrangement is capable of interpretation, e.g. in Basilica B at Philippi the baptistery is at the east end of the south wall and opening out of it is a long narrow chamber; the fact that the far wall of this is shaped as an apse indicates that it had a special function, viz. to enshrine the episcopal throne for the chrism or act of confirmation.

As long as the unction and/or laying on of hands was part of the one rite there was no need to question its exact meaning. But when confirmation became a separate act, it had to be interpreted. The general theory was that chrismation bestowed the Spirit,[16] but the view that was eventually to prevail in the Middle Ages was that it was a means of 'strengthening' for the Christian life.

Eucharist

As with baptism so with the eucharist, there was an overall similarity of structure. Every rite continued to have two parts: the ministry of the Word and the ministry of the sacrament. Almost every rite included a Preface and Sanctus, an Institution Narrative and the Our Father. Every rite preserved the shape of the Last Supper in that they included the bringing of the bread and wine, the taking of them, their blessing, the fraction and their distribution. The tendency, however, was to overlay the primitive pattern with elaborations, consisting of prayers and litanies and this occasionally led to a change of sequence so that differentia were created.

The primitive synaxis had been essentially a ministry of the word and contained nothing of a strictly devotional character. Elements of this nature were added to the original nucleus from the fifth century onwards in the form of an introduction which included different features in different parts of Christendom. The majority of the Greek and western rites after the fifth century have an entrance chant. The note of worship was provided in many eastern liturgies by the Trisagion – a threefold repetition of 'Holy God, Holy Mighty, Holy Immortal, have mercy upon us' – which was inserted in the Constantinopolitan order between 430 and 450. In the West, at Rome, Symmachus (498–514) introduced the *Gloria in excelsis*, possibly as an imitation of or alternative to the Trisagion. As a consequence of the inclusion of these other elements, the number of lections was gradually reduced. In the fifth century the church of Constantinople abolished the reading from the Old Testament, Rome following suit later in the same century or possibly early in the sixth. The 'Nicene' creed also began to find a place in the synaxis and it would appear to have been first used by Peter the Fuller at Antioch in 473 to emphasize the adherence of the Monophysites to the Council of Nicaea as opposed, by them, to the Council of Chalcedon. In the early sixth century its use spread to Constantinople, and it was adopted in Spain by the third Council of Toledo in 589 as a test for Arians, being recited after the fraction – an unusual position it still retains in the Mozarabic rite. Rome was not eager to accept this innovation and it was not until the eleventh century that the practice spread thither from the Frankish dominions.

These elaborations arose both from a psychological need and from a change of circumstances. The laity came to worship and wanted that note to be sounded from the outset; they demanded and were eventually given some kind of devotional preparation to the sacrament proper. But those who now assembled were all at least nominally Christians; there were no longer present catechumens and interested outsiders who were not members of the Church and with whom, since they had not received the Spirit of adoption through baptism, the faithful could not pray. Prayers – in the form of litanies in the East – thus came to abound in the first half of the service.

Further prayers were also added to the second half, the reason for this being clearly enunciated by Cyril of Jerusalem when he said: 'it will be a very great advantage for souls, for whom supplication is offered up, while the holy and awesome sacrifice lies exposed',[17] i.e. prayer in the presence of the consecrated sacrament is deemed to be most effective. Thus at Antioch, immediately before the Lord's Prayer, the president uttered petitions for the whole earth and for the living and the dead.[18] At Rome a *memento* of the living, being a recitation of the names of the communicants, was closely associated with the offertory; a *memento* of the dead was only included in the ninth century as the antepenultimate paragraph of the canon. Since different prayers and different types of prayer – simple petitions by the president or litanies by a deacon – were adopted, liturgies diverged further from each other and an even greater distinction between those of the West and the East was effected by a dissimilarity in the way the offertory was performed. In the West it was the custom for the bread and the wine to be brought up by the individual worshippers during the service; in the East the gifts were handed in beforehand and from this two practices were eventually to develop, peculiar to the Eastern liturgies: the rite of the prothesis and the Great Entrance. The former was an elaborate preparation of the eucharistic species before the service proper began, while the Great Entrance was the carrying in of the elements to the high altar. A rationale was developed to connect these features – in the rite of the prothesis Christ is slain in a figure by the piercing of the host with a miniature lance; at the Great Entrance the dead Christ is solemnly borne to his altar-bomb and finally, at the Epiclesis, the Spirit is invoked to raise the dead Christ who is then present as the living Lord in the midst of his worshippers.

The divergent ethos of East and West in terms of the mass of the faithful will become apparent if, with the previously described Clementine liturgy[19] in mind, a brief account be now given of the liturgy in North Africa as it may be reconstituted from references in the works of Augustine.[20]

After the conclusion of the intercessions, the deacons receive the offerings from the congregation and place them upon the altar. The bishop greets the people and bursts into thanksgiving – there was apparently as yet no Sanctus – he celebrates the memorial of the death of Christ, repeats the Institution Narrative, and prays for the living and the dead. After the fraction comes the Lord's Prayer, then the Kiss of Peace and a blessing of the people. Distribution takes place, to the singing of a psalm, and the bishop utters a final prayer before the solemn dismissal: 'Go in peace.'

Eucharist doctrine during this period, in relation to the presence of Christ, was of two kinds: the figurative, which stresses the distinction between the elements and the reality they represent, and the conversionist, which affirms a change in the bread and wine. The former view was the more primitive and was represented in the West by Augustine, the latter was an eastern development, exemplified by John Chrysostom and popularized in the West by Ambrose.

Augustine distinguished between the sacrament as a sign and as a reality: the bread and the wine are effective symbols that convey the invisible grace. But that grace or reality is not to be identified with Christ's historical body[21] – it is rather the gift of life. 'I am the food of grown men,' declares the heavenly voice, 'grow and thou shalt feed upon me; nor shalt thou convert me, like the food of thy flesh, into thee, but thou shalt be converted into me.'[22]

Chrysostom was much more materialistic and he could speak of eating Christ[23] and assert that the wine is identical with the blood that flowed from his side.[24] Ambrose, partly under the influence of Greek thought, could ask: 'the word of Christ could make out of nothing that which was not; cannot it then change the things which are into that which they were not?'[25] There is indeed a 'change of nature' – a conception that was to issue in the later doctrine of transubstantiation.

The eucharistic sacrifice, as understood by Chrysostom, involves the identity of that which is offered at the altar with what Christ offered at the Last Supper. The sacrifice is one and in the eucharist the memorial of the cross is made.[26] Augustine linked the theme of sacrifice with the teaching of Hebrews about the heavenly intercession of Christ to the effect that the eucharist is the earthly representation of Christ's eternal self-offering.[27] But Augustine's main stress in eucharistic teaching was upon the unity accomplished by the sacrament, a unity between head and members and between the members themselves, so that by communion the Church, the *totus Christus*, becomes its true self[28] – 'the spiritual benefit which is there understood is unity, that being joined to his body and made his members we may be what we receive.'[29]

Architectural setting

In the West the church-type, which had been adopted under Constantine and was to prevail for some seven hundred years, was the basilica. To describe one is to describe all, due allowance being made for differences in secondary detail. The report of the excavations at Hippo, published in 1958, contains a full account of the *Basilica Pacis* which was the episcopal seat of Augustine. This basilica was an imposing building, 40 metres by 20, divided into nave and two aisles. The elongated apse

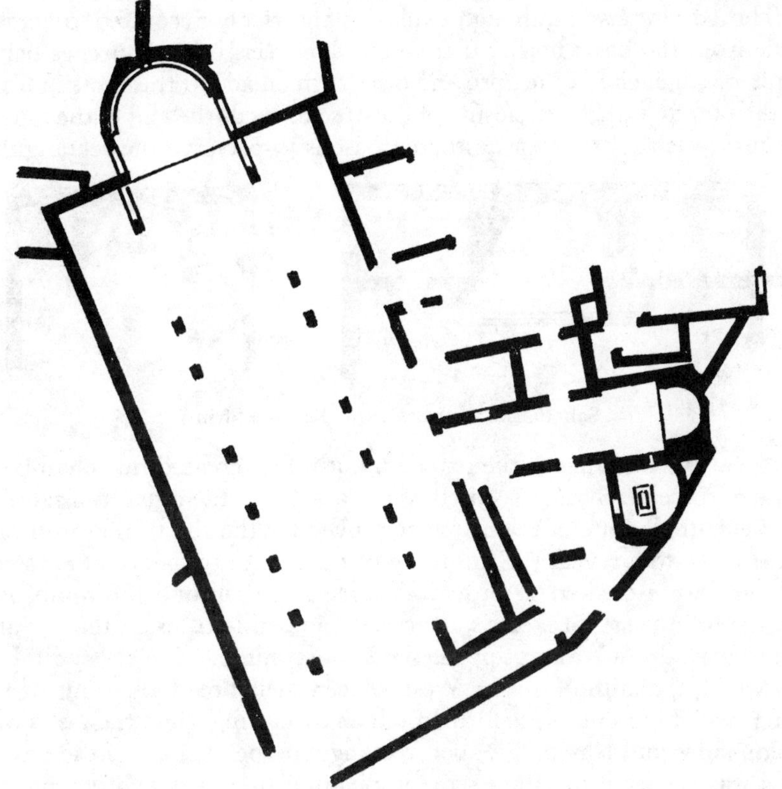

Basilica Pacis at Hippo

had a masonry bench for the presbyters around the wall with a central space for the cathedra. The elevated presbyterium would appear to have been extended forward to the first pilasters, being then fenced with cancelli and containing the altar. Some two yards in front of this towards the central axis of the nave was the ambo. Clerestory lighting was provided through the walls rising above the roofs of the aisles and the floor was decorated with mosaics. Opening off the south aisle was the baptismal complex, consisting of a rectangular font beneath a ciborium, a *chrismarion* with apse, and side rooms with no identifiable function. This basilica was not an isolated building but occupied the centre of a whole block belonging to the Church. Extending eastwards from the baptistery was a bath and then the bishop's residence, while opposite to this on the north side was the *secretarium*, colonnaded and open to the sky in the centre, where Augustine had his library and where most probably the 329 bishops met in October 393. Eastwards again was the monastery for laymen established by Augustine under his predecessor Valerius.

The *Basilica Pacis*, although extensive and richly decorated, diverged little from the basic norm; there were, however, other churches being built which enclosed the apse and others which added transepts in front of the sanctuary. The enclosing of the apse towards the end of the fourth century was probably for aesthetic reasons to preserve the rectangular

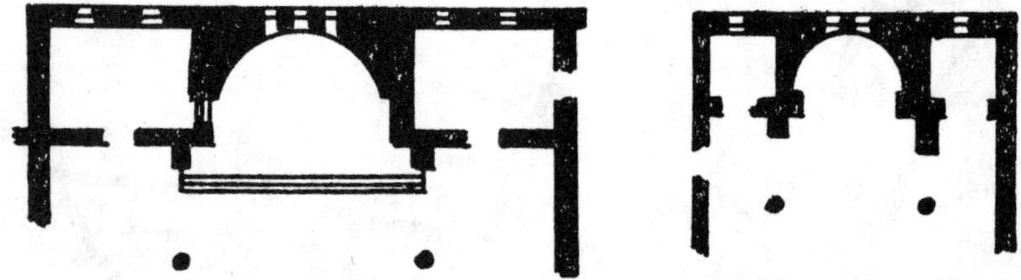

Sanctuaries: (*a*) Brad; (*b*) Kharâb Shems

shape of the building at the exterior, but it also created side chambers. One of these, in Syria, was used as a martyrium, the other as a sacristy and eventually one of them was employed for the rite of the prothesis. Transepts, too, reveal the influence of the cult of the martyrs for some of them were created to provide a large space around the tomb of a patron saint, e.g. St Peter's, Rome. Besides this transept-martyrium, there was also a transept-prothesis, i.e. accommodation for the tables on which the faithful, in the West, placed their bread and wine at the offertory. Transepts were formed either by cutting short the aisles and colonnades and leaving an open rectangle perpendicular to the nave – this was the plan in Rome – or by bending the aisles and colonnades outwards at right angles near the east end and then turning them

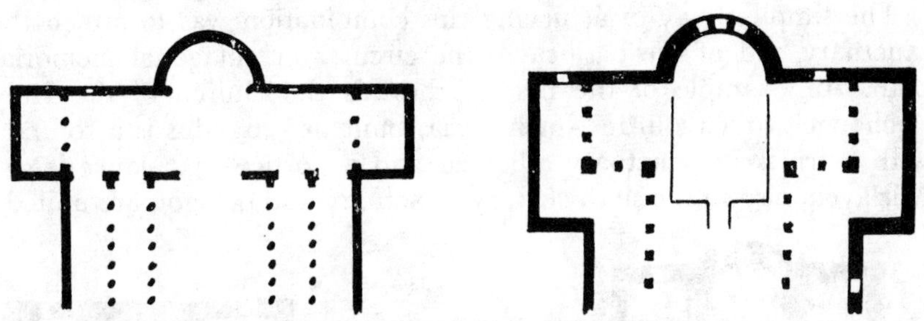

Transepts: (*a*) St Peter's, Rome; (*b*) Basilica A, Philippi

through another right angle to join the east wall, thus providing a free space in the centre – a feature of a number of Greek basilicas.

The cult of the saints not only influenced the formation of transepts, it also affected the shape of the altar and, in the East, even of the whole building. When the pilgrim Egeria visited the reputed burial place of Job at Carneas, she noted that the church had been erected in such a way that 'the body should lie under the altar'.[30] It was usual for a vertical shaft to connect the altar with the tomb and access to it was obtained by means of an opening in the side of the table facing the nave; this opening was closed by a grating of stone or metal which was called the *fenestella confessionis*. The pierced slab of the *fenestella* had a small door large enough to allow the passage of an arm and by this means small objects, such as handkerchiefs, were brought into contact with the tomb; it was these *brandea* that were exported as relics. In those churches where the tomb was too far below the surface to be readily accessible perforated plates, *cataractae*, were inserted across the shaft, objects being placed upon them. There were, of course, many churches dedicated in honour of saints whose bodies lay elsewhere; accordingly the practice arose of enclosing in the altar some small relics and the altar therefore assumed the shape of a box. Since the altar now acted as a kind of tomb, the practice developed of making it of stone and this usage spread with such rapidity that by 517 the council of Epaon prohibited wooden altars entirely.[31]

The translation of relics which began in the latter half of the fifth century allowed the cult of the martyrs to leave the cemeteries and the new buildings erected in the East to enshrine their remains naturally perpetuated the traditional form of the martyria, with its centralized plan and its resemblance to a tomb. As the edifice was also to be used for the regular celebration of the liturgy, which requires not a vertical axis but a horizontal perspective, the architects were faced with the problem of modifying the primitive form in order to combine it with the basilica; hence arose the centralized church as distinct from the centralized martyrium.

The simplest way of achieving this combination was to attach the sanctuary end of the basilica to the circular or octagonal memorial plan. An example of the first of these is the church of the Holy Archangels at Fa'loul in North Syria, built in 526 – this is a rotunda with a tripartite sanctuary adjoined and a portico to balance it. At Mir'âyeh, also in the sixth century, sanctuary and octagon are united;

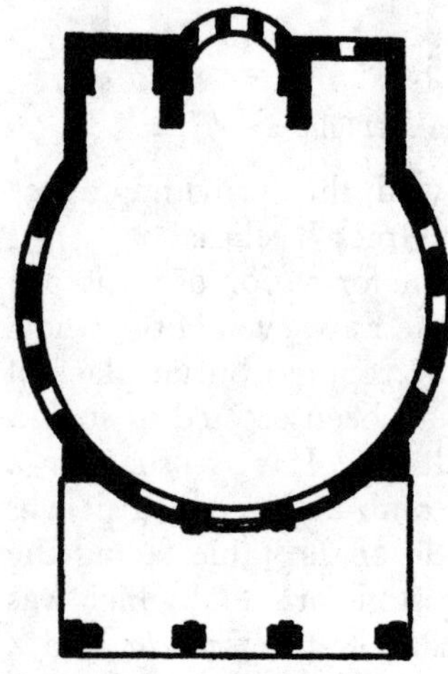

Centralized Church at Fa'loul

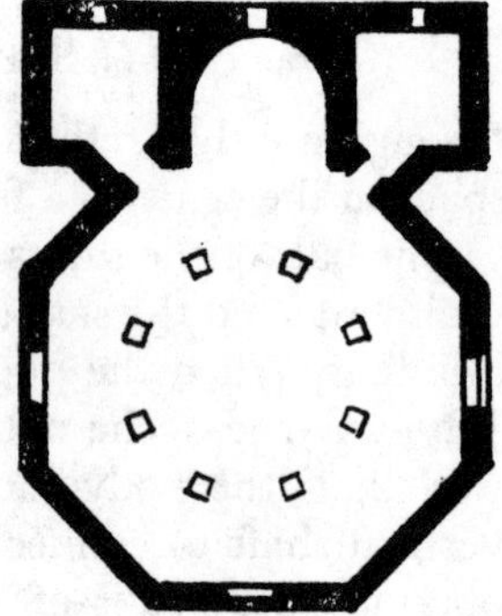

Centralized Church at Mir'âyeh

the interior is too destroyed to allow certainty about its disposition, but it probably had pillars to carry a dome, which was another almost invariable element of the centralized building. The most outstanding example of this arrangement is S. Vitale, Ravenna (526–47), which consists of two concentric octagons with bema and apse extending beyond the perimeter to the East. Yet it was the dome over a square that was to become the characteristic form of the Byzantine church building, a key construction in this development being SS. Sergius and Bacchus at Constantinople, for which Justinian was responsible. In Asia and the Balkans the domed basilica became common, e.g. at Kasr Ibn Wardân, but the supreme example was S. Sophia, dedicated in 537, which has its central dome abutted by two half domes to east and west.

The dome was also in itself an ideal feature for mosaic decoration which now proliferated, covering also the walls and the apse. A new monumental art was in the process of being created with individualized figures and a concern for detail. Scenes from the gospels were represented, as in S. Apollinare Nuovo at Ravenna (520–30) or the great apisdal mosaic of the ascension in SS. Cosma e Damiano at Rome (526–30); patron saints and apostles were depicted as in S. Pudenziana

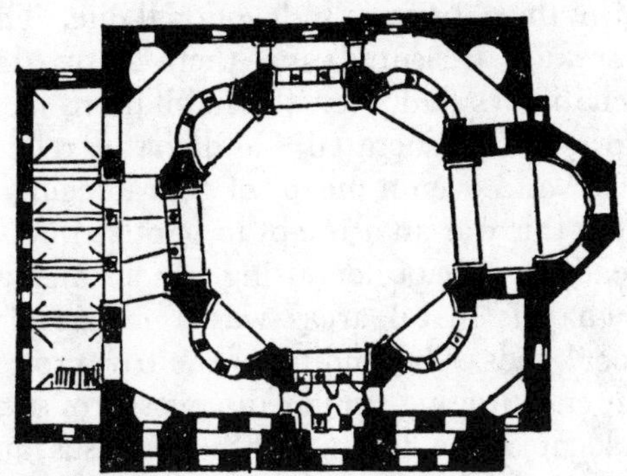

Domed square: SS. Sergius and Bacchus, Constantinople

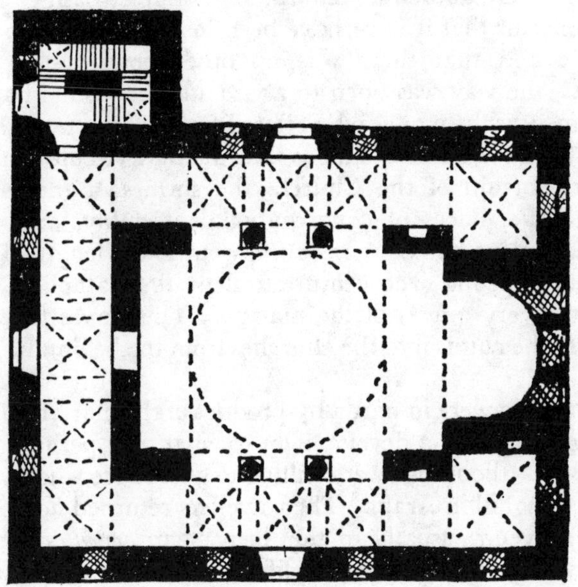

Domed Basilica at Kasr Ibn Wardân

(402–17) and S. Agnes (625–38) in Rome. Even contemporary scenes appeared as in the offertory processions showing Justinian and Theodora with their suites in S. Vitale, Ravenna. If these seem a far cry from the simplicity of the house-church, they testify to the desire to impress the worshipper with a knowledge of holy things and to express devotion in terms of the most beautiful works of man's hands that could be offered.

Martyr-cult and pilgrimages

The cult of the saints, which so influenced architecture, also became an important item in the Christian's devotional life. The relics of the martyrs were carefully treasured and their cultus defended on the grounds that their bodies had been the habitations of the Holy Spirit and were therefore to be venerated[32] and that a relic is a protection against evil spirits[33] and even a means of guaranteeing public safety.[34] To a certain extent this was an attempt to baptize into Christianity the already widespread practice of honouring famous men and heroes, and the creation of chapels in all areas was a means of displacing the worship of the local gods. The finding of the true cross by Helena also played its part in encouraging similar discoveries of sacred remains, as when Ambrose located the tomb of SS. Gervasus and Protasius at Milan.[35] Care was indeed exercised by the Church authorities to see that the relics were authentic, and so, for example, Basil records of the body of Dionysius that it must have been his since the tomb was easily recognizable and that there was no other body resting nearby.[36] Nevertheless, the way was open to abuse and Augustine had occasion to censure mendicant monks who offered for sale the supposed limbs of martyrs.[37] There was also a danger that the matryr cult would replace the regular worship of the Church, the shrines of the saints being preferred to the places of congregational assembly, and indeed an Egyptian document, the *Canones Basilii*, went to the length of condemning 'uncultured people who venture to deny the Catholic Church and its law at the very graves of the martyrs'. This serves to explain the movement of the cultus into the churches from the beginning of the fifth century.

Pilgrimages too were in part a by-product of the martyr-cult; indeed, the fourth century saw a development of what may perhaps be termed pilgrimage-itis – thousands were willing to go and see what was reputed to be Job's dunghill in Arabia. The travellers returned home each with his or her souvenir, usually in the form of an *ampulla* or small flask decorated with a scene from the life of Christ or of the saints and containing holy oil, i.e. oil that had been allowed to percolate through a sarcophagus containing sacred remains. Constantine's Holy Land plan also provided a stimulus to pilgrimages and rendered many eager to see the very ground where Christ was born, lived, died and ascended. A third factor that increased the number making these journeys was the reputation of individual living saints and of the monks in particular. The fame of Simeon Stylites brought crowds to the foot of his column and as far west as Rome itself small images of him were placed in the vestibules of shops which, it was believed, he would then guard and protect. The deserts of Nitria and elsewhere ceased to be impenetrable wastes as visitors came to learn more of the ascetic life from those who were practising it. By this means the monastic ideals and the liturgical practices of the monasteries and of the holy places were made familiar to all parts of the Church.

Hours of Prayer

During the third and fourth centuries Christians had been expected to offer prayers at certain hours of the day and night; this practice, however, was a private exercise for individuals and their families. The history of the transformation of this cycle of private prayer into a cycle of public worship is by no means clear, but from the late fourth century onwards two of these hours, morning and evening, were conducted publicly day by day in the large churches. So in the *Apostolic Constitutions* the bishop is exhorted to 'assemble the church' for morning and evening prayer,[38] and at Jerusalem, according to Egeria, vigils consisting of psalms and readings were common, together with prayers at daybreak. Yet the fact that it is recorded as an innovation that Chrysostom initiated a service after nightfall for the men who had had no opportunity for Christian devotion during the day indicates that the practice was not yet universal.[39]

The main impetus to the development came from the monastic movement. Living together as a community the monks said prayer in common at all hours of the day and this issued in the regulated offices of Benedict which became the pattern for the western Church. Benedict also provided for the singing of hymns, thus incorporating a feature which had become popular in the late fourth century, pioneered by Ambrose of Milan.

The Agape

While the daily office was developing, there was one devotional practice that was suffering a decline, viz. the agape. Love feasts were held on three main occasions: at marriages, funerals and on the feast days of martyrs.[40] The first took place in private houses, but the other two were celebrated in cemeteries and near the tombs of the martyrs. Special *triclinia* were indeed constructed in close proximity to the *hypogea* for funeral meals and one such is still to be seen at the entrance to the catacomb of Domitilla in Rome. Churches and martyria were also used for these feasts, primarily with the intention of controlling and regularizing them. Nevertheless, with the rapid increase of Church membership the primitive sense of brotherhood became less acute and social distinctions began to reassert themselves, so that the agape developed into a social entertainment for the wealthy or a mere dole of food for the poor. Gregory of Nazianzus was led to complain: 'If we come together to satisfy the belly and to enjoy the changing and fleeting pleasures, and so turn this place of temperance into one of gluttony and satiety . . . I do not see how our conduct corresponds with the occasion.'[41] Augustine saw the bad effects that such behaviour would have on the proclamation of the gospel, because 'those debaucheries and lavish banquets in cemeteries are usually believed by a sensual and ignorant populace to be not only commemorations of martyrs, but even consolations to the dead.'[42] 'These drunkards,' he declared, 'persecute the saints as much with cups as the furious pagans did with stones.'[43] Hence the synod of Laodicea, while permitting the agape in the private house, forbade its being held in churches: 'it is not permitted to hold love-feasts, as they are called, in the Lord's house or churches, nor to eat and spread couches in the house of God.'[44] In 397 the third Council of Carthage not only repeated this but also ordered that all Christians should 'as far as may be be debarred from entertainments of this kind'.[45] The bishops took steps to implement these canons; Ambrose at Milan instructed the doorkeepers to turn away anyone bringing food[46] and Augustine wrote to Valerius of Hippo to induce him to follow this example on the grounds that the agape had become indistinguishable from heathen banquets and was therefore to be discouraged.[47]

Nevertheless the agape persisted and in the same year as the Council of Carthage, Pammachius held a great funeral banquet in St Peter's at Rome in honour of his deceased mother Paulina.[48] In the fifth century common meals were held in the Thebaid every Saturday night[49] and Theodoret reports yearly feasting in honour of the martyrs.[50] Gregory the Great was prepared to allow them at the dedication of churches, especially in the case of the newly converted English.[51] Even after the final condemnation at the Trullan or Quinisextan Council of 692, canon 74 of which repeats the enactment of Laodicea, adding the words 'those who dare to do this must either cease or be excommunicated', even after this traces of it persisted in the *eulogia* or blessed bread which was taken to absent members of the congregation.

The history of the agape is a story of progressive secularization and is illustrative of the liability of the social life of the Church to become degraded. The danger of this can be best appreciated by examining that social life itself.

SOCIAL LIFE

Since Christianity was now the official religion of the empire, both East and West, all citizens were nominally Christians. Indeed, Augustine could say of Hippo: 'there are houses in our town in which there is not a single pagan to be found, and there is not a single house where there are no Christians.'[1] Consequently all trades and professions were now represented within the Christian community. Slavery persisted since no attempt was made to reconstruct the social order – which is what its abolition would have involved – but there was a constant effort on the part of the Church to ennoble the existing relations between masters and servants. Nevertheless, distinctions of wealth and rank were not easily set aside within the community. Inevitably there was a large number who were poor and many who were illiterate.[2] The cultured minority retained the Hellenistic contempt for work as a slavish task and regarded technical ability in a craft as much inferior to the ability to read.[3] Hence the repeated insistence of a man such as Chrysostom on the nobility of manual labour on the grounds that what was good enough for the apostles should be sufficient for any Christian.[4]

Food, clothing and leisure

The excessive luxury that had characterized the pagan upper classes was a constant source of concern to the clergy when they found it still practised by members of their own flocks. Chrysostom frequently condemned the gluttony that was prevalent,[5] despising the pork haggis, pheasants, snow-white loaves and Tyrian wine of the gourmands,[6] while Jerome's advice on a suitable menu was as follows:

> As for food, he should not be allowed such as is difficult to digest. The preparation of vegetables, fruit and pulse is easy and does not require the skill of an expensive cook: our bodies are nourished by them with little trouble on our part. He will not have his stomach inflated or overloaded if he eats only one or two dishes, and those inexpensive ones: such a condition comes of pampering the taste with variety. The smells of the kitchen may induce us to eat, but when hunger is satisfied they make us their slaves. Hence gorging gives rise to disease: and many persons find relief for the discomfort of gluttony in emetics – what they disgraced themselves by putting in, they with still greater disgrace put out.[7]

Augustine's diet consisted of vegetables and cereals, with a little wine, and meat for the sick or when guests were present. The solemnity of the occasion was marked for him by a couplet that he had inscribed in his dining-room:

> Whoever loves to detract from the good name of those absent,
> Let him know that there is no place for him at this table.[8]

The Church was fighting a continual battle against the standards of the world which were infecting the lives of the faithful and blunting the summons to self-denial and discipline. The extent to which this infection was spreading may be appreciated from the fact that even the consecrated virgins and widows were following contemporary fashions in dress. Augustine, Jerome and Chrysostom all complain bitterly of this capitulation to worldly caprice.

According to Augustine: 'there is a certain aim of pleasing, either by more elegant dress than the necessity of so great a profession demands, or by a remarkable manner of binding the head, whether by bosses of hair swelling forth or by coverings so yielding that the fine network below appears.'[9]

According to Jerome: 'their robes have but a narrow purple stripe (plebeian in contrast to patricians who have broad ones); their head-dress is somewhat loose, so as to leave the hair free. From their shoulders flutters the lilac mantle which they call 'maforte'; they have their feet in cheap slippers and their arms bound in tight-fitting sleeves.'[10]

According to Chrysostom: 'the virgins study appearance in a common garment more than those who wear gold. For when a very dark coloured robe is drawn closely round the breast with a girdle, with such nicety that it may neither spread into breadth nor shrink into scantiness but be between both; and when the bosom is set off with many folds, this is just as alluring as any silken dresses. And when the shoe, shining with its blackness, ends in a sharp point, and imitates the elegance of painting, so that even the breadth of the sole is scarcely visible – or when, though they do not indeed paint their faces, they spend much time and care on washing it, and spread a veil across the forehead, whiter than the face itself – and above that, put on a hood of which the blackness may set off the white by contrast – isn't there in all this the vanity of dress? What can I say to the perpetual rolling of the eyes? to the putting on of the stomacher so artfully as sometimes to conceal, sometimes to disclose the fastening? For this too they sometimes expose, to show the exquisiteness of the cincture, winding the hood entirely round the head. Then like the players, they wear gloves so closely fitted that they seem to grow upon the hands.'[11]

The right and proper use of leisure came also within the Church's purview. At Hippo, for example, where attendance at church was high, when any festival coincided with a special performance in the theatre many preferred the latter.[12] Towards the theatre itself the Fathers continued to manifest the utmost scorn. To Chrysostom it was the seat of pestilence, the gymnasium of incontinence and a school of luxury, Satan being the author and architect of it. Gross comedies, indecent ballets and ribald pantomime were the rule; marriage was constantly mocked, even the eucharist was burlesqued,[13] and the *pièce de résistance* was often the frolics of nude courtesans in specially constructed swimming pools.[14] Their songs were unashamedly coarse, with such a theme as how a woman loved a man and, not obtaining him, hanged herself.[15] Indeed, there seemed little in the conduct of the theatrical profession either on or off the stage that did not call forth the severest strictures of the Christian moralist. In one particular only had the Church's teaching had any effect – gladiatorial combats had been discontinued. Under Honorius an eastern ascetic named Telemachus or Almachius came to Rome and, attending a show in the amphitheatre, threw himself between two contestants, only to be stoned to death by the spectators, furious at being deprived of their sport. Honorius, informed of this happening, forthwith declared that all bloody contests were to cease.[16] But this small success only stresses the magnitude of the task that still lay before the Church, a task made even greater by the incursion of the barbarian tribes – merely to baptize these did not render them immediately Christian in either spirit or conduct.

CONCLUSION

No certain answer can be given to the question: when did the period of the Early Church come to an end? History is a continuum and one so-called period grows out of its predecessor and merges into its successor by almost imperceptible degrees. Towards the end of the fifth century the Church possessed a structure, an inner life, a system of beliefs and a social concern which rendered it easily identifiable. Its success within the empire had been remarkable, as it advanced from the position of a persecuted minority to the status of a vast and powerful body able to challenge and even to dominate the civil power. Yet its victory was only momentary and new tasks presented themselves – much of Europe was still pagan; in the West society was disintegrating and such standards as had been achieved were in danger of collapsing; in the East divisions were apparent. Ahead lay the restoration of the ancient empire of the West under Charlemagne, the schism between East and West, the labours of a Boniface, the struggle of the papacy for supremacy. . . . The vitality and new life of the original impetus given in Palestine was still to persist, and although it might ebb and flow it was to be renewed in the centuries to come.

NOTES

CHAPTER I: THE ORIGINS OF CHRISTIANITY

The Background

1. II Sam. vii. 16.
2. M. Black, *The Scrolls and Christian Origins* (London, 1961), p. 6.
3. The Herodians equally pursued a policy of political prudence, but their principal aim was the furtherance of the sovereignty of the house of Herod.
4. This is based on the commonly accepted assumption that the community of the Dead Sea Scrolls at Qumran was Essene.
5. T. H. Gaster, *The Scriptures of the Dead Sea Sect* (London, 1957), p. 258.
6. *B. J.* ii. 13. 4.
7. *Ant. Jud.* xviii. 5. 2.
8. Mk. i. 6; II Kings i. 8.
9. Lk. iii. 7, 9.
10. Lk. iii. 16a, 17.

Sources

1. xx. 9. 1.
2. The Talmud consists of the Mishnah or codified oral law together with the commentary upon it known as the Gemara.
3. *Ep.* x. 96.
4. xv. 44.
5. xxv. 4.
6. Gal. iv. 4.
7. Rom. i. 3.
8. Rom. xv. 8.
9. Gal. i. 19.
10. Gal. ii. 9.
11. I Cor. vii. 10.
12. I Cor. v. 7.
13. I Cor. xi, 23–27.
14. I Thess. ii. 14.
15. Rom. vi. 6.
16. Col. ii. 14.
17. I Cor. xv. 1–7.
18. vii. 58.
19. Gal. i. 18, 19.
20. For a synopsis in English see J. M. Thompson, *The Synoptic Gospels* (Oxford, 1929) and in Greek A. Huck, *Synopsis of the First Three Gospels* (Oxford, 1949).
21. Acts xx. 35.
22. R. M. Grant and D. N. Freedman, *The Secret Sayings of Jesus* (London, 1960), pp. 44–51.
23. Mk. ii. 23, 24.
24. Mk. xii. 13–17.
25. Mk. ix. 14–29.
26. Lk. xii. 22 f.
27. Lk. xv. 11–32.
28. Mk. i. 16–20.
29. Mk. vi. 1–6.
30. Matt. vi. 25.
31. Mk. iv. 41.
32. M. Kähler, *Der sogenannte historische Jesus und der geschichtliche, biblische Christus* (1896) ,2nd edition, p. 80.
33. I Cor. i. 23; ii. 2.
34. Acts x. 37–40.
35. M. Bloch, *The Historian's Craft* (Manchester, 1954), p. 115.
36. T. A. Roberts, *History and Christian Apologetic* (London, 1960), p. 173.
37. i. 1–4, N.E.B.
38. Mk. viii. 17–21; Lk. xxiv. 8; Jn. ii. 22.
39. xx.31.

The Message and Ministry of Jesus

1. Mk. i. 9–11.
2. vi. 14.

The Message and Ministry of Jesus—cont.

3. Lk. x. 23f.
4. Lk. xi. 20.
5. Lk. xiii. 20f.
6. Mk. iv. 26–29.
7. Matt. xiii. 44.
8. Lk. xvi. 1–8.
9. Matt. xxii. 2–14.
10. *The Message of Jesus* (London, 1939), p. 168.
11. Exod. viii. 19.
12. Lk. xi. 20.
13. Mk. iii. 27.
14. Is. lxi. 1f; Lk. iv. 18–21.
15. Lk. vii. 22.
16. Mk. vi. 32–44; Enoch lxii. 14.
17. Lk. xii. 13–21.
18. Mk. xii. 28.
19. Lk. xviii. 9–14.
20. Matt. v. 21f.
21. ii. 6.
22. ii. 16.
23. ii. 18.
24. iii. 6.
25. iii. 22.
26. viii. 11.
27. xi. 28.
28. xii. 13–17.
29. Mk. viii. 31; ix. 31; x. 33f.
30. Mk. xi. 7–10.
31. xii. 16.
32. Mk. xi. 15–18.
33. The arguments for and against identifying this meal with the Passover may be studied in A. J. B. Higgins, *The Lord's Supper in the New Testament* (London, 1952); J. Jeremias, *The Eucharistic Words of Jesus* (Oxford, 1955).
34. *Leg. ad Caium*, 301f.
35. *B.J.* ii. 9. 3f; *Ant.* xviii. 3. 1f; 4.1.
36. xiii. 1.
37. Mk. xv. 26.
38. Mk. viii. 29ff.
39. Lk. xxiv. 21.
40. *He That Cometh* (Oxford, 1956), p. 303.
41. R. Bultmann, *Theology of the New Testament* (London, I, 1952), p. 26.
42. Mk. ii. 10.
43. Mk. viii. 31.
44. Mk. viii. 38.
45. ix. 5.
46. xlii. 1–4; xlix. 1–6; l. 5–9; lii. 13–liii. 12.
47. Arguments against: M. D. Hooker, *Jesus and the Servant* (London, 1959); arguments for: O. Cullmann, *The Christology of the New Testament* (London, 1959), pp. 51–82.
48. Acts viii. 32–35; I Peter ii. 21–24.
49. xiv. 24.
50. xxvi. 28.
51. V. Taylor, *Jesus and His Sacrifice* (London, 1937), p. 141.
52. A. E. J. Rawlinson, *The New Testament Doctrine of the Christ* (London, 1926), p. 50.
53. T. W. Manson, *The Teaching of Jesus* (Cambridge, 1931), p. 113.
54. Cullmann, *op. cit.*, p. 283.
55. Mk. ii. 5, 7.
56. E. Hoskyns and N. Davey, *The Riddle of the New Testament* (London, 1931), p. 222.

CHAPTER II: THE APOSTOLIC AGE

The Background

1. Acts xviii. 15.
2. iii. 22, 23.
3. *Nat. Hist.* II. 22.
4. Suetonius, *Tiberius*, 69.
5. Apuleius, *Metamorph.* XI, 25.
6. The date of the inception of Gnosticism is much debated. Some scholars (e.g. R. Bultmann, *Theology of the New Testament*, I (London, 1952) place it relatively early in the first century, and consider that it has had important influences on the New Testament, others (e.g. A. Richardson, *An Introduction to the Theology of*

the New Testament, London, 1958) are sceptical.

7. *c.Cel.*, ii, 30.

8. II Cor. xi. 26.

9. *Ann.* xv. 44.

10. Theophilus, *Ad Autol.* iii. 4.

Sources

1. J. P. Audet, *La Didaché : instruction des apôtres* (Paris, 1961); he dates this document between 50 and 70.
2. Gal. i.
3. Acts ix. 1–9.
4. These epistles raise several critical problems, which do not require detailed consideration for the purposes of the text. The main problems are:
   (i) the destination and date of *Galatians* – was it addressed to Christians in North *or* South Galatia?
   (ii) the genuineness of *II Thessalonians* and *Colossians.*
   (iii) the unity of *I* and *II Corinthians*: Paul probably wrote four letters to Corinth, and some critics consider that sections of these have been combined to form the two extant epistles.
   (iv) Were the captivity epistles written while Paul was under arrest at Rome, or were they sent during another imprisonment, e.g. at Ephesus (cf. G. S. Duncan, *St. Paul's Ephesian Ministry*, London, 1929)? For a careful survey of these problems see H. F. D. Sparks, *The Formation of the New Testament* (London 1952).
5. Col. iv. 14.
6. e.g. Acts xvi. 10.
7. i. 8.
8. Jude 3, 17.
9. Eusebius, *H.E.* vii. 25.

Expansion and Development

1. Rom. vi. 23.
2. Gal. v. 18.
3. i. 3.
4. i. 12.
5. iii. 14.
6. vi. 4.
7. Gal. iv. 4–6.
8. ii. 1–4.
9. xx. 22.
10. For the reasons for preferring the Johannine chronology see J. G. Davies, *He Ascended into Heaven* (London, 1958), pp. 47–56.
11. Acts ii. 28f.
12. Acts ii. 36.
13. C. H. Dodd, *The Apostolic Preaching and Its Development* (London, 1936). If Dodd overstates the case for the reliability of the speeches in Acts (see M. Dibelius, *Studies in the Acts of the Apostles*, London, 1956), his definition of the 'gospel' of Paul, on the basis of the epistles, nevertheless provides details of a very early form of the preaching.
14. Matt. xxviii. 10, 16; Mk xvi. 7; Jn. xxi.
15. Acts i. 15–26.
16. vi. 7.
17. iii. 17.
18. vii. 2–53.
19. viii. 14–7.
20. xi. i.–18.
21. Matt. x. 5f.
22. Acts xi. 19.
23. xiii. 1–3; Rom. i. 16.
24. Acts xiii, xiv. Barnabas was probably the leader, since not only is his name given first, but the people of Lystra took him for Zeus and Paul for Hermes (xiv. 12); it follows from this that Paul was the chief spokesman.
25. Acts xv. We touch here upon a very complex problem, viz. the relationship between Paul's visits to Jerusalem, as recorded in Acts and in his letters. Acts lists five visits (ix. 26; xi. 30; xv; xviii. 22; xxi. 5), the letters three (Gal. i. 18; ii. 1; Rom. xv. 25). The position adopted in the

Expansion and Development—cont.

text is that Acts ix. 26 and Gal. i. 8 refer to the first visit, that Acts xi. 30 and Gal. ii. 1 refer to the second visit, and that Galatians was written before the third visit (Acts xv).
26. Rom. ix–xi.
27. Gal. iii. 28.
28. Gal. iii. 29.
29. Rom. vii. 12f.
30. Gal. iii. 24.
31. Acts xv. 36–xviii. 22.
32. xviii. 23–xxi. 16.
33. I Cor. ix.
34. II Cor. xi. 4.
35. I Cor. xvi. 1f.; Rom. xv. 26.
36. Acts xxi. 17– xxviii. 31.
37. *I Clem.* 5.
38. This is based upon the account of Josephus (*Ant.* xx. 9, 1) in preference to that of Hegesippus (Eusebius, *H.E.* ii. 23).
39. For a full account, see Josephus, *B.J.* iii–vii.
40. *H.E.* iii. 5. 3. The historicity of this withdrawal has been questioned (S. G. F. Brandon, *The Fall of Jerusalem and the Christian Church* (London 1951), pp. 168–73), but I remain unconvinced by these counter arguments.
41. Mk. xiii. 14.
42. J. Parkes, *The Foundations of Judaism and Christianity* (London, 1960), p. 225.
43. Justin, *Dial.* 108.
44. Eusebius, *H.E.* iii. 11.
45. Mk. iii. 14.
46. Acts i. 15–26.
47. I Cor. ix. 1.
48. Acts xiv. 14.
49. vi. 1–6.
50. Numb. xi.
51. Acts xv. 6.
52. xiv. 23.
53. xx. 28.
54. I Thess. i. 1.
55. Mk. x. 45.
56. Rom. xi. 13.
57. Phil. i. 1.

Beliefs

1. I Cor. ix. 12.
2. Rom. i. 1, 3.
3. I Jn. iv. 8f.
4. Rom. v. 8.
5. Heb. i. 1f.
6. I Cor. viii. 4.
7. I Tim. ii. 5.
8. Gal. iv. 8.
9. I Cor. viii. 5f.
10. Rom. ix. 26; Heb. iii. 12; Rev. vii. 2.
11. Acts iii. 21.
12. I Cor. i. 27.
13. Acts iii. 25.
14. Rom. iii. 6.
15. II Cor. i. 9.
16. Deut. vii. 8.
17. I Cor. v. 7.
18. Rom. iii. 25. N.E.B.
19. II Cor. v. 19.
20. Gal. iv. 7.
21. II Cor. v. 17.
22. Rom. vi. 23.
23. Rom. vi. 10.
24. iv. 15.
25. ix. 24.
26. vii. 25.
27. xiv. 9.
28. i. 14.
29. C. H. Dodd, *Interpretation of the Fourth Gospel* (Cambridge, 1953), p. 282.
30. iii. 16.
31. i. 29.
32. xii. 32.
33. Gal. iv. 4.
34. Phil. ii. 6–8.
35. Col. i. 15f.
36. Wisdom vii. 26.
37. Prov. viii. 23.
38. Wisdom ix. 2.
39. I Cor. i. 24.
40. i. 3. cf. Wisdom vii. 25f.
41. ii. 14, 17.
42. I Jn. i. 1.
43. Jn. x. 30.
44. x. 38.

45. W. F. Howard, *Christianity according to St. John* (London, 1943), p. 19.
46. Lk. i. 35.
47. x. 45.
48. I Kings xviii. 12.
49. Acts viii. 39.
50. xv. 28.
51. xiii. 2.
52. Rom. viii. 9.
53. Rom. viii. 26, 34.
54. I Cor. xii. 11.
55. Gal. iii. 5.
56. II Cor. i. 12.
57. xv. 26.
58. xvi. 7.
59. xv. 26.
60. xvi. 13–5.
61. I Cor. iii. 16.
62. Eph. ii. 22.
63. I Peter iv. 14.
64. ii. 5.
65. Lev. xxvi. 11f.
66. II Cor. vi. 16.
67. Gal. iii. 29.
68. Col. iii. 12; I Peter i. 1.
69. Rom. i. 7.
70. Phil. iii. 3.
71. I Peter ii. 9.
72. Eph. v. 30.
73. I Cor. xii. 27.
74. e.g. Col. i. 18; Eph. iv. 15.
75. Hos. ii. 14–7; Ezek. xvi.
76. Mk. ii. 20.
77. v. 22–32.
78. xxii. 17.
79. I Cor. x. 11.
80. I Cor. xv. 50.
81. Phil. iii. 21. N.E.B.
82. I Cor. xv. 38.
83. I Cor. xv. 44.
84. II Thess. ii. 15.
85. Rom. vi. 17.
86. I Cor. xii. 3.
87. I Jn. ii. 22.
88. Rom. viii. 34.
89. I Cor. viii. 6.
90. II Cor. xiii. 14.

Worship

1. II Cor. ix. 12.
2. ii. 17.
3. xii. 1.
4. Acts vi. 9.
5. Acts iii. 1.
6. Acts xxii. 17.
7. *Manual of Discipline*, iii. 4f.; iv. 21; v. 13; *Zadokite Document*, x. 10–13.
8. Lev. i. 3f.
9. I Jn. ii. 20; Gal. iii. 27.
10. Acts viii. 36.
11. Acts xvi. 13ff.
12. Acts xvi. 33.
13. Col. ii. 11f.
14. II Cor. i. 22.
15. I Cor. iii. 16.
16. Heb. vi. 4.
17. I Cor. xii. 13.
18. Rom. vi. 3f.
19. Eph. ii. 6.
20. Gal. iii. 26f.
21. Jn. iii. 5.
22. I Thess. v. 5; II Cor. v. 17.
23. Acts ii. 38.
24. ii. 42.
25. I Cor. xi. 20.
26. H. Lietzmann, *Messe und Herrenmahl* (Berlin, 1926): English Translation, *Mass and Lord's Supper* (Leiden, from 1953).
27. Acts ii. 46.
28. Rom. xiv. 17.
29. Mk. xiv. 25.
30. See above p. 23.
31. I Cor. xi. 23ff.
32. Jude 12; according to one reading, the *agape* is also mentioned in II Peter ii. 13.
33. Acts xx. 7.
34. Col. iv. 16.
35. I Cor. xvi. 2.
36. I Cor. xvi. 20.
37. Rev. i. 10.
38. Acts ii. 46.
39. I Cor. xvi. 19.
40. Col. iv. 15.
41. Philemon 2.
42. I Cor. xi. 25.
43. Is. lxv. 13.
44. I Cor. x. 17.

Worship—cont.

45. Rev. xix. 19.
46. I Cor. x. 3; Jn. vi. 49f.
47. Jn. vi. 50.
48. C. F. D. Moule, *Worship in the New Testament* (London, 1961), p. 24.
49. I Cor. xiv. 26.
50. I Cor. xiv. 26, 33.
51. Rom. viii. 15.
52. I Cor. xvi. 23.
53. Rom. i. 25.
54. Col. iii. 16.
55. Lk. xviii. 1.
56. Gal. iv. 6.
57. Rom. viii. 26.
58. I Jn. v. 14.
59. Acts iv. 29.
60. Rom. x. 1.
61. Phil. i. 9.
62. Col. i. 9.
63. II Cor. xiii. 7.
64. Acts vii. 60.
65. Mk. xi. 25.
66. Matt. xxiv. 27.

Social Life

1. Rom. vii. 17.
2. I Cor. xi. 23.
3. I Thess. iv. 1.
4. Phil. ii. 3–8.
5. Rom. vi. 1–14.
6. P. Carrington, *The Primitive Christian Catechism* (Cambridge, 1940); E. G. Selwyn, *The First Epistle of St. Peter* (London, 1949), pp. 363–466.
7. I Thess. iv. 7. N.E.B.
8. I Peter i. 15f.
9. II Cor. vi. 17; Is. lii. 11.
10. Heb. xiii. 14.
11. I Peter ii. 11.
12. Gal. iii. 28.
13. W. A. Beardslee, *Human Achievement and Divine Vocation in the Message of Paul* (London, 1961), p. 62.
14. Philemon 16.
15. I Thess. ii. 9.
16. Eph. iv. 28.
17. I Thess. iv. 11f.
18. Col. iii. 23f.
19. I Cor. i. 26.
20. Acts ix. 43; xvi. 14; xvi. 33; xviii. 3.
21. I Peter ii. 18.
22. Acts xiii. 12; xvii. 4, 12; xviii. 8.
23. James i. 10.
24. Col. iv. 14.
25. Phil. iv. 22.
26. Eph. v. 18.
27. Rom. xiii. 13.
28. Phil. iii. 19.
29. Rom. xvi. 18.
30. Rom. xiv. 17.
31. I Peter iii. 3f.

CHAPTER III: THE APOSTOLIC FATHERS AND THE SECOND CENTURY

The Background

1. *De Is.* xxiii.
2. Lucian, *Alexander.*
3. Apuleius, *Metamorph.* XI. 4.
4. Spart. *Hadr.*, 16. 7.
5. *Apologia*, 55.
6. R. M. Grant, *Gnosticism: An Anthology* (London, 1961), p. 149.
7. Irenaeus, *Adv. Haer.* i. 6. 4.
8. *The Secret Book of John* (Grant, *op. cit.*, p. 70).
9. Acts viii. 9–24.
10. Irenaeus, *Adv. Haer.* i. 23. 1. The relevant texts are all translated in Grant, *op. cit.*
11. *ibid.*, i. 23. 5.
12. Irenaeus, *op. cit.* i. 26, 3; 28–31; Hippolytus, *Ref.* v. 7–10.
13. Irenaeus, i. 24. 1f.; 28.
14. Two contradictory accounts are preserved of Basilides' teaching, by Irenaeus (i. 24. 3–7) and Hippolytus (vii. 20–7); in the view of most scholars the latter represents Basilides' genuine teaching.

15. Irenaeus, i. 15. 3.
16. i. 1–8.
17. The principles are set out in Ptolemy's *Letter to Flora* and are applied in Heracleon's commentary on John (J. A. Robinson, *The Fragments of Herakleon* [Cambridge, 1891]).
18. Acts xvii. 28.
19. Gal. iii. 19.
20. *Adv. Marc.* iv. 5. This treatise by Tertullian is the main source for the teaching of Marcion.
21. The evidence for a persecution under Domitian is slight and by no means certain (R. L. P. Milburn, 'The Persecution of Domitian', *C.Q.R.*, CXXXIX, 1945, pp. 154–64).
22. *Ep.* X. xxxiv.
23. *Ep.* X. xciii.
24. *Ep.* X. xcvi.
25. *Ep.* X. xcvii.
26. Eusebius, *H.E.* iii. 32.6; Ignatius, *Epistolae.*
27. Eusebius, however, places this incident in the first year of Antoninus Pius (*H.E.*, iv. 10).
28. Eusebius, *H.E.* iv. 9.
29. *C.I.L.* vi. 1001.
30. Justin, *II Apol.* 2.
31. *Mart. Poly.*
32. Eusebius, *H.E.* iv. 16.7.
33. *Acta Justini et Sociorum.*
34. Eusebius, *H.E.* v. 1.
35. *Passio Martyrum Scillitanorum.*
36. Tertullian, *ad. Scap.* 3.
37. *ibid.*, 5.
38. *Acta S. Apollonii.*
39. Hippolytus, *Ref.* ix. 12.

Sources

1. The *Epistle to Diognetus* is usually included, but as this is a late second century apology it is considered below.
2. Eusebius, *H.E.* iv. 23.11.
3. Tertullian, *de Praes.* 32.
4. 9.4.
5. *H.E.* iv. 3.2.
6. For an account of these see below, pp. 87ff.
7. *Haer.* xxiii. 3–7.
8. Eusebius, *H.E.* v. 20.5ff.

Expansion and Development

1. *ad Rom.* 9.
2. *Ep.* X. xcvi.
3. I *Apol.* 16.
4. *ad Graec.* 29.
5. Origen, *c. Cel.* iii. 55.
6. *Octav.* 10.
7. Justin, *I Apol.* 11.
8. *Octav.* 9.
9. Clement, *Strom.* 3.10.
10. *Haer.* xlviii. 1.
11. *Chronicon.*
12. Didymus, *de Trin.* III. xli. 3; Jerome, *Ep.* 41.4.
13. Epiphanius, *Haer.* xlviii. 4.
14. 13.
15. Eusebius, *H.E.* v. 17.4.
16. 82.
17. *Adv. Haer.* v. 6.2.
18. Epiphanius, *Haer.* xlviii. 1.
19. Jerome, *op. cit.*
20. *Comm. in Gal.* II. *Praef.*
21. Eusebius, *H.E.* v. 23–5.
22. *ad Rom.* 9.
23. *ad Mag.* 3.
24. *ad Smyrn.* 8.
25. *I Clem.* 42, 44.
26. *ad Trall.* 3.
27. *ad Phil.* 8.
28. *Adv. Haer.* iii. 3.3; iv. 26.51.
29. Eusebius, *H.E.* iv. 22.3. The list has been preserved by Epiphanius, *Haer.* xxvii. 6.
30. *Adv. Haer.* iii. 3.3.

Beliefs

1. *Adv. Haer.* i. 10.1.
2. *Mand.* I. I.
3. *Supp.* 8.2.
4. Theophilus, *Ad Aut.* II. 4.
5. *ad Graec.* 4. 1, 2.
6. Ignatius, *ad Pol.* 3.

Beliefs—cont.

7. Justin, *Dial.* 107.3.
8. *I Clem.* 59.2.
9. *ad Eph.* 19.
10. *Adv. Haer.* v. 21.1,3.
11. *ibid.* v. *praef.*
12. *Adv. Haer.* iii. 18.7.
13. *Dial.* 61.
14. *Adv. Haer.* iv. 20.1.
15. *Dial.* 128.
16. *I Apol.* 46.
17. *ibid.* 14.
18. *ad Aut.* 2.22.
19. Tatian, *Or.* 5.1f.
20. *Categ.* 2.1b,6–7.
21. *Dial.* 128.4.
22. I *Apol.* 13.
23. *ad Aut.* 2.15.
24. Ignatius, *ad Eph.* 9.
25. Justin, *Dial.* 87.
26. Athenagoras, *Supp.* 10.
27. Ignatius, *ad Smyrn.* 8.
28. Irenaeus, *Adv. Haer.* iii. 24.1.
29. *ad Diog.* 1.
30. Aristides, *Apol.* 2.
31. Irenaeus, *Adv. Haer.* v. 32.2.
32. *ibid.* iv. 33.7.
33. *ibid.*
34. *ad Eph.* 19.
35. *ad Philad.* 9.
36. 6.16.
37. *Dial.* 78, 87, 116, 121.
38. *Adv. Haer.* iii. 18.2; iv. 34.2.
39. 5, 8.
40. 21.
41. *Dial.* 49.
42. *ibid.* 5.
43. xx. 4.
44. Eusebius, *H.E.* iii. 39.
45. *Dial.* 80.
46. *Adv. Haer.* v. 34.2.
47. xvii. 32.
48. I *Apol.* 18.
49. *Or.* 6.
50. *Adv. Haer.* iv. 18.5; v. 1.1; v. 6.12.
51. e.g. *Demon.* 6; *Adv. Haer.* i. 10.1.
52. *Dial.* 132.
53. cf. Justin, I *Apol.* 61.

Worship

1. 7.
2. I *Apol.* 61.
3. *Adv. Haer.* i. 21.4.
4. 5.
5. Hermas, *Sim.* 8.2.
6. 1.1–3.
7. 25.8.
8. 8.16; 29.6.
9. *Adv. Haer.* i. 21.4.
10. i. 25.6.
11. Irenaeus, *Dem.* 42.
12. Ignatius, *ad Pol.* 6.
13. Justin, *Dial.* 44.
14. *ibid.* I *Apol.* 61.
15. *ibid. Dial.* 43.
16. Theophilus, *ad Aut.* 2.16.
17. Irenaeus, *Dem.* 3.
18. I *Apol.* 65.
19. *ibid.* 67.
20. It is questionable how far the Sanctus was an element in the second century rite, since indisputable evidence for its use is not available before the fourth century. It is doubtful if I *Clem.* 34 refers to it (W. C. Van Unnik, 'I Clem. and the "Sanctus",' *Vig. Christ.*, V, 1951, pp. 204–48), and while Rev. iv. 8 has the form found in the later liturgies it may be the source of these rather than the reflection of contemporary practice. If the Sanctus were employed in the second century, then Justin's words may be taken to suggest that it preceded the thanksgiving or 'consecration' prayer; the president 'gives praise and glory to the Father of the universe, through the name of the Son and of the Holy Spirit, and offers thanks at considerable length' (I *Apol.* 65).
21. Irenaeus, *Adv. Haer.* i. 13.2.
22. *ad Smyrn.* 6.
23. *ad Eph.* 13; *ad Philad.* 4.
24. *ad Eph.* 20.
25. I *Apol.* 66.

26. *Adv. Haer.* iv. 18. 5.
27. i. 11; Justin, *Dial.* 41; Irenaeus, *Adv. Haer.* iv. 17.5.
28. *ad Smyrn.* 8.
29. 9, 10.
30. xxii. 17f.
31. vi. 6.
32. *Mand.* 4.3.
33. i. 8f.
34. v. 16.
35. 4.14; 14.1.
36. *ad Phil.* 14.
37. *ad Pol.* 1.
38. *Mand.* 9.
39. 8.2f.
40. Dan. vi. 10; Ps. lv. 17.
41. 3.
42. *Sim.* 5.1.
43. *Sim.* 5.4.
44. Matt. xxv. 40.
45. II Cor. viii. 9.
46. *Didache* 8.1.
47. Hermas, *Sim.* 5.1.

Social Life

1. 5.1, 2.
2. II Cor. vi. 17; Is. lii. 11.
3. See above p. 65.
4. *Barnabas*, 19.
5. *ibid.*, 20.
6. *Didache*, 1.4.
7. *ibid.* 2.2.; *ad Diog.* 5.6.
8. *Didache*, 3.5.
9. Eusebius, *H.E.* v. 5.
10. Irenaeus, *Adv. Haer.* iv. 30.1.
11. *Acta Justini* 4.
12. Hippolytus, *Ref.* ix. 12.
13. 4.
14. *Octav.* 30; Eusebius, *H.E.* v. 1.26.
15. *Octav.* 38.
16. Hermas, *Mand.* 12.2.
17. Eusebius, *H.E.* v. 1.5.
18. 12.
19. 37; cf. Tatian, *Or.* 22–4.

CHAPTER IV: THE CENTURY OF ADVANCE

The Background

1. *adv. Gent.* i. 24.
2. Murder was the fate of Caracalla (211–7), Macrinus (217–8), Elagabalus (218–22), Maximus Thrax (235–8), Gordianus (238–44), Gallienus (260–8), Aurelian (270–5), Florian (276), Probus (276–82), Carus (282–283) and Carinus (283–5).
3. Severus Alexander (222–35), Philip (244–9) and Decius (249–51), each fell in battle.
4. *Vita Sev.* xvii. 1.
5. Eusebius, *H.E.* vi. 1.1.
6. *Passio S. Perpetuae.*
7. *Vita Sev.* xxix. 2.
8. Cyprian, *Ep.* 75.10.
9. Eusebius, *H.E.* vi. 36.3.
10. *ibid.* vi. 34.
11. *ibid.* vi. 41.3–6.
12. *c. Cel.* iii. 15.
13. *In Matt. Comm.* 39.
14. *Chron.* ii. 32.
15. Cyprian, *de Lap.* 8.
16. *ibid. Ep.* 55.2.
17. *ibid. de Lap.* 27.
18. Eusebius, *H.E.* vii. 21.9f.
19. *ibid.* vii. 11.10.
20. Cyprian, *Ep.* 80.1.
21. *Acta proconsularia* 3–6.
22. T. Ruinart, *Acta Martyrum Sincera* (Amsterdam, 1713), pp. 264–8.
23. Eusebius, *H.E.* vii. 12.
24. *ibid.* vii. 13.
25. *ibid.* viii. 4.3.
26. Lactantius, *de Mort. Per.* 10.12.
27. Eusebius, *H.E.* vi. 8–10; *Mart. Pal.* iii. 1.
28. *Acta SS. Saturnini*, etc., 2. 10.
29. Eusebius, *Mart. Pal.* 9.2.
30. *ibid.*, *H.E.* viii, 17.
31. Lactantius, *op. cit.* 52.
32. Eusebius, *op. cit.* ix. 3.

The Background—cont.

33. Athanasius, *Hist. arian. ad. monachos* 64.
34. *op. cit.* 44.
35. *Cod. Theod.* II. 8.1.; *Cod. Just.* III. 12.2.

Sources

1. Jerome, *De vir. ill.* 53.
2. *Strom.* i. 5.
3. Eusebius, *H.E.* vi. 8.
4. *Adv. Ruf.* ii. 22.
5. Eusebius, *H.E.* vi. 23.
6. *Adv. Prax.* 5; *De monog.* 11.

Expansion and Development

1. Eusebius, *Mart. Pal.* 3.3.
2. *H.E.* viii. 6.9.
3. Eusebius, *Vita Const.* iv. 8.
4. Eusebius, *H.E.* vii. 7.5.
5. Possibly, however, Asia Minor provided the base for the evangelization of these islands.
6. Eusebius, *Vita Const.* iv. 43.
7. *Adv. Jud.* 7.
8. *Ep.* 67.1.6.
9. Augustine, *De Baptismo* 13.
10. *Ep.* 59.10.
11. Eusebius, *H.E.* vii. 26.3.
12. *Ad Donat.* 3f.
13. Gregory of Nyssa, *Panegyric.*
14. *Ref.* ix. 12.
15. Cyprian, *Ep.* 55.
16. *Ep.* 43.
16. Eusebius, *H.E.* vi. 43.8f.
18. Cyprian, *Ep.* 59.9.
19. *Ep.* 68.
20. Socrates, *H.E.* iv. 28. The desire of certain Novatianists to re-enter the Church gave rise to the Baptismal Controversy, which almost issued in a schism between Rome and Carthage; for details see below, p. 149.
21. See below, pp. 173–6.
22. *de Unit.* 1.
23. *ibid.* 11.
24. *ibid.* 5.
25. *Ep.* 66.8.
26. *Ap. Trad.* iii. 4f.
27. Cyprian, *Ep.* 41.2. The Presbyters were paid monthly (*Ep.* 39.5.)
28. *Ap. Trad.* viii. 2.
29. Cyprian, *Ep.* 38.1.
30. *ibid. Ep.* 67.4.
31. *ibid.*
32. *Ap. Trad.* ix. 3.
33. *ibid.* xxx.
34. Cyprian, *Ep.* 52.1.
35. Ignatius, *Ad Smyrn.* 11.
36. Eusebius, *H.E.* vii. 11.24.
37. *Ap. Trad.* ix. 11; xxiii. 1; Cyprian, *De Lap.* 25.
38. i. 3.
39. *Apol.* I. 67.
40. *De Praes.* 41.
41. *Ap Trad.* xii.
42. *Ep.* 39.1.
43. Cyprian, *Epp.* 38; 39.
44. Cyprian, *Epp.* 8; 9; 20; 36; 45; 77; 79.
45. *Ap. Trad.* xxx.
46. Eusebius, *H.E.* vi. 43.11.
47. Cyprian, *Epp.* 52.59.
48. *ibid.* 7.
49. *ibid.* 77.3; 78.1.
50. *ibid.* 69.15; 75.10.
51. 39.4.
52. 38.2.
53. Acts ix. 39.
54. Acts vi. 1.
55. I Tim. v. 9.
56. Justin, *Apol.* I. 68.
57. *Ap. Trad.* xi. 5.
58. iii. 2.
59. iii. 6.
60. iii. 7.
61. iii. 8.
62. A. Harnack, *Sources of the Apostolic Canons* (London, 1895), p. 20.
63. iii. 12.
64. iii. 12f.
65. *P.G.* 10.1566.
66. *P.G.* 18.577–81.
67. Eusebius, *H.E.* v. 16.17.

68. *ibid.* v. 16.10; 19f.
69. *ibid.* v. 23, 24.
70. *ibid.* vii. 29.1.
71. *The Letters of Dionysius of Alexandria*, ed. C. L. Feltoe (Cambridge, 1904).
72. Cyprian, *Ep.* 75.17.
73. *Ep.* 67.5.
74. 68.
75. Mansi, I. 925.7.

Beliefs

1. Hippolytus, *Ref.* vii. 35; Eusebius, *H.E.* v. 28.6.
2. Novatian, *de Trin.* 30.
3. Irenaeus, *Adv. Haer.* v. 1.3.
4. H. J. Lawlor, 'The Sayings of Paul of Samasota', *J.T.S.*, XIX, 1918, pp. 20-45, 115–20.
5. Hippolytus, *c. Noetum*, 1.
6. *ibid.* 2.
7. Hippolytus, *Ref.* ix. 7.
8. Tertullian, *Adv. Prax.* 29.
9. Epiphanius, *Haer.* vi. 2.1, 4ff; Pseudo-Ath. *c. Ar.* 4.25.
10. Athanasius, *de Sent. Dion.* 4.14–18.
11. *ibid.* 17.
12. *Adv. Prax.* 3.
13. See above, p. 97.
14. *Adv. Prax.* 2.
15. H. A. Wolfson, *The Philosophy of the Church Fathers*, I (Mass. 1956), pp. 312ff.
16. *Adv. Prax.* 12.
17. *ibid.* 2.
18. *ibid.* 7; *Adv. Hermog.* 3.
19. *c. Noet.* 15.
20. *de Trin.* 31.
21. *In Ioh.* x. 37.246.
22. *de Orat.* 15.1.
23. *c. Cel.* viii. 12.
24. *de Prin.* 1.2.4.
25. *In Ioh.* xiii. 25.151.
26. Photius, *bibl. cod.* 106.
27. Basil, *Ep.* 210.5.
28. *Apol.* 21.
29. *de Praes.* 13.
30. *de Bapt.* 11.
31. *Apol.* 21.
32. *de Carn. Christ.* 5, 10–13, 18.
33. *Adv. Prax.* 27.
34. *ibid.*
35. *de Trin.* 13.
36. *Hom. in Lev.* 1.3; *in Rom.* 3.8.
37. *c. Cel.* vii. 17.
38. *In Matt.* 16.8.
39. *In Ioh.* 1.20.124.
40. *c. Cel.* vi. 68.
41. *de Prin.* 2.9.6.
42. *ibid.* 2.6.3–5.
43. *c. Cel.* i. 60.
44. *ibid.* iii. 41.
45. *In Ierem. hom.* 15.6.
46. *de Pud.* 21.
47. *Ep.* 66.8.
48. *Ep.* 49.2.
49. *de Unit.* 6.
50. *Strom.* 7.11.68; 17.107.
51. *de Orat.* 20.1.
52. *In Cant.* 2.
53. *In Ioh.* x. 20.
54. *c. Cel.* v. 14.
55. *de Res. Carn.* 35.
56. *de Virg.* 17.
57. *Paed.* 1.4.10; 6.46.
58. *c. Cel.* v. 18.
59. *ibid.* vi. 29.
60. *ibid.* vii. 32.
61. *ibid.* v. 23.
62. *ibid.* vii. 32.
63. *adv. Gent.* 1.40, 58; 2. 52.
64. *Symp.* 9.5.
65. Eusebius, *H.E.* vii. 24,25.
66. *adv. Marc.* 3.16.
67. *de Unit.* 2.
68. *de Mort.* 2.
69. *Prot.* 11.
70. *c. Cel.* vii. 17.
71. *Ap. Trad.* xxi. 12–18.
72. *Ep.* 69.7.
73. *ibid.* 75.10.
74. Eusebius, *H.E.* vii. 9.2

Worship

1. *de Bapt.* 2.
2. *ibid.* 20.
3. *de Res. Carn.* 8.
4. *Ep.* 70.2.

Worship—cont.

53. xxxvi.
5. *Ep.* 73.6.
6. xvii–xxii.
7. Ed. Connolly, pp. 146–7.
8. Eusebius, *H.E.* vi. 43.15.
9. *de Bapt.* 18.
10. *Ep.* 58.2.
11. *Epp.* 69–75.
12. The Roman position is argued in the anonymous tract *de Rebaptismate.*
13. *de Bapt.* 4.
14. *de Cor.* 3.
15. *de Monog.* 10; *de Exhort. Cast.* 11.
16. *de Praes.* 36; *Apol.* 32.
17. *de Anima* 9.
18. *Apol.* 39.
19. *de Orat Dom.* 18.
20. *adv. Marc.* 4.40.
21. *de Spec.* 25.
22. *de Mortal.* 1; *de Op. et Elee.* 15; *de Orat. Dom.* 3; *Ep.* 63.17; *de Lap.* 25.
23. Clement, *Strom.* 6.14; *Paed.* 3.11; Origen, *c. Cel.* iii. 50; *in Rom.* x. 33; *in Luc. hom.* 39; *in Lev. hom.* 13.3.
24. iv, xxiii.
25. x.
26. xxiii.
27. *adv. Marc.* 3.19.
28. *de Orat. Dom.* 18.
29. e.g. *in Numb.* xvi. 9; *de Orat.* 27.1–5.
30. *Ep.* 63 *passim.*
31. *C.S.E.L.* xxvi. 186.
32. Eusebius, *H.E.* vii. 30.
33. Lampridius, *Vita Alex.* xlix.
34. Lactantius, *de Mort. Persec.* 15.
35. *de Schism. Donat.* ii. 4.
36. Eusebius, *H.E.* viii. 1.2.
37. Connolly, pp. 119f.
38. Tertullian, *Apol.* 39; Cyprian, *Epp.* 1; 63.16; *de Op. et Elee.* 15.
39. xxv.
40. *de Jejun.* 17.
41. *Paed.* 2.4.
42. *de Lap.* 2.
43. Dionysius, *Ep. ad Basil*; Connolly, p. 183.
44. *de Jejun.* 14.
45. *in Ps.* 37; *Hom.* 2.6.
46. Hippolytus, *Ref.* ix. 12.20–6; Origen, *de Orat.* 28.8f.
47. *Ep.* 55.6, 7, 20f.
48. *de Orat. Dom.* 20.
49. *Strom.* 7.7, 12.
50. Tertullian, *de Orat.* 14; Clement, *Strom.* 7.7; Origen, *de Orat,* 32.
51. Tertullian, *de Cor. Mil.* 3.
52. Tertullian, *de Orat.* 19; *ad Uxor.* 2.5; *de Spec.* 5; Hippolytus, *Ap. Trad.* xxxii. 1–4.

Social Life

1. *c. Cel.* iii. 9.
2. Cyprian, *Ep.* 80.1.
3. Canons 2, 56.
4. xvi.
5. I Cor. vii. 20.
6. I Thess. iv. 11.
7. *de Idol.* 5, 6, 12.
8. *Ep.* 2.2.
9. Clement, *Paed.* 2.1., 2.
10. *ibid.*
11. *de Cultu Fem.* 1.2.
12. *Paed.* 2.10.
13. *de Habitu Virg.* 12.
14. Clement, *Paed.* 3.11; Connolly, p. 10.
15. Elvira, *c.* 79.
16. Connolly, p. 11.
17. Clement, *Paed.* 3.4.

CHAPTER V: FROM NICAEA TO CONSTANTINOPLE

The Background

1. *Cod. Theod.* IX. xvi. 3.2 and 1; XVI. x. 1.
2. *ibid.* XVI. x. 4.
3. Ammianus Marcellinus XXII. v. 2.
4. *Chron.* ad ann. 365.
5. *Ep.* 42.
6. Gregory Naz. *Orat.* iv. 111; Sozomen, *H.E.* v. 16.1–3.

7. Sozomen, *H.E.* v. 10, 11.
8. *Ep.* 49.
9. *Kephalaia* 154.
10. *Vita Const.* iii. 33.
11. Athanasius, *Hist. Arian.* 44.
12. S. Severus, *Chron.* II. 47–51; *Dial. S. Mart.* ii (III), 11–13.

Expansion and Development

1. Eusebius, *Vita Const.* iv. 24.
2. *ibid.* iv. 13.
3. *ibid.* iv. 54.
4. Sozomen, *H.E.* v. 15.
5. S. Severus, *Vita S. Mart. passim.*
6. Theodoret, *H.E.* iv. 18.
7. *ibid.* iv. 21.
8. Rufinus, *H.E.* xi. 6.
9. Epiphanius, *Haer.* 70.
10. Philostorgius, *H.E.* ii. 5.
11. Faustus Byz. iii-vi.
12. Rufinus, *H.E.* i. 9; Sozomen, *H.E.* ii. 24; Philostorgius, *H.E.* iii. 4.
13. Athanasius, *Apol. c. Arian.* 71; Epiphanius, *Haer.* 68.
14. Athanasius, *op. cit.*, 11f., 63f., 74, 76, 83, 85.
15. *ibid.* 65.
16. Optatus, *de Schism. Don.* i. 13f.
17. *ibid.* i. 15–19.
18. *ibid.* i. 22.
19. *ibid.* 23–6.
20. *ibid.* app. ii.
21. Augustine, *Ep.* 43.20.
22. *ibid. c. Litt. Parm.* i. 13.
23. Optatus, app. i.
24. Augustine, *Ad Don. post Coll.* 54.
25. Optatus, iii. 4.
26. Epiphanius, *Haer.* 69.6.
27. Athanasius, *de Syn.* 16.
28. *ibid. c. Arian.* i. 6.
29. *Dem. Evang.* v. i. 20.
30. For the sources and the reasons for adopting this order of events, see W. Telfer, 'When did the Arian Controversy begin?' *J.T.S.*, XLVII, 1946, pp. 129–42.
31. Socrates, *H.E.* i. 13.
32. Athanasius, *de Decret. Nic. syn.* 33.
33. Theodoret, *H.E.* i. 21.
34. Athanasius, *Apol. c. Arian.* 7, 10.
35. *ibid.* 20.
36. *ibid. de Synod.* 22.
37. Four creeds are traditionally associated with this council; only this one can be regarded as the official statement.
38. *de Synod.* 29.
39. Athanasius, *Hist. Arian.* 15.
40. S. Severus, *Hist. Sac.* ii. 39.
41. Athanasius, *op. cit.* 31f.
42. Theodoret, *H.E.* xvi. 1–27.
43. Athanasius, *op. cit.* 42–6.
44. Hilary, *c. Const.* 2.
45. *Hist. Aceph.* iii. 4.
46. Athanasius, *Apol. de fuga sua*, 22–4.
47. *de Synod.* 10.
48. Epiphanius, *Haer.* 73.2–11.
49. Sozomen, *H.E.* iv. 16.
50. *ibid.* iv. 16.1–55.
51. Athanasius, *de Synod.* 8.
52. Hilary, *Frag.* vii. 3.
53. Socrates, *H.E.* ii. 39.
54. Sozomen, *H.E.* iv. 24.
55. Athanasius, *Tom. ad Antioch.*; Liberius, *Ep.* 363.
56. Athanasius, *Ep.* 55.
57. Sozomen, *H.E.* vi. 7, 12.
58. *Hist. Aceph.* xv.
59. Athanasius, *Ep. ad Serap.* 1.1, 10.
60. Socrates, *H.E.* ii. 45; Sozomen, *H.E.* iv. 27.3f.
61. *Orat.* 20.
62. *Cod. Theod.* XVI. v. 5; i. 2.
63. Theodoret, *H.E.* i. 22.2.
64. Sozomen, *H.E.* iv. 28.5–7, 10.
65. *ibid.* v. 13.1–3.
66. Theodoret, *H.E.* v. 23.2.
67. Sozomen, *H.E.* vii. 15.1.
68. Socrates, *H.E.* iii. 9.5–8.
69. *Ep.* 90.
70. *Vita Antoni, passim.*
71. *Consul. Zacch. et Apoll.* iii. 3.
72. Athanasius, *Vita Ant.* 60; Palladius, *Hist. Laus.* 8.
73. Palladius, *op. cit.* 17.
74. *Ep.* 22.11.
75. Jerome, *Vita Hilar.*
76. *Ep.* 223.2.
77. *Reg. fusius tract., passim.*

Expansion and Development—cont.

78. Ambrose, *Ep.* 63.66f.
79. Paulinus, *Vita Ambr.* 9.
80. Connolly, pp. 109–19.
81. *Cod. Theod.* I. xxvii. 2.
82. *Const. Sirm.* I.
83. *Ep.* 82.
84. Canons 6, 7.
85. Canon 5.
86. Canon 3.
87. Ammian. Marcell. XXVII. iii. 12–15.
88. *Et hoc Gloriae vestrae, P.L.* 13.575–84.
89. *ibid.* 583–8.

Beliefs

1. Athanasius, *de Syn.* 16.
2. Epiphanius, *Haer.* 69.6.
3. Athanasius, *Or. c. Arian.* ii. 25.
4. *ibid.* i. 6.
5. Athanasius, *de Syn.* 51.
6. *ad Serap.* 1.28.
7. *Or. c. Arian.* iii. 4.
8. *ibid.* iii. 41.
9. *ibid.* iii. 4.
10. *ad Serap.* 1.24.
11. *ibid.* 1.27.
12. *ibid.* 1.2.
13. *Or.* 31.10.
14. cf. Amphilochius, *Frag.* 15.
15. Gregory Naz. *Or.* 25.16; 26.19; 29.2.
16. G. L. Prestige, *God in Patristic Thought* (London, 1936), p. 249.
17. Quoted by J. N. D. Kelly, *Early Christian Doctrines* (London, 1958), p. 282.
18. *de Incarn.* 8.3; 3.3.
19. *ibid.* 18.1.
20. Cf. *Tom. ad Antioch.* 7.
21. *Ep. ad Diocaes.* 2.
22. *ad Iov.* 3.
23. *Frag.* 108; 109; 49; 52.
24. *Frag.* 36.
25. *ad Dion.* 6.
26. *ad Iov.* 1.
27. *de Unione* 13.
28. *Ep.* 2; *Frag.* ii.
29. *Ep.* 101.7.
30. *de Trin.* 10.19.
31. *ibid.* 9.38; 12.6.
32. *ibid.* 10.23–32.
33. *de Incarn.* 54.
34. *ibid.* 20.
35. *Or. c. Arian.* i. 38.
36. *de Incarn.* 20.
37. *Or. Cat.* 27.
38. *ibid.* 25.
39. *ibid.* 17–23.
40. *Carmen Theol.* x. 65f.
41. *P.G.* 11.1713–1884.
42. *Comm. in Ps. cxxix.* 9.
43. *Dem. Evang.* 1.10.
44. *Cat.* 13.1.
45. *Hom. in Ps. xxviii.* 5.
46. *Or. c. Arian.* iii. 22.
47. *In illud 'Tuncipse'* (*P.G.* 44.1317).
48. *Cat.* 18.22–8.
49. *de Schism. Donat.* 2.9; 1.3f.; 2.1.
50. Greek text in J. N. D. Kelly, *Early Christian Creeds* (London, 1950), p. 103.
51. *ibid.* pp. 293f.

Worship

1. Eusebius, *Vita Const.* iii. 30f.
2. E. C. Whitaker, *Documents of the Baptismal Liturgy* (London, 1960), pp. 74–6.
3. *Mystag.* i. 1.
4. *ibid.* ii. 1–3.
5. *ibid.* ii. 4.
6. *ibid.* iii. 1, 4.
7. *ibid.* iv. 8.
8. *Procat.* 1.
9. *ibid.* 15.
10. 7.41–5.
11. 7.43.5, 45.3.
12. *Or.* 40.27.
13. All the texts cited are conveniently printed in P. F. Palmer, *Sacraments and Worship* (London, 1957), pp. 63–83.
14. *In Matt. hom.* 82.4.
15. *Or. cat.* 37.
16. *Or.* 2.95.
17. *Lib. Pont. Vita Sylv.*
18. *Ap. Const.* 2.57.
19. *P.G.* 26.1412.
20. References in J. G. Davies, *Holy Week, A Short History* (London, 1963).

Social Life

1. *Ap. Const.* 4.11.
2. *ibid.* 4.2.
3. O. Marucchi, *Epigrafia christiana* (Milan, 1910), pp. 222–35.
4. 8.32.
5. e.g. Athanasius, *Exp. in Ps. xiv*; Cyril, *Catech.*
6. *ibid.* 4.26.
7. *Or.* 8.10.
8. *Ep.* 2.6.
9. *Ap. Const.* 1.3.
10. *ibid.* 2.62.
11. Laodicea canon 55.
12. *ibid.* canon 25.
13. Gregory Naz., *Or.* 8.12.
14. *ibid.*, *Or.* 43.35.
15. *Epp.* 94, 142, 143.
16. Basil, *Ep.* 93.

CHAPTER VI: FURTHER ADVANCE

The Background

1. *C.I.L.* VI. 102.
2. *Cod. Theod.* XVI. x. 10–12.
3. *ibid.* XVI. x. 13, 14, 19.
4. Ambrose, *Epp.* 40–1.
5. *ibid.*, *Ep.* 51; *de Ob. Theod.* 34.

Sources

1. The information concerning the life of Chrysostom is mainly contained in the biography by Paulinus.
2. *Retract.* 2.67.

Expansion and Development

1. Augustine, *de Civ.* 18.54.
2. Sozomen, *H.E.* vii. 15.
3. Theodoret, *H.E.* v. 22.
4. Procopius, *de Aedif.* 6.11.
5. Gregory, *Dial.* 2.8.
6. Paulinus, *Vita* 36.
7. *P.L.* 13.549–58.
8. Paulinus, *Carm.* xvii. 213–61.
9. Theodoret, *H.E.* v. 31.
10. *Epp.* 206f., 221, 226.
11. *de Catech. rud.*, written *c.* 400.
12. It is surveyed in two articles by E. A. Thompson, 'Christianity and the Northern Barbarians' and 'The Conversion of the Visigoths to Catholicism', *Nottingham Mediaeval Studies*, I, 1957, pp. 3–21; IV, 1960, pp. 4–35.
13. The date is disputed.
14. Orosius, vii. 42.
15. Cyril of Scythopolis, *Vita S. Euth.*
16. Theodoret, *H.R.* 36.
17. *Cod. Just.* I. iii. 35.
18. *P.O.* V. 311.
19. For a full account, together with references, see W. H. C. Frend, *The Donatist Church* (Oxford, 1952).
20. *Ep.* 93.5, 17.
21. *de Carn. Christ.* 7; *adv. Marc.* 4.19.
22. *adv. Helvidium.*
23. Jerome, *Ep.* 61.
24. *Apol. c. Rufinus*, 3.33.
25. Jerome, *ad Ioh. Hier.* 11.
26. *Ep.* 51.1.
27. *Ep.* 125.18.
28. Origen had some supporters in the West; Orosius reports that a fellow Spanish cleric named Avitus had been to Jerusalem and returned with the doctrines of Origen (*Consultatio*, 3).
29. *Ep.* 140.83.
30. Augustine, *Ep.* 157.22.
31. *de Gest. Pelag.* 23.
32. *Ep.* 133.3.
33. Orosius, *Apol.* 1–6.
34. *de Gest. Pelag.*
35. Augustine, *Epp.* 175, 176.
36. Zosimus, *Epp.* 2, 3.
37. Prosper, *c. Collatorem*, 5.3.
38. Cassian, *de Inc. Chr.* 1.4f.
39. *Ep.* 219.1.
40. Bede, *H.E.* i. 17.
41. Cf. Augustine, *de Gratia et lib. arb.* and *de Corrept. et Gratia*, both written in 427.
42. Augustine, *Ep.* 217.1.

Expansion and Development—cont.

43. Mansi, VIII. 711–9.
44. *Ep.* 2.
45. *Ep.* 3.
46. Mansi, IV. 545–52.
47. *ibid.* IV. 1123.
48. Socrates, *H.E.* vii. 35.
49. *ibid.* vii. 34.
50. W. A. Wigram, *The Assyrian Church* (London, 1910), cap. 8.
51. Mansi, VI. 744.
52. *ibid.* 839, 867.
53. Leo, *Ep.* 77; Theodoret, *Epp.* 138–40.
54. Mansi, VI. 563–938.
55. Evagrius, *H.E.* iii. 4, 14.
56. Theodoret, *H.E.* iv. 11. Photius, *Cod.* 52.
57. Socrates, *H.E.* iv. 23; Sozomen, *H.E.* vi. 30.
58. Abbreviated from *Inst.* 4.32–42.
59. J. Chapman, *Saint Benedict and the Sixth Century* (London, 1929).
60. Theodoret, *R.H.* 26.
61. Palladius, *Dial.* 3.
62. *ibid.* 5.
63. Possidius, *Vita Aug.* 24.
64. *Ep.* 126.9.
65. *Ep.* 19.2.
66. Canon 5.
67. Toledo, 597, canon 2.
68. *Epp.* 2, 6.
69. *Ep.* 25.
70. *Ep.* 30.
71. *Epp.* 13–15.
72. Mansi, III. 830ff.; Caelestine, *Ep.* 2.
73. *P.L.* 54.141–56.

Beliefs

1. xiv. 10.
2. For full references see F. H. Dudden, *The Life and Times of Saint Ambrose* (Oxford, 1935), pp. 566–80.
3. *de Trin.* 7.7.
4. *adv. Prax.* 9.
5. *de Trin.* 7.6.
6. *adv. Ar.* 1.63.
7. *de Trin.* 11–14.
8. *Or.* 28.4.
9. *Metaph.* V. 6.1015b.36–1016a.1.
10. *de Gen. et Corr.* I. 10.328a.27–8.
11. Plutarch, *de Comm. Not. adv. Stoicos*, 37.
12. *Sermo* 1.
13. *Heracl.* (ed. Nau), 210.
14. Theodoret, Eranistes, *Dial.* II (*P.G.* 83, 153 D).
15. *ibid.* 157 A.
16. *Ep.* 46 (ad Succens. 2).
17. *c. Nest.* 2 prooem.
18. *ibid.*
19. *Ep.* 28. 3–5.
20. *Def. Fidei Chal.*
21. *c. Nest. et Eutych., passim.*
22. iii. 2; cf. iii. 11.
23. iii. 18.
24. *Sermo* 192.2.
25. *de Civ. Dei*, 18.51.1.
26. *Sermo* 265.6.7.
27. *Ep.* 61.2.
28. *de Util. cred.* 35.
29. *Ep.* 93.7.23.
30. *de Civ. Dei*, 20.10.
31. *Sermo* 341.
32. *Sermo* 263.
33. *Sermo* 144.4.
34. *Or.* 37.13.
35. *Ps. cxviii. expos.* xv. 36.
36. *ibid.* vii. 8.
37. *de Excess. Satur.* 2.6.
38. *Expos. ev. Luc.* 2.84.
39. *Exhort. virg.* 43.
40. *Enarr. in ps.* lxxxix.4.
41. *Enchir.* 27.
42. *c. Iul.* 6.49f.
43. *In ps.* l. 7.
44. *In Phil.* i. 29f.
45. *In Is.* liii. 5–7.
46. *Confess.* 10.69.
47. *de Incarn. unigen.* (*P.G.* 75.1213).
48. *In II Thess.* ii. 8f.; *in I Cor.* xv. 52.
49. *de Fide et Symb.* 15.
50. *de Civ. Dei*, 20.1.
51. *ibid.* 20.2.
52. *c. Ioh. Hier.* 3.
53. Cf. *de Anim. et Resurr.*
54. *Hom.* 40.2. (*P.G.* 61.349).
55. *Enchir.* 84.

Worship

1. Narsai, *Hom.* 22.
2. Augustine, *Serm.* 215.1; 216.1f.; 294.11f.
3. Narsai, *op. cit.*
4. Ambrose, *de Myst.* 2.5–7.
5. *ibid.* 6.31–33.
6. Augustine, *Ep.* 54.7.
7. *Liber ad Baptizandos*, Woodbrooke Studies, ed. A. Mingana, VI, 1933, p. 47.
8. *ibid.*, p. 110.
9. Cyril of Alexandria, *In Nah.* ii. 2ff.
10. *c. Duas Epp. Pelag.* 3.3.5.
11. *op. cit.*
12. *de Sacramen*, 2.7.23.
13. *In Ioh. Hom.* 26.
14. *de Sacramen.* 3.1.1.
15. *In Ep. ad Rom.* x. 4.
16. cf. Cyril of Alexandria, *In Is.* xxv. 6f.
17. *Mystag.* 5.9.
18. Chrysostom, *In I Cor. Hom.* 41.4.
19. See *supra*, pp. 205f.
20. References collected in F. Van der Meer, *Augustine the Bishop* (London, 1961), pp. 397–402.
21. *Enar. in ps.* xcviii. 9.
22. *Confess.* 7.10.
23. *In Ioh. Hom.* 46.3.
24. *In I Cor. Hom.* 24.1–4.
25. *de Myst.* 9.52.
26. *In Heb. Hom.* 17.3.
27. *Enar. in ps.* xxxix. 8.
28. *Sermo* 272.
29. *Sermo* 57.7.
30. *Peregrin.* xvi. 6.
31. Canon 26.
32. Augustine, *de Civ. Dei*, 1.12.
33, Paulinus, *Ep.* 31.
34. Basil, *Hom. in sanctos XL martyres*, 8.
35. *Ep.* 32.
36. *Ep.* 197.
37. *de Op. Monach.* 28.
38. 8.35, 37.
39. Palladius, *Dial.* 5.
    Theodoret, *Evang. verit.* 1.8.
40. Gregory Naz. *Carm.* 10; Paulinus, *Ep.* 13.
41. *Or.* 6.4.
42. *Ep.* 22.6.
43. *Enar. in ps.* lix.
44. Canon 28.
45. Canon 30.
46. Augustine, *Confess.* 6.2.
47. *Ep.* 22.
48. Paulinus, *Ep.* 13.
49. Sozomen, *H.E.* vii. 19.
50. *H.E.* iii. 11.
51. *Lib.* I. *ep.* 14; II. *ep.* 76.

Social Life

1. *Sermo* 302.21.
2. Augustine, *Ep.* 213.6.
3. Augustine, *de Div. Quaest. LXXXIII. Lib. Unus*, 83 *q.* 78.
4. *In I Cor. Hom.* 20.
5. *In Coloss. Hom.* 1.
6. Palladius, *Dial.* 12.
7. *c. Iov.* II. 10.
8. Possidius, *Vita Aug.* 22.
9. *de Virg.* 34.
10. *Ep.* 22.
11. *In I Tim. Hom.* 8.
12. Augustine, *Sermo* 51.1f.
13. *In Matt. Hom.* 6.
14. *ibid., Hom.* 7.
15. *In I Thess. Hom.* 5.
16. Theodoret, *H.E.* v. 26.

SELECT BIBLIOGRAPHY

(Except where otherwise stated, the place of publication is London)

I

THE ORIGINS OF CHRISTIANITY AND THE NEW TESTAMENT

1. Background

M. Black, *The Scrolls and Christian Origins* (1961); R. Bultmann, *Primitive Christianity in its Contemporary Setting* (1956); F. V. Filson, *The New Testament against its Environment* (1950); E. Hoskins and N. Davey, *The Riddle of the New Testament* (1931); S. Mowinckel, *He that Cometh* (Oxford, 1956); J. Parkes, *The Foundations of Judaism and Christianity* (1960); R. H. Pfeiffer, *History of New Testament Times* (New York, 1949).

2. Sources

Guides. R. G. Heard, *An Introduction to the New Testament* (1950); A. M. Hunter, *Introducing the New Testament* (1945); C. F. D. Moule, *The Birth of the New Testament* (1962); H. F. D. Sparks, *The Formation of the New Testament* (1952).

Gospels: GENERAL. R. Bultmann, *The History of the Synoptic Tradition* (Oxford, 1963); M. Dibelius, *From Tradition to Gospel* (1934); B. Gerhardsson, *Memory and Manuscript* (Uppsala, 1961); B. H. Streeter, *The Four Gospels* (1930); V. Taylor, *The Formation of the Gospel Tradition* (1933).

SPECIFIC. C. K. Barrett, *The Gospel according to St. John* (1955); J. M. Creed, *The Gospel according to St. Luke* (1930); C. H. Dodd, *The Interpretation of the Fourth Gospel* (1953); G. D. Kilpatrick, *The Origins of the Gospel according to St. Matthew* (Oxford, 1948); R. H. Lightfoot, *The Gospel Message of St. Mark* (Oxford, 1950); D. E. Nineham, *Saint Mark* (1963); J. M. Robinson, *The Problem of History in Mark* (1957).

Acts and Epistles: C. K. Barrett, *Luke the Historian in Recent Study* (1961); H. J. Cadbury, *The Making of Luke-Acts* (1927); M. Dibelius, *Studies in the Acts of the Apostles* (1956); A. M. Farrer, *A Rebirth of Images* (1949); P. N. Harrison, *The Problem of the Pastoral Epistles* (Oxford, 1921); K. Lake, *The Earlier Epistles of St. Paul* (2nd ed. 1927); F. J. Leenhardt, *The Epistle to the Romans* (1961); A. H. McNeile, *St Paul* (Cambridge, 1920); C. L. Mitten, *The Formation of the Pauline Corpus of Letters* (1955); E. G. Selwyn, *The First Epistle of St. Peter* (2nd ed. 1947); C. S. C. Williams, *A Commentary on the Acts of the Apostles* (1957).

3. Jesus

Ministry. G. Bornkamm, *Jesus of Nazareth* (1960); J. G. Davies, *He Ascended into Heaven* (1958); R. H. Fuller, *The Mission and Achievement of Jesus* (1954); G. Hebert, *The Christ of Faith and the Jesus of History* (1962); G. Ogg, *The Chronology of the Public Ministry of Jesus* (Cambridge, 1940); J. M. Robinson, *A New Quest of the Historical Jesus* (1959); A. Schweitzer, *The Quest of the Historical Jesus* (1910); V. Taylor, *The Life and Ministry of Jesus* (1954); P. Winter, *On the Trial of Jesus* (Berlin, 1960).

Miracles. J. Kallas, *The Significance of the Synoptic Miracles* (1961); A. Richardson, *The Miracle-Stories of the Gospels* (1941).

Teaching. M. Dibelius, *The Message of Jesus* (1939); C. H. Dodd, *Parables of the*

Kingdom (1935); M. D. Hooker, *Jesus and the Servant* (1959); J. Jeremias, *The Parables of Jesus* (1954); *The Unknown Sayings of Jesus* (1957); W. G. Kümmel, *Promise and Fulfilment* (1957); T. W. Manson, *The Teaching of Jesus* (1931); R. Otto, *The Kingdom of God and the Son of Man* (1943); E. F. Scott, *The Ethical Teaching of Jesus* (New York, 1946).

4. Paul

W. D. Davies, *Paul and Rabbinic Judaism* (1948); M. Dibelius, *Paul* (1953); G. S. Duncan, *St. Paul's Ephesian Ministry* (1929); A. M. Hunter, *Paul and his Predecessors* (1940); W. L. Knox, *St. Paul and the Church of Jerusalem* (Cambridge, 1925), *St. Paul and the Church of the Gentiles* (Cambridge, 1939); A. D. Nock, *St. Paul* (Oxford, 1938); W. M. Ramsay, *St. Paul the Traveller and Roman Citizen* (18th ed., 1935).

5. Beliefs

General. R. Bultmann, *Theology of the New Testament*, 2 vols. (1952–8); A. Richardson, *An Introduction to the Theology of the New Testament* (1958).

Christ. L. Cerfaux, *Christ in the Theology of St. Paul* (New York, 1959); O. Cullmann, *The Christology of the New Testament* (1959); A. J. Rawlinson, *The New Testament Doctrine of the Christ* (1926).

Holy Spirit. C. K. Barrett, *The Holy Spirit and the Gospel Tradition* (1947); J. G. Davies, *The Spirit, the Church and the Sacraments* (1954); E. Schweizer, *Spirit of God* (1960).

Atonement. V. Taylor, *Jesus and His Sacrifice* (1937), *The Atonement in New Testament Teaching* (1940), *Forgiveness and Reconciliation* (1941).

Church. E. Best, *One Body in Christ* (1955); L. Cerfaux, *The Church in the Theology of St. Paul* (New York, 1959); C. Chevasse, *The Bride of Christ* (1940); J. A. T. Robinson, *The Body* (1952); K. L. Schmidt, *The Church* (1950).

Formulation of Belief. O. Cullmann, *The Earliest Christian Confessions* (1949); V. H. Neufeld, *The Earliest Christian Confessions* (Leiden, 1963).

6. Worship

General. P. Carrington, *The Primitive Christian Catechism* (Cambridge, 1940); O. Cullmann, *Early Christian Worship* (1953); D. G. Delling, *Worship in the New Testament* (1962); C. F. D. Moule, *Worship in the New Testament* (1961).

Baptism. G. R. Beasley-Murray, *Baptism in the New Testament* (1962); O. Cullmann, *Baptism in the New Testament* (1950); W. R. Flemington, *The New Testament Doctrine of Baptism* (1948).

Eucharist. A. J. B. Higgins, *The Lord's Supper in the New Testament* (1952); J. Jeremias, *The Eucharistic Words of Jesus* (Oxford, 1955).

II

THE EARLY CHURCH

1. General Histories

L. Duchesne, *Early History of the Christian Church*, 3 vols. (1924); A. Fliche and V. Martin, edd., *Histoire de l'Eglise* (Paris, 1934–); H. M. Gwatkin, *Early Church History to A.D. 313*, 2 vols. (1909); B. J. Kidd, *A History of the Church to A.D. 461*, 3 vols. (Oxford, 1922); J. Lebreton and J. Zeiller, *The History of the Primitive Church*, 4 vols. (1942–8; translation of Fliche and Martin); H. Lietzmann, *Geschichte der Alten Kirche*, 4 vols. (Berlin, 1932–; ET. 1937–51).

2. Background

Philosophy. A. H. Armstrong, *An Introduction to Ancient Philosophy* (1947); F. Copleston, *A History of Philosophy*, II (1950).

Pagan Religion. S. Angus, *The Mystery Religions and Christianity* (New York, 1925); C. N. Cochrane, *Christianity and Classical Culture* (Oxford, new ed. 1957); F. Cumont, *The Mysteries of Mithra* (1903); T. R. Glover, *The Conflict of Religions in the Early Roman Empire* (1909); M. Laistner, *Christianity and Pagan Culture* (Ithaca, 1951); A. Momigliano ed., *Paganism and Christianity in the Fourth Century* (Oxford, 1963).

Gnosticism. E. C. Blackman, *Marcion and His Influence* (1948); F. C. Burkitt, *Church and Gnosis* (Cambridge, 1932); F. L. Cross, ed., *The Jung Code* (1955); J. Doresse, *The Secret Books of the Egyptian Gnostics* (1960); R. M. Grant, *Gnosticism and Early Christianity* (New York, 1959); R. M. Wilson, *The Gnostic Problem* (1958).

Church, State and Persecutions. P. Allard, *Histoire des Persécutions* (Paris, 1885); J. B. Bury, *History of the Later Roman Empire*, 2 vols. (1889); L. H. Canfield, *The Early Persecutions of the Christians* (New York, 1913); S. L. Greenslade, *Church and State from Constantine to Theodosius* (1954); A. H. M. Jones, *Constantine and the Conversion of Europe* (1948); N. Q. King, *The Emperor Theodosius and the Establishment of Christianity* (1961); A. J. Mason, *The Historic Martyrs of the Primitive Church* (1905); E. J. Martin, *The Emperor Julian* (1919); E. M. Pickman, *The Mind of Latin Christendom* (1937); L. T. Taylor, *The Divinity of the Roman Emperor* (Middleton, Conn., 1931); H. Workman, *Persecution in the Early Church* (4th ed., 1923).

3. Sources

Texts. *Die griechischen christlichen Schriftsteller* (Berlin, 1897); J. P. Migne, *Patrologia latina* (Paris, 1844–55); *Patrologia graeca* (Paris, 1857–66).

Translations. *Ancient Christian Writers* (Westminster, 1946–); *Ante-Nicene Christian Library* (Edinburgh, 1866–72); *Library of the Fathers* (Oxford, 1838–88); *Select Library of Nicene and Post-Nicene Fathers* (Oxford and New York, 1886–1900).

Guides. B. Altaner, *Patrology* (1960); F. L. Cross, *The Early Christian Fathers* (1960); J. Quasten, *Patrology* (Utrecht, 1950–).

Individual Writers. A. d'Alès, *La théologie de Saint Hippolyte* (Paris, 2nd ed., 1929); C. Baur, *John Chrysostom and His Times*, 2 vols. (1959); E. W. Benson, *Cyprian, His Life, His Times, His Work* (1897); C. Bigg, *The Christian Platonists of Alexandria* (Oxford, rev. ed. 1913); O. Chadwick, *John Cassian* (Cambridge, 1950); J. Daniélou, *Origen* (1955); E. Fleury, *Saint Grégoire de Nazianze et son temps* (Paris, 2nd ed., 1930); J. Ferguson, *Pelagius* (Cambridge, 1956); F. Holmes Dudden, *The Life and Times of Saint Ambrose*, 2 vols. (Oxford, 1935); J. Lawson, *The Biblical Theology of Saint Irenaeus* (1948); W. K. Lowther Clarke, *Saint Basil the Great* (Cambridge, 1913); R. B. Tollington, *Clement of Alexandria*, 2 vols. (1914); F. Van der Meer, *Augustine the Bishop* (1961); D. S. Wallace-Hadrill, *Eusebius of Caesarea* (1960).

4. Expansion and Development

Missionary Endeavour. A. Harnack, *The Expansion of Christianity in the First Three Centuries*, 2 vols. (1905); K. S. Latourette, *A History of the Expansion of Christianity*, I. (1947); A. D. Nock, *Conversion* (Oxford, 1933); F. Van der Meer and C. Mohrmann, *Atlas of the Early Christian World* (2nd ed., 1960).

Schism. W. H. C. Frend, *The Donatist Church* (Oxford, 1952); S. L. Greenslade, *Schism in the Early Church* (1953); P. de Labriolle, *La crise montaniste* (Paris, 1913).

Ministry. A. Ehrhardt, *The Apostolic Succession in the First Two Centuries of the Church* (1953); C. Gore, *The Church and the Ministry* (rev. ed. 1936); C. Jenkins and K. D. Mackenzie, edd., *Episcopacy Ancient and Modern* (1930); K. E. Kirk, ed., *The Apostolic Ministry* (1946); H. B. Swete, ed., *Essays in the Early History of the Church and Ministry* (1918); W. Telfer, *The Office of a Bishop* (1962).

Roman Primacy. E. Caspar, *Geschichte des Papsttums*, 2 vols. (Tubingen, 1930–33);

T. G. Jalland, *The Church and the Papacy* (1944); B. J. Kidd, *The Roman Primacy to 461* (1936).

Parochial System and Councils. G. W. O. Addleshaw, *The Beginnings of the Parochial System* (York, 1953); C. H. Hefele, *A History of the Christian Councils*, 4 vols. (Edinburgh, 1883–96).

Monasticism. O. Chadwick, *Western Asceticism* (1958); H. Delehaye, *Les saints stylites* (Brussels, 1927); H. B. Workman, *The Evolution of the Monastic Ideal* (2nd ed., 1927).

5. *Beliefs*

General Histories of Doctrine. J. F. Bethune-Baker, *An Introduction to the Early History of Christian Doctrine* (1903); A. Harnack, *History of Dogma*, 7 vols. (1894–9); J. N. D. Kelly, *Early Christian Creeds* (1950), *Early Christian Doctrines* (1958); G. L. Prestige, *Fathers and Heretics* (1940); H. E. W. Turner, *The Pattern of Christian Truth* (1954).

God. H. M. Gwatkin, *Studies of Arianism* (Cambridge, 2nd ed., 1900); G. L. Prestige, *God in Patristic Thought* (2nd ed., 1952); A. E. J. Rawlinson, ed., *Essays in the Trinity and the Incarnation* (1928).

Christ. J. F. Bethune-Baker, *Nestorius and his Teaching* (Cambridge, 1908); J. A. Dorner, *History of the Development of the Doctrine of the Person of Christ* (Edinburgh, 1878); J. Liébaert, *La doctrine christologique de saint Cyrille d'Alexandrie avant la querelle nestorienne* (Lille, 1951); F. Loofs, *Nestorius and his Place in the History of Christian Doctrine* (Cambridge, 1914); R. L. Ottley, *The Doctrine of the Incarnation* (1896); C. E. Raven, *Apollinarianism* (Cambridge, 1923); H. M. Relton, *A Study in Christology* (1917); R. V. Sellers, *Two Ancient Christologies* (1940), *The Council of Chalcedon* (1953); A. R. Vine, *An Approach to Christology* (1948).

Holy Spirit. J. G. Davies, *The Spirit, the Church and the Sacraments* (1954); C. R. B. Shapland, *The Letters of Saint Athanasius concerning the Holy Spirit* (1951); H. B. Swete, *The Holy Spirit in the Ancient Church* (1912).

Atonement. G. Aulen, *Christus Victor* (1931); J. K. Mozley, *The Doctrine of the Atonement* (1915); H. E. W. Turner, *The Patristic Doctrine of Redemption* (1952).

Church. G. Bardy, *La théologie de l'église*, 2 vols. (Paris, 1945–7); G. G. Willis, *Saint Augustine and the Donatist Controversy* (1950).

Man. J. B. Mozley, *A Treatise on the Augustinian Doctrine of Predestination* (1855); F. R. Tennant, *The Sources of the Doctrines of the Fall and Original Sin* (Cambridge, 1903); J. Turmel, *Histoire du dogme du péché originel* (Mâcon, 1904); N. P. Williams, *The Ideas of the Fall and of Original Sin* (1927).

Eschatology. J. T. Darragh, *The Resurrection of the Flesh* (1921).

6. *Worship*

General. L. Duchesne, *Christian Worship, Its Origins and Evolution* (5th ed., reprint. 1956); T. S. Garrett, *Christian Worship* (Oxford, 1961); J. A. Jungmann, *The Early Liturgy* (1959).

Baptism. K. Aland, *Did the Early Church Baptize Infants?* (1963); A. Benoit, *Le baptême chrétien au second siècle* (Paris, 1953); J. Jeremias, *Infant Baptism in the First Four Centuries* (1960); G. W. H. Lampe, *The Seal of the Spirit* (1951); P. Lundberg, *La typologie baptismale dans l'ancienne église* (Uppsala, 1942); A. J. Mason, *The Relation of Confirmation to Baptism* (2nd ed., 1893).

Eucharist. G. Dix, *The Shape of the Liturgy* (1945); J. A. Jungmann, *The Mass of the Roman Rite* (New York, 1959); H. Lietzmann, *Mass and Lord's Supper* (Leiden, 1953); G. A. Michell, *Eucharistic Consecration in the Primitive Church* (1948); *Landmarks in Liturgy* (1961); J. H. Srawley, *Early History of the Liturgy* (Cambridge, 1913); D. Stone, *A History of the Doctrine of the Holy Eucharist*, 2 vols. (1909).

Penance. R. C. Mortimer, *The Origins of Private Penance* (Oxford, 1939); O. D. Watkins, *A History of Penance* (New York, reprint. 1961).

Calendar. A. A. McArthur, *The Evolution of the Christian Year* (1953); J. G. Davies, *Holy Week. A Short History* (1963).

Prayer. F. Cabrol, *La prière des premiers chrétiens* (Paris, 1929); E. G. Jay, *Origen's Treatise on Prayer* (1954).

Agape. J. F. Keating, *The Agape and the Eucharist in the Early Church* (1901).

Martyr Cult. H. Delehaye, *Les légendes hagographiques* (Brussels, 3rd ed., 1927), *Les origines du culte des martyrs* (Brussels, 2nd ed., 1933).

Architectural Setting: Baptism. W. M. Bedard, *The Symbolism of the Baptismal Font in Early Christian Thought* (Washington, 1951); J. G. Davies, *The Architectural Setting of Baptism* (1963); A. Khatchatrian, *Les baptistères paléochrétiens* (1962).

Eucharist. H. C. Butler, *Early Churches in Syria* (Princeton, 1929); J. W. Crowfoot, *Early Churches in Palestine* (1941); J. G. Davies, *The Origin and Development of Early Christian Church Architecture* (1952); A. Grabar, *Martyrium*, 2 vols. (Paris, 1946); S. Gsell, *Les monuments antiques de l'Algérie*, 2 vols. (Paris, 1901); J. Lassus, *Sanctuaires chrétiens de Syrie* (Paris, 1947); P. Lemerle, *Philippes et la Macédoine orientale* (Paris, 1945); G. Leroux, *Les origines de l'édifice hypostyle* (Paris, 1913); E. Marec, *Monuments chrétiens d'Hippone* (Paris, 1958).

7. *Social Life*

R. H. Barrow, *Slavery in the Roman Empire* (1928); C. J. Cadoux, *The Early Church and the World* (Edinburgh, 1925); J. Carcopino, *Daily Life in Ancient Rome* (1941); J. G. Davies, *Daily Life in the Early Church* (1952), *Social Life of Early Christians* (1954); S. Dill, *Roman Society from Nero to Marcus Aurelius* (1904); E. von Dobschutz, *Christian Life in the Primitive Church* (1904); M. M. Fox, *The Life and Times of St. Basil the Great as revealed in his Works* (Washington, 1939); A. T. Geoghegan, *The Attitude towards Labour in Early Christianity and Ancient Culture* (Washington, 1945); T. A. Goggin, *The Times of St. Gregory of Nyssa as reflected in the Letters and the Contra Eunomium* (Washington, 1947); M. E. Keenan, *The Life and Times of St. Augustine as revealed in his Letters* (Washington, 1935).

INDEX